Data-Centric Systems and Applications

Springer
Berlin
Heidelberg
New York
Hong Kong
London
Milan
Paris
Tokyo

Gustavo Alonso • Fabio Casati
Harumi Kuno • Vijay Machiraju

Web Services

Concepts, Architectures and Applications

With 143 Figures

Springer

Gustavo Alonso
Dept. of Computer Science
ETH Zentrum, 8092 Zürich
Switzerland

Fabio Casati
Harumi Kuno
Vijay Machiraju
Hewlett-Packard
1501 Page Mill Road, MS 1142
Palo Alto, CA, 94304
USA

Library of Congress Cataloging-in-Publication Data applied for

Die Deutsche Bibliothek - CIP-Einheitsaufnahme
Bibliographic information published by Die Deutsche Bibliothek
Die Deutsche Bibliothek lists this publication in the Deutsche
Nationalbibliografie; detailed bibliographic data is available in the
Internet at <http://dnb.ddb.de>.

ACM Subject Classification (1998): H.3.5, D.2.11, D.2.12, H.4.1, K.4.4

ISBN   978-3-642-07888-0

Springer-Verlag Berlin Heidelberg New York
Is a part of Springer Science+Business Media

springeronline.com

© Springer-Verlag Berlin Heidelberg 2010
Printed in Germany

The use of designations, trademarks, etc. in this publication does not imply, even in the absence of a specific statement, that such names are exempt from the relevant protective laws and regulations and therefore free for general use.

Cover Design: KünkelLopka, Heidelberg

Printed on acid-free paper   45/3111   5 4 3

To Steffi, Ana, and Alejandro.
GA

To SiSi and to my family, for their patience
and their gratifying enthusiasm.
FC

To my family for their patient and loving support.
HK

To my beloved parents, and my wife Anu
for her love and encouragement.
VM

Preface

Motivation for the Book

When confronted with technological advances, we often overestimate their potential in the short term and underestimate what will actually happen in the long term. Short-term hype results from the desires of industry, academia, funding agencies, and financial institutions to make the most of new ideas in as short a time span as possible. Long-term unpredictability reflects the chaotic nature of the process whereby society adopts new technologies.

Web services are no exception to this rule–neither in the current hype nor in the lack of a clear understanding of how they will evolve. This makes it extremely difficult to get a coherent picture of what Web services are, what they contribute, and where they will be applied. Nevertheless, Web services are likely to play a crucial role both in the short and in the long term. In the short term, Web services have the potential to solve many of the interoperability problems that have plagued application integration efforts, as they can be seen as an attempt to standardize the interfaces of middleware platforms. By itself, this would already be a significant contribution. In the long term, Web services could become the basis for a seamless and almost completely automated infrastructure for electronic commerce and wide area, cross-enterprise application integration. Many developers, researchers, and users have been attracted to the notion of Web services precisely because of this highly ambitious goal.

The question is then how to distinguish between what can be done today and what Web services may become in the more or less distant future. This is by no means an easy question to answer. For instance, the rapidly growing body of literature and specifications is no guarantee that the functionality they describe will be supported by current or future products. In many cases, existing specifications ignore the complexities of implementing the functionality they describe and build upon other specifications that have not yet been standardized. More often than not, existing Web services specifications simply state how properties of Web services could be expressed rather than how they can be implemented, or even whether it is feasible or reasonable to implement them. This makes it difficult to determine the exact state of the art in Web services and to distinguish between reality and long-term research and development objectives.

But if the state of the art is unclear, the future of Web services is even fuzzier, as the uncoordinated proliferation of specifications raises doubts about Web services having a clear direction. Recently, concerns have been raised about the fact that Web services standards are being proposed by different groups that may not have an interest in yielding influence to other organizations, e.g., OASIS (Organization for the Advancement of Structured Standards), W3C (World Wide Web Consortium), and WS-I (Web Services Interoperability Organization). In several instances, such bodies are developing competing standards addressing the same problem. Furthermore, many existing specifications covering different aspects of Web services have not been proposed as open standards. The fact that the authors of those specifications have indicated that they will pursue a *RAND* (reasonable and non discriminatory) licensing policy, thereby implying they will charge fees for use of the standard, can have a dramatic impact on the actual adoption of those specifications. RAND licenses will certainly make the adoption process slower and will inevitably trigger the emergence of competing standards that will further fraction the efforts around Web services. Such a process will make it difficult for Web service technology to converge toward a common goal in the long term.

Goals of the Book

This book is an attempt at taking a step back to regain some perspective on Web services as well as to clarify the state of the art and the potential of Web services. This is not an easy task. Web services are still at a very early stage of development and hence there is very little evidence of what their true value will be. To avoid being snared in the low-level and continually evolving details of current specifications, the book focuses on the problems that Web services try to solve rather than on how Web services can be implemented using this or that programming language.

Currently, Web services are no more than the latest attempt to master the complexity of enterprise application integration. Some would even say that Web services are simply a standardization effort that builds upon decades of experience in developing and deploying middleware systems. Indeed, the main line of argument followed in this book is that Web services are, by design, evolutionary rather than revolutionary. This is why the first part of the book discusses conventional middleware and enterprise application integration. Only by understanding how Web services extend current middleware platforms can we hope to understand the forces that are defining and shaping the current efforts around Web services.

Of course, it is very well possible that Web services will trigger a radical change in the way we think about middleware and application integration, or in the way we use the Internet. In that case, Web services will evolve into something yet unforeseen. Before that stage is reached, however, Web services need to provide solutions to the many complex problems that have plagued application integration efforts in the past. In the second part of the book we take a close look at these problems and discuss in great detail if and how Web services can help to tackle them.

Our Approach

Our main concern in this book has been to deliver a coherent, concise, and accurate picture of the state of the art and future evolution of Web services. In pursuing this goal, a key decision was to avoid turning the book into a lengthy commentary on existing specifications spiced up with examples of XML encoding. Since this approach differs from much of the available literature on the topic, the reader is entitled to an explanation on why we have chosen to adopt this particular format.

Our reasons are both pedagogical and practical. First, on the practical side and in terms of how to deal with the available specifications, we have tried to be comprehensive and reflect what is available at the time of publication. Yet, our goal is not to simply describe these specifications. We aim at giving a critical overview of the specifications: what is provided, why it is provided, what is the model behind the specification, what is missing, why it is missing, and which are the available alternatives. Hence, we are not so much interested in illustrating how to implement a "Hello world!" Web service, but rather in understanding the concepts underlying the technology. When looking at a particular specification, both the basic as well as the most advanced ones, our main objective has been to clarify the approach taken by Web services and to examine to what extent this approach can succeed in view of past efforts. Web services as they are now may disappear in a few years, but the problems that Web services are trying to tackle will not go away. Whether the solution is called Web services or something else, what matters is to have a solid understanding of the problems that must be solved and of the constraints associated with realistic solutions. Following this idea, we have organized the book along the problems that need to be solved rather than around the specifications available today.

On the pedagogical side, we have opted for including what we thought would be most useful to a reader who is interested in going beyond XML encoding of existing specifications. Accordingly, we use XML very sparingly and prefer abstract descriptions rather than lengthy XML examples. In our opinion, including pages and pages of XML does not contribute to the understanding of Web services and leaves little room for a critical appraisal of the technology. Moreover, it might even soon become a pointless exercise. If

Web services succeed, their XML representation will be just a low-level detail hidden to all but a few system developers occupied with the Web service infrastructure. At that stage, it will be far more important to have a deep understanding of how and when to use Web services than to be able to write and parse XML by hand.

Organization of the Book

Following this approach, the book is organized in two parts. The first part covers conventional middleware with an emphasis on the problems that need to be solved and the approaches followed by different forms of middleware. Specifically, it covers the architecture of distributed information systems (Chapter 1), a variety of middleware platforms (Chapter 2), an overview of the problem of enterprise application integration (Chapter 3), and concludes with a discussion of the basic technologies that enable applications to be integrated over the "Web" (Chapter 4). The second part covers Web services. It starts with a general introduction to Web services (Chapter 5). With the basic aspects covered, the book addresses increasingly more complex aspects of application integration using Web services. Chapter 6 provides a critical overview of basic Web service technologies and standards (such as SOAP, WSDL, UDDI). Chapter 7 discusses coordination protocols, including an in-depth coverage of WS-Coordination, WS-transactions, and RosettaNet. Chapter 8 describes the problem of service composition and some of the existing specifications in this area (focusing in particular on BPEL). The final chapter (Chapter 9) puts into perspective all the ideas discussed in previous chapters and speculates on how Web services may evolve in the future.

Intended Audience

The book is intended for those interested in a critical overview of what Web services are and what they might become. First and foremost, this book was written for those involved in deciding when and how to resort to Web services. We make a distinct effort to relate Web services to the problems and ideas typical of middleware and enterprise application settings. These settings are the most obvious candidates for using Web services, but there is a clear need for separating the hype from the facts. By presenting Web services as what they are (i.e., a natural step in the evolution of enterprise application integration platforms), and by closely relating Web services to existing middleware platforms, we expect that practitioners will find this book a valuable reference when evaluating the potential of Web service technology.

For this same reason, the book can be of help in establishing research priorities in this area. We certainly hope that it will bring some clarity in terms of what can be done today with Web services and where more work

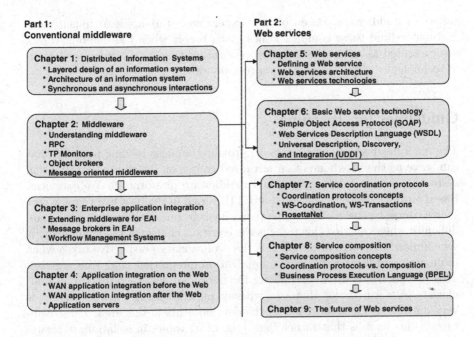

Part 1:
Conventional middleware

Chapter 1: Distributed Information Systems
* Layered design of an information system
* Architecture of an information system
* Synchronous and asynchronous interactions

Chapter 2: Middleware
* Understanding middleware
* RPC
* TP Monitors
* Object brokers
* Message oriented middleware

Chapter 3: Enterprise application integration
* Extending middleware for EAI
* Message brokers in EAI
* Workflow Management Systems

Chapter 4: Application integration on the Web
* WAN application integration before the Web
* WAN application integration after the Web
* Application servers

Part 2:
Web services

Chapter 5: Web services
* Defining a Web service
* Web services architecture
* Web services technologies

Chapter 6: Basic Web service technology
* Simple Object Access Protocol (SOAP)
* Web Services Description Language (WSDL)
* Universal Description, Discovery, and Integration (UDDI)

Chapter 7: Service coordination protocols
* Coordination protocols concepts
* WS-Coordination, WS-Transactions
* RosettaNet

Chapter 8: Service composition
* Service composition concepts
* Coordination protocols vs. composition
* Business Process Execution Language (BPEL)

Chapter 9: The future of Web services

is needed in order to have the necessary basis for pursuing more ambitious endeavors. We believe that Web services have, to a certain extent, become an outlet for ideas that proved impractical in the past. It is not at all clear that Web services will make these ideas any more feasible than they were before. Hence, although proposals around topics such as the Semantic Web, dynamic marketplaces, and automatic contract negotiation and enforcement are all very appealing, we do not discuss them in great detail. The reason is that all these ideas heavily depend on Web services not only being widely adopted but also evolving far beyond the current state of the art. Clarifying the current state of the art is a difficult enough task as it is without also engaging in speculative exercises. We hope that by clearly pointing out the limitations of Web services technology we have experienced in industrial settings, we will motivate researchers to tackle some of the many open problems that still remain in this area. That will create a solid foundation for further work exploring more visionary issues.

Last but not least, we have made a considerable effort to organize the book in such a way so as to facilitate it being used in an advanced course on distributed information systems. It is certainly not meant to compete with books that cover specific forms of middleware. Its purpose is instead to provide a unified view that confers meaning to what is typically presented to students as a conglomerate of separated and independent issues. The book can be used as the main reading source for a course on middleware and enterprise application integration, with more specific details provided directly by looking at the wealth of product information and white papers available on almost every aspect of middleware. Based on our experience, students learn much more and understand these complex issues much better when the different topics are presented as an evolutionary process rather than as a random collection of technologies and implementation techniques.

Guidelines for Teaching

The book has been designed so as to provide the basic reading material that can serve as the backbone of an advanced course on distributed information systems, covering from conventional middleware platforms to Web services. Based on the experience gathered at ETH Zürich in the past five years, where such a course has been offered on a yearly basis by one of the authors, the main difficulty when covering this topic is the constant change in the technology. A very important aspect of the book is the evolutionary perspective taken when discussing middleware, enterprise application integration, and Web services. This perspective is often lost among the details of how each individual middleware platform works. However, without understanding this evolution it is very difficult to make sense out of the developments in this area. The advantage of this book is that rather than presenting topics in isolation, it always frames each technology in relation to previous systems and with a view to motivate the systems that followed. By focusing on the problems to solve and the constraints imposed on the potential solutions to the problems, students can gain a deeper understanding of middleware and be much better prepared for the rapid changes that will continue to occur in this area.

To achieve this effect, we recommend organizing such a course as follows. Assuming a 14 week course, with 2 hours of teaching and 2 hours of exercises a week, the material should be divided into two parts corresponding to the two parts of the book. Depending on what aspects the course wants to emphasize, the assignment of time to each topic can vary. A good first approximation is to devote seven weeks to the first part of the book: middleware and application integration. The first two weeks should cover Chapter 1 of the book. The next three weeks should devote two hours each to selected middleware platforms, covering their purpose, architecture, underlying technology, precursor systems, limitations, and leading up to the next natural step in improving such platforms. A good selection is TP and object monitors, workflow systems, and message oriented middleware (Chapters 2 and 3). With this background, students can then move on to the challenges imposed by the Internet and the need to interconnect heterogeneous middleware platforms. This material should be covered in another two weeks using Chapter 4. The remaining seven weeks should be devoted to analyzing Web services in detail, starting by discussing SOAP, UDDI, and WSDL (one week each), and then moving on to more advanced topics such as coordination protocols and composition (four weeks in total to cover the basic problems and existing solutions).

In this program, the book provides the glue that keeps the course together and relates the different parts of the lecture. It includes enough material to cover all these topics without having to resort to other textbooks. A good working methodology is to ask students to read the corresponding chapter before the lecture, and use the lecture to go into the details of each particular topic. Lectures and the chapters of the book can be easily complemented with one or two articles covering concrete products or technologies in more depth, so as to give students a solid link to actual systems. The material in the book is sufficiently self contained to let students read it on their own while devoting the lectures to pursuing certain topics in more depth (e.g., distributed transaction processing or concrete programming examples in one of the middleware platforms). The book also includes a companion Web site (http://www.inf.ethz.ch/~alonso/WebServicesBook) where students and professors can find additional reading material and presentations on selected topics.

In terms of exercises, in a 14-week course, a useful and very rewarding approach for the students is to develop, step by step, a complex application integration project. As an example of what could be done, at ETH Zürich we organize the exercises as a series of three projects that build upon the previous one. The first project involves developing clients for well defined services. Depending on the emphasis of the course, one can use conventional middleware services like stored procedures or RPC services; it is also possible, however, to start directly by building clients for well-established Web services. This gives students a feeling for how services are used and what basic problems need to be addressed. It also allows for the introduction of important notions such as response time, throughput, and benchmarking. The second project asks students to implement their own service by either developing it from scratch or by wrapping an existing service to make it conform to a given interface type (e.g., wrap a set of Web pages as a Web service). This gives students a taste of the problems related to interface mismatches, session and state information, persistence, connection pools, and a wide range of other important issues. The project can be used to illustrate techniques that vary from the most prosaic ones such as screen-scraping to advanced research topics such as adaptive middleware and run-time modification of information infrastructures. The third and final project asks students to use a complex middleware platform (e.g., a workflow tool) to compose clients and services into a sophisticated business process (which again can be done using conventional services or Web services, depending on what aspects the course wants to emphasize). Based on the business process developed, students can be asked to perform exhaustive execution analysis, suggest optimizations, and critically evaluate the tools at their disposal for developing the process. If services to be composed are dynamically selected from a UDDI registry, then students can also appreciate the opportunities and the difficulties of performing dynamic binding, even in simple settings. These exercises, when combined with the use of the book in the lecture, give students a very good basis for appreciating the advantages of using middleware and the implications of increasing complexity as they need to rely on additional layers of middleware to implement the projects.

Acknowledgements

Books are born as a result of a coordinated and focused effort by the authors. However, the knowledge behind the ideas presented is often the result of a long learning process whereby ideas discussed with many people mature to the point in which it is possible to give them concrete shape. This has certainly been the case for this book. In this regard, we would like to thank the former and current graduate students of the Information and Communication Systems Research group at ETH Zürich for many useful discussions on the topics covered in the book and for useful input on how to improve the presentation of some of the material. We are also grateful to our colleagues in HP Labs for the many useful and enlightening discussions on Web services. They helped us to unveil which are the key issues behind Web services as well as how to present them. We also thank colleagues in the HP business units for sharing their insights about industrial applications of Web service technology and about the problems that Web services can and cannot solve in such scenarios.

Special mention should be given to the editors of this book series, Stefano Ceri and Mike Carey, as well as Barbara Pernici, who acted as a reviewer. Their comments were extremely helpful in making this a better book. We would also like to thank Ralf Gerstner of Springer-Verlag, who showed infinite patience on the face of many delays on our side and was always very helpful during the editing process. We thank Mike Lemon, Rena Takahashi, and David Pietromonaco for their gracious help with the indexing and proof-correcting process. Finally, we thank Heidy Schümperlin and Dan Muntz for proofreading several chapters of this book.

Zürich, Switzerland,   *Gustavo Alonso*
Palo Alto, California,   *Fabio Casati*
Palo Alto, California,   *Harumi Kuno*
Palo Alto, California,   *Vijay Machiraju*
                                                             July, 2003

Contents

Part I

Conventional Middleware

1

Distributed Information Systems

Web services are a form of distributed information system. Many of the problems that Web services try to solve, as well as the design constraints encountered along the way, can be understood by considering how distributed information systems evolved in the past. As part of this evolution process, a key aspect to keep in mind is that while the technology has changed, the problems that need to be solved are to a large extent the same. Thus, the first step toward looking at Web services from the correct perspective is to develop a comprehensive understanding of distributed information systems.

In this chapter we introduce the most basic aspects of distributed information systems: their design, architecture, and communication patterns. We do so in an abstract manner, to avoid the distractions created by the myriad of details found in individual systems and products. The objective is to identify a number of design guidelines and concepts that in subsequent chapters will help the reader compare Web services with traditional information systems.

The chapter begins by addressing several aspects related to the design of an information system (Section 1.1). First we discuss the different layers involved and how they can be designed in either a bottom-up or a top-down manner. Throughout this book we will deal almost exclusively with information systems designed bottom-up. It is therefore important that we establish from the beginning what this implies in terms of how information systems are organized. We then describe possible architectures for an information system (Section 1.2). We follow a historical perspective from 1-tier to N-tier architectures placing special emphasis on why they appeared and their advantages as well as drawbacks. The relations between these different tiers are very important elements in the evolution of distributed information systems, and the issues raised here appear again and again throughout the book. The chapter concludes with a discussion on the differences between synchronous and asynchronous interaction as well as of the consequences of using each of them (Section 1.3).

1.1 Design of an Information System

In spite of the complexity and variety of distributed information systems, we can abstract a few characteristic design aspects. Understanding these aspects will be a great help when we get into detailed descriptions of how concrete systems work and operate.

1.1.1 Layers of an Information System

At a conceptual level, information systems are designed around three layers: *presentation, application logic,* and *resource management* (Figure 1.1). These layers may sometimes exist only as design abstractions in the minds of developers who, for performance reasons, produce nevertheless tangled implementations. In many cases, however, these layers are clearly identifiable and even isolated subsystems, often implemented using different tools.

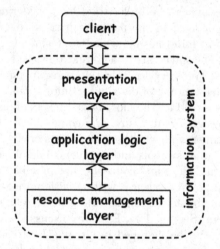

Fig. 1.1. The different layers of an information system

In general, we define the three layers as follows:[1]

- **Presentation layer.** Any information system needs to communicate with external entities, be they human users or other computers. A large part of this communication involves presenting information to these external entities and allowing the external entities to interact with the system by submitting operations and getting responses. The components of an information system that are devoted to these tasks form the *presentation layer.* The presentation layer may take many guises. For example, it could

---

[1] There have been many alternative definitions, but they are all equivalent. See, for instance, [86] for definitions in the context of the so-called *three-ball model.*

be implemented as a graphical user interface, or it could be a module that formats a data set into a given syntactical representation. The presentation layer is sometimes referred to as the *client* of an information system, which is not exactly correct. All information systems have clients, which are entities that use the services provided by the information system. The clients can be completely external and independent of the information system. In this case, they are not part of the presentation layer. The best examples of this design are systems accessed through Web browsers using plain HTML documents. The client is a Web browser that only displays the information prepared by the Web server.

The presentation layer of the information system in this case is the Web server and all the modules in charge of creating the HTML documents (e.g., a Java servlet). It can also be the case that the client and presentation layers are merged into one. This is typical of *client/server* systems that, being so widely used, are a source of the confusion between the client and the presentation layer. In these systems, there is an actual program that acts as both presentation layer and client. To continue with the Web browser example, *Java applets* are an instance of clients and presentation layer merged into one.

- **Application logic layer.** Information systems do more than simply deliver information and data. The vast majority of systems perform some data processing behind the results being delivered. This processing involves a program that implements the actual operation requested by the client through the presentation layer. We refer to these programs and to all the modules that help to deploy and run such programs as the *application logic layer*. We also often refer to these programs as the *services* offered by the information system. A typical example of such a service is a program that implements a withdrawal operation from a bank account. This program takes the request, checks whether there are enough funds, verifies whether withdrawal limits are exceeded, creates a log entry for the operation, performs the operation against the current balance, and gives the approval for handing out the money. All these steps are opaque to the client but reflect the logic behind a withdrawal operation *from the point of view of the service provider* (the bank, in this case). Depending on the complexity of the logic involved and on the selected implementation technique, this layer can also be referred to as *business processes, business logic, business rules*, or simply *server*. In all cases, these names apply only to particular implementations. Hence, in the following we use the term *application logic* to refer to this layer.

- **Resource management layer.** Information systems need data with which to work. The data can reside in databases, file systems, or other information repositories. A conventional *resource management layer* encompasses all such elements of an information system. From a more abstract perspective, the resource management layer deals with and implements the different data sources of an information system, independently of the nature of these data sources. In a restrictive interpretation of the term, the resource management layer is also known as *data layer* to indicate that it is implemented using a database management system. For instance, again using the banking example, the resource management layer could be the account database of the bank. This perspective, however, is rather limiting as it considers only the data management aspects. Many architectures include as part of the resource management layer any external system that provides information. This may include not only databases, but also other information systems with presentation, application, and resource management layers of their own. By doing so, it is possible to build an information system recursively by using other information systems as components. In such architectures, the resource management layer refers to all the mechanisms and functionality used to interact with these low-level building blocks.

1.1.2 Top-down Design of an Information System

When designing an information system, a very useful strategy is to proceed *top-down*. The idea is to start by defining the functionality of the system from the point of view of the clients and of how the clients will interact with the system. This does not imply that the design starts by defining the user interfaces. Rather, it means that design can be almost completely driven by the functionality the system will offer once it becomes operational. Once the top-level goals are defined, the application logic needed to implement such functionality can then be designed. The final step is to define the resources needed by the application logic. This strategy corresponds to designing the system starting from the topmost layer (the presentation layer), proceeding downwards to the application logic layer, and then to the resource management layer (Figure 1.2).

Top-down design focuses first on the high-level goals of the problem and then proceeds to define everything required to achieve those goals. As part of this process, it is also necessary to specify how the system will be distributed across different computing nodes. The functionality that is distributed can be from any of the layers (presentation, application logic, or resource management). To simplify system development and maintenance, distributed information systems designed top-down are usually created to run on homogeneous computing environments. Components distributed in this way are known as *tightly coupled*, which means that the functionality of each component heavily depends on the functionality implemented by other components. Often, such components cannot be used independently of the overall system. That is, the design is component-based, but the components are not stand-alone (Figure 1.3).

Parallel database management systems are an example of top-down design. A parallel database is designed so that different parts of its functionality

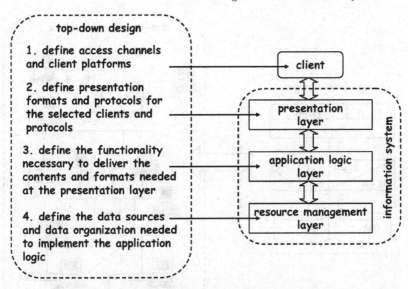

Fig. 1.2. Top-down design of an information system

can be distributed and, hence, used in parallel. Each distributed element is typically designed to work exclusively within the context of one particular parallel database and, as such, is only a subpart of a whole without meaning of its own. In the vast majority of such systems, the design focuses on how to build the system on a set of homogeneous nodes (e.g., PCs running Linux) as heterogeneity would make the design significantly more complex.

Top-down design has considerable advantages. In particular, the design emphasizes the final goals of the system and can be tailored to address both functional (what operations the system supports) and non functional issues (such as performance and availability). The drawback of top-down design is that, in its full generality, it can only be applied to systems developed entirely from scratch. As a result, few information systems are nowadays designed in a purely top-down fashion.

1.1.3 Bottom-up Design of an Information System

Bottom-up designs occur from necessity rather than choice. Information systems are built nowadays by integrating already existing systems, often called *legacy applications* or *legacy systems*. A system or an application becomes legacy the moment that it is used for a purpose or in a context other than the one originally intended. Any information system will inevitably become a legacy system at one point or another during its life time.

The problem with legacy systems is how to integrate their functionality into a coherent whole. This cannot be done top-down because we do not have the freedom of selecting and shaping the functionality of the underlying

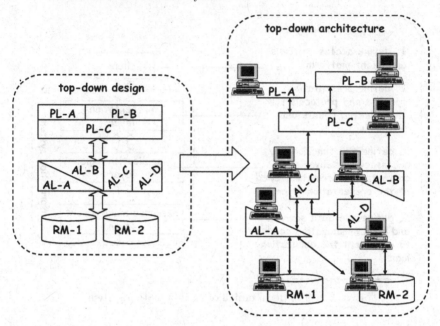

Fig. 1.3. Architecture of a top-down information system. The acronyms PL, AL, RM denote the presentation layer, application logic layer, and resource management layer. PL-A, AL-A, RM-1, and so on indicate distinct modules within each layer

systems. The functionality provided by these components is predefined and, more often than not, cannot be modified. Re-implementing the functionality provided by legacy systems so that a top-down approach can be used is in most cases not a viable option due to the development and deployment efforts required.

As a result, when legacy systems are involved, the design is mostly driven by the characteristics of the lower layers. What can be done with the underlying systems is as important as the final goal. That is, designers start by defining high-level goals as in a top-down design. Unlike in top-down designs, the next step is not necessarily defining the application logic (Figure 1.4). Rather, the next step is looking at the resource management level (which is where the legacy systems are) and figuring out the cost and feasibility of obtaining the necessary functionality from the basic components. The underlying components are then *wrapped* so that proper interfaces are made available and can be exposed to the application logic layer. Only then is it possible to design the application logic. The result is a bottom-up process where developers proceed from the resource management layers upwards toward the application logic layer and the presentation layer. In fact, bottom-up designs often begin with a thorough investigation of existing applications and processes, followed by an analysis and restructuring of the problem domain until it becomes clear which high-level objectives can be achieved.

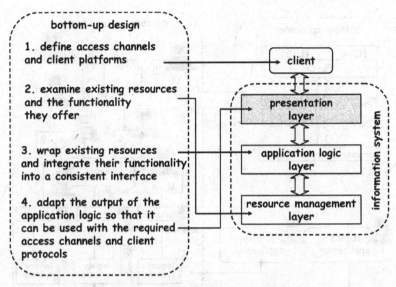

Fig. 1.4. Bottom-up design of an information system

By design, bottom-up architectures yield *loosely coupled* systems, where most components can also be used as stand-alone systems independent of the rest of the system. Often, part of the problem is how to use the legacy system as a component and, at the same time, maintain its functionality as a stand-alone system (Figure 1.5).

It does not make much sense to talk about advantages and disadvantages when discussing bottom-up designs. In many cases there is no other choice. Bottom-up design is often frequently dictated by the need to integrate underlying legacy systems. Nearly without exception, most distributed information systems these days are the result of bottom-up designs. This is certainly the case for the systems we discuss in this book. To a large extent, we find that the advantage of Web services lies in their ability to make bottom-up designs more efficient, cost-effective, and simpler to design and maintain.

1.2 Architecture of an Information System

The three layers discussed above are conceptual constructs that logically separate the functionality of an information system. When implementing real systems, these layers can be combined and distributed in different ways, in which case we refer to them not as conceptual layers, but rather as *tiers*. There are four basic types of information systems depending on how the tiers are organized: *1-tier*, *2-tier*, *3-tier*, and *N-tier*.

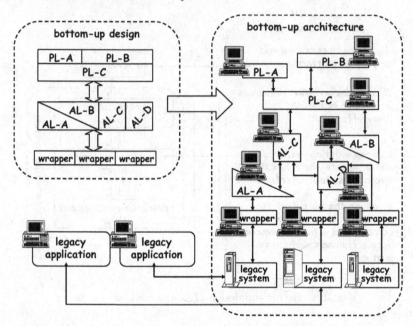

Fig. 1.5. Architecture of a bottom-up information system. The acronyms PL, AL, RM denote the presentation layer, application logic layer, and resource management layer. PL-A, AL-A, RM-1, etc. indicate distinct modules within each layer

1.2.1 One-tier Architectures

From a historical perspective, 1-tier architectures are the direct result of the computer architectures used several decades ago. These were mainframe-based and interaction with the system took place through dumb terminals that only displayed the information as prepared by the mainframe. The main concern was the efficient use of the CPU and of the system.

Information systems running on such hardware settings had no choice but to be monolithic. That is, the presentation, application logic, and resource management layers were merged into a single tier because there was no other option; hence the name 1-tier architectures (Figure 1.6). As an example of what this implies, interaction with the system was through dumb terminals, which were barely more than keyboards and computer screens. These dumb terminals were the clients. The entire presentation layer resided in the mainframe. It controlled every aspect of the interaction with the client, including how information would appear, how it would be displayed, and how to react to input from the user.

Many such systems are still in use today and constitute the canonical example of legacy systems. Because they were designed as monolithic entities, 1-tier information systems do not provide any entry point from the outside except the channel to the dumb terminals. Specifically, such systems do not

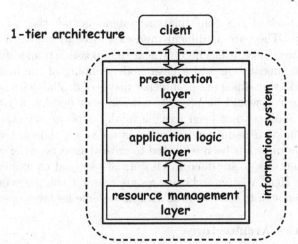

Fig. 1.6. One-tier architectures combine all layers in a single tier. In many early systems, the client in the figure was a dumb terminal

provide an application program interface (API), a stable service interface that applications or other systems can use to interact with the system in question. Therefore, they can only be treated as black boxes. When they need to be integrated with other systems, the most popular method is the dreaded *screen scraping*. This method is based on a program that poses as a dumb terminal. It simulates an actual user and tries to parse the *screens* produced by the 1-tier system. In this way it is possible to extract the necessary information in an automated manner. Needless to say, this procedure is neither elegant nor efficient. It is also highly ad hoc and, therefore, quite expensive to develop and maintain. In this regard, 1-tier architectures illustrate very well the notion of legacy system.

There are, however, obvious advantages to 1-tier systems. For instance, designers are free to merge the layers as much as necessary to optimize performance. Where portability is not an issue, these systems liberally use assembly code and low level optimizations to increase throughput and reduce response time. Moreover, since the entire system shares a single execution context, there are no penalties in the form of context switches and calls between components. Since there is no need to publish and maintain an interface, there is also no reason to invest in complex data transformations or to worry about compatibility issues. These characteristics can result in extremely efficient systems whose performance remains, in many cases, unmatched. Another advantage of historical 1-tier architectures is essentially zero client development, deployment, and maintenance cost. Of course, this was a side effect of the technology available at the time. Nevertheless, it is important to keep this aspect in mind since other architectures incur significant deployment costs because of the complexity of the clients.

The drawback of 1-tier information systems is that they are monolithic pieces of code. They are as difficult and expensive to maintain as they are efficient. In some cases, it has become next to impossible to modify the system for lack of documentation and a clear understanding of the architecture as well as for lack of qualified programmers capable of dealing with such systems [184]. Although it would be possible nowadays to develop a 1-tier system, the software industry has been moving in the opposite direction for many years. Even modern mainframe software is no longer monolithic, especially since the mainframe has been relegated to critical aspects of the system while more mundane chores are done in clusters of personal computers (PCs) or workstations. Hence, 1-tier architectures are relevant nowadays only to those unfortunate enough to have to deal with mainframe legacy systems.

1.2.2 Two-tier Architectures

Two-tier architectures appeared when as computing hardware started to be something more than a mainframe. The real push for 2-tier systems was driven by the emergence of the PC. Instead of a mainframe and dumb terminals, there were large computers (mainframes and servers) and small computers (PCs and workstations). For designers of information systems it was no longer necessary to keep the presentation layer together with the resource management and application logic layers. The presentation layer could instead be moved to the client, i.e., to the PC (Figure 1.7).

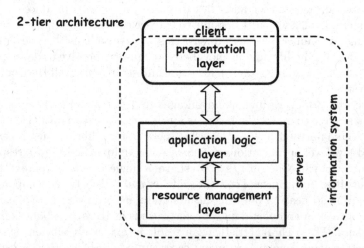

Fig. 1.7. Two-tier architectures separate the presentation layer from the other two layers. The result is a client/server system where the client has the ability to further process the information provided by the server

Moving the presentation layer to the PC achieves two important advantages. First, the presentation layer can utilize the computational power available in a PC, freeing up resources for the application logic and resource management layers. Second, it becomes possible to tailor the presentation layer for different purposes without increasing the complexity of the system. For instance, one could build one presentation layer for administration purposes and another for ordinary users. These presentation modules are independent of each other and as such can be developed and maintained separately. Of course, this is not always possible and depends on the nature of the presentation layer. Web servers, for instance, cannot be moved to the client side.

Two-tier architectures became enormously popular, particularly as *client/ server* architectures [124, 162]. The *client* in client/server typically corresponds to the presentation layer and the actual client software, while the server encompasses the application logic and resource management layers. The client can take many different forms and even implement functionality that otherwise would have been in the server. Depending on how complex the client is, architectures consider *thin clients* (clients with only minimal functionality) and *fat clients* (complex clients that provide a wide range of functionality). Thin clients have the advantage of making the client easier to port, install, and maintain. They also require less processing capacity at the client machine and can therefore be used from a wider range of computers. Fat clients are much more sophisticated and offer richer functionality. The drawback is that they have a large footprint, since they are large pieces of code requiring considerable resources on the client machine. In either case, 2-tier architectures are what led many people to identify the presentation layer with the client on which it runs.

Client/server systems were involved in a positive feedback loop with many advances in computer and network hardware. As PCs and workstations became more powerful (faster CPUs, more memory and disk space, color displays, and so on), the presentation layer could be made more and more sophisticated. Increasingly sophisticated presentation layers, in turn, demanded faster and better computers and networks.

Client/server systems are also associated with many key developments in software for distributed systems. Intimately related to client/server systems is the notion of remote procedure call (RPC), discussed in Chapter 2, a programming and communication mechanism that allowed client and sever to interact by means of procedure calls. Perhaps even more importantly, client/server architectures and mechanisms such as RPC forced designers of distributed systems to think in terms of published interfaces. In fact, in order to develop clients, the server needed to have a known, stable interface. This resulted in the development of the application program interface (API), a concept that has radically changed the way information systems are designed. An API specifies how to invoke a service, the responses that can be expected, and possibly even what effects the invocation will have on the internal state of the server. Once servers had a well-known and stable APIs, it was possible to develop all sorts of clients for it. As long as the API was kept the same, developers could change and evolve the server without affecting the clients.

Through these concepts, client/server architectures became the starting point for many crucial aspects of modern information systems (Figure 1.8). The individual programs responsible for the application logic became *services* running on a *server*. The service interface defined how to interact with a given service and abstracted the details of the implementation. The collection of service interfaces made available to outside clients became the *server's* API. The emphasis on interfaces engendered the need for standardization, a process that is increasingly important today. In many respects, Web services are the latest outcome of these standardization efforts.

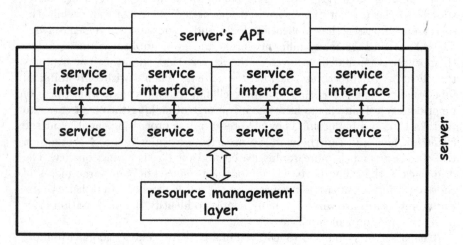

Fig. 1.8. Internal organization of the application logic layer in a 2-tier system

From a technical point of view, 2-tier systems offer significant advantages over 1-tier systems. By keeping the application logic and the resource management layers together it is still possible to execute key operations faster, since there is no need for context switches or calls between components. The same type of optimizations used in 1-tier systems are also possible in 2-tier systems. Two-tier systems also support development of information systems that are portable across different platforms, since the presentation layer is independent of the server. System designers can thus provide multiple presentation layers customized to different types of clients without worrying about the server.

The problems of client/server systems are well known, although they are not really intrinsic to the architecture itself. One obvious problem is that a single server can only support a limited number of clients, and may eventually be unable to support as many clients as needed. For example, clients need connections and authentication and require the server to maintain the context of the interaction. The server should also run the application logic and resource management layers. Typical servers do not run on mainframes but on machines that are both less expensive and less powerful, which has led to the perception that 2-tier architectures have limited scalability. This is certainly also true of 1-tier systems, but 1-tier systems did not have to meet the performance demands of today's environments, and surviving 1-tier systems have the advantage of running today on platforms that are much more powerful than most servers in 2-tier systems.

Another typical disadvantage of 2-tier architectures is the legacy problem that arises when 2-tier systems are used for purposes other than those for which they were originally intended. These problems started when designers realized the potential of the client. Once the client became independent of the server (independent in the sense of being a separate piece of code, possibly developed by people other than those who developed the server), it could be further developed on its own. One such development was to use the client to connect to different servers, thereby integrating their services (Figure 1.9). This is in principle a good idea, but it uses the wrong architecture. For a client to connect to different servers, it needs to be able to understand the API of each server. This makes the client bigger and more complex. It also makes it dependent on two systems, thereby reducing its useful lifetime since the client must now be updated if changes are made to either server. In addition, since the two servers need not know anything about each other, the client becomes responsible for the integration. The client must combine the data from both servers, deal with the exceptions and failures of both servers, coordinate the access to both servers, and so on. In other words, an extra application layer appears but it is embedded in the client. Such an approach quickly becomes unmanageable as the client increases in both size and complexity. Furthermore, the ad hoc procedure of customizing the client to a new server must be repeated from scratch for every possible combination of servers.

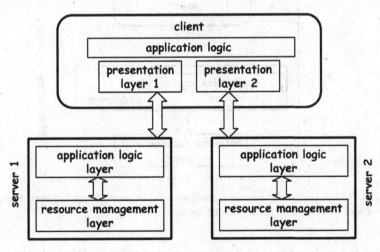

Fig. 1.9. The client is the integration engine in 2-tier architectures

Thus, in spite of their success, 2-tier architectures have acquired a reputation for being less scalable and inflexible when it comes to integrating different systems. These limitations are not intrinsic to 2-tier architectures but they are an indication of the advances in information technology that continually shift the demands on distributed systems.

1.2.3 Three-tier Architectures

The new requirements that 2-tier systems could not address were the result of the proliferation of servers with published, stable interfaces and the increase in network bandwidth provided by local area networks (LANs). The former created *islands of information* where a set of clients could communicate with a server but could not communicate with other servers. The latter made it technically possible to think about integrating different servers. What was missing was the proper architecture to do so.

Three-tier architectures are best understood when considered as a solution to this architectural problem. As we have just seen, this problem cannot be addressed at the client level. Three-tier architectures solve the problem by introducing an additional tier between the clients and the servers. This additional tier is where the integration of the underlying systems is supported and where the application logic implementing this integration resides (Figure 1.10).

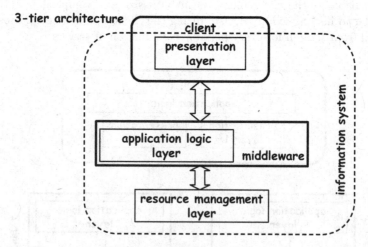

Fig. 1.10. Three-tier architectures introduce a middleware layer between the presentation and the resource management layers

Three-tier architectures are far more complex and varied than client/server systems and are therefore all the more difficult to characterize. At an abstract level, however, 3-tier architectures are usually based on a clear separation between each of the three layers. The presentation layer resides at the client as in 2-tier architectures. The application logic resides at the middle tier. Also for this reason, the abstractions and infrastructure that support the development of the application logic are collectively known as *middleware* [26]. The resource management layer is composed of all servers that the 3-tier architecture tries to integrate. The catch in this description is that the servers at the resource management level may in turn each have their own application logic and resource management layers. From the perspective of such resource management servers, the programs running within the application logic layer of the 3-tier architecture are mere clients working in a client/server setting (Figure 1.11).

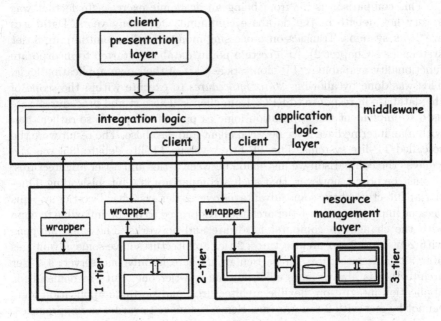

Fig. 1.11. Integration of systems with different architectures using a 3-tier approach

Although 3-tier architectures are mainly intended as integration platforms, they can also be used in exactly the same setting as 2-tier architectures. By comparing these architectures, it is possible to gain a better understanding of what 3-tier architectures imply. As already observed above, in 2-tier systems the application logic and the resource management layers are co-located, which has performance advantages and disadvantages. The advantage is that communication between these two layers is very efficient. The disadvantage is that a powerful server is needed to run both layers. If the system needs to scale, increasingly powerful servers must be obtained, which becomes very expensive and, at a certain point, is no longer possible without resorting to a mainframe.

We can turn a 2-tier system into a 3-tier system by separating the application logic from the resource management layer [67, 89]. The advantage is that now scalability can be accomplished by running each layer in a different server. In particular, the application layer can be distributed across several nodes so that it is even possible to use clusters of small computers for that layer. Furthermore, 3-tier systems offer the opportunity to write application logic that is less tied to the underlying resource manager and, therefore, more portable and reusable. The disadvantage is that the communication between the resource manager layer and the application layer becomes much more expensive.

This comparison is far from being an academic exercise. In fact, it was a very hot debate in the database community for many years. Databases are 2-tier systems. Transaction processing monitors (TP monitors) are 3-tier systems (see Chapter 2). At a certain point, databases started to incorporate functionality available in TP monitors as part of their own application logic. This was done by allowing *stored procedures* to execute within the scope of the database in response to RPCs from clients. These stored procedures were used to implement the application logic as part of the database rather than within an intermediate layer between client and database. The result were the so-called TP-lite systems. The TP-heavy versus TP-lite debate [85] was the same as the comparison we just made between 2-tier and 3-tier architectures. It must be noted, however, that such a comparison is a bit misleading. One-tier architectures have some advantages over 2-tier systems. Two-tier systems became important when 1-tier architectures proved to be too inflexible to cope with the changes in computer hardware and networks. The same happens with 2-tier and 3-tier architectures; 2-tier architectures have some advantages over 3-tier architectures. In particular, if there is only one server, a 2-tier architecture is always more efficient than a 3-tier one. But the demand for application integration, flexible architectures, and portable application logic cannot be met with 2-tier systems. Hence the move toward 3-tier approaches.

Three-tier systems introduced important concepts that complemented and extended those already provided by 2-tier architectures. For instance, resource managers were forced to provide clear interfaces so that they could be accessed by application logic running at the middleware layer. There was also a need to make such interfaces more or less standard so that application logic code could access resource managers in a uniform manner. Such is the origin of the open database connectivity (ODBC) [135] and the java database connectivity (JDBC) [190] interfaces, which were developed so that application logic code at the middleware level could access databases in a standard manner. Thus, while 2-tier architectures forced the definition of application logic layer APIs, 3-tier architectures forced the creation of resource management APIs.

Three-tier systems are at their best when dealing with the integration of different resources. Modern middleware infrastructure provides not only the location for developing the integration logic that constitutes the middle tier but also the functionality necessary to endow this middle tier with additional properties: transactional guarantees across different resource managers, load balancing, logging capabilities, replication, persistence, and more. By using a middleware system, the designers of the application logic can rely on the support provided by the middleware to develop sophisticated interaction models without having to implement everything from scratch. This emphasis on the properties provided at the middleware level triggered another wave of standardization efforts. For instance, a common standard emerged to be able to commit transactions across different systems (e.g., X/Open [197], Chapter 2). There were even attempts to standardize the global properties and the interfaces between middleware platforms by using an object-oriented approach (e.g., CORBA, Chapter 2).

The main advantage of 3-tier systems is that they provide an additional tier where the integration logic can reside. The resulting performance loss is more than compensated for by the flexibility achieved by this additional tier and the support that can be provided to that application logic. The performance loss when communicating with the resource management layer is also compensated for by the ability to distribute the middleware tier across many nodes, thereby significantly boosting the scalability and reliability of the system.

The disadvantages of 3-tier architectures are also due to a legacy problem. Two-tier systems run into trouble when clients wanted to connect to more than one server. Three-tier systems run into trouble when the integration must happen across the Internet or involves different 3-tier systems. In the case of integration across the Internet, most 3-tier systems were just not designed for that purpose. They can be made to communicate across the Internet but the solution is more a hack than anything else (we discuss these solutions in detail in Chapter 4). In the case of having to integrate different 3-tier systems, the problem is the lack of standards. In Chapter 5 we see how Web services try to address this problem.

1.2.4 N-tier Architectures

N-tier architectures are not a radical departure from 3-tier systems. Instead, they are the result of applying the 3-tier model in its full generality and of the increased relevance of the Internet as an access channel. N-tier architectures appear in two generic settings: linking of different systems and adding connectivity through the Internet. In the former setting, and as shown in Figure 1.11, the resource layer can include not only simple resources like a database, but also full-fledged 2-tier and 3-tier systems. In these last two cases, we say the system is an N-tier or multi-tier architecture. In the latter case, N-tier architectures arise, for example, from the need to incorporate Web servers as part of the presentation layer (Figure 1.12). The Web server is treated as an additional tier since it is significantly more complex than most presentation layers. In such systems, the client is a Web browser and the presentation layer is distributed between the Web browser, the Web server, and the code that prepares HTML pages. Additional modules might also be necessary, such as the *HTML filter* shown in the figure, to translate between the different data formats used in each layer. The HTML filter in the figure translates the data provided by the application logic layer into HTML pages that can be sent to a browser.

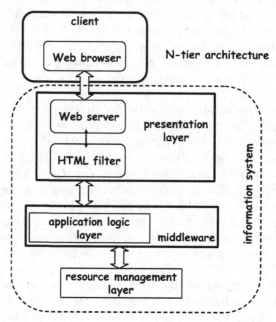

Fig. 1.12. An N-tier system created by extending a 3-tier system by adding a Web server to the presentation layer

As N-tier systems demonstrate, the architecture of most information systems today is very complex and can encompass many different tiers as successive integration efforts build systems that later become building blocks for further integration. This is in fact the main disadvantage of the N-Tier model: there is too much middleware involved, often with redundant functionality [185], and the difficulty and costs of developing, tuning, maintaining, and evolving these systems increases almost exponentially with the number of tiers. Many N-tier systems today encompass a large collection of networks, single computers, clusters, and links between different systems. As Figure 1.13 suggests, in an N-tier system it might be difficult to identify where one system ends and the next starts. Remote clients access the system via the Internet after going through a firewall. Their requests are forwarded to a cluster of machines that together comprise the Web server (clusters of machines are a very typical configuration for the layers of 3-tier and N-tier systems; they provide higher fault tolerance and higher throughput for less cost than a single machine with equivalent processing capacity). Internally, there might be additional clients spread out all over the company that also use the services of the system either through the Web server or by directly accessing the application logic implemented in the middleware. It is also very common to see the application logic distributed across a cluster of machines. There might even be several middleware platforms for different applications and functionalities coexisting in the same system. Underlying all this machinery, the often-called *back end* or *back office* constitutes the resource management layer. The back end can encompass a bewildering variety of systems, ranging from a simple file server to a database running on a mainframe and including links to additional 2-, 3-, and N-tier systems.

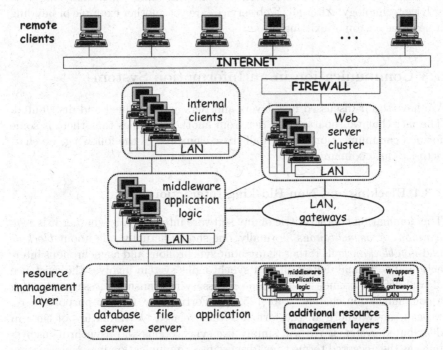

Fig. 1.13. N-tier systems typically encompass a large collection of networks, gateways, individual computers, clusters of computers, and links between systems

1.2.5 Distributing Layers and Tiers

The attentive reader may have noticed a pattern when discussing the advantages and disadvantages of each architecture. The progress from 1-tier to N-tier architectures can be seen as a constant addition of tiers. With each tier, the architecture gains flexibility, functionality, and possibilities for distribution. The drawback is that, with each tier, the architecture introduces a performance problem by increasing the cost of communicating across the different tiers. In addition, each tier introduces more complexity in terms of management and tuning.

This pattern does not occur by chance. It is an intrinsic characteristic of the tier system. When new architectures for information systems appear, they are invariably criticized for their poor performance. This was the cause of discussions about TP-heavy versus TP-lite. This was why CORBA was criticized, and this is also why Web services are criticized. A loss in performance caused by the additional tiers must be offset by the gain in flexibility; when that happens, the new architecture prevails. The evolution from 1-tier to N-tier systems is a good reference to keep in mind when analyzing Web service technology: After all, Web services are yet another example of building a new tier on top of existing ones.

1.3 Communication in an Information System

We have so far discussed how layers and tiers are combined and distributed. The fact that we separate one tier from another assumes that there is some form of communication between all these elements. In the following, we characterize this communication.

1.3.1 Blocking and Non Blocking Interactions

The dominating characteristic of any software interaction is whether it is *synchronous* or *asynchronous*. Formally, one should actually talk about *blocking* and *non blocking* calls rather than about synchronous and asynchronous interaction. The formal definition of a synchronous system involves the existence of well-defined bounds for the time necessary to transmit messages through a communication channel [146, 125, 54]. Fortunately, for our purposes here, we can safely ignore all the formal details related to the nature of time in distributed systems. We will simply use synchronous and asynchronous systems as the accepted terms when discussing communication in an information system.

We say that an interaction is synchronous, or blocking, if the parties involved must wait for the interaction to conclude before doing anything else; otherwise, the interaction is asynchronous, or non blocking. Note that concurrency and parallelism have nothing to do with synchrony. For instance, a server can start a thread every time a client makes a request and assign that thread to that client. The server can thus deal concurrently with many clients. Synchrony, in this case, refers to how the code at the client and the code in the server thread interact. If the code at the client blocks when the call is made until a response arrives, it is a synchronous interaction. If, instead of blocking after making the call, the client moves on to do something else, the interaction is asynchronous. Simple as these definitions are, the choice between synchronous and asynchronous interaction has important practical consequences.

1.3.2 Synchronous or Blocking Calls

In synchronous interactions, a thread of execution calling another thread must wait until the response comes back before it can proceed (Figure 1.14). Waiting for the response has the advantage of simplifying the design a great deal. It is easier for the programmer to understand as it follows naturally from the organization of procedure or method calls in a program. For instance, while a call takes place, we know that the state of the calling thread will not change before the response comes back (since the calling thread will wait for the response). There is also a strong correlation between the code that makes the call and the code that deals with the response (usually the two code blocks are next to each other). Logically it is easier to understand what happens in a synchronous system since the different components are strongly tied to each other in each interaction, which greatly simplifies debugging and performance analysis. As a result, synchronous interaction has dominated almost all forms of middleware. For instance, when the presentation layer moved to the client in 2-tier systems this was generally done through synchronous remote procedure calls. Similarly, when the application logic and the resource management layer were separated, most systems used synchronous calls for communication between both layers.

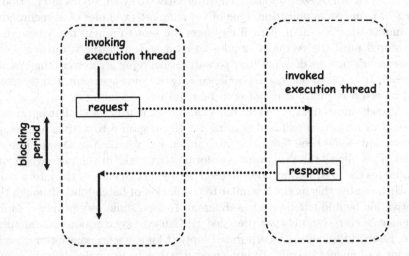

Fig. 1.14. A synchronous call requires the requester to block until the response arrives

All these advantages, however, can also be seen as disadvantages–especially if the interaction is not of the request-response type. The fact that the calling thread must wait can be a significant waste of time and resources if the call takes time to complete. Waiting is a particular source of concern from the performance point of view. For example, a waiting process may be swapped out of memory, thereby significantly increasing the time it takes to process the response when it arrives. Since this can happen at each tier, the problem is aggravated as more tiers are added to the system. Similarly, since every call results in a new connection, there is the danger of running out of connections if there are too many outstanding calls. Finally, the tight integration between the components imposed by synchronous interaction may be impossible to maintain in highly distributed, heterogeneous environments. It is also very complex to use when there are many tiers involved. In terms of fault tolerance, synchronous interactions require both the caller and the called to be online at the time the call is made and to remain operational for the entire duration of the call. This has obvious implications because of the reduced fault tolerance (for a call to succeed, both the caller and the called must work properly) and the more complex maintenance procedures (for system upgrades, everything must be taken offline since one part will not work without the other). Again, these problems become more acute as the number of tiers increases.

1.3.3 Asynchronous or Non Blocking Calls

In some cases, such as when we need to work interactively, these limitations are unavoidable. In a wide range of applications, however, it is not at all necessary to work synchronously. The alternative to synchronous interaction is asynchronous communication. One of the simplest examples of asynchronous communication is e-mail. E-mail messages are sent to a mail box where they are stored until the recipient decides to read and, eventually, answer them. The sender's process does not have to wait until a reply is received; there is not necessarily a one-to-one correspondence between messages sent and received, and indeed a response may not even be required.

Asynchronous distributed systems can be built using a similar approach. Instead of making a call and waiting for the response to arrive, a message is sent and, some time later, the program checks whether an answer has arrived. This allows the program to perform other tasks in the meanwhile and eliminates the need for any coordination between both ends of the interaction.

Historically, this model is similar to the notion of batch jobs, although the motivation behind batch jobs was different. In fact, some very primitive forms of client/server systems that preceded RPC used asynchronous communication. Later, TP monitors incorporated support for asynchronous interaction in the form of queues in order to implement batch jobs in predominantly online environments (Figure 1.15). Today, the most relevant asynchronous communication systems are *message brokers* (Chapter 2), typically used in N-tier architectures to avoid overly tight integration between multiple tiers.

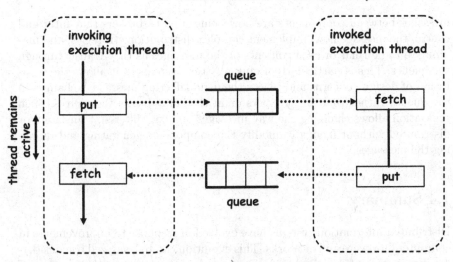

Fig. 1.15. An asynchronous call performed through queues allows the caller to continue working while the request is processed

Asynchronous communication can also be used for online interaction. In practice, asynchronous communication is used in a multitude of applications that would normally be implemented using mechanisms such as RPC, but that are prevented from doing so by design constraints (e.g., when the number of open connections would be too high if synchronous RPC were used). In such cases, the request is sent asynchronously, but the sender actively waits for and expects a response. In this mode of operation, asynchronous interaction can be effectively used to reduce problems with connection management, dependencies between components, fault tolerance, or even format representation. Asynchronous interaction is most useful, however, when the communication pattern is not of the request-response type. Examples of such applications include information dissemination (a server that periodically sends information to a collection of clients) and event notification (systems in which interaction between components does not occur through explicit calls or explicit exchanges of messages but through the publication of *events* or signals that inform those interested that a particular system state has been reached). Another example is a publish/subscribe system, where components continuously make information available by *publishing* it to the system, while other components indicate their interest on parts of the published information by *subscribing* to it. The system is then in charge of matching published information to subscriptions and delivering the information to the subscribers.

Asynchronous interaction requires messages to be stored at some intermediate place until they are retrieved by the receiver. Such intermediate storage opens up the possibility of implementing additional functionality that no longer needs to be made part of the individual components. Following this idea, many queuing systems that were used in the past simply to forward messages between components are now being used as brokers that filter and control the message flow, implement complex distribution strategies, and manipulate the format or even contents of the messages as they transit through the queues. This is particularly useful in N-tier systems as it allows the separation of design concerns and places the logic affecting message exchanges in the queues rather than in wrappers or in the components themselves. Such separation allows changing the way messages are, e.g., filtered, translated, or distributed without having to modify the components generating and receiving the messages.

1.4 Summary

Distributed information systems have evolved in response to improvements in computer hardware and networks. This evolution can be analyzed by considering distributed information systems as a stack of three abstract layers: presentation, application logic, and resource management. When mainframes were the dominant computer architecture, the three layers were blurred into a single tier running on a centralized server. Once local area networks appeared and PCs and workstations became powerful enough, it was possible to move part of the system's functionality to the clients. The result was client/server architectures with two tiers: the presentation layer, which resided at the client, and the application logic and resource management layers, which resided at the server. Such 2-tier architectures were the first step toward modern distributed information systems. Many important concepts were developed around 2-tier systems, including RPC, service interfaces, and APIs, to name just a few.

The proliferation of information servers and the increase in network bandwidth subsequently led to 3-tier architectures, which introduce a middleware layer between the client and the server. It is in this middleware layer that the effort of integrating different information services takes place. Thanks to the middleware approach, 3-tier architectures opened the way for application integration, a higher form of distributed information system.

These ideas are crucial for understanding many of the middleware platforms that are discussed in the next two chapters. The middleware platforms we discuss there reflect this evolution and illustrate very well how system designers have tried to cope with the complexities and challenges of building systems with an increasing number of tiers. The different platforms also serve as examples of the different architectures, design alternatives, and communication trade-offs that we have discussed in this chapter.

The basic ideas described in this chapter are also very important to understand Web services and to put them in the proper context. Web services are just one more step in this evolutionary process–the latest one and probably quite significant–but a step nonetheless. In many ways, Web services are a response to problems that cannot be easily solved with 3-tier and N-tier architectures. Web services can also be seen as yet another tier on top of existing middleware and application integration infrastructure. This new tier allows systems to interact across the Internet, with the standardization efforts around Web services trying to minimize the development cost associated to any additional tier. As indicated in the introduction of this chapter, Web services are the latest response to technology changes (such as the Internet, the Web, more available bandwidth, and the demand for electronic commerce and increased connectivity), but the problems they try to solve are still very much the same as those outlined in this chapter.

2

Middleware

Middleware facilitates and manages the interaction between applications across heterogeneous computing platforms. It is the architectural solution to the problem of integrating a collection of servers and applications under a common service interface. Simple as this description is, it still covers a wide range of situations. Obviously, integrating two databases residing on the same LAN is not the same as integrating two complete 3-tier systems residing on different branches of the same company and linked through a leased line. For the same reason, the solutions employed in the latter case cannot be the same if the systems to be integrated are owned by different companies and must communicate through the Internet.

In this and the following two chapters we examine in depth the complete range of integration possibilities. In this chapter we cover *conventional middleware* platforms as used in restricted settings such as LANs or over a collection of subsystems that are physically close to each other. In Chapter 3 we discuss integration when the systems involved are complete applications. Finally, in Chapter 4 we discuss Web technologies and their impact on application integration. In all cases we discuss middleware–often the same form of middleware, except for small extensions needed to cope with the new requirements. Accordingly, in this chapter we cover all the basic aspects of middleware and the most common middleware platforms available today. We try to follow a logical sequence that mirrors to a great extent how these different platforms were developed (Section 2.1). We start with RPC and related middleware (Section 2.2). Then, we cover modern TP monitors (Section 2.3) as transactional extensions to RPC, object brokers (Section 2.4) as the object-oriented version of RPC, object monitors (Section 2.4.6) as the result of merging TP monitors and object brokers, and message-oriented middleware (Section 2.5) as the descendant of asynchronous RPC. For each of these platforms we provide a brief historical perspective, discuss its particular approach to middleware, and compare it to other forms of middleware in order to identify its advantages and disadvantages.

2.1 Understanding Middleware

Middleware platforms fulfill several roles and appear in many guises. It can be difficult to identify the commonalities and get a comprehensive perspective of the functionality each one provides. Before discussing concrete forms of middleware, it is worthwhile to spend some time understanding the general aspects underlying all middleware platforms.

2.1.1 Middleware as a Programming Abstraction

Middleware offers programming abstractions that hide some of the complexities of building a distributed application. Instead of the programmer having to deal with every aspect of a distributed application, it is the middleware that takes care of some of them. Through these programming abstractions, the developer has access to functionality that otherwise would have to be implemented from scratch.

Remote procedure calls (RPCs) are a very good example of why such abstractions are helpful and of how they evolved over time. Imagine we need to write an application where part of the code is intended to run on one computer and another part must run on a different computer. A first, very basic approach, is to use sockets to open a communication channel between the two parts of the application and to use this channel to pass back and forth whatever information is needed. This is not very difficult and is a programming exercise that every student of computer science has probably completed at one time or another. Let us explore, however, what this programming model implies in real settings. First, we need to worry about the channel itself. We need to write the code that creates the channel and all the code to deal with any errors or failures that may occur on the channel. Second, we need to devise a protocol so that the two parts of the application can exchange information in an ordered manner. The protocol specifies who will be sending what, when, and what is the expected response. Third, we need to work out a format for the information being exchanged so that it can be correctly interpreted by both sides. Finally, once the issues described above have been addressed, we must develop the application that uses the communication channel. This involves including all the code necessary to deal with any errors that may occur: erroneous messages, failures of the application at the other side of the channel, recovery procedures to resume operations after failures, and so on.

Most of this work can be avoided by using middleware abstractions and tools. For example, using plain RPC, we can ignore everything related to the communication channel. RPC is a programming abstraction that hides the communication channel behind an interface that looks exactly like a normal procedure call. With RPC, the only thing we need to do is to reformulate the communication between the two parts of the application as procedure calls. The rest is done for us by the middleware implementing the RPC abstraction. The different layers hidden by the RPC abstractions are shown in Figure 2.1, where RPC acts as the programming interface built upon the communication interface provided by the operating system (*sockets*), which in turn is built upon a stack of communication protocols.

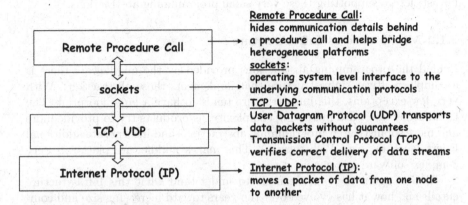

Fig. 2.1. RPC as a programming abstraction that builds upon other communication layers and hides them from the programmer

If we want the middleware to also support the handling of errors and failures, we could use transactional RPC. With transactional RPC we do not need to worry about the state of the invocation or interaction if an error occurs in the middle of it. The underlying middleware guarantees that any partial effects the call may have had are erased as part of the recovery procedure. That way, we do not need to program such clean-up procedures ourselves. Still, this might not be enough (in fact, it isn't). If the application or parts of it fail, transactional guarantees make sure that no unwanted side effects have taken place. However, the application does not necessarily remember when it failed, what things it had already done, and what was left to do. Again, this is something that we would need to program ourselves if we did not use middleware. For this purpose, many modern middleware platforms provide automatic persistence for applications so that, in the event of a failure, they do not lose their state and can quickly resume where they left off.

These are only a few examples of what middleware programming abstractions provide. In all cases, the choice for the programmer is between coding all this functionality from scratch or using a middleware platform. This choice is not always as trivial as it may seem. From the point of view of programming support, the more the middleware can do, the better. Unfortunately, the more the middleware does, the more complex and expensive it becomes. In practice, any non trivial distributed application is built using middleware, but the key to using middleware successfully is to use exactly what one needs and no more. This is not always feasible, since middleware functionality comes bundled in complete platforms. As a result, sometimes designers are better off using a less sophisticated form of middleware that they can extend as needed rather than using a full-featured platform that may offer much more than what is actually needed. The advantages that the middleware provides in terms of programming abstractions are often offset by the cost and complexity of the infrastructure supporting these very same programming abstractions.

2.1.2 Middleware as Infrastructure

Behind the programming abstractions provided by the middleware there is a complex software infrastructure that implements those abstractions. With very few exceptions, this infrastructure tends to have a large footprint. The trend today is toward increasing complexity, as products try to provide more and more sophisticated programming abstractions and incorporate additional layers (such as, e.g., Web servers). This makes middleware platforms very complex software systems.

RPC is again the best example to understand what this infrastructure entails and how it has evolved over the years toward increasing size and complexity (see the next section for more details on RPC). As a programming abstraction, RPC is very simple. Yet, in its simplest form it already requires some basic infrastructure such as an interface definition language, an interface compiler!compiler, and a number of libraries that provide the functionality required to make remote procedure calls. Part of this infrastructure is related to the development of applications using the RPC programming abstraction (the interface definition language and the interface compiler). The other part of the infrastructure is used at run time to execute calls to remote procedures. A similar division between development and run-time support can be found in all forms of middleware.

When a programming abstraction, in this case RPC, turns out to be useful and widely adopted, it starts to be extended and enhanced in different ways. Each extension entails either additional development or run-time support, and has to be general enough to be useful to many different users. These extensions make the programming abstraction more expressive, more flexible, and easier to use. Often, they also make the system more complex and the learning curve steeper. For instance, if RPC clients need to authenticate themselves before they can start to make calls, the infrastructure needs to incorporate mechanisms for dealing with authentication. Similarly, if the addresses of the procedures to invoke are determined dynamically, then a name and directory service is needed. When used, such services need to be installed and kept running in order for RPC to work, thereby adding one more component to worry about. In addition, using a naming service requires additional programming abstractions to deal with the service itself, thereby making the programming interface more complex. As another example, some designers need to have a tighter control of what goes on during an RPC interaction. For these programmers, RPC can be extended with further abstractions that allow direct access to low-level details like the transport protocol used or the parameters of that protocol. The result is additional machinery and a longer list of programming abstractions. More sophisticated users may also need support for multi-threading, automatic logging, transactions, asynchronous RPC, and so on. Once all the required features are accounted for, the programming abstractions have become merely the visible part of a middleware platform that may provide much more than the initial programming abstractions it intended to support. In some cases, part of this functionality may assume a life of its own and become a separate middleware infrastructure. This happened, for instance, with the persistent queuing systems that all TP monitors used to incorporate. Today, such queuing systems have become message brokers.

2.1.3 Types of Middleware

In this chapter we discuss the following forms of middleware:

- **RPC-based systems**. RPC is the most basic form of middleware. It provides the infrastructure necessary to transform procedure calls into remote procedure calls in a uniform and transparent manner. Today, RPC systems are used as a foundation for almost all other forms of middleware, including Web services middleware. For example, the SOAP protocol, often used to support interactions among Web services and discussed in Chapter 6, provides a way to wrap RPC calls into XML messages exchanged through HTTP or some other transport protocol.
- **TP monitors**. TP monitors are the oldest and best-known form of middleware. They are also the most reliable, best tested, and most stable technology in the enterprise application integration arena. In a very gross simplification, TP monitors can be seen as RPC with transactional capabilities. Depending on whether they are implemented as 2-tier or 3-tier systems, TP monitors are classified into *TP-lite* and *TP-heavy* monitors. *TP-lite* systems typically provide an RPC interface to databases. *TP-heavy* monitors are the quintessential middleware platform, providing a wealth of tools and functionality that often matches and even surpasses that of operating systems.
- **Object brokers**. RPC was designed and developed at a time when the predominant programming languages were imperative languages. When object-oriented languages took over, platforms were developed to support the invocation of remote objects, thereby leading to object brokers. These platforms were more advanced in their specification than most RPC systems, but they did not significantly differ from them in terms of implementation. In practice, most of them used RPC as the underlying mechanism to implement remote object calls. The most popular class of object brokers are those based on the Common Object Request Broker Architecture (CORBA), defined and standardized by the Object Management Group (OMG).

- **Object monitors**. When object brokers tried to specify and standardize the functionality of middleware platforms, it soon became apparent that much of this functionality was already available from TP monitors. At the same time, TP monitors, initially developed for procedural languages, had to be extended to cope with object-oriented languages. The result of these two trends was a convergence between TP monitors and object brokers that resulted in hybrid systems called object monitors. Object monitors are, for the most part, TP monitors extended with object-oriented interfaces. Vendors found it easier to make a TP monitor look like a standard-compliant object broker than to implement object brokers with all the features of a TP monitor and the required performance.
- **Message-oriented middleware**. The first forms of RPC middleware had to acknowledge the fact that synchronous interaction was not always needed (see Chapter 1 for a discussion of this topic). Initially this was solved by providing asynchronous RPC. Later on, TP monitors extended this support with persistent message queuing Systems. At a certain point, designers realized that these queuing systems were useful in their own right, and they became middleware platforms on their own under the general name of message-oriented middleware (MOM). Such platforms typically provide transactional access to the queues, persistent queues, and a number of primitives for reading and writing to local and remote queues.
- **Message brokers**. Message brokers are a distinct kind of message-oriented middleware that has the capability of transforming and filtering messages as they move through the queues. They can also dynamically select message recipients based on the message content. In terms of basic infrastructure, message brokers are just queuing systems. The only difference is that application logic can be attached to the queues, thereby allowing designers to implement much more sophisticated interactions in an asynchronous manner.

In this list we omit two important entries–workflow management systems and application servers. Workflow management systems are addressed in Chapter 3, and application servers are discussed in Chapter 4.

2.1.4 Middleware Convergence

It has often been argued that there is too much middleware with competing and overlapping functionality [26, 6, 185]. This refers not so much to the programming abstractions supported, but rather to the underlying infrastructure. The problem arises when, to take advantage of the different programming abstractions, different middleware platforms are used to integrate the same systems. Since each middleware platform comes with its own fixed infrastructure, using several of them amounts to dealing with several such infrastructures. The irony is that a significant percentage of the underlying infrastructure is probably identical across all platforms (RPC-based, in most cases), but is made incompatible by the tailoring of the infrastructure in each product. As a result, there are two obvious trends that can be observed in the evolution of middleware platforms. One is the consolidation of complementary platforms. The other is the emergence of massive product suites that offer, in a single environment, many different forms of middleware.

Object monitors are an example of consolidation. They combine the features and performance of TP monitors with the object-oriented interfaces of object brokers. Another example is the extension of TP monitors or message brokers with support for workflow languages (discussed in detail in Chapter 2) in addition to third-generation programming languages such as C.

There are already many examples of massive product suites combining all the middleware platforms offered by a single vendor. The idea is to simplify multi-tier architectures by resorting to systems that were specifically designed to work together from the start (or where a significant effort has been made to simplify the integration). This is still an ongoing process, but one that is welcome given the integration problems designers face in practice. Essentially every big player in the area has taken this path. The level of integration is certainly not perfect at this stage, but it is reasonable to expect that it will improve and become seamless as new versions of such *all-purpose* middleware platforms appear.

2.2 RPC and Related Middleware

RPC is the foundation underlying the vast majority of middleware platforms available today. In the following, we describe RPC in detail.

2.2.1 Historical Background

RPC was introduced at the beginning of the 1980s by Birell and Nelson as part of their work on the Cedar programming environment [28]. The original paper presented RPC as a way to transparently call procedures located on other machines. This mechanism immediately became the basis for building 2-tier systems, which inherited much of the notation and assumptions used in RPC. In particular, RPC established the notion of client (the program that calls a remote procedure) and server (the program that implements the remote procedure being invoked). It also introduced many concepts still widely used today: *interface definition languages* (IDL), *name and directory services*, *dynamic binding*, *service interface*, and so on. These concepts appear in essentially all forms of middleware and are also a big part of Web services. For instance, about 20 years ago the ANSA Testbench platform provided programmers with a *trading service* to dynamically select a remote procedure based on criteria other than the procedure's signature [9], analogously to what modern name and directory services do.

The strength of RPC was that it provided a clean way to deal with distribution. Moreover, it was based on a concept that programmers at the time knew very well: the *procedure*. RPC made it possible to start building distributed applications without having to change the programming language and the programming paradigm. Initially, RPC was implemented as a collection of libraries. Later on, as more functionality was added, it became a middleware platform on its own. All that was required for a program to become a component of a distributed system was for it to be compiled and linked with the correct set of RPC libraries.

From the very beginning, RPC raised very tough questions about the design and architecture of distributed information systems [196, 54]. Many of these questions are still open. A very heated debate at the time was, for instance, whether RPC should be transparent to the programmer or not. Arguments in favor were based on the simplicity of the concept and the fact that programmers did not need to deal with distribution directly. Arguments against revolved around the fact that including a remote call in a program deeply changed the nature of that program. Forcing programmers to use special constructions for RPC was a way of making them aware of the functional (e.g., using a remote method) and non functional (e.g., performance, reliability) implications of distribution, thereby reducing the opportunities for errors. Most modern RPC systems use a transparent approach.

Today, RPC is at the heart of most distributed information systems [54], and comes in different flavors. For instance, remote method invocation (RMI) is identical to RPC but applies to object methods rather than procedures. Similarly, *stored procedures* are an instance of RPC used to interact with databases. In some cases RPC is used as a low-level primitive used by the system to implement more sophisticated forms of interaction. In other cases, programmers may use it directly to implement distributed applications. However it is used, the mechanisms underlying RPC as well as its implementation have become an intrinsic part of middleware, enterprise application integration, and even Web services.

2.2.2 How RPC Works

The development of a distributed application with RPC is based on a very well defined methodology. For simplicity, we assume here that we want to develop a server that implements a procedure to be used remotely by a single client.

The first step is to define the interface for the procedure. This is done using an interface definition language (IDL) that provides an abstract representation of the procedure in terms of what parameters it takes as input and what parameters it returns as a response. This IDL description can be considered the specification of the services provided by the server. With the IDL description in hand, we can proceed to develop the client and the server (Figure 2.2).

The second step is to compile the IDL description. Any RPC implementation and any middleware using RPC or similar concepts provides such an interface compiler. Typically, compiling the IDL interface produces:

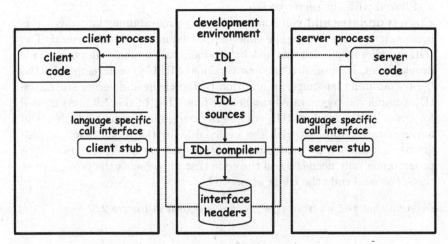

Fig. 2.2. Developing distributed applications with RPC

- **Client stubs.** Each procedure signature in the IDL file results in a client *stub*. The stub is a piece of code to be compiled and linked with the client. When the client calls a remote procedure, the call that is actually executed is a local call to the procedure provided by the stub. The stub then takes care of locating the server (i.e., *binding* the call to a server), formatting the data appropriately (which involves *marshaling* and *serializing* the data[1]), communicating with the server, getting a response, and forwarding that response as the return parameter of the procedure invoked by the client (Figure 2.3). In other words, the stub is a placeholder or *proxy* for the actual procedure implemented at the server. The stub makes the procedure appear as a normal local procedure (since it is part of the client code). The stub, however, does not implement the procedure. It implements all the mechanisms necessary to interact with the server remotely for the purposes of executing that particular procedure.
- **Server stubs.** The server stub is similar in nature to the client stub except that it implements the server side of the invocation. That is, it contains the code for receiving the invocation from the client stub, formatting the data

---

[1] Marshaling involves packing data into a common message format prior to transmitting the message over a communication channel, so that the message can be understood by the recipient. Serialization consists of transforming the message into a string of bytes prior to sending the message through a communication channel.

as needed (which, mirroring the operations at the client stub, involves *deserializing* and *unmarshaling* the call), invoking the actual procedure implemented in the server, and forwarding the results returned by the procedure to the client stub. As with the client stub, it must be compiled and linked with the server code.

- **Code templates and references.** In many programming languages, it is necessary to define at compile time the procedures that will be used. The IDL compiler helps with this task by producing all auxiliary files needed for development. For instance, the first versions of RPC were developed for the C programming language. In addition to the client and server stubs, the IDL compiler also generated the header files (that is, the **.h* files) needed for compilation. Modern IDL compilers even go a step beyond: they can also generate templates with the basic code for the server, such as programs containing only procedure signatures but no implementation. The programmer only needs to add the code that implements the procedure at the server and code the client as needed.

The system that results from this process is shown in Figure 2.3.

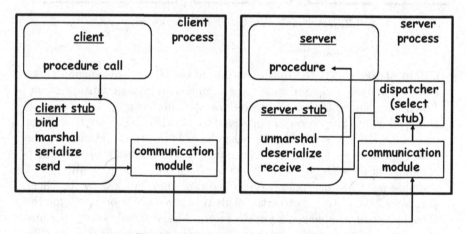

Fig. 2.3. Basic functioning of RPC

RPC stubs can handle all of the network programming details, including timeouts and retransmissions if an unreliable protocol such as the user datagram protocol (UDP) is used. If more control is needed, RPC infrastructures typically provide different RPC interfaces, ranging from very simple to very sophisticated ones, that can be invoked to configure how the interaction should occur. These interfaces are used to implement different types of stubs. The simple interfaces usually provide only three primitives for using RPC: *procedure registration* (making it known to clients that a procedure is available for remote invocation), *procedure call* (actual invocation of the remote procedure), and *procedure call using broadcast* (same as procedure call, but using a broadcast primitive). The advanced interfaces give programmers finer control over the transport protocols and binding procedures.

2.2.3 Binding in RPC

In order for a client to make an RPC, it must first locate and bind to the server hosting the remote procedure. *Binding* is the process whereby the client creates a local association for (i.e., a *handle* to) a given server in order to invoke a remote procedure. Binding can be either *static* or *dynamic*. In static binding, the client stub is hardcoded to already contain the handle of the server where the procedure resides. The form of this handle depends on the environment: It might be an IP address and port number, an Ethernet address, an X.500 address, and so on. When the client invokes the procedure, the stub simply forwards the call to that server.

The advantages of static binding are that it is simple and efficient. No additional infrastructure is needed beyond the client and the server stubs. The disadvantages are that the client and the server become tightly coupled. That is, if the server fails, the client will not work. If the server changes location (because of upgrades, maintenance, etc.), the client must be recompiled with a new stub that points to the right location. Finally, it is not possible to use redundant servers to increase performance because the clients are bound to specific servers. Load balancing must take place at the time that clients are distributed and developed, or else the system may exhibit severe skews in load, with some servers answering most requests while others remain idle.

These disadvantages led the designers of RPC to develop dynamic binding. *Dynamic binding* enables clients to use a specialized service to locate appropriate servers (Figure 2.4). Similar to the consequence of adding new tiers to information systems (Chapter 1), dynamic binding simply adds a layer of indirection to gain flexibility at the cost of performance. This additional layer of indirection, generally called *name and directory server* (also known as a *binder* in earlier RPC implementations), is responsible for resolving server addresses based on the signatures of the procedures being invoked. Thus, when the client invokes a remote procedure, the client stub asks the directory server for a suitable server to execute that procedure. The directory server responds with the address of a server. With that address, the client stub proceeds to complete the invocation.

Dynamic binding creates many opportunities for improving RPC interaction. The directory server could, for instance, keep track of which servers have been invoked and perform load balancing so as to use resources as efficiently as possible. If the server changes location, it is enough to change the entry in the directory server for requests to be rerouted to the new location. The result is the decoupling of the client and the server, which adds a great deal of flexibility when deploying and operating the system. The cost of this flexibility is additional infrastructure such as a directory server, a protocol for interacting

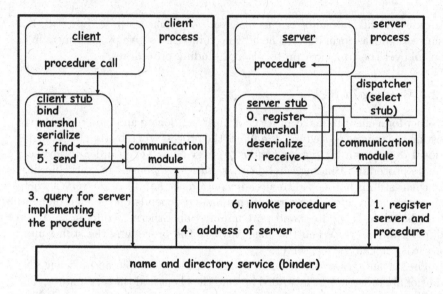

Fig. 2.4. Dynamic binding allows a server to register the procedures it implements (steps 0 and 1). A client can then ask for the address of the server implementing a given procedure (steps 2 and 3), obtain the address from the binder (step 4), and make the call to the procedure (steps 5, 6, and 7), which then proceeds as in the static case

with the directory server, and primitives for registering procedures with the server. These operations are, in principle, hidden from the programmer since they are performed by the stubs. The server stub, for instance, registers the server procedures when the server is started. Similarly, the client stub deals with the directory server when calls are made.

The directory server uses the IDL specification of the procedures to perform dynamic binding. That is, the binding is made based on the procedure's *signature*. However, there is nothing that prevents the binding from happening based on other, possibly non functional criteria. Directory servers supporting sophisticated selection mechanisms were called *traders*. Such ideas are well-explored in the context of RPC; there are even RPC platforms that support such sophisticated binding procedures [54].

RPC systems, however, predominantly worked under the assumption that the implementation of the distribution mechanism should be hidden from the programmer by the stubs. In other words, the programmer is not necessarily aware of whether binding is dynamic or static. This is decided when the system is designed and the stubs created. Such an approach is the basis for the separation between programmers of client and server functionality.

2.2.4 RPC and Heterogeneity

One of the original design goals of RPC was to serve as a mechanism for bridging heterogeneous systems. Because the bulk of the work of dealing with distribution is performed by the stubs, one can develop very complex stubs that enable client programmers to develop software on platforms other than those used by server programmers. That is, the stubs can be used to hide not only the distribution but also the heterogeneity. This was a very appealing feature of RPC. Recall that RPC was instrumental to the development of client/server systems. As we saw in Chapter 1, 2-tier or client/server architectures appeared when information systems started to move away from the mainframe approach. PCs, however, were not powerful enough to run a server; they could only support the client application. Servers required more powerful machines that used CPUs and operating systems (e.g., UNIX) different from those available for clients (e.g., DOS). Hence, when they moved to client/server architectures, information systems became not only distributed but also heterogeneous.

The problem of dealing with heterogeneous client and server systems is that, potentially, there are many different platforms on which the clients and servers could run, and there are many programming languages in which the clients and the servers could be developed. A naive approach would use a different client and server stub set for every possible combination of platforms and languages (i.e., $2 \times n \times m$ stubs are needed for n client and m server platforms). A much more efficient alternative is to use some form of intermediate representation so that clients and servers only need to know how to translate to and from this intermediate representation. The problem of dealing with heterogeneity then becomes a matter of developing client and server stubs for the corresponding platforms (which requires only $n + m$ stubs).

RPC uses IDL not only to define interfaces but also to define the mapping from concrete programming languages to the intermediate representation used in that particular RPC system. One of the reasons for using an IDL rather than simply adopting the syntax of a given programming language (although earlier IDLs showed a marked preference for programming languages such as C) is that the intermediate representation of IDL enables clients and servers to ignore differences in terms of machine architecture, programming languages, and type systems used by each one of them. As a platform independent representation, IDL serves not only for specifying interfaces but also for defining the intermediate representation for data exchanges between clients and servers. This intermediate representation specifies how parameters should be represented and organized before being sent across the network. For instance, Sun's IDL (called XDR) requires calls to be encoded into 4-byte objects, each byte being an ASCII code [54, 183]. It further defines how to use these objects to store the name of the procedure and the values of the parameters. Once marshaled into this format, the data can be serialized and sent through the network. At the other side, the message can be deserialized and unmarshaled to obtain the parameters of the call in whatever internal format is used.

2.2.5 Extensions to RPC

Conventional RPC shares many of the characteristics of a local function call. First, it uses a synchronous, procedural approach. The execution, including the execution of subroutines, is sequential. A client can have only one outstanding call at a time and is blocked until the call returns. At the server, multiple threads can be used to handle several clients concurrently, but each thread is dedicated exclusively to one client. Very early on, designers realized that the limitations of this model prevented the implementation of all forms of interactions needed in a distributed information system. As a result, many extensions to the basic RPC mechanisms have been implemented. The motivation behind these extensions to RPC lies in the same changes that triggered the move toward 3-tier architectures, i.e., the increasing availability of servers with published, stable interfaces spurred the need for architecture and infrastructure to support server integration. In fact, extensions to RPC have resulted in different middleware platforms such as TP monitors, object monitors, queuing systems, or message brokers. Here we discuss *asynchronous RPC* (which underlies message-oriented middleware and message brokers), while in Section 2.3.2 we discuss *transactional RPC* (as the basis for TP monitors).

Asynchronous RPC was one of the first extensions to RPC to support non blocking calls . It allows a client to send a request message to a service without waiting for the response. The communication handler returns control to the client program immediately after sending request, and thus the client thread is not blocked when it makes a call. This allows it to have multiple outstanding calls while still doing other work.

This is relatively easy to implement by changing the way the client stub works. Instead of one single entry point to invoke the procedure, the stub provides two entry points–one to invoke the procedure and one to obtain the results of the invocation. When the client calls the remote procedure, the stub extracts the input parameters and immediately returns control to the client, which can then continue processing. The stub, in the meantime, makes the call to the server and waits for a response. This behavior can be easily achieved by using threads at the client without the programmer of the client having to be aware of it. Later, the client makes a second call to the stub to obtain the results. If the call has returned, the stub placed the results in some shared data structure and the client picks it up from there. If the call has not yet returned, the client receives an error that indicates that it should try again later. If there was an error with the call itself (timeout, communication error, etc.) the client receives a return value that indicates the nature of the problem. In essence, the stubs execute synchronously while giving the illusion of asynchronous execution to the clients and servers using them.

The original motivation for asynchronous interaction in RPC systems was to maintain backward compatibility, so to speak, with functionality provided by 1-tier architectures. In particular, 1-tier architectures typically supported *batch* operations, which cannot be implemented with synchronous RPC; asynchronous RPC provided a means for implementing such operations. Later, designers recognized additional advantages to asynchronous RPC, but also encountered the challenges it posed to programmers. To be truly useful, asynchronous RPC needed a much more sophisticated infrastructure than the stubs provided. For example, because less information about the connection is maintained and requests are decoupled from replies, it can be more difficult to recover from a failure involving asynchronous RPC than traditional RPC. This infrastructure was developed as part of the queuing systems used in TP monitors and later evolved into what we know as message brokers. Because RPC initially lacked the necessary additional support, the use of asynchronous RPC was not as general then as it is today. We revisit this issue in detail when discussing message-oriented middleware (Section 2.5) and message brokers (Section 3.2).

2.2.6 RPC Middleware Infrastructure: DCE

Even without considering extensions to the basic RPC mechanism, RPC already assumes a certain degree of infrastructure for both development and execution. Some of this infrastructure is minimal, particularly in basic implementations of RPC such as Sun's RPC [183]. In other cases, it is quite extensive as in the Distributed Computing Environment (DCE) provided by the Open Software Foundation (OSF) [98] (Figure 2.5). DCE is still in use today in many popular middleware and enterprise integration products. Because it represents an intermediate stage between basic client server and full 3-tier architectures, we devote some time here to understand what DCE provides.

DCE was the result of an attempt to standardize RPC–an attempt that did not succeed. DCE provides not only a complete specification of how RPC should work but also a standardized implementation. The goal of DCE was to give vendors a standard implementation that they could then use and extend as needed for their own products. By using the same basic implementation of RPC, the hope was that the resulting products would be compatible. Many see this as the reason why DCE did not become an accepted standard. When the Object Management Group proposed CORBA as a standard for distributed object platforms (discussed later in this chapter), it had learned from that error and enforced only a specification, not an implementation. However, since many implementations compliant with the CORBA standard are not compatible among themselves, the OSF may have had a point.

The DCE platform provides RPC and a number of additional services that are very useful when developing distributed information systems. These services include:

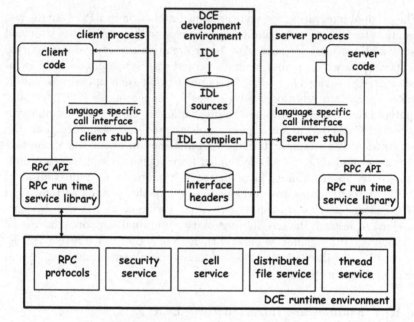

Fig. 2.5. The architecture of DCE

- **Cell directory service.** The Cell directory is a sophisticated name and directory server used to create and manage RPC domains that can coexist over the same network without interfering with each other.
- **Time service.** The Time service provides mechanisms for clock synchronization across all nodes.
- **Thread service.** As pointed out in the explanations above, multi-threading is an important part of RPC systems. DCE supports threads and multiple processors with the Thread service.
- **Distributed file service.** The file service allows programs to share data files across a DCE environment.
- **Security service.** In a shared environment, such as the ones addressed by DCE, it is not feasible to accept procedure calls from arbitrary clients. The Security service solves this problem by providing authenticated and secure communication.

The main architectural characteristics of DCE are shown in Figure 2.5. This figure is a good summary of how RPC works, as well as some of the support needed in real environments. The attentive reader will notice that the figure will appear again under different disguises as we discuss other forms of middleware. This is no accident. Most of the middleware platforms described in this and the next chapters are based on RPC and, in some cases, are direct extensions and enhancements of the RPC mechanism. In fact, many of these platforms are actually built on top of RPC platforms including those that would appear to use different paradigms (like object brokers or message-oriented middleware).

2.3 TP Monitors

Transaction processing monitors, or *TP monitors*, are one of the oldest forms of middleware. Because they have been around for such a long time, they are very well understood and have been studied in great detail [25, 86, 209]. TP monitor products are also the most efficient form of middleware, given that their architectures and internal mechanisms have been optimized for many years. Nowadays, TP monitors are the cornerstone of many N-tier systems and their architectures and functionality are a constant reference for new forms of middleware.

2.3.1 Historical Background

TP monitors predate client/server and 3-tier architectures. One of the earliest TP monitors was IBM's Customer Information and Control Systems (CICS), developed at the end of the 1960s and still in use today. Initially, such TP monitors were designed to allow mainframes to support the efficient multi-plexing of resources among as many concurrent users as possible. As part of this task, they also needed to deal with multithreading and data consistency, thereby extending core functionality with the concept of *transaction*. CICS was the first commercial product offering transaction protected distributed computing [86].

In the same way that the RPC was heavily influenced by the prevailing programming paradigm at the time it emerged, TP monitors owe much of their architecture to the characteristics of early operating systems. In many ways, a TP monitor is an alternative operating system and offers features that compete with those provided by operating systems. At the time, operating systems were rather limited in their capabilities. TP monitors were developed to bypass these limitations. For instance, CICS owed its popularity to the fact that it could create and dispatch a thread an order of magnitude faster than the operating system [86]. CICS, like many other TP monitors that came later, was not only an execution environment with functionality equivalent to that of many operating systems but also a complete development tool. Faithful to the 1-tier architecture, these initial systems were entirely monolithic and ran the complete system as a single operating system process.

With the migration to client/server and 3-tier architectures, TP monitors became more modular but not necessarily simpler. Much of their functionality was separated into components that could be combined in different manners: logging, recovery, persistence, transactional file system, security, communications, and so on. They also became more versatile by offering a wider range of functionality. For instance, CICS was initially a 1-tier system designed for online transactions. Tuxedo, which appeared at the beginning of the 1980s, was originally a 2-tier queue-based system. Eventually, almost all commercial monitors became 3-tier systems that supported batch transactions, online transactions, and even interactive transactions. In the process, it also became clear that programming support was a critical issue. There was no point in providing sophisticated functionality if designers did not have the necessary programming abstractions to use them in practice. As a result, TP monitors started to incorporate their own languages or versions of programming languages. For example, in the early 1990s, Encina introduced *Transactional-C*, a dialect of C where transactions were first-class programming constructs that made it considerably simpler to program in TP monitor environments.

This trend toward increasing complexity and functionality was reversed to a certain extent with the development of *TP-lite* monitors. The idea was to provide the core functionality of a TP monitor (i.e., transactional RPC) as an additional layer embedded in database management systems. This can be done using *stored procedures*, where application logic can be written and run within the scope of the database rather than in an intermediate layer as in conventional TP monitors. The resulting 2-tier architecture was lighter than a TP monitor, but sufficient for those applications whose only resource managers were databases. TP-lite monitors are an extension of the functionality of a database and lack most of the sophisticated functionality of a conventional TP monitor. As such, they cannot be really seen as integration tools but are, nevertheless, still heavily used–especially in conjunction with stored procedures.

For many decades, TP monitors were the absolutely dominant form of middleware. Indeed, they are one of the most successful forms of middleware, enabling many of the operations that we perform in everyday life (such as purchasing a plane ticket or performing a banking transactions) to take place with satisfactory performance and reliability. In fact, they still play this key role today; TP monitors can be found behind most application servers and Web services implementations. There are many commercial implementations of TP monitors, e.g., IBM CICS [97], Microsoft MTS [140], and BEA Tuxedo [17]. These same TP monitors can be found at the heart of modern product suites for enterprise application integration. TP monitors have also played a pivotal role in the development of middleware platforms. Almost all forms of middleware available today have a direct link to one TP monitor or another.

2.3.2 Transactional RPC and TP Monitors

The main goal of a TP monitor is to support the execution of distributed transactions. To this end, TP monitors implement an abstraction called *transactional RPC* (TRPC).

Conventional RPC was originally designed to enable a client to call a server. When there are more than two entities–and therefore more than one procedure call–involved in an interaction (e.g., a client invoking procedures of two servers, or a client talking to a server that is talking to a database), then conventional RPC incorrectly treats the calls as independent of each other. However, the calls are not really independent, which complicates recovering from partial system failures. For example, if the call is to a server that, as part of executing the procedure, invokes some other remote procedure, then the semantics of the call are not defined. If the original call returns with an error, the client has no way of knowing where the error occurred and what changes actually took place. There is no way to distinguish between the case where the error is confined to the first server and the second completes its execution of the procedure, and the case where the error is confined to the second server. Similarly, if a client uses conventional RPC to interact with two different servers, it has no way of maintaining consistency between the two servers unless it implements all necessary mechanisms itself.

As an example, consider an application that withdraws money from one bank account and deposits it into another account. Should the client fail between the two calls, the money would be lost unless the client maintained a persistent state. An elegant solution to this problem was to make RPC *transactional*, that is, to extend the RPC protocol with the ability to wrap a series of RPC invocations into a *transaction*.

The notion of transaction was developed in the context of databases, and refers to a set of database operations that are characterized by the so called ACID properties (atomicity, consistency, isolation, and durability). In particular, the transactional abstraction implies that either all the operations in the set are successfully executed or none of them is. If the client interacting with the database fails or if an error occurs after it has executed some (but not all) of the operations within the transaction, the effect of completed operations is rolled back (undone). Databases typically provide transactional guarantees only for operations interacting with the database (Figure 2.6a). As discussed above for RPC, such properties are also desirable when dealing with data distributed across multiple, possibly heterogeneous systems (Figure 2.6b). This is what transactional RPC provides.

The semantics of transactional RPC is such that if a group of procedure invocations within a transaction are committed (i.e., successfully completed), the programmer has the guarantee that all of them have been executed. If instead the group of invocations is aborted, typically due to some failure, then none of them will have been executed (or better said, the overall effect is *as if* none of them were executed). In other words, TRPC guarantees *at most once* semantics on a group of RPC calls. Other similar extensions to RPC have been proposed, where the goal is to achieve *at least once* or *exactly once* semantics to one or groups of RPC calls.

In more detail, procedure calls enclosed within the transactional brackets (*beginning of transaction* (BOT) and *end of transaction* (EOT) instructions) are treated as one unit, and the RPC infrastructure guarantees their atomicity. This is achieved by using a *transaction management* module that coordinates interactions between the clients and the servers (Figure 2.7). This transac-

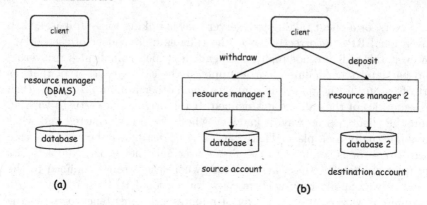

Fig. 2.6. a Database management systems (DBMSs) provide ACID properties for the resources they manage; **b** This is not sufficient for procedures that span multiple heterogeneous resources

tion management module is what gives TP monitors their name, but its most basic functionality can be explained as an extension of the RPC mechanism. Thus, the BOT and EOT commands are treated as calls to the corresponding stub (the client stub or the server stub since the server can also make calls to other services). Assume the transactional program resides at the client and that two RPC invocations are being made to two different servers. When the BOT is encountered, the client stub contacts the transaction manager of the TP monitor to obtain the appropriate transactional identifier and create the transactional context that will be used throughout the sequence of calls. From then on, all outgoing RPC calls carry the transactional context with them. When the client calls one of the servers, the server stub extracts the transactional context, notifies the transaction manager that it is now participating in the transaction, and forwards the call as a normal call. The same is done when the client invokes the second server. When the EOT is reached, the client stub notifies the transaction manager. The transaction manager then initiates a *two-phase commit* (2PC) protocol between the two servers involved, to determine the outcome of the transaction. Once the protocol terminates, the transaction manager informs the client stub, which then returns from the EOT to the client code indicating whether the transaction was successfully committed or not. Figure 2.7 summarizes this procedure.

The 2PC protocol [84, 117] used as part of TRPC was first used commercially within CICS, and was subsequently standardized by the Open Group within the X/Open specification [197]. Today, 2PC is the standard mechanism for guaranteeing atomicity in distributed information systems [86, 209]. In 2PC, the transaction manager executes the commit in two phases: in the first phase, it contacts each server involved in the transaction by sending a *prepare to commit* message, asking whether the server is ready to execute a commit. If the server successfully completed the procedure invoked by the TRPC, it

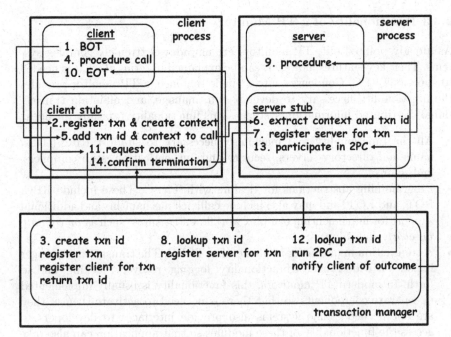

Fig. 2.7. Encapsulating an RPC call within transactional brackets

answers that it is *ready to commit*. By doing this, the server guarantees that it
will be able to commit the procedure even if failures occur. If the server could
not complete the TRPC, it replies *abort*. In the second phase, the transaction
manager examines all the replies obtained and, if all of them are *ready to commit*, it then instructs each server to commit the changes performed as part
of the invoked procedure. If at least one resource manager replied *abort* (or
failed to reply within a specified time limit), then the transaction manager requests all servers to abort the transaction. Fault tolerance in 2PC is achieved
through *logging* (writing the state of the protocol to persistent storage). By
consulting such log entries, it is possible to reconstruct the situation before a
failure occurred and recover the system. What is logged and when depends on
the flavor of 2PC used (*presumed nothing, presumed abort, presumed commit,*
[209]) but it is an important factor in terms of performance, since it must be
done for each transaction executed and since logging implies writing to the
disk (which is a time-consuming operation). 2PC may block a transaction if
the coordinator fails after sending the *prepare to commit* messages but before
sending a commit message to all participants. In those cases, the decision on
what to do with a blocked transaction is typically left to the system administrator, who can decide to either abort or commit the transaction and then
reconcile the state of the system once the coordinator recovers. In practice,
for normal transactions, the probability that the coordinator fails exactly at
that point in time is very small.

2.3.3 Functionality of a TP Monitor

As already pointed out, TP monitors are nowadays extremely complex systems. Their key features, however, can be explained in terms of what is needed to support TRPC. Condensed into a single sentence, a TP monitor provides the functionality necessary to develop, run, manage, and maintain transactional distributed information systems. This functionality typically includes:

- All the functionality and machinery necessary to support RPC (IDLs, name and directory servers, security and authentication, stub compilers, and so on).
- Programming abstractions for dealing with TRPC. These include RPC, BOT, and EOT, and may also include callback mechanisms and additional support for implementing complex workflow structures (such as *on commit*, *on abort*, and so on).
- A transaction manager for implementing TRPC. The transaction manager includes a wide range of functionality: logging, recovery, locking, and so forth. In modern TP monitors, this functionality is usually implemented in separate components so that there is no need to activate them if they are not needed. Some systems also provide interfaces to developers to access the functionality of these modules so that application can also take advantage of it (e.g., to log additional information about the state of the application).
- A monitor system in charge of scheduling threads, assigning priorities, load balancing, replication, starting and stopping components, and so forth. The monitor system provides performance and flexibility to the TP monitor.
- A run-time environment that acts as the computational background for all the applications that use the TP monitor. This run-time environment provides the resources and services applications may need (transactional services, security services, transactional file system, and so on.)
- Specialized components tailored for particular scenarios or systems. These components range from proprietary protocols for interacting with mainframe-based systems to persistent queuing systems for asynchronous interaction.
- A wide variety of tools for installing, managing, and monitoring the performance of all these components.

In addition, each of these elements is likely to come in different flavors and with different interfaces so that it can be used on top of a variety of platforms and in connection with a variety of legacy systems. Like RPC, the programming abstractions available can be used at different levels of complexity. In their simplest form, they merely transform RPC into TRPC. In their most complex form, they allow designers to control almost all aspects of the interaction.

2.3.4 Architecture of a TP Monitor

The typical architecture of a TP monitor is shown in Figure 2.8. The figure abstracts the most salient features of an actual TP monitor and ignores many details related to the way components are interconnected and interact with each other. Components in this architecture include:

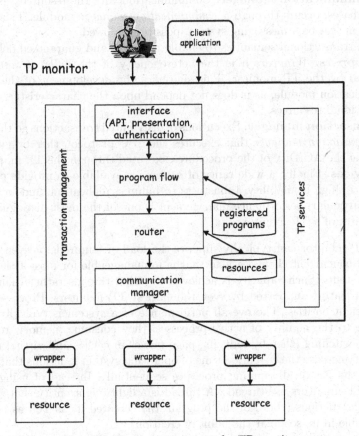

Fig. 2.8. Basic components of a TP monitor

- **Interface.** A client *interface* component provides a programmatic API as well as support for direct access via terminal and authentication.
- **Program flow.** The *program flow* component stores, loads, and executes procedures, possibly written in a language provided by the TP monitor itself. Stored programs typically involve the invocation of operations on logical resources, identified by their name.
- **Router.** The *router* maps each operation to an invocation. The invocation can involve an underlying resource manager (such as a database) or

a local service provided by the TP monitor itself. The router includes a special-purpose database that stores the definition of the mappings between logical resource names and physical devices. In case of changes to the system configuration, the system administrator needs only update this mapping; client applications do not need to be modified, because they access resources based on logical names.

- **Communication manager.** Communication with the resources, such as databases, occurs through a *communication manager* module. This component can be a messaging system, possibly endowed
with transactional semantics to enable rollbacks and guaranteed delivery.

- **Wrappers.** *Wrappers* hide the heterogeneity of the different resources linked by the TP monitor. This simplifies the development of the communication module, as it does not depend upon the characteristics of the individual resources.

- **Transaction manager.** Executions of distributed transactions go through a *transaction manager* that executes the 2PC protocol, thereby guaranteeing the ACIDity of the procedures executed through the TP monitor.

- **Services.** Finally, a wide range of *services* is available to provide performance, high availability, robustness to failures, replication, and so forth. In particular, performance management is one of the most distinguishing features of a TP monitor.

A TP monitor can typically support the load of hundreds or even thousands of concurrent clients, a load that is unmanageable for most 1-tier and 2-tier systems. Such capacity is achieved by using threads rather than processes, a feature supported by even the earliest TP monitors. Processes are heavyweight entities. The overall performance of a system is typically very sensitive to the number of active processes: they consume memory, require context switching (thereby inducing page misses in caches and virtual memory), and increase the execution time of operating system functions that have to scan the list of all running processes sequentially. Instead of using processes, TP monitors use threads. A thread is a lightweight entity that shares all the instructions (code) of the program that created it, as well as all the data visible in its scope at the point of creation.

Once created, each thread gets its own thread identifier, as well as its own registers and stack for local variables, which allows the thread to execute independently. Most TP monitors provide their own thread-scheduling mechanism. In addition to threads, TP monitors provide load-balancing components to improve performance by dynamically distributing the workload across different machines. A large part of the architecture of a TP monitor is devoted to the efficient implementation of all these mechanisms.

2.4 Object Brokers

Object brokers extend the RPC paradigm to the object-oriented world and provide a number of services that simplify the development of distributed object-oriented applications. In a nutshell, object brokers are middleware infrastructures that support interoperability among objects. In the following we describe their basic principles, focusing in particular on *CORBA*, the most well-known object broker architecture.

2.4.1 Historical Background

Object brokers appeared at the beginning of the 1990s as the natural evolution of RPC to cope with object orientation, a programming paradigm that was increasingly gaining acceptance. The purposes of object brokers, especially in the beginning, were exactly the same as those of RPC: hide much of the complexity behind remote invocations by making them look like local calls from a programmer's perspective. The difference was that clients did not have to invoke a procedure, but a method of an object. Since object-oriented models include notions such as inheritance and polymorphism, the function performed by the server object actually depends on the class to which the server object belongs, and therefore different objects may respond in different ways to the invocation of the same method. This means that the middleware had to bind clients with specific objects running on a server and manage the interactions between two objects. This was indeed the main functionality of an object broker. With time, object brokers added features that went beyond basic interoperability, for example including location transparency, sophisticated dynamic binding techniques, object lifecycle management, and persistence.

Probably the best-known example of object broker is the abstraction described in the Common Object Request Broker Architecture (CORBA) specification. CORBA is an architecture and a specification for the creation and management of object-oriented applications that are distributed in a network. It was developed in the early 1990s by the Object Management Group (OMG), a consortium of more than 800 companies. CORBA [153] offers a standardized *specification* of an object broker rather than a concrete implementation, and is agnostic with respect to both the programming language used to develop object-oriented applications and also the operating systems on which the applications run.

CORBA enjoyed tremendous popularity in the mid- and late-1990s: many software vendors have implemented the CORBA specifications, and thousands of applications have been developed on top of this architecture. Indeed, it is almost impossible to speak about object brokers without speaking of CORBA, whose well-defined architecture is also suited to introducing the principles and functionality of an object broker. Object brokers and CORBA are so tightly coupled in the minds of many people in the IT world that some technical dictionaries even go as far as defining object brokers as "a component in the

CORBA programming model" [110]. However, not all object brokers were or are based on CORBA. The most significant and widely used example of non-CORBA object broker are the Distributed Component Object Model (DCOM) and its descendant, COM+ [164], which are specific to the Microsoft operating systems (indeed, they are incorporated into it).

More recently, the interest in CORBA has started to fade as new technologies have emerged. The most relevant of these are .NET from Microsoft and the Java 2 Enterprise Edition (J2EE) platforms and application servers offered by a number of other vendors. The OMG is currently responding to these challenges by enabling interoperability between CORBA and Java [156] and by defining a richer, J2EE-like component model for CORBA objects [158]. Nevertheless, CORBA has always been a hybrid standard that covered not only object-orientation but also many services already offered by other middleware platforms. It is thus very likely that CORBA specifications will eventually be subsumed by other standards.

2.4.2 CORBA: System Architecture

A CORBA-compliant system is made of three main pieces (as shown in Figure 2.9):

- **Object request broker.** The object request broker (ORB) provides basic object interoperability functions.
- **CORBA services.** A set of services, known collectively under the name of *CORBA services* [152], is accessible through a standardized API and provide functionality commonly needed by most objects, such as persistence, lifecycle management , and security.
- **CORBA facilities.** A set of facilities, collectively known under the name of *CORBA facilities* [151], provides higher-level services needed by applications rather than by individual objects. Examples include document management, internationalization, and support for mobile agents. CORBA facilities may also include services specific to a vertical market, such as education, health care, or transportation.

Together, these three components support the development of distributed object applications. The ORB is at the core of this architecture: every interaction between clients and services (user-defined, CORBA services, or CORBA facilities) goes through it.

2.4.3 How CORBA Works

In order to be accessed through an ORB, an object must first declare its interface, so that clients are aware of the methods it provides. How this is done is very similar to the mechanisms already described for RPC. Interfaces are specified in CORBA's IDL . Figure 2.10 shows an example IDL specification

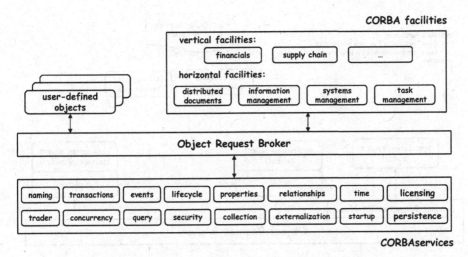

Fig. 2.9. High level view of the CORBA architecture

defining the interface of an object that provides supply chain-related operations (note the similarity to Figure 2.5 in terms of use of stubs, IDL compilers, etc.; except for the different notation, the concepts are practically identical). In addition to method declarations, and unlike the IDLs for RPC systems, CORBA's IDL supports many object-oriented concepts such as inheritance and polymorphism. As with RPC, IDL specifications can be fed to an IDL compiler that generates a *stub* and a *skeleton*. The stub is a proxy object that hides the distribution and makes method calls in the client look as if they were local instead of remote. The stub code includes the declarations of the methods provided by the object implementation and is linked with the client code to obtain the executable client application. The skeleton, on the other hand, shields the server object from all issues concerning the distribution, so that it can be developed as though function calls were coming from a local object (Figure 2.10).

Technically, to develop a client object that interacts with a given server, all a programmer needs to know is the server's IDL interface. Of course, the developer must be aware of the semantics of the interface methods as well as of other constraints (such as a specific ordering in which the methods should be invoked to achieve a certain goal). These aspects are not formalized and are assumed to be described by other means, such as through comments in the IDL specifications or by exchanging descriptive documents.

2.4.4 CORBA: Dynamic Service Selection and Invocation

The interoperability mechanism described above requires clients to be statically bound to an interface. In fact, the IDL compiler statically generates a stub that is specific to a given service interface. In addition to this form of

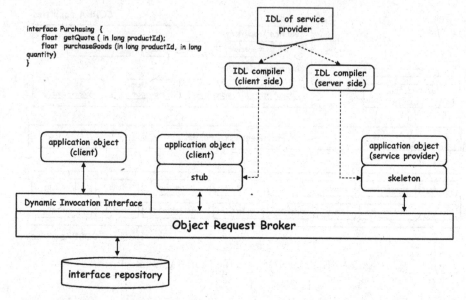

Fig. 2.10. IDL specifications are compiled into skeletons on the server side and into stubs on the client side

interface binding, CORBA allows client applications to dynamically discover new objects, retrieve their interfaces, and construct invocations of this object on the fly, even if no stub has been previously generated and linked to the client. This capability is based on two components: the *interface repository* and the *dynamic invocation interface*. The interface repository stores IDL definitions for all the objects known to the ORB. Applications can access the repository to browse, edit, or delete IDL interfaces. An ORB can have many interface repositories, and the same repository can be shared across ORBs; however, the OMG specifications require each ORB to have at least one interface repository. The dynamic invocation interface provides operations such as *get_interface* and *create_request* that can be used by clients to browse the repository and dynamically construct the method invocation based on the newly discovered interface.

The ability to dynamically construct a method invocation based on a dynamically discovered interface solves only part of the dynamic service invocation problem. It assumes that clients have already identified the service they need. How can they do that? In CORBA, references to service objects are obtained through the Naming and Trader services. The relationship between the Naming and the Trader services is analogous to the one between telephone white and yellow pages. The Naming service allows for the retrieval of object references based on the name of the service we need (e.g., *PurchaseBooks*). The Trader service, on the other hand, allows clients to search for services based on their *properties*. Services can in fact advertise their properties with the trader. Different services can have different properties, describing non-functional characteristics of the service. With the Trader, clients are not only able to look for objects implementing a certain interface (e.g., the Purchasing interface described above), but also for objects whose properties have specified values (e.g., companies selling history or archaeology books).

Although the capability of using CORBA to perform dynamic service selection and invocation is very intriguing, in practice it is rarely used. Constructing dynamic invocations is in fact very difficult, not so much from a technical perspective (it just requires a few more steps with respect to using statically generated stubs), but from a semantic one. One problem is that, to search for services, the client object must understand the meaning of the service properties, which in turn requires a shared ontology among clients and service providers. Furthermore, if the client has not been specifically implemented to interact with a certain service, it is difficult that it is able to figure out what the operations of the newly discovered service do, what is the exact meaning of their parameters, and in what order they should be invoked to obtain the desired functionality. We revisit these issues when discussing service discovery in Chapter 6, to compare CORBA-based service selection and invocation with the techniques adopted in the Web services domain.

2.4.5 CORBA: Encapsulation

One of the most significant features of CORBA, and of object brokers in general, is *encapsulation*. The notion of encapsulation refers to the hiding of the internal details of an object from its clients. It is a very important abstraction since it allows a service provider to change the details of the service implementations without requiring changes to the client. Encapsulation was present to a certain extent in RPC and TP monitors since they also work based on well-defined interfaces and use IDLs in a manner similar to CORBA. Yet, encapsulation fits more naturally with the object-oriented model used in CORBA.

In Chapter 1, we saw that APIs are the basic ingredient of encapsulation, but there are many other forms in which encapsulation can manifest itself. An example is CORBA's independence from programming languages and operating systems. In CORBA, and unlike in RPC systems and most TP monitors, client and server objects do not need to be implemented in the same programming language and do not need to run on top of the same operating system. Moreover, the client does not even need to know in which language the server object has been implemented or on which environment the server object is running, and vice versa. As we pointed out earlier, all a client needs to know about a server is the latter's IDL specification. Since all method calls flow through the ORB, invocation parameters are converted into a common data representation independent of the specific programming language and operating system, and are converted again by the skeleton prior to invoking the programming language-specific methods on the server side. Therefore, developers on both the client and the server side are free to change not only the implementation logic, but also the language in which clients and servers are implemented and the operating system on top of which they run, as long as the IDL stays the same.

One could argue that this is in principle also possible with RPC and TP monitors. Note, however, that while the IDL is always the same regardless of which programming language is used for implementing the objects, IDL compilers are not all identical to each other. Each compiler compiles to a different language, and how this compilation takes place plays a crucial role in determining compatibility. For instance, the skeleton must invoke the server object's methods and such an invocation is programming language-specific. The big advantage of CORBA over previous uses of the concept of IDL is that the mappings from IDL to different programming languages are also standardized. This ensures that an object implementation can be ported across ORBs of different vendors independently of the language used. It was this standardization effort that made encapsulation much more effective in CORBA than in RPC systems and TP monitors.

Another form of encapsulation provided by object brokers is location independence. As discussed above, when clients need to invoke a service supporting a certain interface, they access the ORB to retrieve a reference to the server object. An object reference is a logical identifier for a server object, assigned as the object is created. Conceptually, the reference has no relation to the physical address of the object. From the client's perspective, it is just an opaque identifier. It is the job of the ORB to maintain the correspondence between the object reference and the actual object location. The reference remains valid until the server object is destroyed, even if the object changes physical location during its lifetime. In addition, objects not only can change physical address but they can even be running on top of a different ORB, perhaps provided by another ORB vendor. In fact, in addition to providing specifications for interoperability among objects, CORBA also supports interoperability among ORBs [153]. Every CORBA-compliant ORB is required to speak the General Inter-ORB Protocol (GIOP). GIOP can be implemented on top of different transports. CORBA requires that a CORBA-complaint ORB supports at least GIOP over TCP/IP, which is referred to as Internet Inter-ORB Protocol (IIOP). Through this protocol, an ORB can forward invocations initiated by one of its clients to another ORB, where the invoked object resides, as long as the two ORBs are aware of each other's existence.

2.4.6 TP Monitors+Object Brokers = Object Monitors

Object monitors [31] are a good example for understanding the evolution of middleware platforms and the hype around commercial products. Very often, new forms of middleware appear that are just slightly modified versions of already existing products. Object monitors are the best example of this. The very name implies what object monitors really are: an *object* broker and a TP-*monitor*. This marriage between object brokers and TP monitors was an obvious step to take at the time and, in many cases, the only feasible way to obtain commercially competitive products.

Part of the problem encountered by object brokers, particularly in the case of CORBA, is that the only real novelty they offered was object orientation as a way to standardize interfaces across different systems and programming languages. In fact, CORBA was meant to be implemented on top of conventional middleware platforms such as DCE, TP monitors, and even primitive forms of message-oriented middleware. Unfortunately, programming paradigms are a small part of the picture in a distributed information system. Many of the CORBA *services* were mere specifications that took quite a long time to be implemented in real products. The Object Transactional Service (OTS) of CORBA is probably the most illustrative case of the dilemma faced by object brokers. OTS essentially described what TP monitors had been doing very successfully for many years before CORBA appeared. Since the first commercial products available were typically systems implemented almost from scratch, when compared with already existing middleware platforms, object brokers were extremely inefficient and lacked key functionality such as transactions. This turned out to be a decisive factor limiting the adoption of object brokers.

The way out of this dilemma was to actually use TP monitors and other forms of middleware with an additional layer that would make them object-oriented (and, in some cases, CORBA compliant). When TP monitors were used, the result were object monitors. In terms of functionality, however, object monitors offered very little over what TP monitors already offered. This was the first step toward the assimilation of object broker ideas into other forms of middleware. Java, C#, and the middleware environments around them represent the culmination of this convergence process.

2.5 Message-Oriented Middleware

The previous chapters and sections have presented interoperability concepts and techniques that are mainly based on synchronous method invocation, where a client application invokes a method offered by a specific, although possibly dynamically selected, service provider. When the service provider has completed its job, it returns the reply to the client. In this section we explore abstractions supporting more dynamic and asynchronous forms of interaction, along with the corresponding middleware platforms.

2.5.1 Historical Background

Message-oriented middleware is often presented as a revolutionary technology that may change the way distributed information systems are built. The idea is, however, not new. Originally, asynchronous interaction was used to implement batch systems. RPC implementations already offered asynchronous versions of RPC, and many TP monitors had queuing systems used to implement message-based interaction. For instance, the first versions of the TP monitor Tuxedo were based on queues. Furthermore, the notion of a persistent queue was already well understood at the beginning of the 1990s [27].

Modern message-oriented middleware is, for the most part, a direct descendant of the queuing systems found in TP monitors. In TP monitors, queuing systems were used to implement batch processing systems. But as TP monitors were confronted with the task of integrating a wider range and larger numbers of systems, it quickly became obvious that asynchronous interaction was a more useful way to do this than RPC. As computer clusters started to gain more ground as platforms for distributed information systems, the queuing systems of TP monitors started to play a bigger role when designing large information systems. Eventually they became independent systems on their own. Today, most large integration efforts are done using message-oriented middleware. As discussed in Chapter 6, messages may also become the preferred way of implementing Web services.

Some of the best-known MOM platforms include IBM WebSphere MQ (formerly known as MQ Series) [100], MSMQ by Microsoft [137], or WebMethods Enterprise by WebMethods [213]. CORBA also provides its own messaging service [155].

2.5.2 Message-Based Interoperability

The term *message-based interoperability* refers to an interaction paradigm where clients and service providers communicate by exchanging *messages*. A message is a structured data set, typically characterized by a *type* and a set of <name,value> pairs that constitute the message *parameters*. The type used to be system dependent; nowadays, most products use XML types. As an example, consider a message that requests a quotation from a vendor about the price of a set of products. The message parameters include the name of the requesting company, the item for which a quote is being requested, the quantity needed, and the date on which the items should be delivered at a specified address. In general, the language for defining message types varies with the messaging platform adopted.

```
Message quoteRequest {
  QuoteReferenceNumber: Integer
  Customer: String
  Item: String
  Quantity: Integer
  RequestedDeliveryDate: Timestamp
  DeliveryAddress: String
}
```

To show how message-based interoperability works, we assume that an application receives the customers' requests for a quote and has to transfer them to a quotation system, to retrieve the quote, and notify the requesting customer. This interaction is depicted in Figure 2.11. We refer to the quotation system as being the service provider, while the application receiving the customer's request is the client in this case.

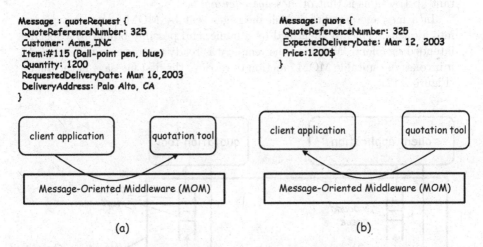

```
Message : quoteRequest {
    QuoteReferenceNumber: 325
    Customer: Acme,INC
    Item:#115 (Ball-point pen, blue)
    Quantity: 1200
    RequestedDeliveryDate: Mar 16,2003
    DeliveryAddress: Palo Alto, CA
}
```

```
Message: quote {
    QuoteReferenceNumber: 325
    ExpectedDeliveryDate: Mar 12, 2003
    Price:1200$
}
```

(a)   (b)

Fig. 2.11. Example of message-based interoperability: an application sends a message to a quotation tool (**a**). The tool serves the request by sending another message (**b**)

With message-based interoperability, once clients and service providers agree on a set of message types, they can communicate by exchanging messages. To request a service, the client application sends a message (for example, a *quoteRequest* message) to the desired provider. The service provider will receive the message, perform appropriate actions depending on the message content (for example, determine a quote), and send another message with the required information back to the client.

The class of middleware applications that support message-based interoperability is called *message-oriented middleware* (MOM). Note that although we use the terms client and service provider, this distinction is blurred in pure message-oriented interactions, at least from the perspective of the middleware. Indeed, to the MOM, all objects look alike; i.e., they send and receive messages. The difference between "clients" and "service providers" is purely conceptual and can only be determined by humans who are aware of the semantics of the messages and of the message exchange. This is different with respect to the other forms of interaction discussed earlier, where objects acting as clients invoke methods provided by other objects, acting as servers.

2.5.3 Message Queues

MOM, per se, does not provide particular benefits with respect to other forms of interactions presented earlier in the book. However, it forms the basis on which many useful concepts and features can be developed, considerably simplifying the development of interoperable applications and providing support for managing errors or system failures. Among these, one of the most important abstractions is that of *message queuing*.

In a message queuing model, messages sent by MOM clients are placed into a queue, typically identified by a name, and possibly bound to a specific intended recipient. Whenever the recipient is ready to process a new message, it invokes the suitable MOM function to retrieve the first message in the queue (Figure 2.12).

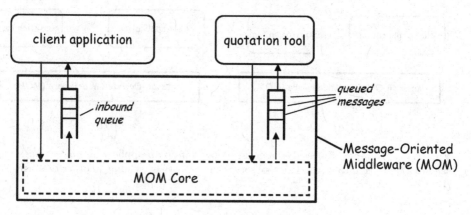

Fig. 2.12. Message queuing model

Queuing messages provide many benefits. In particular, it gives recipients control of when to process messages. Recipients do not have to be continuously listening for messages and process them right away, but can instead retrieve a new message only when they can or need to process it. An important consequence is that queuing is more robust to failures with respect to RPC or object brokers, as recipients do not need to be up and running when the message is sent. If an application is down or unable to receive messages, these will be stored in the application's queue (maintained by the MOM), and they will be delivered once the application is back online and pulls them from the queue. Of course, this also means that the messaging infrastructures must themselves be designed to be very reliable and robust with regard to failures. Queued messages may have an associated expiration date or interval. If the message is not retrieved before the specified date (or before the interval has elapsed), it is discarded.

Queues can be shared among multiple applications, as depicted in Figure 2.13. This approach is typically used when it is necessary to have multiple applications provide the same service, so as to distribute the load among them and improve performance. The MOM system controls access to the queue, ensuring that a message is delivered to only one application. The queuing abstraction also enables many other features. For example, senders can assign *priorities* to messages, so that once the recipient is ready to process the next message, messages with higher priorities are delivered first.

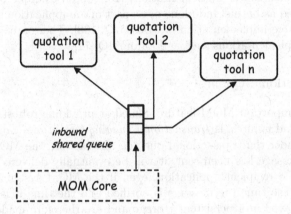

Fig. 2.13. Message queuing model with shared queues

2.5.4 Interacting with a Message Queuing System

Queuing systems provide an API that can be invoked to send messages or to wait for and receive messages. Sending a message is typically a non blocking operation, and therefore once an object has sent a message to another object, it can continue processing. Receiving a message is instead often a blocking operation, where the receiving object "listens" for messages and processes them as they arrive, typically (but not necessarily) by activating a new dedicated thread, while the "main" thread goes back to listen for the next message. Recipients can also retrieve messages in a non blocking fashion by providing a callback function that is invoked by the MOM each time a message arrives. Note therefore that this approach, unlike basic RPC, is naturally asynchronous.

Java programmers can use an industry-standard API for interacting with MOM systems: the Java Message Service (JMS) [194]. In JMS, a message is characterized by a *header*, which includes metadata such as the message type, expiration date, and priority; by an optional set of *properties* that extend the header metadata attributes, for example, to support compatibility with a specific JMS implementation; and a *body*, which includes the actual application-specific information that needs to be exchanged. In JMS, as in most MOM systems, addressing is performed through queues: senders (receivers) first *bind* to a queue, i.e., identify the queue to which they want to send messages (receive messages from), based on the queue name. Then, they can start sending (retrieving) messages to (from) the queue.

As already indicated, JMS is simply an API and not a platform. In fact, several, but not all, MOM products are JMS compliant. JMS can be implemented as a stand-alone system or as a module within an application server (Chapter 4). For instance, the Java Open Reliable Asynchronous Messaging (JORAM, an open source implementation) [109], is an example of a system that can be used as both stand-alone or as part of an application server. Another open source implementation is *JBossMQ* [108]. There are also several commercial implementations such as FioranoMQ [71].

2.5.5 Transactional Queues

Another very important MOM feature, aimed at providing robustness in the face of errors and failures, is *transactional queuing* (sometimes called reliable messaging). Under the transactional queuing abstraction, the MOM ensures that once a message has been sent, it will be eventually delivered once and only once to the recipient application, even if the MOM system itself goes down between the time the message is notified and the time it is delivered. Messages are saved in a persistent storage and are therefore made available once the MOM system is restarted.

In addition to providing guaranteed delivery, transactional queuing provides support for coping with failures. In fact, recipients can bundle a set of message retrievals and notifications within an *atomic* unit of execution. As described earlier, an atomic unit identifies a set of operations that have the all-or-nothing property: either all of them are successfully executed, or none are. In case a failure occurs before all operations in the atomic unit have been executed, all completed operations are rolled back (undone). In message queuing, rolling back a message retrieval operation corresponds to placing the message back in the queue, so that it can be then consumed again by the same application or, in case of shared queues, by other applications. From the perspective of the sender, transactional queues mean that messages sent within a sender's atomic unit are maintained in a persistent storage by the MOM and are made visible for delivery only when the execution of the atomic unit is completed. Therefore, rolling back message notifications simply involves deleting the messages from the persistent storage.

For example, assume that a set of quotation applications $A = \{a_1, a_2, ..., a_n\}$ retrieves *quoteRequest* messages from a queue, and that the message retrieval operation is within an atomic unit that also involves getting pricing and availability information from the product suppliers, preparing a *quote* message, and sending the message back to the requester. If an application a_j retrieves message $quoteRequest_k$ and is unable to obtain the quote, either because the application a_j itself fails, or because for any reason it is unable to obtain pricing and availability information from suppliers, then message $quoteRequest_k$

is put back into the queue, so that other applications in set A can later retrieve message $quoteRequest_k$ again in an attempt to fulfill the request.

We observe here that although transactional queuing is a very useful mechanism to overcome short-lived failures, additional higher-level abstractions are in general needed to manage exceptional situations: indeed, putting a message back in the queue does guarantee that the message is not discarded and that it will be eventually processed again, enabling service providers to overcome problems that have a short time span. However, if the inability to process the message correctly is due to a cause other than a temporary failure, placing the message back in the queue neither addresses the problem nor provides feedback to the requester about the inability to complete the service. For example, if application a_j is unable to determine a quote because no supplier can deliver the requested goods by the specified delivery date, then rolling back the operations and putting the message back in the queue is not going to help in any way.

2.6 Summary

There are two important aspects to middleware that are sometimes blurred, but that should be differentiated. On the one hand, middleware provides programming abstractions for designing distributed applications. These abstractions can range from more sophisticated communication models (e.g., remote procedure calls instead of sockets), to transactions, queues for asynchronous interactions, or automatic properties conferred to the code (e.g., security or persistence). On the other hand, middleware implements the functionality provided by the programming abstractions. This might include transactional support, specialized communication primitives, name and directory services, persistence, and so on. Here we are no longer discussing the programming abstractions, but rather the mechanisms necessary to implement such programming abstractions. The type of middleware, its capabilities, and how it is used depend very much upon these two aspects.

In practice, however, middleware platforms differ much more in terms of the programming abstractions they provide than in their underlying infrastructure. In this chapter we took an evolutionary perspective when discussing the different forms of middleware available today. We started with RPC and progressed to TP monitors, object brokers, and message-oriented middleware. In this progression it is important to keep in mind the motivation behind each step. RPC provides a very basic form of distribution that initially was devised to avoid having to deal with the low-level communication interfaces available in UNIX (sockets). Soon, the designers of RPC realized that additional infrastructure was necessary to support a higher level of programming abstraction. TP monitors took advantage of RPC to extend to distributed environments the functionality they offered in large computers. By doing so, they became the predominant form of middleware, a role that they still enjoy

today. Changes in programming paradigms and the increasing opportunities
for distribution triggered the emergence of object brokers. At the same time,
object brokers became the second attempt to standardize middleware platforms (the first was DCE, which tried to standardize the implementation for
RPC). For practical reasons, few object brokers made it on their own. Their
ideas and specifications were eventually taken over by TP monitors and have
been by now almost completely superseded by the .NET and J2EE initiatives.
Finally, to cope with the increasing use of cluster-based architectures and the
greater demand for enterprise application integration solutions, the queuing
systems found in TP monitors became stand-alone systems that soon evolved
toward MOM systems and later into what we know today as message brokers.
As we will see in Chapter 3, message brokers play a crucial role among the
platforms used for enterprise application integration.

3

Enterprise Application Integration

Middleware and enterprise application integration (EAI) are not completely orthogonal concepts. They are, however, distinct enough to warrant separate treatment. As we saw in Chapter 2, middleware constitutes the basic infrastructure behind any distributed information system. Initially, middleware was used to construct new systems and to link to mainframe-based systems (2-tier architectures). Later, it was used to distribute the application logic and to integrate the many servers created by 3-tier architectures.

When the systems involved were compatible and comparable in their functionality and did not involve many platforms, middleware could be used without further ado to integrate the servers. Unfortunately, for more ambitious projects, plain middleware was not enough. The main limitation was that any concrete middleware platform makes implicit assumptions about the nature of the underlying systems. When these systems are very different in nature and functionality, using conventional middleware to integrate them becomes rather cumbersome, and in some cases simply infeasible.

EAI can be seen as a step forward in the evolution of middleware, extending its capabilities to cope with application integration, as opposed to the development of new application logic. Such extensions involve some significant changes in the way the middleware is used, from the programming model to the marked shift toward asynchronous interaction. In this chapter we examine how these extensions came about and how they facilitate large scale integration. In the first part, we discuss in detail the problem of application integration (Section 3.1). Then we address the use of message brokers as the most versatile platform for integration (Section 3.2), and conclude with a review of workflow management systems as the tools used to make the integration logic explicit and more manageable (Section 3.3).

3.1 From Middleware to Application Integration

The difference between conventional middleware and EAI can sometimes be rather subtle. To understand the differences in terms of requirements and actual systems, it helps to differentiate between application development and application integration.

3.1.1 From a Mainframe to a Set of Servers

In Chapter 1, we discussed in detail how client/server systems came to be. As the available bandwidth increased and PCs and workstations became increasingly powerful, the client/server paradigm gained momentum. Functionality that was previously only available in a single location (the mainframe) began to be distributed across a few servers. At the same time, companies became more decentralized and more geographically dispersed and also started to increasingly rely upon computers. As a result, information servers established their presence everywhere within a company. Because of the limitations of client/server architectures, these servers were effectively information islands; clients could communicate with servers, but the information servers did not communicate with each other. At a certain point, this severely limited the ability to develop new services and introduced significant inefficiencies in the overall functioning of the enterprise.

When 3-tier architectures and middleware emerged, they addressed two issues. First, by separating the application logic layer from the resource management layer, the resulting architecture became more flexible. This approach gained even more relevance when systems began to be built on top of computer clusters instead of powerful servers, a trend that was markedly accentuated by the Web. Second, they served as a mechanism for integrating different servers. In this regard, middleware can be seen as the infrastructure supporting the middle tier in 3-tier systems. As such, it is the natural location for the integration logic that brings different servers together. For instance, the accepted way to integrate different databases was to use a TP monitor.

3.1.2 From a Set of Servers to a Multitude of Services

The use of middleware led to a further proliferation of services. In fact, 3-tier architectures facilitate the integration of different resource managers and, in general, the integration of services. The functionality resulting from this integration can be then exposed as yet another service, which can in turn be integrated to form higher-level services. This process can go on ad infinitum, leading to a proliferation of services. The big advantage is that each new layer of services provides a higher level of abstraction that can be used to hide complex application and integration logic. The disadvantage is that now integration is not only integration of resource managers or servers, but also the integration of services. Unfortunately, while for servers there has been a significant effort to standardize the interfaces of particular types of servers (e.g., databases), the same cannot be said of generic services. As long as the integration of services takes place within a single middleware platform, no significant problems should appear beyond the intrinsic complexity of the system being built. Once the problem became the integration of services provided by different middleware platforms, there was almost no infrastructure available that could help to reduce the heterogeneity and standardize the interfaces as well as the interactions between the systems.

Thus, while 3-tier architectures provided the means to bridge the islands of information created by the proliferation of client/server systems, there was no general way to bridge 3-tier architectures. Enterprise application integration appeared in response to this need. Middleware was originally intended as a way to integrate servers that reside in the resource management layer. EAI is a generalization of this idea that also includes as building blocks the application logic layers of different middleware systems.

3.1.3 An Example of Application Integration

Behind any system integration effort there is a need to automate and streamline procedures. During the late 1980s and the 1990s, enterprises increasingly relied on software applications to support many business functions, ranging from "simple" database applications to sophisticated call center management software or customer relationship management (CRM) applications. The deployment of information systems allowed the automation of the different steps of standard business procedures. The problem of EAI appears when all these different steps are to be combined into a coherent and seamless process.

To understand what this entails, consider the problem of automating a *supply chain*. A supply chain is the set of operations carried out to fulfill a customer's request for products and services. Simplifying and abstracting the procedure, a basic supply chain comprises the following steps: *quotation, order processing*, and *order fulfillment*. Quotation involves processing a *request for quotes* (RFQ) from a customer. In an RFQ, the customer queries the company about the price, availability, and expected delivery dates of particular goods. Based on this information, the customer may eventually place a purchase order with the company. Order processing involves the analysis of the purchase order placed by the customer. This includes verifying that the purchase order corresponds to a previously given quote and that it can be fulfilled under the conditions requested by the customer. It also involves placing the order internally to schedule the manufacturing of the goods, purchase the necessary components, and so on. Order fulfillment includes several steps: *procurement, shipment*, and *financial aspects*. Procurement is the actual acquisition of components and manufacturing of the requested product. Shipment is the delivery of the product to the customer. The financial aspects include invoicing the customer, paying suppliers, and so forth.

An actual supply chain is much more complex and involves many more steps. We can nevertheless already understand the difficulties of EAI using this basic example. Each one of the steps mentioned is likely to be implemented and supported using a different information system. For instance, companies maintain extensive customer, product, and supplier databases. Responding to an RFQ may involve checking the availability of the product, their production schedule, and even checking with suppliers for delivery dates and prices for the required components. In many cases, each of these databases is a separate system that may even reside in a different geographic location. Processing the purchase order may involve interacting with a warehouse control system that indicates the current stock levels of the requested product and where it can be obtained. As part of the order fulfillment step, the purchase order may be forwarded to a manufacturing system. In this case there might be many additional steps to purchase components from suppliers, arrange for delivery dates, schedule the production and testing, and so on, all of them involving more interactions implemented using different information systems. Finally, shipment and billing also require more or less complex interactions with invoice databases, purchase order archives, and the like. Of the systems involved, some are home-grown, others are based on off-the-shelf packages, and yet others are the result of previous integration efforts. Moreover, each has different characteristics:

- Each system may run on a different operating system (e.g., Windows, Linux, Solaris, HP-UX, or AIX).
- Each system may support different interfaces and functionality. For example, some will be transactional, while others will not understand transactions; some will use a standard IDL to publish interfaces, others would use a proprietary syntax, etc.
- Each system may use a different data format and produce information that cannot be easily cast into parameters of a procedure call (e.g., a complex multimedia document).
- Each system may have different security requirements (for example, some systems may require authentication based on X.509 certificates, while others may need a simple username/password authentication).
- Each system may use a different infrastructure as well as different interaction models and protocols (e.g., a DCE installation, a TP monitor, a CORBA-based system, etc.).

Automating the supply chain implies bringing all these disparate systems together. To make matters worse, EAI is also complicated by non technical challenges: the systems to be integrated are typically owned and operated by different departments within a company. Each department is autonomously managed, and uses its systems to perform a variety of department-specific functions whose needs and goals are not necessarily aligned with those of the integrating application.

In spite of all these difficulties, it is often critical to automate the supply chain. When it is not automated, all the operations that involve going from one step to the next in the chain are carried out manually (Figure 3.1). When that is the case, the whole process involves a lot of repetitive human labor, exchange of paper documents, inefficiencies, and errors. Orders are difficult to monitor and track. It is difficult, if not impossible, to have an overall view of operations and to give information about the status of an order. Any tracking or monitoring can only be done through the cumbersome procedure of following the paper trail left behind by the process. Such inefficiencies strongly affect the quality of the supply chain and severely harm the ability to sustain growth. In the following we describe the middleware technologies that facilitate the integration of such coarse-grained, heterogeneous components.

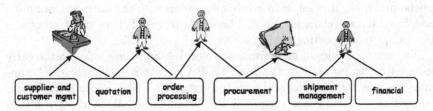

| supplier and customer mgmt | quotation | order processing | procurement | shipment management | financial |

Fig. 3.1. Manual implementation of a supply chain where human users act as relays between the different steps by extracting data from one system, reformatting it, and feeding it into the next

3.2 EAI Middleware: Message Brokers

Traditional RPC-based and MOM systems create point-to-point links between applications, and are thus rather static and inflexible with regard to the selection of the queues to which messages are delivered. Message brokers address this limitation by acting as a broker among system entities, thereby creating a (logical or physical) "hub and spoke" communication infrastructure for integrating applications. Message brokers provide flexibility in routing, as well as other features that support the integration of enterprise applications. This functionality, together with asynchronous messaging, is exactly what is needed in generic EAI settings, and message brokers are thus emerging as the dominant EAI tool used today.

3.2.1 Historical Background

Message brokers are direct descendants of the platforms for message oriented middleware discussed in Chapter 2. They are derived from the new requirements posed by EAI, in terms of supporting the integration of heterogeneous, coarse-grained enterprise applications such as enterprise resource planning (ERP) and CRM systems. Indeed, as soon as the problems behind EAI (exemplified in the previous section) were recognized, the limitations of using MOM systems to support EAI become manifest. Specifically, MOM did not provide support for defining sophisticated logic for routing messages across different systems and did not help developers to cope with the heterogeneity.

In response to these needs, message brokers extend MOM with the capability of attaching logic to the messages and of processing messages directly at the middleware level. In message-oriented middleware the task of the middleware is to move messages from one point to another with certain guarantees. A message broker not only transports the messages, but is also in charge of routing, filtering, and even processing the messages as they move across the system. In addition, most message brokers provide *adapters* that mask heterogeneity and make it possible to access all systems with the same programming model and data exchange format. The combination of these two factors was seen as key to supporting EAI.

The first examples of modern message brokers were developed in the early and mid-1990s, as soon as the need for EAI was recognized. In the beginning, the area was dominated by startup companies such as ActiveSoftware, founded in 1995 and later acquired by WebMethods. With time, software heavyweights such as IBM entered this profitable area, typically by enhancing existing MOM infrastructure. The final "blessing" came from the Java Message Service, a Java API that provides a standard way to interact with a message broker, as least for the basic message broker functionality [194]. Examples of leading commercial implementations of EAI platforms today are Tibco ActiveEnterprise [199], BEA WebLogic Integration [18], WebMethods Enterprise [213], and WebSphere MQ [100].

3.2.2 The Need for Message Brokers

To better understand the limitations of RPC-based and basic MOM systems, let us again consider the execution of a supply chain operation where a company receives a *purchase order* (PO) from a customer and needs to fulfill it. Many different systems will need to process the PO, including, for instance, inventory management applications (to check availability), ERP systems to manage payments, and the shipping application that interfaces with the shipping department to arrange for delivery of the goods. With RPC and message queuing systems, the application that receives and dispatches the PO needs to get a reference (either statically or dynamically) to these three PO processing applications and either invoke one of their methods or send them a message (Figure 3.2). Now, assume that because of a change in the business or IT environment, company policies require additional applications to be notified of the PO. An example of such an application could be a *month-end closing* system that performs book-keeping operations and provides monthly summaries of revenues and profits. In this case, the dispatching application needs to be modified to cope with the change and include the code for notifying this additional system.

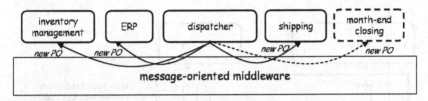

Fig. 3.2. With RPC or message-based interoperability, applications need to be changed if they need to interoperate with a new system (*dashed*)

As another even more "dynamic" example, consider an application that monitors the stock market and interoperates with other applications interested in stock price changes, such as systems that manage investments for stock brokers. In such a scenario, the number of applications interested in stock price modifications changes continuously, as a result of changes in the number of brokers or in the brokers' investing strategies. Therefore, using a basic MOM system to achieve interoperation between the stock monitor and the brokers' applications would be extremely complex, involving the generation of many messages whose number and destination queues are a priori unknown and continuously changing. The problem becomes even more complex if not one but multiple applications can generate the *new PO* or *stock price change* messages, as all these applications then need to be changed.

3.2.3 Extending Basic MOM

The cause of the problem in the above examples is that, in a basic MOM system, the responsibility for defining the receiver of a message lies with the sender. As we have seen, this sort of point-to-point addressing scheme becomes increasingly complex to manage as the number of senders and recipients grows and as the environment becomes more dynamic.

Message brokers are enhanced MOM systems that attempt to overcome this limitation by factoring the message routing logic out of the senders and placing it into the middleware (Figure 3.3). In fact, with a message broker, users can define application logic that identifies, for each message, the queues to which it should be delivered. In this way, senders are not required to specify the intended recipients of a message. Instead, it is up to the message broker to identify the recipients by executing user-defined rules.

The advantage of this approach is that regardless of how many applications can dispatch *new PO* or *stock price change* messages, there is now a single place where we need to make changes when the routing logic for these messages needs to be modified. Later in this section we will see that, using message brokers, there are ways to avoid even this maintenance effort.

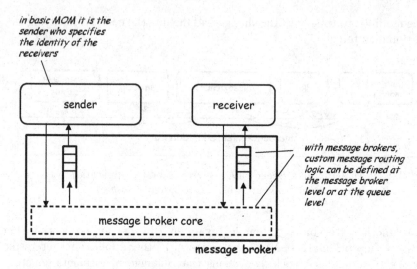

Fig. 3.3. Message brokers enable users to define custom message routing logic

Routing logic can be based on the sender's identity, on the message type, or on the message content. It is typically defined in a rule-based language, where each rule includes a Boolean condition to be evaluated over the message data and an action defining the queues to which messages satisfying the condition should be delivered. This logic can be defined at the message broker level or at the queue level. If defined at the message broker level, it applies to all messages that are then routed accordingly. If it is associated with a specific queue, it defines the kind of messages that the queue is interested in receiving.

The above discussion shows that message brokers can *decouple* senders and receivers. Senders do not specify and are not aware of which applications will receive the messages they send, and, conversely, receivers may or may not be aware of which applications are capable of sending messages to them.

Note that MOM systems that support shared queues also provide a limited form of decoupling, in that applications send messages to queues rather than to specific recipients. However, with shared queues, each message is delivered to at most one application. Applications taking messages from a shared queue are typically of the same type (or different threads of the same process), and shared queues have the purpose of load balancing. Indeed, shared queues may be combined with message brokering to provide both decoupling and load balancing: messages can be delivered to several queues, depending on the routing logic (decoupling). Multiple threads or applications can then share the load of retrieving and processing messages from a queue (load balancing).

Since in MOM systems (and in message brokers) communication between applications goes through a middle layer, it is possible to implement even more application-specific functionality in this layer, going beyond routing rules. For example, another reason for associating logic with queues is to enable the definition of *content transformation* rules. Refer again to the PO processing example: in that case, routing is only part of the problem. Another issue to be handled is that different applications support different data formats. For example, an application may assume that the weight of goods to be shipped is expressed in pounds, while another may require the weight to be expressed in kilograms. By defining content transformation rules and by associating them with the queue, it is possible to factorize these mappings in the message broker, as opposed to having each application perform them. Every application pulling messages from the queue will now receive the weight expressed in kilograms, as desired. By assigning different transformation rules to each queue, we can accommodate the needs of different applications without modifying these applications.

In general, there is no limit to the amount of application logic that can be "embedded" into the broker or into the queue. However, placing application logic into the broker is not always a good idea. In fact, although on the one hand we make applications more generic and robust to changes, we embed the integration logic into the message brokers' queues. Distributing such logic into the queues makes it difficult to debug and maintain, as no tools are provided to support this effort. Another problem is that of performance: although message brokers tend to be quite efficient, if they have to execute many application-specific rules each time a message is delivered, the overall latency and throughput is degraded. Finally, another limitation of message brokers is their inability to handle large messages. This is perhaps due to the fact that they have been designed to support OLTP-like interactions, which are short-lived and have a light payload. Whenever they are used to route large messages, their performance is greatly affected.

3.2.4 The Publish/Subscribe Interaction Model

Thanks to the possibility of defining application-specific routing logic, message brokers can support a variety of different message-based interaction models. Among those, perhaps the most well-known and widely adopted one is the *publish/subscribe* paradigm. In this paradigm, as in message-based interaction, applications communicate by exchanging messages, again characterized by a type and a set of parameters. However, applications that send messages do not specify the recipients of the message. Instead, they simply *publish* the message to the middleware system that handles the interaction. For this reason, applications that send messages are called *publishers*. If an application is interested in receiving messages of a given type, then it must *subscribe* with the publish/subscribe middleware, thus registering its interest. Whenever a publisher sends a message of a given type, the middleware retrieves the list of all applications that subscribed to messages of that type, and delivers a copy of the message to each of them.

Figure 3.4 exemplifies publish/subscribe interaction in the PO processing example described above. As the figure shows, the PO processing application simply needs to send a message to the message broker, publishing a notification that a new PO has been received. All applications interested in new PO notifications will then receive the message, provided that they subscribed to the *new PO* message type prior to the time the message was sent.

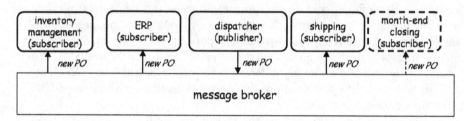

Fig. 3.4. Publish/subscribe models make interoperability more flexible and robust to changes

In a publish/subscribe model, subscribers have two main ways to define the messages they are interested in receiving. The first is to specify a message *type*, such as *new PO*. In simple cases, the type namespace is flat and is defined by a string. More sophisticated systems may allow the types' namespace to be structured into a type/subtype hierarchy of arbitrary depth. For example, if we assume that the type hierarchy is encoded by means of dot-separated strings of the form *type.subtype.subsubtype...*, then a legal message type name could be *Supply Chain.new PO*. With structured types, subscribers not only can register their interest in messages having a specific type and subtype, but can also subscribe to messages whose type T has another type A as ancestor in the type hierarchy. For example, a subscription to *Supply Chain.new PO* specifies interest in receiving all messages related to new purchase orders, while *Supply Chain.** is a more general subscription that declares interest in all supply chain-related messages, including but not limited to new purchase orders.

The second form of subscription is parameter-based: subscribers specify the messages they want to receive by means of a boolean condition on the message parameters. For example, the condition *type="new PO" AND customer="ACME Co." AND quantity>1200* specifies a subscription to all *new PO* messages related to orders by *ACME Co.* whose volume is above 1200 units.

Virtually every message broker today supports the publish/subscribe interaction paradigm. There have even been attempts to standardize the programming abstractions and the interfaces (APIs) between applications and publish/subscribe middleware infrastructure. JMS [194] is one such effort that is part of Java-related standards from Sun. The JMS specifications include a publish/subscribe API in addition to a point-to-point one. In JMS, publications and subscriptions are based on the notion of *topic*. A topic is analogous to a message broker's queue: it is identified by a string (such as "new PO"), and it is the entity to which clients bind to send and receive messages. The difference between topics and queues is that multiple recipients can subscribe to the same topic and receive the same message.

3.2.5 Distributed Administration of a Message Broker

Message broker systems include support for an *administrator*, a distinguished user that has the authority to define (1) the types of messages that can be sent and received, and (2) which users are authorized to send and/or receive a message and to customize routing logic. Administrators are also present in MOMs, but they are more relevant in message brokers due to the decoupling between senders and receivers that, in general, causes the senders to be unaware of which applications will receive the message. Publish/subscribe systems may, however, allow publishers to define limitations on the set of users that can receive a certain message.

Message broker architectures are naturally extensible to meet the needs of communication-intensive applications that span different administrative domains (possibly corresponding to different departments or companies). In fact, it is possible to compose several message brokers, as shown in Figure 3.5. In this architecture, a message broker (say, message broker MB-A) can be a client of another message broker MB-B, and vice versa. If a client of MB-B wants to receive messages sent by clients of MB-A, then it subscribes with MB-B. In turn, MB-B subscribes for the same message type with MB-A. When one of MB-A clients publishes the message of interest, then MB-A will deliver it to MB-B, in accordance with the subscription. As soon as MB-B receives the message, it will deliver it to all of its clients that subscribed for such a message. Note that from the perspective of MB-B, MB-A is conceptually just like any other subscriber. The only difference is that it belongs to a different administrative domain, and therefore the administrator of broker MB-A will set up subscription and publication permissions for this client accordingly. System administration and security are kept simple and modular with this approach, since each message broker administrator only needs to determine which messages can be sent to or received from another domain.

3.2.6 EAI with a Message Broker

Figure 3.6 shows the basic principles on which most EAI platforms are based. There are two fundamental components:

- **Adapters.** Adapters map heterogeneous data formats, interfaces, and protocols into a common model and format. The purpose of adapters is to hide heterogeneity and present a uniform view of the underlying heterogeneous world. A different adapter is needed for each type of application that needs to be integrated

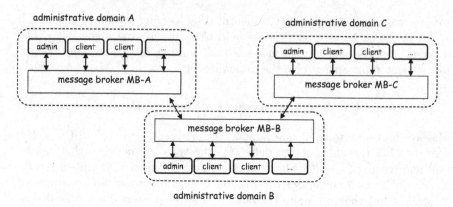

Fig. 3.5. Clients can interoperate through multiple message brokers distributed across different administrative domains

- **Message broker.** A message broker (or a MOM) facilitates the interaction among adapters and therefore, ultimately, among the back-end systems that need to be integrated.

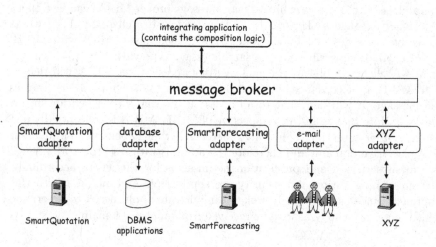

Fig. 3.6. High-level architecture of typical EAI systems

If an EAI platform is in place and the adapters for all the systems to be integrated have been deployed, then EAI-based application integration amounts to:

1. Developing an application (often in Java or C) that implements the integration logic. This application interacts with the message broker (and

consequently with the back-end systems accessible through the message broker and the adapters) by publishing and receiving messages.
2. Configuring the adapters so that they subscribe to the appropriate messages and perform the appropriate action on the back-end system.

We next present a simple example based on a quotation scenario that shows how applications can be built on top of EAI platforms. Assume that the application logic for processing requests for quotes involves:

1. Receiving the quote from the customer
2. Accessing the quotation system to obtain a quote
3. Inserting quote information into a forecasting system (i.e., a system that, based on previous quotes, predicts the order volume)
4. Sending the quote back to the customer

Steps 1 and 4 are not discussed here; they involve interactions with the customer and occur either via traditional methods (fax or e-mail), or via the Internet, possibly in the form of interactions among Web services. We focus instead on steps 2 and 3, which involve the integration of enterprise applications.

Figure 3.7 shows the main components of the solution and illustrates the flow of messages among those components. The *RFQ processing* application executes the business logic required for handling requests for quotes, performing the steps described above. In particular, it interacts with the two back-end systems (*SmartQuotation* and *SmartForecasting*) via the EAI platform, by sending messages. It is therefore a client of the EAI message broker, and it is specifically developed for the EAI platform being used. To obtain a quote from the SmartQuotation system, the RFQ processing application publishes a *quoteRequest* message (or, in JMS terminology, sends a message on the *quoteRequest* topic) and expects to receive a *quote* message as reply by the quotation system. To enter a forecast, it publishes a message of type *newQuote*.

The *SmartQuotation Adapter* is an EAI client that enables access to the *SmartQuotation* system via messages. In this example, we assume that the adapter has been configured to:

- Subscribe to messages of type *quoteRequest*.
- Invoke the *getQuote* function provided by the quotation system each time a *quoteRequest* message is received. The parameters required for the function invocation are extracted from the message.
- Publish a *quote* message as the function execution terminates and returns a reply. The message parameters are taken from the return value of the *getQuote()* function.

The adapter to the forecasting system needs to be configured in an analogous way. In particular, it subscribes to *newQuote* messages, and invokes the

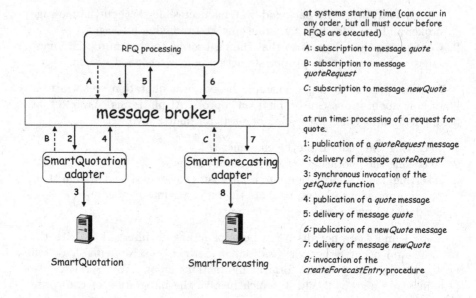

Fig. 3.7. Message exchanges and procedure invocations during the processing of a request for quote

procedure *createForecastEntry* on the *SmartForecasting* system, which will cause the new forecast to be created.

Adapters are typically configured through graphical user interfaces (GUIs) that allow users to define the messages that the adapter can publish or to which it should subscribe, as well as how to map messages to method invocation on the back-end system. If adapters for the back-end systems are not provided "out of the box" by the EAI vendor, then they must be developed. EAI platforms typically include tools that help users in this effort, such as "skeletons" of adapters that can be reused and configured for bridging the message broker with a back-end system.

Once all the adapters have been configured, the process logic can be implemented by writing an RFQ processing application that:

- Subscribes to messages of type *quote*.
- Publishes *quoteRequest* messages as a quote is requested.
- Extracts relevant parameters as a *quote* message is received, and creates and publishes a *newQuote* message.

Observe that, in an alternative approach, the forecasting tool could subscribe to *quote* messages and invoke the *createForecastEntry* when such messages are received, as opposed to having to go through the RFQ processing application. However, "hiding" the process logic in the adapter configurations can make the process difficult to design and maintain, as users would have to examine each adapter in detail to understand and reconstruct if and how they interact. This problem quickly becomes unmanageable as the number of adapters grows.

3.2.7 A Critical View of Message Brokers as EAI Platforms

Message brokers are not the only way to tackle the problem of enterprise application integration. As discussed in Chapter 2, TP monitors also provide a limited form of application integration functionality. However, message brokers have been in many cases designed explicitly for this purpose, and as such provide more application integration functionalities in terms of the number and type of available adapters, of their customization and extensibility, and of adapter development tools. As a result, integration through a message broker entails a number of benefits that, of course, depend of the concrete scenario and the functionality to be implemented but that are typically characterized as:

- **Lower development cost.** Integration is simpler and can be done more quickly. The integration is simpler because systems are loosely coupled and the biggest part of the integration effort can be localized in the adapters. This is in contrast with the tightly integrated systems resulting from using TP monitors or object brokers.
- **Lower opportunity costs.** Since integration is done more quickly, the automation (and the corresponding cost savings) can be achieved sooner. This directly affects the ability to implement new services and expand the capabilities of the overall infrastructure of the enterprise. It is also possible to react more rapidly to demands for new services, and more services can thus be offered than if alternative solutions (i.e., RPC-based middleware platforms) were used.
- **Lower maintenance effort.** The use of adapters has the effect of extracting the interaction with external systems as an orthogonal concern and localizing the related logic in a single module: the adapter. This offers significant advantages from the software engineering point of view. For instance, if new versions of existing systems are introduced, the EAI vendor will very likely provide new adapters for them. The application that executes the integration logic will thus not have to be changed substantially since the interaction between the integration logic and the underlying applications happens through the adapters.

Despite these advantages, message brokers are not a panacea for all application integration problems. Indeed, there are many drawbacks to implementing EAI solutions using message brokers. The main issue is that software licenses are extremely expensive. An EAI message bus, along with its development and management tools, may cost several hundreds of thousands of dollars, or even millions of dollars. In addition, each adapter costs additional significant amounts of money. Besides licensing costs, companies need to invest in the training of IT personnel and acquire the resources necessary for the installation and operation of the tool. Finally, while the development of applications that compose existing systems is certainly made easier if an EAI tool is available, it is still a significant effort. In fact, developers must still code the application integration logic, configure the adapters, and even develop adapters for those systems not supported by the message broker-based EAI platform.

These reasons often discourage small and medium enterprises from adopting EAI platforms, and even from performing the integration at all. The situation is different for large companies: first, they are typically faced with very complex integration problems, both because they require the integration of many systems, and because the autonomy of the departments and business units is often a cause of heterogeneity in the choice of the back-end systems. Such problems are quite challenging without automated support. In addition, large companies can afford the investment required by a message broker-based EAI platform, both in terms of software licenses and in terms of operation and maintenance costs, and can leverage these investments across many different integration projects. In the near future, however, the situation may change rapidly, particularly as a result of the adoption of the Web service standards that are discussed in Chapters 6 to 8. Such standards may greatly facilitate the integration efforts and considerably simplify the design and use of the integration middleware.

3.3 Workflow Management Systems

The previous section showed how message brokers can address one of the enterprise process automation problems: that of hiding the heterogeneity and the distribution of enterprise systems to provide a uniform view to the applications that integrate those systems. Workflow management systems (WfMSs) tackle the other side of the application integration problem: that of facilitating the definition and maintenance of the integration logic.

3.3.1 Historical Background

WfMSs have their origins in the domain of *office automation*. The first WfMS implementations were aimed at automating administrative processes based on paper documents, such as travel expense reimbursement or review of project proposals. The goal was to use an electronic version of the document rather than a paper copy, and use the WfMS to take care of routing the document from one point to another [202, 35]. Many initial implementations were e-mail-based (e.g., [128, 82]) and later substituted by Web-based forms. Workflows that implement such office procedures are called *administrative workflows* [79] and are widely used today in document processing and document management suites.

As workflow technology matured and, at the same time, the need for enterprise application integration arose, companies started to realize that WfMS could be used not only to control how to dispatch information among (human) participants of an administrative process, but also to define the business logic necessary to integrate heterogeneous and distributed systems. This is indeed the most interesting and challenging aspect of WfMS, and it is the one on which we focus the attention in this section. Workflow management systems that implement such business logic are called *production workflows* [105, 121]. The interest in production workflows was at the time related to an emphasis on *business process reengineering* [90, 76], a need to understand the processes of a company and optimize them along several dimensions.

In many ways, production workflows act as EAI tools in that they automate the control and data flow between different applications. However, although they were very well suited for the task of routing information, they did not have the kind of support for heterogeneity that EAI platforms had (e.g., the adapters). Therefore, it was natural to combine WfMS with EAI platforms into a single system, where the EAI platform hides the heterogeneity and provides basic interoperability support, while the WfMS supports the definition of the business logic that governs the integration. This is possible due to the WfMS's ability to make complex application logic explicit and expressed in a high level language (typically graphical) rather than encoded in a programming language. This trend started in the late 1990s and is still ongoing. In fact, today virtually every middleware vendor has a WfMS as well as a message broker in its portfolio. In most cases, the WfMS extends already existing middleware with the possibility of using processes as a way to describe the integration logic. Examples of leading commercial workflow systems include WebSphere MQ Workflow by IBM [104], Vitria Business-Ware [208], Tibco BPM [198], BEA WebLogic Integration [19], and Microsoft BizTalk Orchestration [139].

WfMSs have also been the target of several standardization efforts. The most widely known standardization consortium in this space is the Workflow Management Coalition (WfMC) [221]. It was formed in the mid-1990s with the objective of standardizing workflow definition languages and the APIs to access the WfMS. The beginning was very promising, with virtually every workflow vendor actively involved in the activity of the coalition. With time, however, interest in the WfMC started to fade, as only a few vendors actually supported the proposed standards. We will see in Chapter 8 that these standardization efforts are now being revived in the context of Web service composition, although their success in that context is still unclear at this stage.

3.3.2 Workflow Definition

Before discussing a WfMS in detail, we introduce some terminology that is used in this and later chapters. We define a *business process* as a collection of activities performed by human users or software applications that together constitute the different steps to be completed to achieve a particular business objective. Examples of business processes include the procedures for travel expense reimbursements within a company, the procedure for hiring new employees, or the procedures to process purchase orders from clients. The terms *workflow*, *workflow process*, or sometimes simply *process* refer to a formal, executable description of a business process. A *workflow management system* is a software platform that supports the design, development, execution, and analysis of workflow processes.

Typically, a workflow is specified by a directed graph (called a *flow graph*) that defines the order of execution among the nodes in the process. Nodes can be of one of the following types:

- **Work node.** Work nodes represent work items to be performed by a human or automated resource.
- **Routing node.** Routing nodes define the order in which work items should be executed, and allow the definition of parallel or conditional activation of work nodes.
- **Start and completion nodes.** Start and completion nodes denote the starting and ending points of the workflow.

By combining and configuring these different nodes, developers can specify the work to be done, the order in which the work activities should be executed, and to whom (or to what) the work should be assigned. A *workflow instance* is an execution of a workflow. A workflow may be instantiated several times, and several instances of the same or of different workflows may be concurrently running.

As an example, Figure 3.8 shows a workflow that models a supply chain process, and specifically the steps to be executed by a vendor in order to provide a quote to a customer. The example is in fact a more complex (and realistic) version of the one described in Section 3.2.6. The graphical representation is based on a variation of UML activity diagrams [154]. In the figure, rounded boxes represent work nodes, filled circles represent start and completion nodes, and the other symbols (diamonds and horizontal lines) represent routing nodes. Specifically, diamonds model conditional executions, while horizontal bars denote parallel activation of the subsequent nodes. The graphics next to the work nodes informally depict the kinds of resources to which the work is assigned (e.g., a human, an application, a DBMS, or the e-mail system).

The semantics of the flow in Figure 3.8 are as follows: as a new workflow instance is started, work node *check if offered product* verifies whether the products mentioned in the request for quote are already offered by the vendor.

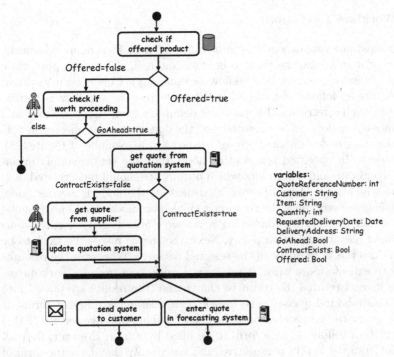

Fig. 3.8. A sample workflow specification that models a quotation process

In case of new products, a decision is made as to whether it is worth procuring this new product and placing it among the ones being offered, or whether instead the related business is so small that it is not worth the extra effort that would be required to serve this customer's request. In the first case, the company identifies a supplier, gets a quote, and updates the quotation system. Otherwise the customer is informed that the request cannot be fulfilled, and the process terminates.

Once the quote has been determined, either because of the request sent to the supplier or because of an existing agreement (in case of products already offered by the vendor), it is sent to the customer and inserted into the company's forecasting application. It will be retrieved if and when the customer accepts the quote and places the order. The figure also shows that the workflow has a set of variables, whose values are local to each instance, that are used to exchange data among work nodes and to determine the value of routing conditions.

Many other models have been proposed in the literature. These include approaches in which workflows are specified by variations of Petri nets [205], state and activity charts [219], or hierarchical activity decomposition [48]. However, most commercial systems provide models based on directed flow graphs (at least at the GUI level), such as the one depicted in Figure 3.8, since this model appears to be more intuitive for users.

3.3.3 Workflow Execution

Workflow instances are executed by a *workflow engine.* The engine is basically a scheduler: it schedules the work to be done and assigns it to an appropriate executor (called a *resource* in workflow terminology). Concisely, a workflow engine works as follows (Figure 3.9): Whenever a new workflow is instantiated, the engine retrieves the workflow definition from the repository and determines the node(s) to be executed, i.e., the ones that are connected in output to the start node (*Check if offered product* in the example of Figure 3.8). If the node to be executed is a routing node, then the engine simply evaluates the condition and determines which output arc should be activated, and therefore which node should be executed next. If the node is a work node, then the engine determines the resource to which the node should be assigned for execution, possibly by contacting a *resource broker* that executes some user-defined resource selection policy. Next, the engine places the work to be executed into the work queue of the selected resource. Whenever the resource is ready to execute more work, it retrieves a work item from its work queue, executes it, and returns the result to the engine (the results are placed into the engine's inbound queue). The "work" can take many different forms: it can be a query to be executed on a database, a short message service (SMS) to be sent to a cellphone, or a form to be filled by a user. However, they all look alike from the WfMS perspective, and specifically they have the form of messages sent to a resource. How the resource carries out the work is irrelevant to the WfMS.

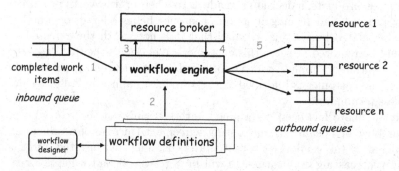

Fig. 3.9. Scheduling and assignments are the basic tasks of a WfMS, and specifically of the WfMS engine, which is at the heart of a WfMS

Note that resources do not necessarily have to pull work from the work queue in a first-in-first-out fashion: in general, they have the freedom of selecting the work item they want to execute next. We also observe that although the "pull" model described above is the one adopted by most systems (especially when resources are humans), workflow engines can also *push* work to the resources, typically by invoking a specified method of the resource API.

The engine continuously monitors the inbound queue to process work node completion messages. In particular, for each message in the inbound queue, the engine determines the next node to be executed based on the flow graph and on the workflow instance execution state, and then proceeds with resource assignment as discussed above.

3.3.4 Workflows as Programming in the Large

As the previous sections have shown, a workflow is similar to a program written in a third-generation language (3GL). In fact, it is basically characterized by the invocation of several functions in an order specified by some flow logic. The effect of loops and conditional statements is modeled here by inserting appropriate routing nodes. In addition, as in programming languages, a workflow can have variables (data items) that can be passed as input to or taken as output from work node invocations. These variables are used to evaluate routing conditions and to pass data among nodes.

Despite these similarities, workflows also present significant differences with respect to programming languages. The first is that of scale. Typically, procedures invoked in the context of a computer program are short-lived. Instead, workflows typically compose coarse-grained activities and applications that can last hours or days. A second, very important difference is the granularity at which composition takes place in workflow management systems when compared to programming languages. Workflow systems compose large software modules, typically entire applications and, quite often, complex N-tier systems. In this regard, workflow systems embody the idea of *megaprogramming* [216] as a shift in software engineering toward programming as an exercise in composition of large modules (i.e., *megamodules*) rather than programming from scratch. When viewed from this perspective, workflow can be seen as the programming language for enterprise application integration. This seems, in fact, to be the implicit assumption behind the widespread adoption of WfMSs in conjunction with EAI tools.

As the language for EAI, workflows need to incorporate functionality that goes well beyond what can be typically found in programming languages. For instance, a consequence of workflows being long-lasting is the need for sophisticated failure-handling techniques. If a computer program fails for any reason, the typical solution is to restart it. If a transactional application fails, then the solution consists in rolling back the partial execution and again restarting it. However, neither of these solutions is satisfactory in workflow management. Indeed, since executing a workflow can be very expensive in terms of time and money, restarting from scratch (with or without rolling-back the partial execution) is often not a desirable option. In addition, providing atomicity in a workflow is not as easy as in database applications or message queuing, since the unit to be rolled back is not a database update or a message retrieval, but can be any kind of action, such as sending a letter to a customer. Rolling back this kind of operation may cause work to be lost and is also difficult because the appropriate rollback action depends on the actions that need to be undone. Furthermore, because workflow applications are typically long-lived, it is not acceptable to hold (lock) the database resources necessary to be able to perform a rollback in case the need arises, as this would cause an excessive delay for other applications that need to access the same data.

To support failures, WfMSs provide a set of modeling abstractions and the relative system support:

- **Forward recovery.** WfMSs maintain the workflow instance execution state in a persistent storage. If the system fails, when it recovers from the failure it will be able to continue the execution of the workflow instances that were active at the time of the failure. The only work lost is the one performed by nodes that were active at the time of failure and had not yet communicated their results back to the WfMS.

- **Backward recovery.** WfMSs also provide backward recovery to support those cases in which it is not possible to complete a workflow and the partial execution needs to be undone. Backward recovery is supported through transactional abstractions that closely resemble those of *sagas* [78]: the idea is to associate with each work node a *compensating* activity whose execution semantically undoes the effects of the work node. For example, the compensation for sending a quote to a customer would involve sending another message to the customer stating that the quote is no longer valid. Backward recovery then involves executing compensating activities for each completed fork node, in the reverse order of forward execution [4, 220].

- **Exception-handling languages.** Some WfMSs, especially prototypes developed in academia, offer additional primitives for handling exceptions. These include mechanisms for capturing events that can occur asynchronously with respect to the control flow (i.e., can happen at any time during a workflow execution). An example of such an event is a customer canceling a request for quote. Mechanisms to detect "exceptional" occurrences range from additional workflow node types, such as *event nodes*, [88] to event-condition-action (ECA) rules [45, 59] and Java-style *try-catch-throw* constructs, or variations thereof [217].

- **Deadlines.** Being tools for composing and integrating applications, WfMSs must deal with the problem of applications that, after being invoked, fail to respond. This problem is known as *deadline expiration*. The usual way to deal with this problem is to associate a time-out with each step of the process. Once the step is invoked, time starts running. If, when the time-out is reached, the application has not finished or has not responded in any way, the WfMS can then take corrective action. For instance, the job can be rescheduled, execution stopped, or a message sent to a system administrator indicating the problem.

Another important difference between conventional programming and workflows lies in the resource that executes the procedure. In a programming

language, the resource is always the computer, and specifically the micropro-
cessor. In a workflow the resource can be human and can vary depending on
the work to be executed and on the nature of the workflow instance. For example, in our sample workflow, step *check if worth proceeding* may be assigned
to a different manager depending on the type of product being requested.
This ability to dynamically assign work nodes to different resources requires
the possibility of defining *resource rules*, that is, specifications that encode
the logic necessary for identifying the appropriate resource to be assigned to
each work node execution. Rules are typically defined over the workflow instance state and over the value of workflow variable, and return the resource
to which the work should be assigned. Most WfMSs come with an internal
resource broker that can execute simple resource rules. We discuss resource
selection and exception handling in more detail in Chapter 8, when we present
service composition models.

3.3.5 Integration of WfMSs with Other Middleware Technologies

WfMSs have a tight relationship with the interoperability models and systems presented earlier in the book. In particular, workflow technology has
many characteristics that resemble those of *TP monitors*. For example, they
execute distributed transactions on top of autonomous systems, they manage
resource naming and binding, and they include performance management and
load-balancing functionalities, thereby enabling the concurrent execution of
thousands of complex transactions. In addition, WfMS architectures, just like
TP monitors, include a single operating system process (the workflow engine)
that manages all workflow instances, thereby avoiding overloads of the execution platform with a large number of operating system processes. WfMSs,
however, put an emphasis on programming in the large, on dynamic resource
selection and assignment, and on exception handling, as opposed to focusing
on the execution of transactional RPC. WfMSs also leverage ORB-style brokers, MOMs, or publish/subscribe systems. At least one of these technologies
is part of any WfMS architecture, to enable interoperability among WfMS
components.

As noted before, WfMSs and EAI platforms are complementary. While EAI
tackles the composition problem from the side of heterogeneity, to make all
components look alike and therefore easier to integrate, workflow technology
focuses on the workflow language and on the management of the workflows
that perform the integration. This is also due to historical reasons: many
WfMSs were originally developed for the purpose of automating and controlling administrative processes, such as expense approvals or automatic employee reimbursements, where the "components" are typically humans, and
the "adapters" are simple Web interfaces or the e-mail system.

Enterprise applications may therefore be created by first deploying an EAI
tool to hide the heterogeneity of component blocks, and by then leveraging a
WfMS to design and enact the composition logic. The resulting architecture is

shown in Figure 3.10. In this approach, all workflow steps are assigned to the same "resource", the WfMS/EAI adapter, which takes work items from the WfMS work queue and publishs a message to the bus. The "real" assignment is then done by the message broker, based on the subscriptions by back-end system adapters. The adapters also collect work results and publish them back to the message broker, who delivers them to the WfMS/EAI adapter and, ultimately, to the WfMS inbound queue. Therefore, the development of a workflow application that uses an EAI platform involves designing the flow through the WfMS graphical development environment and configuring the adapters so that they subscribe to the appropriate messages, invoke the required API on the back-end system, and publish a message with the execution results back to the message broker when the back-end system has completed its job.

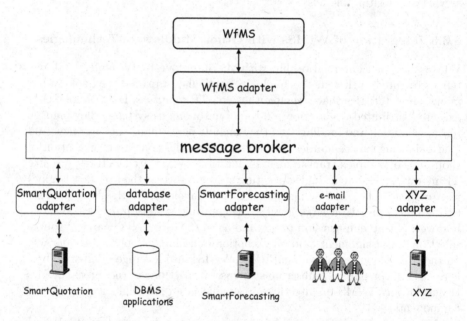

Fig. 3.10. Workflow and EAI technologies can be combined to automate business processes across the enterprise. The workflow is used to implement the integration logic (*upper box*) and the actual interaction between the components takes place though the message broker

3.3.6 Benefits and Limitations of WfMS

The functionalities provided by the WfMS components like the ones described above offer many benefits with respect to coding the process logic for those application integration problems involving the composition of coarse-grained applications and human actions. In particular, they enable rapid process design and maintenance, failure and exception handling, as well as catering for performance and high availability. Workflow design is also typically supported by a graphical development environment that, in combination with the model, aims at enabling the definition of complex business processes through point-and-click interfaces.

Perhaps for the above reasons, WfMSs raised a lot of interest in both industry and the research community when they began to emerge. This interest led to the development of literally dozens of workflow models, systems, and research prototypes. However, at least in the beginning, WfMSs did not live up to their promises and expectations. Some of their problems and limitations were common to those of EAI platforms: expensive software licenses, complex installation and operation, and long development cycles to actually automate real business processes. In the case of WfMSs, these problems were compounded by the fact a WfMS had to implement a complete middleware platform to provide the necessary run-time environment. As a result, WfMSs turned out to be heavyweight platforms, difficult to operate and maintain. In addition, WfMSs proved to be most useful with repetitive, well-defined processes (i.e., that could be subjected to formalization using a workflow language). Unfortunately for WfMSs, these types of processes were in many cases already automated using conventional middleware. That some processes were not automated already was more because they required functionality that neither middleware platforms nor workflow systems could readily support (for example, integration across wide area networks or integration of widely heterogeneous applications).

Nowadays, the interest in workflow systems and, more generally, in technologies for composing coarse-grained software applications is rising again. An example is the increasing use of the workflow model in cluster and grid computing [16, 2, 44, 123, 163]. Another is the influence of workflow systems in the work being done around Web services composition. In Chapter 8, when presenting service composition models and systems, we will look back at the drawbacks of WfMSs mentioned above, and discuss why WfMS-like composition technologies are more likely to succeed in that context.

3.4 Summary

All middleware is about application integration. Nevertheless, the term *EAI platform* is used to refer specifically to software systems that facilitate the integration of heterogeneous, coarse-grained applications. The platforms of choice nowadays for this purpose are message brokers and workflow management systems. There are, however, marked differences between these platforms and how they are being adopted. Message brokers play a much more important role in EAI. Workflows seem to drift in and out of fashion, depending on the technology that is being emphasized at the given moment. The reason for this state of affairs is directly related to the fact that while application integration provides many benefits, it often presents a non trivial design challenge. In particular, developers now face the problem of gluing together different, independently developed systems. This raises issues ranging from how to enable interactions and data exchange to how to design, implement, and execute the integration logic that specifies which applications need to be invoked and in what order.

The success of message brokers lies in their use of an asynchronous communication model and a loosely coupled architecture for application integration that locates the necessary code to interact with existing systems in an adapter. This approach considerably simplifies the design and provides a great deal of flexibility when addressing these issues, in stark contrast with RPC-based systems where the integration effort must often take place in the application itself. If that is not possible, the use of wrappers typically leads to an ad hoc asynchronous solution equivalent to using a message broker. Workflow management systems, on the other hand, should be seen as complementary technology. As an integration tool, a workflow management system can only follow the approach of either an existing middleware platform or a message broker. As a result, when WfMSs are advertised as integration tools, they are often a disappointment since they do not have anything new to offer. The strength of WfMSs is the ability to make the integration logic explicit and, in some cases, hide many of the complexities of this integration logic behind visual languages and sophisticated development interfaces. It is in this role as the language for megaprogramming that workflow management systems become an intrinsic part of integration efforts. Proof of this is the increasing relevance of workflow models as languages for expressing complex interaction between Web services, a topic that is discussed in detail in Chapter 8.

One question that may arise after reading this chapter is, if message brokers have been so successful as tools for enterprise application integration, why do we need anything else? The answer to this question is twofold. On the one hand, the type of integration discussed so far has been implicitly limited to LANs. As it is easy to imagine, the problems of application integration are significantly amplified when we consider integration across enterprises and over the Internet. On the other hand, although current technology provides tremendous benefits, existing platforms are still very expensive and quite complex to use and maintain. The integration is far less "seamless" than most vendors suggest. Even with an adequate integration platform, there is still considerable programming overhead each time a remote invocation takes place. We are not yet at the point where we can have *plug and play* application integration, which is the ultimate goal in this area. One of the biggest problems that stands in the way of this goal is the lack of standardization, both at the middleware and at the component level. How to solve the problems of integration across wide area networks and of standardization will be the topic of the following chapters.

4

Web Technologies

In Chapter 3, we have studied the need for integrating enterprise applications in order to achieve business process automation. The need to integrate, however, is not limited to the systems within a single company. The same advantages that can be derived from automating a company's business processes can be obtained from automating business processes encompassing several companies. Hence, it should not come as a surprise that there is as much interest in inter-enterprise application integration as there is in intra-enterprise application integration. This chapter serves as a transition between the chapters that precede, which focus on intra-enterprise application integration and on middleware services, and the chapters that follow, which describe Web services for inter-enterprise application integration. The purpose of this chapter is to introduce the basic Web technologies that are used to implement the "Web" portion of Web services.

The Web emerged as a technology for sharing information on the Internet. However, it quickly became the medium for connecting remote clients with applications across the Internet, and more recently (with the advent of Web services) a medium for integrating applications across the Internet. Some of the same technologies that enabled information sharing and integration of remote clients also form the basis for inter-enterprise application integration. That is why, in this chapter, we start by examining the core Web technologies (Section 4.1). We then follow that with a discussion of Web technologies for creating remote clients (Section 4.2). The initial set of technologies for moving the client to remote locations emerged as mechanisms for wrapping local information systems. However, as the popularity of using the Web for building client/server systems increased, traditional middleware platforms were forced to provide the ability to "Web-enable" their applications. In Section 4.3, we discuss one such middleware platform–J2EE-based application servers. Finally, in Section 4.4, we initiate a discussion of some of the Web technologies that were aimed at inter-enterprise application integration. These technologies are precursors to Web services, which are the focus of discussion for the rest of this book.

4.1 Exchanging Information over the Internet

The Internet is a global system of computer networks. In 1969, the Advanced Research Projects Agency (ARPA) connected the computer systems of Stanford Research Institute, UCLA, UC Santa Barbara, and the University of Utah together, across the United States, in a small network called the ARPANET.

ARPANET allowed the connection of autonomous computing systems, which gave rise to the first standards organizations for governing this network. These standards groups developed protocols such as Transmission Control Protocol (TCP), which handles the conversion between messages and streams of packets, and the Internet Protocol (IP), which handles the addressing of packets across networks. TCP/IP is the defining technology of the Internet, because it enables packets to be sent across multiple networks using multiple standards (e.g., Ethernet, FDDI, X.25, etc.).

4.1.1 Before the Web

Two of the earliest standards for exchanging information through the Internet were the telnet protocol [166] and electronic mail's Simple Mail Transfer Protocol (SMTP) [215]. Each of these protocols specifies a different way to directly connect accounts on different systems, regardless of the underlying operating systems and computers involved. The SMTP protocol was eventually extended with Multi-purpose Internet Mail Extensions (MIME), which support the exchange of richer data files, such audio, video, and images data. Soon after telnet and electronic mail emerged, the File Transfer Protocol (FTP) was published (in 1973) [167]. FTP supports file transfers between Internet sites, and allows a system to publish a set of files by hosting an FTP server. One of the innovations of FTP was that although it required authentication, it also permitted anonymous users to transfer files. This meant that users were no longer required to have accounts on all systems that were to be connected. FTP led to the development of the first Web-like distributed information systems, such as Archie [69] (in the late 1980s), which can be thought of as using FTP to create a distributed file system, and Gopher, an early application protocol that provided a simple client/server system and graphical user interface (GUI) for publishing and accessing text files over the Internet [129].

4.1.2 The Web

The core Web technologies as we know them today, i.e., HTTP, HTML, Web servers, and Web browsers, are an evolution of these early technologies. The HyperText Transfer Protocol (HTTP), is a generic, stateless protocol that governs the transfer of files across a network [70]. It was originally developed at the European Laboratory for Particle Physics (CERN). HTTP is generic in that it also supports access to other protocols such as FTP or SMTP. The same team at CERN that developed HTTP and other related concepts also came up with the name World Wide Web (also known as the Web) [23, 24]. Later, further development was taken over by the World Wide Web Consortium (W3C) with the goal of promoting standards for the Web.

HTTP was designed to support hypertext (the ability to interconnect documents by inserting links between them as part of the document contents). In particular, HTTP supports the HyperText Markup Language (HTML), which defines a standard set of special textual indicators (markups) that specify how a Web page's words and images should be displayed by the Web browser.

Information is exchanged over HTTP in the form of documents, which are identified using Uniform Resource Identifiers (URIs). The exchanged documents can be static (where the resource itself is returned) or dynamic, meaning that the content of the document is generated at access time. Every resource accessible over the Web has a Uniform Resource Locator (URL) that identifies the location of the resource (a file if the resource is a document or a program if the resource is a program that will produce the document) and describes how to access it. Thus, a URL provides the name of a protocol to be used to access the resource, an address (which can be either a domain name or an IP address) of a machine where the resource is located, and a hierarchical description of the location of the resource on that machine (similar to a directory path).

The HTTP mechanism is based on the client/server model, typically using TCP/IP sockets. An HTTP client (e.g., *a Web browser*) opens a connection to an HTTP server (*a Web server*) and sends a request message consisting of a *request method*, URI, and protocol version, followed by a "MIME-like message" (HTTP is not strictly complaint with MIME [70]). The server then returns a response message consisting of a status line (indicating the message's protocol version and a success or error code), followed by a MIME-like message (usually containing the requested document) and closes the connection. Prior to HTTP version 1.1, a separate TCP connection needed to be established to fetch the individual elements of an HTML page—even when they were all located on the same server (meaning that a separate TCP connection had to be established for every access). With version 1.1, HTTP requires servers to support persistent connections, in order to minimize the overhead associated with opening and closing connections.

The request method indicates the actual operation to perform on the server side. Typical methods include *OPTIONS* (send information about the communication options supported by that particular server), *GET* (retrieve whatever document is specified in the request or, if the request specifies a program, retrieve the document produced by the program), *POST* (append or attach the information included in the request to the resource specified in the request), *PUT* (store the information included in the request in the location specified as part of the request), and *DELETE* (delete the resource indicated in the request).

As shown in Figure 4.1, one or more intermediaries, such as a proxy (forwarding agent), gateway (receiving agent), or tunnel (relay point), may lie between the client and the server. RFC 2616 defines a proxy as *an intermediary program which acts as both a server and a client for the purpose of making requests on behalf of other clients*; a gateway as *a server which acts as an intermediary for some other origin server for the requested resource*; and a tunnel as *an intermediary program which is acting as a blind relay between two connections* [70]. That is to say, a proxy acts on behalf of a client, a gateway acts on behalf of a server, and a tunnel simply connects two networks (e.g., bridges the security mechanisms that might insulate a network, as discussed later in Section 4.4.3). Both the proxy and the gateway potentially process the URLs and content of the messages that they handle; the tunnel does not. Proxies, gateways, and tunnels are all essential concepts that allow HTTP applications to face the integration challenges posed by the Web environment, such as firewalls, load balancing, data translation, etc.

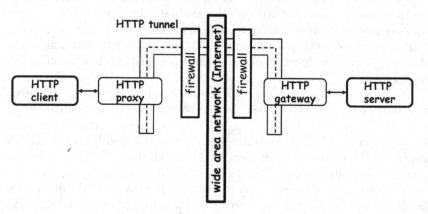

Fig. 4.1. Interaction between a HTTP client and a HTTP server could pass through several intermediaries

4.1.3 Limitations of HTTP

Despite its advantages, HTTP is subject to a number of limitations, many of which have been addressed by corresponding extensions to the HTTP protocol. First, ordinary HTTP does not encrypt data before sending it; if someone were to use a network sniffer to intercept messages between the HTTP server and client, they would be able to "read" those messages. Netscape therefore developed the Secure Sockets Layer (SSL), a protocol that uses public key encryption to protect data transferred over TCP/IP. HyperText Transfer Protocol over Secure Sockets Layer (HTTPS), also known as HTTP over SSL, allows the Web server and client to use SSL to authenticate to each other and establish an encrypted connection between themselves [148]. As shown in Figure 4.2, HTTPS runs on top of SSL, and requires both the server and the browser to be SSL-enabled.

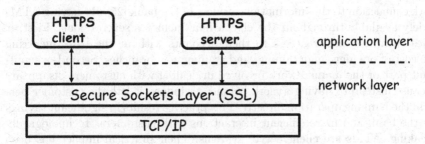

Fig. 4.2. HTTPS servers and clients encrypt the pages that they exchange

Second, HTTP is stateless, meaning that the protocol does not provide any support for storing information across HTTP transactions. Even if they are sent from the same client to the same server, there is no indication of any relationship between two different requests. The application developer is thus responsible for storing and managing the state information. One way for an HTTP server to store information on an HTTP client's machine is to use *HTTP cookies* [149], which are small data structures that a Web server requests the HTTP client to store on the local machine (the actual location of this storage depends on the Web browser being used). The cookies are then used to maintain state information by creating a trace on the local machine of any information needed across different invocations. For example, an e-commerce storefront site might use a cookie to keep track of which items a customer has looked at in a session.

4.2 Web Technologies for Supporting Remote Clients

The original intent of the core Web technologies was to enable linking and sharing documents. But, it was quickly realized that by wrapping local information systems to expose their presentation layer using HTML documents, one could leverage the core Web technologies to have clients that are distributed across the Internet.

4.2.1 Need for Supporting Remote Clients

Conventional 3-tier architectures (and conventional middleware in general) are designed to operate within a single company. This means that the clients of the system will be operated mostly by employees of the company and that data exchanges occur within the safe boundaries of the company. However, there is in principle no reason why the system could not be opened to other users (for instance, to customers) if the need arises.

The automatic teller machines (ATMs) used in banks are an excellent example of the advantages of doing so. An ATM is basically a PC with a network connection to the information services of the bank [25]. By having ATMs widely available throughout the city, a bank achieves several goals. First, it gives customers easier access to their accounts without the bank incurring the cost of opening, maintaining, and staffing new branches. Second, a significant part of the manual work involved in dealing with customers disappears because instead of having a clerk behind a window, it lets the customer perform the banking operation directly. This practice results in significant savings for the bank and more efficient interactions with customers. Technologically speaking, ATMs are client/server systems. Their practical impact has been very significant.

The extension of 3-tier architectures to enable even further integration possibilities can be analyzed in light of the ATM example. ATMs provide a great service. However, there are limitations for how many ATMs can be installed and maintained in a cost effective manner. No matter how hard a bank tries, customers must travel from their homes or work place to the nearest ATM to complete their banking operations. This would not be necessary if a "personal" ATM machine could be installed at everyone's home and office. That way, customers would have access to their bank accounts, any time they wanted, without having to visit an ATM. Giving the ATM to the customer, so to speak, helps extend its functionality. In addition to depositing or withdrawing money, one could also use the personal ATM to invest in stock, transfer funds to other accounts, make payments, and carry out many other financial operations. Once the user owns the client (rather than sharing it with other users), there are no constraints on the time the customer might take to complete an operation or on the complexity of the information the bank can display. The possibilities are almost endless, to the point that customers may never need to visit the bank in person to perform a financial operation.

The resulting architecture is depicted in Figure 4.3. Such interactions are called *business-to-consumer* (B2C), indicating that the business allows consumers to access their information services directly. Although technically feasible and not overly complicated, implementing this in practice is not as easy as simply running the client on a remote computer. Users wanting to take advantage of the opportunity would need to have a specialized client for every company they wanted to interact with, which is not a practical solution. Moreover, if the middleware-based systems are already quite complex to maintain and administer, this complexity would grow enormously if the clients were not local but rather distributed all over the Internet, many of them running completely outside the control of the middleware platform or its administrators.

One of the biggest contributions of the Web has been precisely to provide a universal client for such extensions. Nowadays, architectures like that in Figure 4.3 are implemented not by moving the client to the remote computer

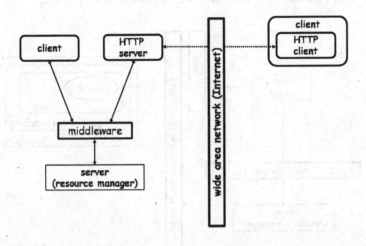

Fig. 4.3. Extending a 3-tier architecture by removing the client to a remote location across the Internet

but by letting the remote computer use a Web browser as a client. Using the Web to implement remote clients effectively places a virtual ATM on any computer with a Web browser. Since Web browsers are standard tools, no application-specific clients need to be installed. Companies can take advantage of the existence of such a standard client by using widely available tools for building a browser-based access channel for their application. In practice this has given rise to new Web technologies for wrapping local information systems to support the new access channel.

4.2.2 Applets

One of the first problems faced when using the Web infrastructure as the medium for implementing remote clients is that Web browsers were originally intended only to display static documents returned by HTTP calls, and it is thus difficult to build sophisticated application-specific clients for Web browsers. One answer to this problem was to introduce *applets*. Applets are Java programs that can be embedded in an HTML document. When the document is downloaded, the program is executed by the Java virtual machine (JVM) present in the browser. Hence, the way to turn the browser into a client is to send the client code as an applet. This, of course, suffers from the limitation of having to download the code every time the client is used. Nevertheless, for applications based on thin clients, it is a very common solution.

Figure 4.3 should thus be understood as the client being implemented as an applet and running on a Web browser, as shown in Figure 4.4.

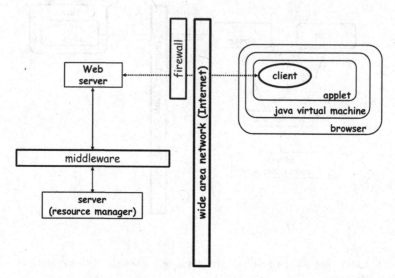

Fig. 4.4. Applets as a way to implement remote clients

Applets have the significant advantage of turning a Web browser into an application-specific client without complex configuration or installation procedures. However, because applets exist only for the lifetime of a particular browser instance, they are transient, and are thus inadequate for supporting complex client code or frequent interactions. An alternative is to use a specialized client that is not based on a browser but contains the necessary code to interact with a Web server through HTTP. Such an approach does not have any of the limitations of applets but requires a specialized client. In this case, the advantages and disadvantages are identical to those of client/server systems, discussed in Chapter 1.

4.2.3 Common Gateway Interface

Thus far, we have only discussed the case where the Web server returns a static document (possibly containing embedded applet code to be executed on the client). But if we view Web servers as interfaces to distributed information systems, they must be able to serve up content from dynamic sources (e.g., publish information retrieved from a database). The issue then is, for example, how a Web server can respond to a request (triggered by addressing a URL) by invoking an application that will automatically generate a document to be returned.

One of the first approaches to solve this problem was to use the Common Gateway Interface (CGI) [147], a standard mechanism that enables HTTP servers to interface with external applications, which can serve as "gateways" to the local information system. CGI assigns programs to URLs, so that when the URL is invoked the program is executed. Arguments or additional information needed by the program (such as parameters or path information) are sent as part of the invoked URL. CGI programs can be written in a variety of programming languages, and are typically placed in a special directory so that the Web server can identify them as programs (as opposed to static content). Thus, when a request for a URL goes to that directory, the Web server knows it must start a program rather than return an HTML page. From the URL received, the Web server extracts any information it may need to pass on to the program (i.e., parameters for a query or arguments for the program) and starts the program as a separate process[1]. These programs can then be used to interact with the underlying middleware (see Figure 4.5).

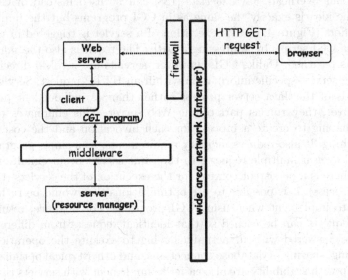

Fig. 4.5. CGI programs as a way to with an application on the server side through a URL

For example, CGI programs often serve as an interface between a database and a Web server, allowing users to submit complex queries over the database through predefined URLs. The parameters of the query are embedded into the URL. When the Web server receives the request for the URL, it will run a program that will act as a client of the database and submit the query.

---

[1] Fast-CGI reduces some of the overhead associated with the creation of new processes by allowing calls to be made to an already running process rather than creating a new process for every invocation of the URL.

The program executes the query, then packs the query results into a HTML document to be returned to the remote browser.

4.2.4 Servlets

From a performance point of view, CGI programs involve a certain overhead. First, a separate process is usually created for each instance. The creation of the process takes time and requires a context switch in the operating system to pass control to the CGI program. The result is an increase in the overall response time of the system. In addition, multiple requests result in multiple processes being created, all of them competing for resources such as database connections or memory (multiple requests to the same CGI program result in the program being loaded in memory once for every request), thereby limiting the scalability of the system.

To avoid this overhead, Java *servlets* [188] can be used instead of CGI programs. The idea is exactly the same as in CGI programs but the implementation differs (Figure 4.6). The execution of a servlet is triggered in the same way as a CGI script: by addressing a URL. The result is also the same: a document is returned. Unlike CGIs, however, servlets are invoked directly by embedding servlet-specific information within an HTTP request. Servlets run as threads of the Java server process rather than as independent processes. Moreover, they run as part of the Web server. This eliminates the overhead of having to create a process for each invocation and the cost of context switching. It also reduces memory requirements, as a single program image is used even if multiple requests to the same servlet occur simultaneously. Since there is a persistent context for the execution of the servlets (the Java server process), it is possible to use optimizations that would be rather cumbersome to implement when using CGI programs. For instance, results of previous requests can be cached so that identical requests from different clients can be answered without actually having to execute the operation. Session tracking, sharing of database connections, and other typical optimizations that help with scalability are also easier to implement with servlets than with CGI programs. Not discussed in this chapter but closely related to CGI and Servlets are server page technologies such as Active Server Pages (ASP) [134], JavaServer Pages (JSP) [189], and ASP.NET, which embed code to be interpreted on the server side into HTML pages.

4.3 Application Servers

The increasing use of the Web as a channel to access information systems forced middleware platforms to provide support for Web access. This support is typically provided in the form of *application servers*.

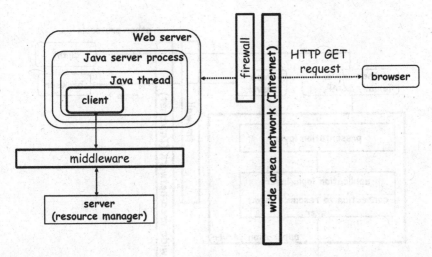

Fig. 4.6. Servlets as a way to interaction with an application on the server side through a URL

4.3.1 Middleware for Web Applications

Application servers are equivalent to the middleware platforms discussed in earlier chapters. The main difference is the incorporation of the Web as a key access channel to the services implemented using the middleware.

Incorporating the Web as an access channel has several important implications. The most significant one is that the presentation layer acquires a much more relevant role than in conventional middleware. This is a direct consequence of how HTTP and the Web work, where all forms of information exchange take place through documents. Preparing, dynamically generating, and managing these documents are thus a big part of what an application server needs in order to extend a middleware platform to one with Web access capabilities. This is typically done by merging the presentation layer related to the Web with the application layer of the middleware platform (Figure 4.7). The reason to integrate the Web presentation layer and the application layer is to allow the efficient delivery of content through the Web as well as to simplify the management of Web applications. Connectivity to the resource management layer is achieved through standard connection architectures and APIs, such as JDBC [190] and ODBC [135] (as it is done in middleware platforms and EAI architectures).

4.3.2 J2EE as the Core of an Application Server

The core functionality of an application server can be described by examining one of the two competing frameworks for Web-based middleware: SUN's J2EE and Microsoft's .NET. In terms of functionality, J2EE- and .NET-based application servers are very similar. Hence, for the purposes of this book, we just

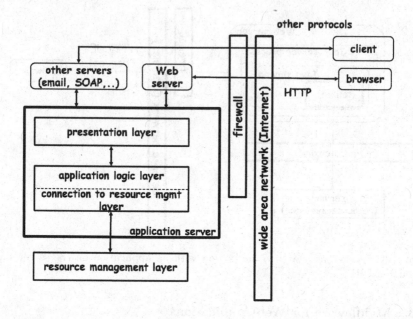

Fig. 4.7. Application servers cover both the application logic and presentation layer

use one of them (J2EE) to illustrate what application servers are all about. The ideas presented should also apply to .NET without major changes.

Figure 4.8 summarizes the main components of the J2EE specification. In addition, J2EE includes other API specifications whose implementation provides functionality commonly needed by application integration projects, such as object brokering and transactional support.

As the complexity of J2EE shows, a significant aspect of application servers is the bundling of more and more functionality within the middleware platform. This is consistent with the trend toward providing integrated support for many different middleware abstractions that we have witnessed in conventional middleware. In fact, as software vendors continue to extend their middleware offerings and package them in many different ways, it becomes hard even to distinguish what is inside an application server and what is not. In many cases, the name originally given to the application server (e.g., WebLogic or WebSphere) has been progressively used to label every middleware component offered by a company. For example, IBM messaging and workflow platforms are now marketed under the name WebSphere MQ, while BEA uses the name WebLogic to label many of its middleware products, such as WebLogic Integration. Sometimes even data warehousing and business intelligence are considered to be part of the application server functionality [161]. Business and marketing reasons therefore contribute to blurring the borders between application servers and other middleware.

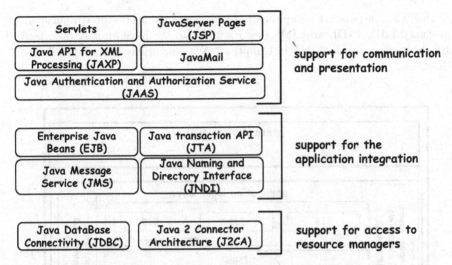

Fig. 4.8. Main API mandated by the J2EE specifications

In the following discussion, we describe the support that application servers provide for the application logic and the presentation layer. Readers interested in more details on application servers than those provided in this chapter can draw from many different resources. For J2EE, the best source of information is the Java Web site [191]. In particular, a short introduction to J2EE is available at [192], while a longer and more detailed version is provided by [29]. Information on commercial application servers is as usual available from the vendors' Web sites. Leading application servers are BEA WebLogic [18], IBM WebSphere [99], Microsoft .NET [165], Sun One [195], and Oracle 9i AS [160]. A more complete list of vendors as well as a comparison of the features provided by J2EE-based application servers is available from [73].

4.3.3 Application Server Support for the Application Layer

At the application layer, application servers conceptually resemble conventional middleware. The functionality provided is similar to that of CORBA, TP monitors, and message brokers. This is why application servers are not limited to Web-based integration, but can also be used for EAI. The goal of application server vendors is in fact to provide a unique environment for hosting all kinds of application logic, whether Web-based or otherwise. As part of this effort, application servers try to provide typical middleware functionality (e.g., transactions, security, persistence) in an automatic manner when the application is deployed in a given server. In this way, application developers do not need to handle this functionality themselves, as these properties are acquired on the fly by deploying a program within an application server.

In J2EE, the support for application logic concentrates on three main specifications: EJB, JNDI, and JMS (see Figure 4.9). We have already discussed
the abstractions behind JMS in Chapter 3. We now briefly describe EJB and
JNDI.

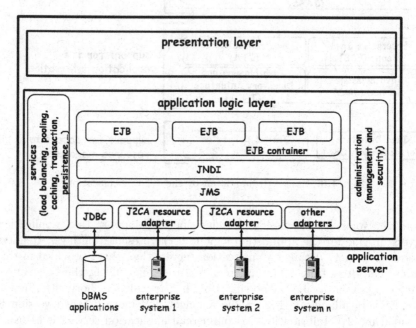

Fig. 4.9. Application servers support the application logic layer

The Enterprise JavaBeans (EJB) specification is at the heart of J2EE, in
that the EJB is where the bulk of the application logic resides. An EJB is a
server-side component that delivers application-specific functionality such as
responding to a request for a quote or processing a purchase order. The EJB
specification defines three different types of beans, based on how they interact
with other components and on how they manage state and persistence:

• **Session beans** handle a session with a client. They can be *stateful* or
  stateless. Stateful beans maintain the state of a conversation with a client.
  The typical example of a stateful bean is an online shopping cart. Stateless
  beans do not maintain any state, and therefore the same stateless bean
  can be reused for different clients.
• **Entity beans** live beyond the boundaries of a session with the client. They
  have a state, stored in a database or in another persistent storage. EJB
  persistence can be managed by the bean itself (meaning that the developer
  must write SQL or other statements to save the state in a database) or
  it can be managed by the EJB platform, meaning that developers do not

have to write any additional code, and the system will take care of the persistence of objects.

- **Message-driven beans** are the latest addition to the EJB family. They cater to asynchronous interaction with clients, unlike session or entity beans, which instead interoperate in an RPC-like fashion. Asynchronous interaction is achieved through messaging, with message driven beans acting as clients to a JMS message bus.

The *EJB container* provides the environment in which the beans run. All interactions between the EJB and other objects go through the container. Thanks to this mediation role, the container can provide a number of services. For example, it supports transactions, freeing developers from having to define transaction boundaries and implement the related code. Transactions can be managed by the container, according to properties assigned to the EJB methods at deployment time. That is, it is possible to "label" an EJB method according to whether it should or should not be run within transactional boundaries and, if it should be run, whether the method should be executed within the transaction of the EJB client (if any) or whether a new transaction should be created. Other container services include persistence (for entity beans) and security.

Binding to EJBs is done through a Java Naming and Directory Interface (JNDI) directory. JNDI defines an interface for directory services, without mandating any implementation. Using JNDI, clients can bind to servers based on the object name. In the case of EJBs, binding to a server actually involves binding to an object that provides the interface for interacting with a server.

In addition to supporting the development and execution of application logic, J2EE (and an application server in general) addresses the problem of connecting to the resource layer. The approach is once again based on standard APIs and architectures. In particular, J2EE leverages two standards in this space: the above-mentioned JDBC and the J2EE Connector Architecture (J2CA). JDBC is an API that enables developers to access almost any tabular data source by executing SQL commands from a Java program. JDBC methods can be called from an EJB or directly from a servlet, bypassing the access to the application logic layer. J2CA is a generalization of this approach, in that it defines how to build *resource adapters*, i.e., Java components that interface EJB and other Java applications with a resource manager. Each resource adapter is characterized by *contracts* with the application and with the J2EE platform. The application contract essentially defines the API that Java applications can use to access the resource manager. The contract with the platform describes the properties of the resource adapter so that the J2EE platform can support connection pooling, XA transactions, and security.

Besides implementing J2EE (or other specifications in the non-Java world), application servers also offer services that simplify the administration and management of the applications and provide for performance and high availability. For example, they can cache objects that are frequently needed, distribute the load among pools of objects, or continuously check that an application is running and restart it upon a failure. They also provide object administration and security, defining which user has access to which applications and enforcing access restrictions.

The previous discussion has shown that EJB platforms (and application servers in general) provide many different services that relieve programmers from having to perform a number of tasks. What could previously be done only manually can now be done automatically by the EJB platform. Analogous features are provided (or are being designed) for other distributed object models, such as COM+, or by CORBA (refer, for example, to the discussion on the CORBA Component Model [158]). This is important not only because it speeds up application development, but also because it facilitates their management, thereby reducing the so-called "Total Cost of Ownership." For these reasons, EJBs and other analogous approaches are enjoying a wide popularity today.

Just as compilers needed some time to improve to a point where they could match or even surpass human beings in how they provide their services, EJB platforms are currently improving how they automatically manage persistence, transactions, and other functionality [114]. Today, there is still a trade-off between ease of development and performance. This is true not only for EJB, but also holds for application servers in general. Application servers cannot match, for example, the performance of TP monitors. TP monitors are an excellent platform for supporting high load applications whose characteristics are rather static, as the configuration and deployment phase can be delicate and time consuming. Application servers, on the other hand, try to make systems easier to develop and easier to evolve.

4.3.4 Application Server Support for the Presentation Layer

The support for the presentation layer and for the document as the basic unit of transfer is what differentiates application servers from conventional middleware. CGI programs take a somewhat black box approach in implementing the presentation layer of a Web application, in the sense that they try to link to the middleware platform without requiring changes to it. The resulting architectures have the advantage that they can be used on top of systems that were not prepared to handle wide area integration. For example, legacy systems for which new clients are written can become Web-enabled simply by wrapping that client with a CGI program. In spite of their obvious practical uses, true integration cannot really be achieved unless the middleware platform cooperates. That is, middleware should not be treated as a black box but modified to provide the necessary support to make its services accessible through the Web.

CGI programs offer a crude way to achieve this. Application servers implement similar mechanisms that are slowly evolving toward more sophisticated implementations that make the transition between documents and arguments more efficient, flexible, and manageable. They provide a variety of presentation features to support the delivery of dynamically generated, personalized content (i.e., documents) to different types of clients. A modern application server supports the following types of clients (as depicted in Figure 4.10):

- **Web browsers**, including both those requesting plain HTML pages and those downloading and executing applets.
- **Applications**, such as those encountered in conventional middleware.
- **Devices**, such as mobile phones or PDAs.
- **E-mail programs.**
- **Web services clients**, i.e., applications that interact with the server through standard Web services protocols.

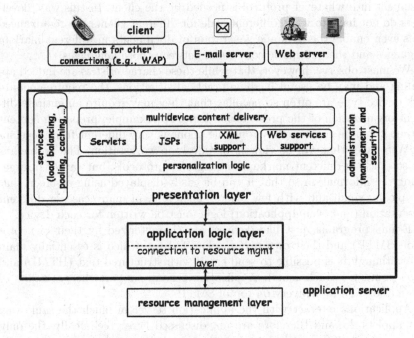

Fig. 4.10. Application server support for the presentation layer

Web browsers are by far the most common type of clients. They interact with the application servers (via the Web server) through HTTP or HTTPS and receive statically or dynamically generated HTML pages. Static pages are in plain HTML while dynamic pages include servlets, JSPs, and ActiveX controls. In both the .NET and the J2EE world, these dynamic components are integrated with the application logic layer. For example, application server development tools simplify the linkage of JSP fragments with the EJBs in the application layer (through the EJB container) providing the data. The JSP then arranges the data into a format suitable for presentation to the client (typically a Web browser). If the client is an applet rather than a Web browser, the communication with the application server may occur through protocols other than HTTP. For example, applets may interact with an application server through RMI (Remote Method Invocation) or CORBA/ IIOP.

Web browsers are not the only way users can access the information provided by a Web site. Other types of clients exist and are expected to be increasingly used in the near future. Examples of such clients are mobile phones and PDAs. These devices may use presentation languages different from HTML and protocols different from HTTP or IIOP. For instance, mobile phones have adopted the Wireless Application Protocol (WAP) to interact and the Wireless Markup Language (WML) as a presentation language. Application servers aim at transparently supporting different protocols, by wrapping the document into whatever protocol is needed by the client. In this way, developers do not have to write different code for different clients. More advanced tools even enable the dynamic generation of documents in different markup languages and the automatic conversion between those languages.

We must observe, however, that while these characteristics are indeed appealing and may be useful in some practical situations, the requirements of each device type are often so peculiar that they may require an entirely different organization of the presentation logic. For example, preparing content so that it can be consumed by a mobile phone is very different from developing Web pages that will be viewed on a desktop workstation. The problem is not so much in different markup languages or protocols, but rather in organizing the information so that it can be easily displayed using a screen that is typically small and with few colors. Therefore, in many cases a different presentation (and even application) logic must be written for each device.

E-mail programs, just like devices, are characterized by their own protocol (SMTP) and their own text markup format, which is essentially plain text, although it is possible to send email with structured text (HTML) and richer content (attachments). Application servers support the packaging of information and its delivery on top of SMTP.

Applications interact with the application server in much the same way that applets do, and therefore are not discussed here. Technically, the only difference is that the applet's code is downloaded from the server on the fly and, coming from an external entity, is by default not trusted and runs with security constraints.

The fifth type of client is the Web services client. It requires yet another protocol (SOAP) as well as other languages and infrastructures. Application server support for interaction with Web services clients includes facilities for creating, parsing, and validating XML documents, as well as for packaging and unpackaging messages to be delivered through SOAP. This type of client will be discussed in the following chapters.

Besides supporting different types of clients, application servers also aim at supporting different types of users. In fact, one of the features provided by such systems is *personalization*, i.e., the ability to provide different content and different renderings of the content based on the user to which this content should be delivered. This is often achieved through the definition of a set of condition/action rules: the condition identifies whether the request (and the requestor, if information about the user is available) conforms to a certain profile. For example, the condition can test whether the request comes from a US Internet address or whether the requestor is a "premium" customer. The action part defines the content that should be delivered to requests satisfying the condition, and how this content is structured. For example, it can cause US news to be shown, and at the top of the page rather than at the bottom.

In general, personalization features can be quite sophisticated, going beyond the simple example described above. Indeed, there are many platforms that have exactly this as their main focus and selling point. Examples of Web application development environments with emphasis on personalization include ATG Dynamo [12], WebRatio [214], and Broadvision [37]. Some of these platforms later evolved to provide support for application logic (such as ATG Dynamo), while others focused on Web application development (and run on top of other application servers, e.g., WebRatio). At the same time, vendors that initially focused on the application logic layer are progressively adding personalization features, thereby supporting the architecture depicted in Figure 4.10. Note that Web servers (and the other communication servers) may or may not be included in a vendor's offering. Most application servers can work with many different Web servers, such as Microsoft Internet Information Server, Apache, or Netscape Enterprise Server.

As the figure shows, at this level the application server also provides a number of services that help manage performance, availability, and security, as well as an administration console to manage servlets, JSPs, and other components that populate the presentation layer.

4.4 Web Technologies for Application Integration

HTTP can be directly used to allow different information systems to interact with each other across the Internet. It is not a perfect solution and has considerable limitations, but the techniques developed for HTTP formed the basis for how Web services were developed later.

4.4.1 Architectures for Wide Area Integration

When integrating systems that are separated by a wide area network, there are a number of strategies that, in principle, can be pursued. To better understand the available strategies, consider a 3-tier architecture built using a middleware platform similar to those discussed in Chapter 2. Such a system has three layers: client, middleware, and resource managers. The available strategies are given by all possible combinations of these three layers; one can integrate systems at the client level, at the middleware level, by connecting clients directly to the remote middleware platform, by connecting resource managers to the remote middleware platform, etc. (Figure 4.11). Which of these strategies is the most appropriate for a given situation depends on a number of factors, among which the level of standardization and the communication protocols available play a crucial role.

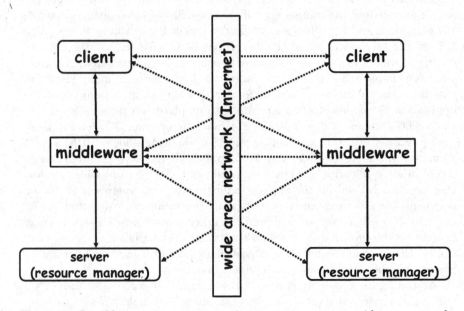

Fig. 4.11. Possible ways to connect two 3-tier systems across a wide area network

Before the emergence of the pervasive Web, only two of these options were realistic due to the protocols available at the time and the lack of standardization. The first option was to use specialized clients to integrate systems at the client level by exchanging messages. The second option was to integrate the middleware layers directly, so far as their compatibility permitted, by forwarding invocations directly to the remote system. The advent of the Web introduced the option of the Web browser as a universal client (as discussed above in Section 4.2.1).

4.4.2 Middleware Extensions

From the point of view of application integration, the Internet requires additional middleware layers between clients and servers or between servers. To allow existing platforms to interact through the Internet, conventional middleware platforms were simply extended to support the Internet as one more access channel. Some of these extensions are at the core of Web services.

Initially, most middleware platforms were designed to work on a single Local Area Network (LAN). As the number of LANs within companies started to grow, and different branches of the same company implemented their own middleware-based systems, the need arose for different middleware platforms to communicate with each other. When such interactions take place across company boundaries, they are called business-to-business (B2B) transaction exchanges. The idea behind electronic business-to-business exchanges is to fully automate the interactions between companies. For instance, instead of having to manually handle a purchase order, company A places the order electronically directly with company B. At company B, the order can then be immediately processed and a confirmation sent to A. Electronic exchanges are much faster and more cost effective than paper-based ones. They are also less prone to errors and can log data exchanges for monitoring and analysis. Companies can react faster, have a much more accurate picture of ongoing activities, and avoid much of the overhead of interacting with each other.

Technically, implementing this kind of interaction requires the ability to invoke services residing in a different company. Conceptually, this is relatively easy to do, and thus there is a strong temptation to implement Internet-wide integration using a simple extension of conventional communication protocols. This was in fact the path originally followed by conventional middleware platforms. The best example of how this approach works is CORBA. CORBA supports access to remote objects located within a given *domain*, i.e., under the control of an object request broker (ORB). Internet-wide integration is then achieved by linking together several ORBs. This is done through a General Inter-ORB Protocol (GIOP) that specifies how to forward calls from one ORB to another and get responses back. The GIOP protocol is then further specialized by using yet another protocol (the Internet Inter-ORB Protocol, IIOP) to translate GIOP calls into TCP/IP calls that can be made across the Internet. Such an approach is simple and very powerful, resulting in architectures like the one shown in Figure 4.12. The problem is that the assumptions underlying this design rarely hold when the interaction occurs across the Internet. For example, ORBs will probably be unable to communicate with each other directly since they most likely will be hidden behind firewalls, which impose significant restrictions on communications. Another issue that remains unsolved by merely extending the communication protocol to connect two ORBs is that of agreeing upon interface definitions and data formats to be used by the two applications. Finally, a directory server is required to enable service discovery, and, especially in inter-organizational settings, it may not be clear where this server should reside and who should manage it. As we will see in the next chapter when discussing the architecture of Web services, these problems are a big part of what Web services try to solve.

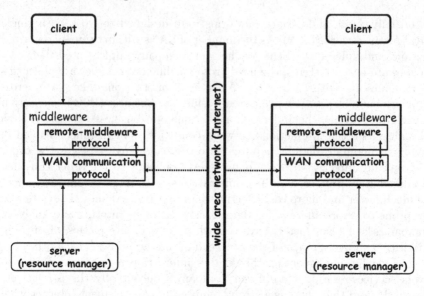

Fig. 4.12. Direct integration of middleware platforms

4.4.3 Firewalls and Tunneling through HTTP

Firewalls present a special challenge to integrating inter-enterprise systems across the Internet. Almost every organization today protects its internal networks, data, and computing resources by placing them behind a firewall. The firewall acts as a barrier against unwanted network traffic. In doing so, it blocks many communication channels. Almost all forms of communication usually employed by conventional EAI products cannot traverse a well-configured firewall. Thus, designers cannot rely on RPC, RMI, or GIOP/ IIOP to bind the different components of their distributed application.

In traditional middleware-based designs, this problem almost never appears because all components operate within the same network or across networks with transparent gateways between them. Thus, it is relatively easy to bind to services, to exchange data, and to control all ongoing interactions between clients and services, between services and the resource manager, and among services. It is also relatively easy to re-route requests to bypass failures, to balance the load in the system, to account for replicated services, and so on. The basic design principle is that every component of the system trusts and knows every other component. Similarly, firewalls are not a problem in message-based systems; protocols like SMTP can get through a firewall since the responsibility for secure interaction can be placed on the software processing the messages.

For architectures such as those depicted in Figures 4.3 and 4.12, firewalls change the design space in two ways. First, no direct communication between the systems to be integrated is generally possible–at least not with the protocols employed by existing middleware platforms. Second, firewalls are there for a good reason: parties outside the firewall are not trusted. The problem of not having a direct communication channel is compounded by a necessary lack of trust on all traffic generated outside the firewall. As a result, the degree of interaction cannot be the same as if the systems were residing in the same intranet.

The widely accepted solution to get through the firewall is to trick the firewall into believing that traffic which otherwise would be blocked is actually allowed. This is done by a technique known as *tunneling*, whereby protocols which would be blocked by the firewall are hidden under protocols that are accepted by the firewall. In other words, a call in one protocol that cannot get through the firewall is encapsulated (tunneled) within a call of another protocol that can get through the firewall. The best known examples of this strategy are tunneling through HTTP or SSH (Secure SHell). As mentioned earlier, in the case of HTTP, tunneling involves using an intermediary to convert the original message into an HTML or XML document, sending the document using HTTP, and extracting the message from the document once it reaches the recipient. Once inside the firewall, the message is fed to the middleware with the techniques and tools described in the previous chapters. The reply is treated in the same way and hence both sites can continue using whatever protocol they need in spite of the fact that firewalls would prevent that protocol from getting through. The resulting architecture is rather cumbersome (Figure 4.13) as it requires an additional layer and introduces one more level of indirection.

In spite of its shortcomings, tunneling has become the de facto solution to the problem of bypassing firewalls. Tunneling is used both by conventional middleware systems (e.g., GIOP/ IIOP over HTTP) and modern Web services (e.g., SOAP tunneling of RPC over HTTP). In almost all cases, tunneling takes place through HTTP since this is one of the very few protocols that are allowed through firewalls. In this case, firewalls have reinforced the role of the Web as the universal gateway between remote systems, as tunneling through HTTP usually assumes there is a Web server on both ends of the communication.

4.4.4 Common Data Representation: EDIFACT

The possibility of using FTP, SMTP, or HTTP for the automatic exchange of messages between companies gave raise to another important challenge: that of identifying a common syntax and semantics for the data exchanged between applications.

The basic assumption underlying any interaction between two parties is that they are each able to interpret the information contained in the data being exchanged. In conventional middleware platforms, the problem of data representation is hidden behind IDLs. In such systems, the IDL fulfills two roles. First, IDL is used to define interfaces. Second, the implementation of

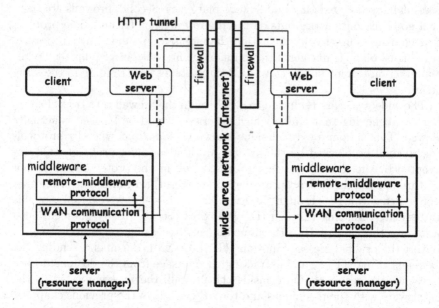

Fig. 4.13. Business to business interactions at the middleware level using tunneling

the IDL uses an intermediate data representation that specifies how each data type used in IDL is represented in a machine-independent manner. This intermediate data representation helps bridge differences between operating systems and computer architectures (e.g., the use of *little endian* and *big endian* representations).

In message-based systems, the format and semantics of the messages or files exchanged are typically determined by the EDIFACT standard (Electronic Data Interchange For Administration, Commerce and Transport) [66]. EDIFACT provides standard templates for messages and for the contents of the messages. For messages, it defines the different parts of a message and how to organize its contents so that it can be properly parsed by the recipient. In principle, the message is in fact a document rather than a message in the conventional middleware sense. An EDIFACT message will typically contain the following fields (among other optional fields):

- **Interchange Header**, indicating the version of EDIFACT used in the message, IDs of sender and recipient, passwords, date, time, and other control information.
- **Message Header**, indicating the type of message (e.g., an invoice) and other qualifiers.
- **User Data Segments**, the payload.
- **Message Trailer**, used to end a message and check its completeness.

- **Interchange Trailer**, used to end an interchange and check its completeness.

Each of the fields is identified by a three letter code; the fields are separated by characters that are indicated in the message itself. The message is encoded in plain text (ASCII) and is handled at both ends of the communication by a *converter*, which translates the message into the application specific format and vice versa.

In addition to defining the format of the message, EDIFACT also defines an extensive collection of standardized message types. Examples of such messages include *Quality data, Purchase order response* message, *Order status enquiry* message, *Order status report* message, and so on. For each message type, EDIFACT defines a standard structure that can be seen as a record with placeholders for all the information associated with that type of message. Each of these placeholders is again identified in the text with a three-letter code. For an invoice, for instance, the placeholders correspond to information like payment instructions, item description, payment terms, and currency. In addition, for each one of these fields, a number of standard codes are used to transmit information. For the payment instructions, for instance, the numeric codes used identify different payment modalities: *Direct payment, Letter of guarantee, Open account for payment, Available with issuing bank*, and so on. Using this information, messages can be parsed and treated as standard forms.

By providing a universal standard representation for different types of commercial exchanges, EDIFACT facilitates performing those exchanges electronically. Parsers can be constructed to automatically extract the information from an EDIFACT message and pass it on to the application as needed. The downside of the approach taken by EDIFACT is that it tries to provide a universal representation for messages related to commercial exchanges. It attempts to provide a universal form for each one of those exchanges. The result is a very complex standard and often unnecessarily complicated forms. In many cases, applications only use a fraction of the information the message could carry, although the machinery necessary to process the messages is tailored for the general case.

In addition, EDIFACT can only be used for exchanges that have been standardized. Any other type of information requires ad hoc development on the systems to be integrated. Since EDIFACT was conceived for commercial exchanges, this was not a severe limitation when it appeared. With the Web, however, the picture changed radically as the type of information available became too varied and rich for any such standardization attempts. Nevertheless, EDIFACT is widely used in many application areas where the set of messages defined already covers most, if not all, of the needed exchanges. As mentioned above, EDIFACT-based systems will eventually be combined with Web services both in terms of syntax representation and software support for the exchange and processing of messages.

4.4.5 XML

The widespread use of the Web made it very difficult to standardize all forms of Internet exchanges. EDIFACT's success became very difficult to extend to other areas simply because of the large variety of information that is being exchanged. It is impossible to formalize every single message that will ever be exchanged. In the context of the Web, the answer to this problem is the eXtensible Markup Language (XML). XML addresses the data representation problem by focusing on the syntax, rather than the semantics, of the documents exchanged. Unlike predecessors such as EDIFACT, which provide standard templates for message content, XML provides a standard way to define the structure of documents that is suitable for automatic processing.

On the one hand, having a clearly defined structure helps users understand the semantics of the different parts of a document. On the other hand, having a standard way to encode the structure enables the development of tools that parse documents and extract their content as well as their structure. For example, an XML parser can identify that a document includes elements customer, product ID, and delivery date, and can extract the content associated with these elements to then create an object or send a message to the underlying middleware. There are in fact a number of freeware tools that perform these functions, and Java has defined APIs for different kinds of XML document parsers [144].

Another form of automated support for XML documents is *validation*. The XML standard defines the rules to which every document must conform in order to be well formed. In addition, it is possible to define document types, and state that a document conforms to a certain document type. For example, it is possible to state that a document should consist of an element request_for_quote that has customer, product ID, and delivery date as sub-elements. These and other restrictions on the structure of a document can be specified by Document Type Definitions (DTDs) [210] or XML schemas [211]. Once document types have been defined, it is possible to declare that a document is of a given type. Automated tools can then verify (validate) whether the structure and content of a document is consistent with what is prescribed by its type (schema) definition. Note that having a DTD or a schema does not provide any semantic information: stating that a certain element should be present in a document is by no means sufficient to clarify its semantics and how the information is expected to be consumed by the recipient.

To compare the differences in approaches, consider how an invoice is represented in EDIFACT and in XML. EDIFACT provides a universal invoice form containing all information that could possibly be associated with an invoice. This invoice form is the same for all applications and the meaning of each field in the form is defined in the standard. XML, on the other hand, does not define a universal invoice form. Together with the invoice, an application needs the DTD for that invoice so that it can extract the information. Different applications might use completely different invoices, whose type is specified by different DTDs. Moreover, what each field in the invoice means is not determined by XML. The assumption is that once the information has been extracted, there is a program that will understand the semantics of the tags and labels associated with the XML document.

However, by providing a syntax along with parsing and validation tools, XML lays the foundation on which semantics can be defined. Standardization consortia can then specify XML document types (through DTDs and schemas) as well as define the meaning (semantics) of each of the document elements or attributes, often in plain English, which can be exchanged among parties having a common interest in the content. For example, the RosettaNet consortium has defined a number of documents types and their semantics for performing electronic B2B transactions in the IT domain (RosettaNet will be discussed in more detail in Chapter 8).

4.5 Summary

It took decades to develop the tools necessary to implement reasonable multi-tier architectures within companies. Some of these tools are still evolving and a few problems still need to be resolved, but one can safely say that we know how to build multi-tier architectures that are robust, efficient, and extensible. Because of this knowledge and the effort invested, it is not surprising that vendors, designers, and developers tried to use this same technology for integrating applications across the Internet. This is important to keep in mind because, in many cases, it does not really matter that an interaction happens to take place via the Internet. In almost any client/server system one can easily remove the client far away, across the Internet, and make it work with the server in a way as if both were operating on a LAN. The real problem is not how to connect the systems but rather how to handle the architectural implications and design constraints that result from using the Web as the communication channel between the systems to integrate.

In this chapter we have discussed these design constraints and explored existing solutions. These solutions are in many cases the foundation for Web services. In understanding current technology, it is very important to keep in mind that the transition from existing to new systems is always gradual. There is too much invested in existing systems to redesign them anew. We have seen in this chapter the technologies developed during such a gradual transition phase. In the next chapter we will see how these technologies are evolving from straightforward extensions of existing middleware platforms to comprehensive solutions for developing, deploying, and maintaining Web services.

Part II

Web Services

5

Web Services

In previous chapters we have discussed the architecture of information systems (Chapter 1), middleware and enterprise application integration (Chapters 2 and 3), and the basics of Web technology (Chapter 4). These chapters have shown a chronological evolution of the technology used for EAI and for building distributed applications. All these technologies have been rather successful in addressing several of the problems created by application integration. The success, however, has been restricted to certain settings (e.g., LAN-based systems, homogeneous middleware platforms, etc.). True application integration requires tools that go one step beyond what conventional middleware and EAI platforms have achieved. Web services and the associated technology are being leveraged to take such a step.

To establish the context for the rest of the book, we provide in this chapter an introduction to Web services. We look at Web services as a way to expose the functionality of an information system and make it available through standard Web technologies. The use of standard technologies reduces heterogeneity, and is therefore key to facilitating application integration. Furthermore, we show that Web services naturally enable new computing paradigms and architectures, and are specifically geared toward service-oriented computing, a paradigm often touted in the past but never quite realized.

This chapter is structured along a continuum that goes from the needs that motivate the introduction of Web services to the solutions that Web services provide. We begin by showing the limitations of conventional technology in tackling some of the application integration challenges, thereby raising the need for a novel technology–a need addressed by Web services. We then describe the essential concepts behind Web services and how they tackle the application integration problem (Section 5.1). Next, we provide an overview of Web services middleware, focusing in particular on the functionality that this middleware must provide to support the development of distributed applications based on Web services (Section 5.2). Finally, we discuss Web services architectures (Section 5.3).

5.1 Web Services and their Approach to Distributed Computing

Before describing the problems Web services try to solve and how they address them, we define what Web services are.

5.1.1 Defining Web Services

The term *Web services* is used very often nowadays, although not always with the same meaning. Nevertheless, the underlying concepts and technologies are to a large extent independent of how they may be interpreted.

Existing definitions range from the very generic and all-inclusive to the very specific and restrictive. Often, a Web service is seen as an application accessible to other applications over the Web (see e.g., [72, 133]). This is a very open definition, under which just about anything that has a URL is a Web service. It can, for instance, include a CGI script. It can also refer to a program accessible over the Web with a stable API, published with additional descriptive information on some service directory.

A more precise definition is provided by the UDDI consortium, which characterizes Web services as *"self-contained, modular business applications that have open, Internet-oriented, standards-based interfaces"* [203]. This definition is more detailed, placing the emphasis on the need for being compliant with Internet standards. In addition, it requires the service to be open, which essentially means that it has a published interface that can be invoked across the Internet. In spite of this clarification, the definition is still not precise enough. For instance, it is not clear what it is meant by a modular, self-contained business application.

A step further in refining the definition of Web services is the one provided by the World Wide Web consortium (W3C), and specifically the group involved in the Web Service Activity: *"a software application identified by a URI, whose interfaces and bindings are capable of being defined, described, and discovered as XML artifacts. A Web service supports direct interactions with other software agents using XML-based messages exchanged via Internet-based protocols"* [212].

The W3C definition is quite accurate and also hints at how Web services should work. The definition stresses that Web services should be capable of being "defined, described, and discovered," thereby clarifying the meaning of "accessible" and making more concrete the notion of "Internet-oriented, standards-based interfaces." It also states that Web services should be "services" similar to those in conventional middleware. Not only they should be "up and running," but they should be described and advertised so that it is possible to write clients that bind and interact with them. In other words, Web services are components that can be integrated into more complex distributed applications. This interpretation is very much in line with the perspective we take in this book, and explains why we place so much emphasis on the need to understand middleware as the first step toward understanding Web services.

The W3C also states that XML is part of the solution. Indeed, XML is so popular and widely used today that, just like HTTP and Web servers, it can be considered as being part of Web technology. There is little doubt that XML will be the data format used for many Web-based interactions.

Note that even more specific definitions exist. For example, in the online technical dictionary *Webopedia*, a Web service is defined as *"a standardized way of integrating Web-based applications using the XML, SOAP, WSDL, and UDDI open standards over an Internet protocol backbone. XML is used to tag the data, SOAP is used to transfer the data, WSDL is used for describing the services available, and UDDI is used for listing what services are available"* [110]. Specific standards that could be used for performing binding and for interacting with a Web service are mentioned here. These are the leading standards today in Web services. As a matter of fact, many applications that are "made accessible to other applications" do so through SOAP, WSDL, UDDI, and other Web standards. However, these standards do not constitute the essence of Web services technology: the problems underlying Web services are the same regardless of the standards used. This is why, keeping the above observations in mind, we can adopt the W3C definition and proceed toward detailing what Web services really are and what they imply.

5.1.2 Motivating the Need for B2B Integration

Before describing in more detail what Web services are about, we introduce an example that shows why the middleware and EAI platforms discussed in the previous chapters are not sufficient in certain application integration scenarios. The limitations of these systems are what led to the current efforts around Web services as well as the shift to a service-oriented paradigm in application development.

Consider again the supply chain scenario introduced in Chapter 3. When describing the problem behind supply chain automation, we observed that the main issues were the integration of several autonomous and heterogeneous systems and the automation of business processes spanning across these systems. Until very recently, such processes were executed manually for the most part. The advent of EAI platforms made it possible to automate most of such processes.

In that example, we assumed that all the components belonged to one company. Consider now the same problem in the general case, where the systems are not all running within a company but are instead managed and operated by different companies. Specifically, consider a procurement scenario, where a company (acting as a customer) needs to order goods from another company (a supplier). The supplier then processes the order and delivers the goods, either directly (if it has goods in stock) or by requesting that the goods be shipped by a third party (in this example, a warehouse that serves several

suppliers and delivers goods upon requests). Once the order is processed, the
customer makes the payment.

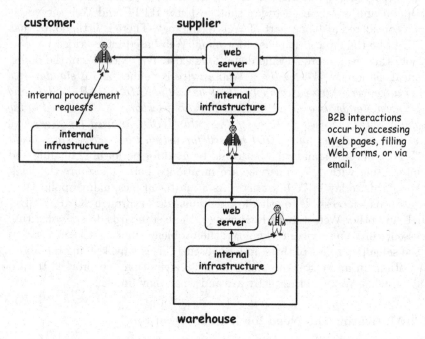

Fig. 5.1. Very often, integration across companies is still done manually

For all the parties involved (customers, suppliers, and the warehouse), it
would be very beneficial if the whole procurement process was automated, all
the way from requesting quotes to processing payments. Today, in all but very
few cases, even if business processes within a company are automated, business
processes across companies are carried out manually. This is exemplified in
Figure 5.1, which emphasizes the fact that the "integration" is performed
manually by means of employees who access the internal systems (for example
to retrieve the list of products to be ordered) and then communicate with
other companies by filling out Web forms (e.g., to order the goods) or via
email or fax. The attentive reader will observe that Figure 5.1 is very similar
to Figure 3.1 of Section 3.1, the only difference being that in this case we
are focusing on a B2B scenario rather than an EAI one. The problems are
similar and the need for automation is driven by the same goals, such as lower
costs, streamlined and more efficient processes, ability to monitor and track
process executions, and ability to detect and manage exceptions. Yet, while
the problems are the same, the solution needed in this case is different. In
fact, none of the technologies that we have described so far either for EAI or

for wide area integration have been able to fully address the challenges posed by the above scenario and become widely adopted.

5.1.3 Limitations of Conventional Middleware in B2B Integration

There are several reasons why conventional middleware platforms cannot be used in this setting. The first one is that in cross-organizational interactions there is no obvious place where to put the middleware. The basic idea for conventional middleware was for it to reside between the applications to be integrated and to mediate their interactions. While the applications were distributed, the middleware was centralized (at least logically), and it was controlled by a single company. Adopting the same solution in this context would require that the customer, supplier, and warehouse agree on using and cooperatively managing a certain middleware platform (e.g., a specific message broker, a specific workflow system, and a specific name and directory server) and on implementing a "global workflow" that drives the whole business process. This approach is presented in Figure 5.2, and is analogous to Figure 3.10 of Section 3.3, which described how EAI middleware can integrate applications.

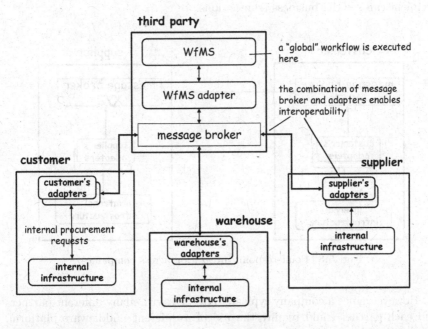

Fig. 5.2. B2B integration performed in the same way EAI is done. While this is conceptually possible, it rarely happens in practice due to lack of trust, autonomy, and confidentiality reasons

While this approach is feasible in some restricted settings (e.g., a very small number of companies that have frequent, close cooperation), in the general case it turns out to be an unlikely proposition. In fact, the lack of trust between companies, the autonomy that each company wants to preserve, and the confidentiality of the business transactions play against the idea of having a centralized middleware hosted by one of the participating companies or by a third party. Each company wants to control its own business operations and how they are carried out, and does not want its business transaction data to be seen by anybody other than its intended recipient.

An alternative solution for a company would be to address the problem in a point-to-point fashion, by separately tackling the integration problem with each of the partners. This means that whenever two parties (the customer and the supplier) want to communicate, they agree on using certain middleware protocols and infrastructure. For example, they can both deploy a message broker and use it to send messages to each other (Figure 5.3), as long as this message broker provides the necessary support for wide area integration (e.g., firewall traversal, discussed in the previous chapter). We have already seen in Section 3.2.5 how two or more applications sitting on top of two distinct but homogeneous message brokers can communicate. With this approach, there is no third party involved and confidentiality is preserved, as only the intended recipient can see the business transactions.

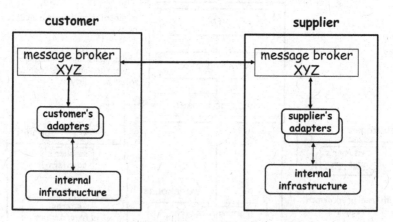

Fig. 5.3. Point-to-point integration across companies

However, since a company typically interacts with many different partners and each partner could require the use of a different middleware platform, this leads to a scenario where a company has to support many heterogeneous middleware systems. The result is that each company must integrate these different middleware systems (not to mention purchasing and maintaining them), which were instead intended to facilitate the integration (Figure 5.4).

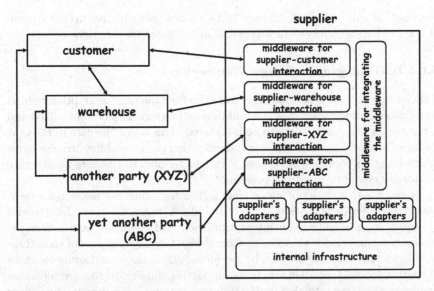

Fig. 5.4. The lack of a central middleware platform means that interactions are managed in a point-to-point manner, possibly using different middleware platforms to communicate with different parties

Another reason that makes conventional middleware unsuitable is that many assumptions that were valid in EAI do not hold here. One such difference is that EAI interactions are typically short lived, while cross-organizational interactions last longer, and sometimes much longer. Rather than calling a procedure, a method, or a function, interactions involve coarse-grained operations lasting possibly for hours or days. As an example of the delays involved, the supplier may confirm that the order has been processed only after the requested goods have been physically picked up by a shipping company. Such delays explain why cross-organizational interactions are mostly implemented as asynchronous exchanges. However, asynchronous interactions introduce their own problems. For example, consider the problem of providing transactional properties to the interaction between two or more parties. If the operations are long-lasting, then conventional protocols such as 2PC are not applicable, as they would lock resources for long period of time and therefore severely limit the possibility of executing concurrent operations. Yet, this are the protocols supported by conventional middleware and EAI tools.

Furthermore, while EAI interactions occur in the same trust domain, cross-organizational interactions occur across trust domains, and there is an implicit lack of trust between interacting entities. Not only does this require authentication and encryption of messages, but it also implies that companies will severely restrict what clients can do on their system. Referring again to the transactional example, service providers will want to control and limit the resources that can be locked, and are certainly not going to give up the control of the locking mechanisms to a possibly malicious outside entity.

5.1.4 B2B Integration before Web Services

The limitations just described arise from the fundamental assumption behind conventional middleware that the middleware platform can be centralized and is trusted by the components to be integrated. This is not the case in B2B exchanges. In addition, the lack of standardization across middleware platforms makes point-to-point solutions (i.e., solutions tailored to concrete middleware platforms) costly to realize in practice.

Note that this does not mean that B2B integration has never been technically possible or was never achieved. Indeed, there are several successful examples of cross-enterprise integration. Some of them are represented by broker companies such as Ariba or CommerceOne. The purpose of these brokers is to facilitate integration by performing functions analogous to those of centralized EAI middleware, from supporting binding to routing messages among the services provided by the different companies. However, the lack of support by major software vendors for the formats and protocols defined by these brokers and the trust-related problems that undermine any centralized solution have resulted in limited acceptance for these solutions.

Other successful examples of B2B integration are systems based on EDIFACT (discussed in the previous chapter). For instance, the US retailer Wal-Mart was able to automate some of its cross-enterprise processes, in particular with respect to co-managing the inventory with its suppliers, setting stock levels, and automatically ordering supplies when in-stock levels were low.

In spite of the success stories, standards like EDIFACT and systems based on such standards have never become widely adopted for a variety of reasons. First, designing such systems is typically an ad hoc endeavor and the result of a one time programming effort. The lack of standards and the lack of an appropriate infrastructure (from middleware to networks) made each one of these systems unique in that each one of them had to implement everything almost from scratch. In addition, the underlying hardware and communication support was very heavy-handed. In terms of networks, before the Web appeared communication often used to take place through leased lines to obtain the necessary bandwidth and security guarantees. In terms of computer cycles, most of these systems were very heavy. As a result, such systems were expensive to develop, almost impossible to reproduce, difficult to maintain, and could not be adapted to new technologies. Moreover, because of the development effort and costs involved, only large companies could afford deploying such systems.

The Internet alleviated some of these design problems by allowing designers to replace leased lines with a network that was pervasive and more cost-efficient. Nevertheless, the lack of standardization at the system and communication protocol levels still remained a significant hurdle in the path toward reducing the cost and complexity of building and deploying such systems. This problem was recognized years ago and there were many standardization attempts but, for reasons not always entirely rational, they had only limited success. At the core of these efforts were technologies that would allow homogeneous middleware platforms to communicate with each other (such as Inter-ORB communication via GIOP/IIOP). These technologies can be easily extended to act as the middleware for the Web. However, as it often happens, these early approaches were never widely used and, in time, were obscured by new developments.

The Web constituted an important step toward facilitating application integration. In fact, it probably was the crucial step toward systems that were more than isolated, ad hoc efforts. The Web brought standard interaction protocols (HTTP) and data formats (XML) that were quickly adopted by many companies, thereby creating a base for establishing a common middleware infrastructure that reduces the heterogeneity among interfaces and systems. However, HTTP and XML by themselves are not enough to support application integration. They do not define interface definition languages, name and directory services, transaction protocols, and the many other abstractions that, as the previous chapters have shown, are crucial to facilitate integration. It is the gap between what the Web provides (HTTP, XML) and what application integration requires that Web services are trying to fill.

5.1.5 B2B Integration with Web Services

The contribution of Web services toward resolving the limitations of conventional middleware involves three main aspects: service-oriented architectures, redesign of middleware protocols, and standardization.

Service-oriented Paradigm

Web services work on the assumption that the functionality made available by a company will be exposed as a service. In middleware terms, a service is a procedure, method, or object with a stable, published interface that can be invoked by clients. The invocation, *and this is very important*, is made by a program. Thus, requesting and executing a service involves a program calling another program.

In terms of how they are used, Web services are no different from middleware services, with the exception that it should be possible to invoke them across the Web and across companies. As a consequence, Web services assume that services are loosely-coupled, since in general they are defined, developed, and managed by different companies. As Web services become more popular and widely adopted, they are likely to lead to a scenario where service-oriented architectures, advocated for many years, finally become a reality. In fact, with Web services, designers and developers are led to think in the direction that "everything is a service," and that different services are autonomous and independent (as opposed to being, for example, two CORBA objects developed by the same team). As we will see, this interpretation has important implications in that it leads to decoupling applications and to making them more modular. Therefore, individual components can be reused and aggregated more easily and in different ways.

Note that not every service available through the Web is a Web service. This is a common mistake that leads to quite a lot of confusion when discussing Web services technology. There is a difference between services in the software sense and services in the general sense, i.e., activities performed by a person or a company on behalf of another person or company. Take as examples bookstores, restaurants, or travel agencies. They all provide services. In some cases, a customer might even be able to obtain such services through the Web server of the company. Strange as it might seem at first, this is not what Web services are about. A Web service is a software application with a published a stable programming interface, not a set of Web pages.

Middleware Protocols

The second aspect of the Web services approach is the redesign of the middleware protocols to work in a peer-to-peer fashion and across companies. Conventional middleware protocols, such as 2PC, were designed based on assumptions that do not hold in cross-organizational interactions. For example, they assumed a central transaction coordinator and the possibility for this coordinator to lock resources ad libitum. As we have seen, lack of trust and confidentiality issues often make a case against a central coordinator, and therefore 2PC must now be redesigned to work in a fully distributed fashion and must be extended to allow more flexibility in terms of locking resources. Similar arguments can be made for all interaction and coordination protocols and, in general, for many of the other properties provided by conventional middleware, such as reliability and guaranteed delivery. What was then achieved by a centralized platform must be now redesigned in terms of protocols that can work in a decentralized setting and across trust domains.

Standardization

The final key ingredient of the Web services recipe is standardization. In conventional application integration, the presence of standards helped to address many problems. CORBA and Java, for example, have enabled the development of portable applications, have fostered the production of low cost middleware tools, and have considerably reduced the learning curves due to the widespread adoption of common models and abstractions. Whenever standardization has failed or proved to be inapplicable due to the presence of legacy systems, the complexity and cost of the middleware has remained quite high and the effectiveness rather low. For Web services, where the interactions occur across companies and on a global scale, standardization is not only beneficial, but a necessity. Having a service-oriented architecture and redefining the middleware protocols is not sufficient to address the application integration problem in a general way, unless these languages and protocols become standardized and widely adopted.

This problem was recognized by major software vendors that have recently showed an unprecedented commitment to standardization. Many standardization efforts in Web services have been initially driven by a small, focused group of companies, and have then been adopted by different organizations such as OASIS (Organization for the Advancement of Structured Standards) or the W3C. These consortia attempt to standardize all the different aspects of the interaction, ranging from interface definition languages to message formats and interaction protocols. We will see many examples of these standards in the following chapters.

This need for standardization is also why we speak today about *Web* services. The Web has itself been characterized by a high degree of standardization, which has allowed it to function and prosper without centralized coordination (with the exception of the Domain Name System or DNS) and has enabled its expansion at an unthinkable rate. Web technologies are now widely accepted and are very successful in enabling the interaction between humans and applications (through Web browsers and Web servers). It is therefore natural for this novel application integration technology to use the Web as its basic foundation and to try to proceed along the same, successful path taken by the Web in terms of standardization.

Observe that the commitment to standardization does not necessarily mean that there will be only one specification for each aspect of the interaction. As we will see throughout the following chapters, sometimes competing and conflicting specifications appear, possibly developed at the same time by different groups or as a result of slightly different needs. This is natural in the early days of a new technology, and does not severely limit its adoption as long as the number of such competing specifications remains relatively small, especially if they eventually converge into one commonly adopted specification. Indeed, the need for a unique solution is already bringing some order in the initially fragmented Web services landscape, and it is likely that in the end a limited number of specifications will emerge as winners.

Figure 5.5 summarizes this discussion on how Web services address the B2B integration problem. The figure shows that each party exposes its internal operations as (Web) services, which therefore act as entry points to the local information systems. The interactions between companies occur in a peer-to-peer fashion (although we will see later in this chapter that some middleware components can indeed be centralized) and take place through standardized protocols, which are designed to provide the interaction with the same properties that conventional middleware provided, but without the presence of a central middleware platform. It will be up to the Web services middleware, as we will see, to facilitate the execution of such protocols and hide from the programmer the complexities intrinsic in application integration problems.

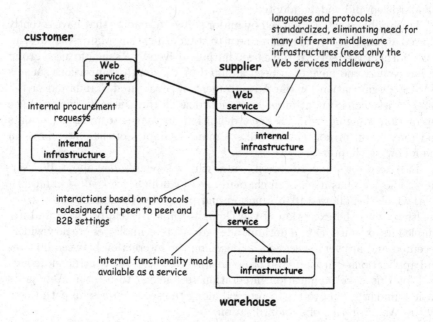

Fig. 5.5. Service-oriented architectures, redesigned (peer-to-peer) middleware protocols, and standardization are the main ingredients of the solution offered by Web services

5.1.6 Web services and EAI

Web services and their technologies are being developed with one specific use in mind: that of being entry points to the local information system. Thus, the primary use of a Web service is that of exposing (through the Web service interface) the functionality performed by internal systems and making it discoverable and accessible through the Web in a controlled manner. Web services are therefore analogous to sophisticated *wrappers* that encapsulate one or more applications by providing a unique interface and a Web access (Figure 5.6). Of course this is a simplification and the reality is a little more complex, but this interpretation helps in clarifying how Web services are used.

We have already encountered and discussed wrappers and adapters in the context of EAI. In particular, we have observed that wrapping components and hiding heterogeneity is the key to enabling application integration. From the perspective of the clients, the wrappers are actually the components to

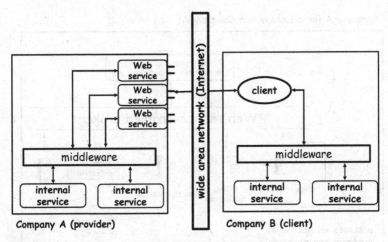

Fig. 5.6. Web services provide an entry point for accessing local services

be integrated, as they are what the integrating application can see of the underlying system.

Having homogeneous components considerably reduces the difficulties of integration. This is also true for Web services, which are indeed wrappers and are homogeneous, in that they interoperate through Web standards. As such, they constitute the base on which we can construct middleware supporting application integration on the Web, by allowing designers to avoid the problems generated by the lack of standardization typical of previous approaches.

This is an interesting aspect of Web services in spite of the fact that most of the literature on the subject is strongly biased toward B2B applications and that B2B integration is what generated the need for Web services. Indeed, Web services do not need to be accessed through the Internet. It is perfectly possible to make Web services available to clients residing on a local LAN (Figure 5.7). At the time of this writing, many Web services are used in this context, i.e., intra-company application integration rather than inter-company exchanges. This trend will be reinforced as software vendors enhance and extend their support for Web services. In fact, if software applications come out of the box with a Web services interface, then their integration is considerably simplified, as all components are homogeneous. Comparing Figure 5.7 with Figure 3.6 of Section 3.2.5, both related to EAI, the reader will notice that there is no need for adapters in this case. Nevertheless, the challenge and ultimate goal of Web services is inter-company interactions. Existing efforts around Web services go in this direction although this is clearly a long-term goal.

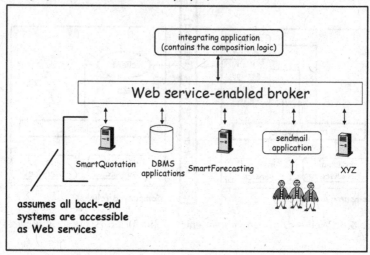

Fig. 5.7. Web services can be also used within the enterprise or even a LAN, to integrate enterprise applications

5.2 Web Services Technologies

After describing what Web services are, we now go into more detail over the different aspects addressed by Web services.

5.2.1 Service Description

Since the Web services approach is centered on the notion of "service", one of the first issues to be addressed by its technology is what exactly a service is and how it can be described. Service description in conventional middleware is based on interfaces and interface definition languages. In that context, IDL specifications are needed to automatically generate stubs and to constitute the basis for dynamic binding. The semantics of the different operations, the order in which they should be invoked, and other (possibly non-functional) properties of the services are assumed to be known in advance by the programmer developing the clients. This is reasonable, since clients and services are often developed by the same team. In addition, the middleware platform defines and constrains many aspects of the service description and binding process that are therefore implicit, and they do not need to be specified as part of the service description. In Web services and B2B interactions, such implicit context is missing. Therefore, service descriptions must be richer and more detailed, covering aspects beyond the mere service interface.

The stack of Figure 5.8 illustrates the different aspects involved in Web services description. The figure essentially shows a stack of languages, where

elements at higher levels utilize or further qualify the descriptions provided
by elements at the lower levels.

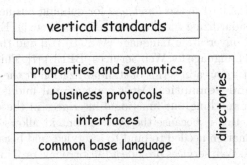

Fig. 5.8. Service description and discovery stack

- **Common base language.** The first problem to be addressed is the definition of a common meta-language that can be used as the basis for specifying all the languages necessary to describe the different aspects of a service. XML is used for this purpose, both because it is a widely adopted and commonly accepted standard and because it has a syntax flexible enough to enable the definition of service description languages and protocols.
- **Interfaces.** Interface definition languages are at the base of any service-oriented paradigm. In Web services, interface definitions resemble CORBA-like IDLs, although there are a few differences between the two. The availability of different interaction modes in the interface definition language and the XML schema-driven type system are two of them. In addition, since (as mentioned above) Web services lack an implicit context (often there is no centralized middleware), their description needs to be more complete. For example, it is necessary to specify the address (URI) of the service and the transport protocol (e.g., HTTP) to use when invoking the service. With this information, it is possible to construct a client that invokes the operations offered by a Web service. The dominant proposal for IDLs in this area is the Web Services Description Language (WSDL) [49].
- **Business protocols.** A Web service often offers a number of operations that clients must invoke in a certain order to achieve their goals. In the procurement example, the customer will have to first request a quote, then order the goods, and finally make a payment. Such exchanges between clients and Web services are called *conversations*. Service providers typically want to impose rules that govern the conversation, stating which conversations are valid and understood by the service. This set of rules is specified as part of the so called *business protocol* supported by the service (where the word "business" is used to differentiate it from a communication protocol). Business protocols are examples of why simple interface

description is not enough in Web services. In fact, to completely describe a service, it is necessary to specify not only its interface but also the business protocols that the service supports. In this regard, there are several proposals to standardize the *languages* for defining business protocols (as opposed to standardizing the protocols, discussed next). Examples are the Web Services Conversation Language (WSCL) [14] and the Business Process Execution Language for Web Services (BPEL) [7]. This is nevertheless a rather immature area in terms of standardization at the time of writing.

- **Properties and semantics.** Most conventional middleware platforms do not include anything but functional interfaces in the description of a service. Again, this is because the system context allows designers to infer other information needed to bind to a service, and because services are tightly coupled. Web services provide additional layers of information to facilitate binding in autonomous and loosely-coupled settings, where the service description is all that clients have at their disposal to decide whether to use a service or not. For instance, this may include non-functional properties such as the cost or quality of a service, or a textual description of the service such as the return policy when making a purchase. This is information that is crucial for using the service but is not part of what we traditionally understand as the interface of the service. In Web services, such information can be attached to the description of a service by using the Universal Description, Discovery, and Integration (UDDI) [20] specification. This specification describes how to organize the information about a Web service and how to build repositories where such information can be registered and queried.

- **Verticals.** All the layers explained so far are generic. They standardize neither the contents of the services nor their semantics (e.g., the meaning of a certain parameter or the effect of a certain operation). Vertical standards define specific interfaces, protocols, properties, and semantics that services offered in certain application domains should support. For example, RosettaNet [171] describes commercial exchanges in the IT world, standardizing all the aspects described above. These vertical standards complement the previous layers by tailoring them to concrete applications, further facilitating the use of standard tools for driving the exchanges. Specifically, they enable the development of client applications that can interact in a meaningful manner with any Web service that is compliant with a certain vertical standard.

5.2.2 Service Discovery

Once services have been properly described, these descriptions must be made available to those interested in using them. For this purpose, service descriptions are stored in a service directory (represented by the vertical pillar in Figure 5.8). These directories allow service designers to register new services and allow service users to search for and locate services. Service discovery can be done both at design-time, by browsing the directory and identifying the most relevant services, and at run-time, using dynamic binding techniques. These directories can be hosted and managed by a trusted entity (centralized approach) or otherwise each company can host and manage a directory service (peer-to-peer approach). In both cases, APIs and protocols are needed for clients to interact with the directory service or for the local directory services to exchange information among themselves in a peer-to-peer fashion. The above-mentioned UDDI specification defines standard APIs for publishing and discovering information into service directories. It also describes how such directories should work.

5.2.3 Service Interactions

Service description and discovery are concerned with static and dynamic binding. Once the binding problem has been addressed, a set of abstractions and tools that enable interactions among Web services is needed. In Web services, these abstractions take the form of a set of standards that address different aspects of the interactions at different levels. Figure 5.9 summarizes these different aspects by presenting them as a protocol stack since, as we will see, each aspect is characterized by one or more protocols defined on top of the lower layers. Unlike the verticals discussed in the previous section, these protocols are useful to any Web service and are therefore implemented by the Web services middleware. As such, they are transparent (for the most part) to the developers, just as the interactions established internally between two CORBA objects are hidden from the programmers, who can then focus on the business logic.

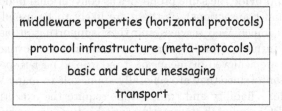

Fig. 5.9. Service interaction stack

The different types of protocols that compose the service interaction stack are:

- **Transport.** From the point of view of Web services, the communication network is hidden behind a transport protocol. Web services consider the use of a wide range of transport protocols, the most common one being HTTP.

- **Messaging.** Once a transport protocol is in place, there needs to be a standard way to format and package the information to be exchanged. In Web services, this role is played by the Simple Object Access Protocol (SOAP) [32]. SOAP does not detail what properties are associated with the exchange (e.g., whether it is transactional or encrypted). It simply specifies a generic message template to add to the top of the application data. Additional specifications standardize the way to use SOAP to implement particular features. For instance, *WS-Security* [13] describes how to implement secure exchanges with SOAP.
- **Protocol infrastructure (meta-protocols).** We have emphasized above that Web services are characterized not only by an interface but also by the business protocols they comply with. While business protocols are application specific, mcuh of the software required to support such protocols can be implemented as generic infrastructure components. For example, the infrastructure can maintain the state of the conversation between a client and a service, associate messages to the appropriate conversation, or verify that a message exchange occurs in accordance to the rules defined by the protocols. Part of the task of the infrastructure is also the execution of *meta-protocols*, which are protocols whose purpose is to facilitate and coordinate the execution of business protocols. For example, before the actual interaction can begin, clients and services need to agree on what protocol should be executed, who is coordinating the protocol execution, and how protocol execution identifiers are embedded into messages to denote that a certain message exchange is occurring in the context of a protocol. *WS-Coordination* [41] is a specification that tries to standardize these meta-protocols and the way WSDL and SOAP should be used for conveying information relevant to the execution of a protocol.
- **Middleware (horizontal) protocols.** Ideally, the Web service middleware should provide the same properties as conventional middleware (e.g., reliability and transactions), as these are likely to be useful in this context as well. Since Web services and their supporting infrastructure are distributed in nature, middleware properties that go beyond basic communication are achieved by means of standardized peer-to-peer protocols, called *horizontal* since they are generally applicable to many Web services. For example, reliability and transactions require the execution of protocols (e.g., 2PC) among the interacting entities. Just like business protocols, horizontal ones can be supported by the meta-protocols described above. However, they are likely to be hidden from the Web service developers and users, and to be entirely managed by the infrastructure. This is why we do not list them as part of the service description stack, but as part of the interaction stack: they are not used to describe a service, but to provide higher-level properties to any sort of interaction. The first protocol of this kind that has been defined is *WS-Transaction* [42], which builds upon WS-Coordination to define how to implement transactional properties when dealing with Web services.

5.2.4 Combining Web Services: Composition

A Web service can be implemented by invoking other Web services, possibly provided by different companies. For example, a reseller of personal computers may offer a Web service that allows customers to request quotes and order computers. However, the implementation of the *requestQuote* operation may require the invocation of several Web services, including for example those provided by PC manufacturers and shippers, for the latest prices and delivery schedules. A Web service implemented by invoking other Web services is called a *composite service*, while a Web service implemented by accessing the local system is called *basic service*. Observe that whether a Web service is basic or composite is irrelevant from the perspective of the clients, as it is only an implementation issue. In fact, they are all Web services and can be described, discovered, and invoked in the same way.

As the number of available Web services continues to grow and as the business environment keeps demanding newer applications that have to be rolled out according to very tight schedules, both the opportunity and the need for service composition technologies provided as part of the Web services middleware arises. These technologies resemble those of workflow systems, and have the potential to enable the rapid development of complex services from basic ones, as well as to simplify the maintenance and evolution of such complex services. In terms of standardization, this area is still rather immature, although the above-mentioned BPEL seems to be emerging as the leading service composition language.

5.3 Web Services Architecture

Now that we have described the main ingredients of Web services middleware, we show how they can be combined in an overall architecture.

5.3.1 The Two Facets of Web Services Architectures

The discussion in the previous section has shown that there are two different aspects to be considered when analyzing Web services architectures.

The first aspect is related to the fact that Web services are a way to expose internal operations so that they can be invoked through the Web. Such an implementation requires the system to be able to receive requests through the Web and to pass them to the underlying IT system. In doing this, the problems are analogous to those encountered in conventional middleware. We will refer to such an infrastructure as *internal middleware* for Web services. Correspondingly, we will use the term *internal architecture* to refer to the organization and structure of the internal middleware (Figure 5.10).

The other facet of Web services architectures is represented by the middleware infrastructure whose purpose is to integrate different Web services. We will refer to such an infrastructure as *external middleware* for Web services (Figure 5.10). Correspondingly, we will use the term *external architecture* to refer to the organization and structure of the external middleware. The external architecture has three main components:

- **Centralized brokers.** These are analogous to the centralized components in conventional middleware that route messages and provide properties to the interactions (such as logging, transactional guarantees, name and directory services, and reliability). However, as we will see, in practice the name and directory server is often the only centralized component present in Web services architectures.
- **Protocol infrastructure.** This refers to the set of components that coordinate the interactions among Web services and, in particular, implement the peer-to-peer protocols (such as the horizontal protocols and the meta-protocols discussed in the previous section) whose aim is to provide middleware properties in those B2B settings where a centralized middleware platform cannot be put in place due to trust and privacy issues.
- **Service composition infrastructure.** This refers to the set of tools that support the definition and execution of composite services.

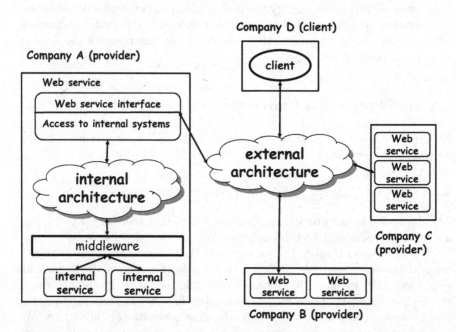

Fig. 5.10. Web services require an internal and an external architecture, along with corresponding middleware support

Observe that, in our definition, whether a component is part of the internal or external architecture is independent, to a large extent, on whether the component is deployed by the service provider or by a third party. Indeed, the same differentiation between internal and external architectures can be made when Web services are used for EAI, i.e., within the same company.

This distinction between internal and external architecture is crucial to understanding much of what is happening around Web services. There are Web services technologies and products that take care solely of the internal architecture of a Web service. There are also technologies and products that address only the external architecture of a Web service. Standardization efforts, however, mainly revolve around the external architecture. In practice both the internal and the external architecture must work together so that a Web service can make its functionality accessible to clients.

5.3.2 Internal Architecture of a Web Service

The easiest way to understand the internal architecture of Web services is to view them as yet another tier on top of the other tiers of the enterprise architecture.

In EAI, conventional middleware is used to build multi-tier architectures. In these architectures, individual programs or applications are hidden behind service abstractions that are combined into higher order programs or applications by using the functionality provided by the underlying middleware. The resulting higher order programs can in turn be hidden behind new service abstractions and can be used as building blocks for new services. Since the composition of service abstractions can be repeated ad libitum, the result is a multi-tier system in which services are implemented atop other services and basic programs. The corresponding architecture is shown in Figure 5.11.

When multiple middleware instances are stacked on top of each other, the middleware used at each level does not need to be the same. The important point is to have compatible service abstractions or to make them compatible using wrappers. The middleware simply acts as the glue necessary to make all the components in a given level interact with each other to form services that can be used by clients or higher levels in the hierarchy. Although it is not strictly necessary, usually the basic components of each middleware instance reside on a LAN and the resulting application also runs on the same LAN.

Web services or, better, the technologies supporting Web services, play the same role as conventional middleware, but on a different scale. The basis for composition is service abstractions very similar in nature to those used in conventional middleware, so that implementing a Web service essentially requires an extra tier on top of the others to enable access using standard Web services protocols. Figure 5.12 shows a typical example of such an internal architecture. Note that the figure emphasizes the fact that the implementation does not occur at the Web services layer, but within conventional middleware.

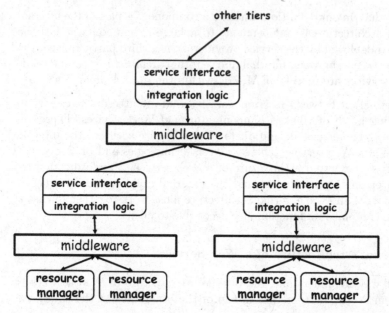

Fig. 5.11. Conventional middleware as an integration platform for basic programs and applications

As observed earlier, Web services are just wrappers. They invoke internal services that implement whatever application logic is needed, and then collect the results.

Today, much of the internal middleware for Web services revolves around packing and unpacking messages exchanged between Web services and converting them into the format supported by the underlying middleware. This is similar to how an application server maps data into HTML pages and back. Observe that the presence of this additional tier and the need for converting messages causes an overhead in processing the messages. This is also why Web services tend to be used for coarse-grained operations, where the overhead caused by the conversion is small compared to the operation execution time.

5.3.3 External Architecture of a Web Service

Using conventional middleware platforms to implement the internal architecture of a Web service is a natural step. However, what we have discussed until now is related to wrapping internal functionality as a Web service, and not to integrating these "wrappers." This aspect, which was addressed by message brokers and workflow management systems (WfMSs) in conventional middleware, should be the job of the external middleware.

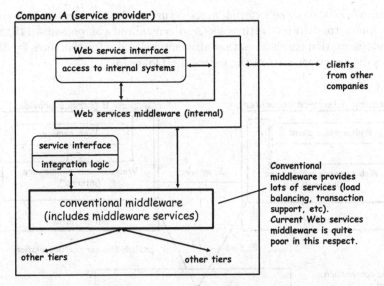

Fig. 5.12. Basic architecture of a set of Web services implemented atop a tiered architecture

However, as we have observed earlier, it is not clear where this middleware should reside. Consider as an example the implementation of name and directory services (this problem was already briefly discussed in Chapter 4). In LAN-based systems, the middleware and the applications developed using the middleware run next to each other. Thus, it is easy for the middleware to provide the necessary brokerage for name and directory services to all parties involved. In Web services, the parties can reside in different locations, and there is therefore no obvious place where to locate the middleware.

There are two solutions to this problem. One is to implement the middleware as a peer-to-peer system where all participants cooperate to provide name and directory services. Conceptually, this is a very appealing approach; but it is not obvious how to provide the degree of reliability and trustworthiness required in industrial strength systems. The other solution is to introduce intermediaries or brokers acting as the necessary middleware. Assuming we find a site somewhere in the network that we can trust and that is reliable enough, the site could act as a name and directory server for Web services. If we see such servers as part of the Web services middleware infrastructure, it follows that the participants and (part of) the middleware may reside at different locations.

Currently, there is only one type of Web services broker that has been standardized and that is used in practice, although to a very limited extent: the name and directory server. As a result, much of the existing literature on the architecture of Web services revolves around such a broker.

Figure 5.13 shows the external architecture of Web services as it is commonly understood today, with respect to centralized components [115, 83]. This representation emphasizes that abstractions and infrastructures for Web services discovery are part of the external middleware.

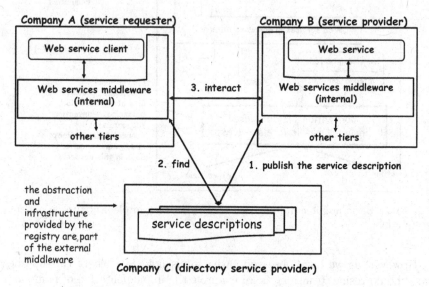

Fig. 5.13. External architecture of Web services

The figure describes how service discovery takes place in a Web service environment. Ignoring the details of the protocols and the syntax underlying the corresponding exchanges, the procedure shown is a normal mechanism for service discovery. It could apply not just to Web services, but also to almost any form of middleware, including the earliest versions of RPC. The idea is for *service providers* to create Web services and to define an interface for invoking them. The service provider also has to generate *service descriptions* for those services. The service provider will then make its services known to the world by *publishing* the corresponding service descriptions in a *service registry*. The information included with the service description is used by the service registry to catalog each service and search for it when requests from *service requesters* arrive. When a service requester tries to *find* a service, it queries the service registry. The service registry answers with a service description that indicates where to locate the service and how to invoke it. The service requester can then *bind* to the service provider by invoking the service. The directory itself is very likely available as a Web service, whose address and interface are assumed to be known a priori by the requester.

What is relevant about Figure 5.13 is not so much the mechanism it describes but the fact that it depicts service discovery as the only component of

Web services middleware. Where are the transaction management features offered by a TP monitor? Where are all the different services offered by CORBA? In some cases they are simply not there, and in others they are there but not in a centralized architecture. As in the case of service registry, a centralized architecture requires brokers that provide a middleware service to be located in well-known locations. But in some cases we do not know how to build such brokers and still provide a sufficient degree of efficiency. In other cases, companies simply cannot permit a broker to mediate their business interactions.

Consider again the example of transaction management. We could use exactly the same approach of conventional middleware and have a centralized transaction broker for Web services, much in the same way the name and directory server operates. Figure 5.13 would be extended by adding a new party corresponding to the hypothetical *transaction broker*, whose implementation would resemble that of brokers in conventional middleware. Such a solution is technically feasible but opens up many issues that are very difficult to sort out in practice. For one, it requires a standard way of running transactions accepted by everybody so that transactional semantics are not violated. Since the transactional semantics at each endpoint of the transaction are dictated by the underlying middleware platform, this amounts to standardizing transactional interactions across middleware tools. There are ongoing efforts to do just that [42] but they have just started and it would be quite some time before middleware platforms follow a common transactional interface.

A much more important constraint is that this approach assumes that all participants trust the broker. Except in restricted settings, this is highly improbable. There is a big difference between consulting a service registry provided by an external company and giving away a complete track of every transaction run as part of the Web services of a company. Companies jealously guard this information and it is not reasonable to assume they will rely on some external system to keep track of it. Even the very basic functionality of service registry that is available in a centralized architecture is not widely used today, as central directories are mostly applicable in closed settings, where there is trust among the companies acting as clients, providers, and directory servers. This may change in the future, if trusted brokers appear that can play a role similar to that played by companies like Yahoo! or Lycos for online shopping.

An alternative solution is to implement our hypothetical transaction broker as a peer-to-peer system. The idea here is that each service requester will have its own transaction manager. When the service requester invokes Web services in a transactional manner, its own transaction manager becomes responsible for orchestrating the execution so that the transactional semantics are preserved. As in the centralized solution, this also requires standardized transactional interaction [42]. However, the functionality provided by this solution will likely be a subset of that provided by conventional middleware systems.

Similar arguments can be made for other components that would normally be centralized in any external architecture. This is why middleware properties are in general provided through peer-to-peer protocols and through an infrastructure that supports the execution of such protocols. Such an infrastructure is part of the external architecture, but it is typically owned and controlled by the service requestor and by the service provider, not by a third party (Figure 5.14).

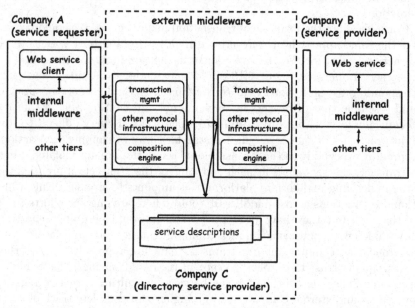

Fig. 5.14. External architecture of a Web service augmented with peer-to-peer protocol execution capabilities and with service composition

Service composition tools are another ingredient of external Web service architectures, likely to gain more importance as technology matures. We consider composition as part of the external architecture since it is about the integration of other Web services. Technically, the service composition infrastructure could be centralized. However, since the implementation is often proprietary and confidential, it is likely that such an infrastructure will be deployed by the service provider, and not by a third party (Figure 5.14).

5.4 Summary

In this chapter we have tried to clarify what Web services are and how they are being built. We have followed the W3C definition of a Web service, described as *"a software application identified by a URI, whose interfaces and bindings are capable of being defined, described, and discovered as XML artifacts.*

A Web service supports direct interactions with other software agents using XML-based messages exchanged via Internet-based protocols." While this definition is quite open in terms of what a Web service can be, current practice indicates that Web services are being used as sophisticated wrappers over conventional middleware platforms. As such, they are an additional tier that allows middleware services to be invoked as Web services. This implies that Web services can be characterized by an internal architecture (supported by internal middleware), defining its connection with the local information systems, and an external architecture (supported by external middleware), defining how Web services discover and interact with each other. The external architecture is particularly critical in that it requires cross-organizational interactions across the Internet, often without centralized control.

The external architecture relies on standards. These standards configure to a large extent the current Web services landscape. In the chapter we have outlined many of these standards and explained how they relate to each other. In the following chapters we will describe these standards in more detail. We will start from the basics (binding and interaction) and then proceed to more advanced topics (and correspondingly more advanced forms of Web services middleware) that become possible, and even necessary, once a basic interoperability infrastructure is in place.

6

Basic Web Services Technology

Many Web services architectures today are based on three components: the service requester, the service provider, and the service registry, thereby closely following a client/server model with an explicit name and directory service (the service registry). Albeit simple, such an architecture illustrates quite well the basic infrastructure necessary to implement Web services: a way to communicate (SOAP), a way to describe services (WSDL), and a name and directory server (UDDI). SOAP, WSDL and UDDI are nowadays the core of Web services. Specifications covering other aspects are typically designed based on SOAP, WSDL and UDDI. This is similar to the way conventional middleware platforms are built, where the basic components are interaction protocols, IDLs, and name and directory services.

In this chapter, we describe in detail each one of these specifications and explain how they relate to each other. We start by elaborating the basic components of this minimalist Web services architecture (Section 6.1). Then, we discuss the role of SOAP as the communication protocol for Web services (Section 6.2). The main point of SOAP is to provide a standardized way to encode different protocols and interaction mechanisms into XML documents that can be easily exchanged across the Internet. The next step is to describe services using WSDL (Section 6.3). WSDL acts as an advanced form of IDL, incorporating several aspects of a service description that are unique to Web services. Then, we introduce UDDI as the specification of the service registry for Web services (Section 6.4). This registry is used by service providers to publish and advertise available services, and by clients to query and search for concrete services.

After covering these three key standards, we discuss how WSDL, SOAP, and UDDI are used to expose internal operations as Web services (Section 6.5). We follow with a discussion on how these different specifications are related to each other and how developments in one area may affect what can be done in others (Section 6.6). We conclude the chapter with a brief description of other related proposals for standards that extend the basic capabilities of WSDL and SOAP to include additional properties and features (Section 6.7).

6.1 A Minimalist Infrastructure for Web Services

The best approach to understanding the basic Web services specifications that will be discussed in this chapter is to gradually address the problems faced when trying to invoke a service across the Internet.

First of all, a common syntax is needed for all specifications. In the case of Web services, this common syntax is provided by XML. Thus, we will find that all standards revolve around XML, with data structures and formats described as XML documents.

Second, there must be a mechanism in place to allow remote sites to interact with each other. The specification of this mechanism involves three aspects: a common data format for the messages being exchanged, a convention for supporting specific forms of interaction (such as messaging or RPC), and a set of bindings for mapping messages into a transport protocol. Note that, in the context of Web services, several different transport protocols could be used. In some cases TCP/IP could be sufficient, in another case one may want to use HTTP to be able to tunnel through firewalls, and in yet another case asynchronous messages exchanged through SMTP (e-mail) could be the best approach. Thus, to remain general enough, the mechanism in question must be able to work with a wide variety of transport protocols so that messages can be translated into whatever underlying protocol is being used. Similarly, the interaction mechanism should allow applications to remain loosely coupled. For this reason, it has to rely on *messages* as the basic unit of communication rather than procedure calls as in RPC. However, whenever required, the mechanism should also allow RPC-style interactions to take place. This is needed, for instance, in cases where the two applications are originally designed on RPC-based middleware and when the simplest way to put them together is by creating an additional layer of RPC calls between the two. In Web services, interactions are based on the Simple Object Access Protocol (SOAP). Using SOAP, services can exchange messages by means of standardized conventions to turn a service invocation into an XML message, to exchange the message, and to turn the XML message back into an actual service invocation (Figure 6.1).

The next obvious step after being able to send messages back and forth is to be able to describe the services (and specifically their interfaces) in a standardized manner. We have already seen the importance of IDL in conventional middleware. In Web services, this role is played by the Web Services Description Language (WSDL). Simply stated, WSDL is an XML-based interface definition language, and fulfills the same purpose as existing IDLs. In addition, it introduces a few extensions that are necessary to cope with the lack of a centralized middleware that manages transport and addressing.

Through WSDL, a designer specifies the programming interface of a Web service. This interface is specified in terms of methods supported by the Web service, where each method could take one message as input and return another as output. In the case of RPC-style interactions, these messages carry

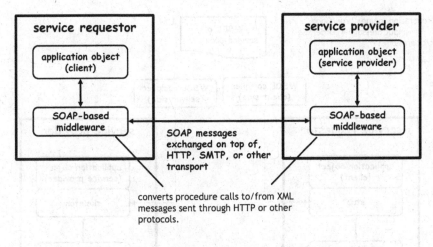

Fig. 6.1. Clients can invoke Web services by exchanging SOAP messages

the input and output parameters of a procedure call. At each site, WSDL is used like conventional IDLs. A WSDL file describing an interface can be compiled into the appropriate programming language to generate the stubs and intermediate layers that make calls to the Web services transparent. In the same way that IDL makes remote procedure calls appear as local procedure calls, WSDL is used to hide a Web service behind some interface, e.g., a method call. That way, users do not need to worry about the fact that they need to invoke a Web service. The Web services infrastructure uses WSDL and SOAP to construct the proxy objects at the requester and provider sides, so that developers can code their applications as if they were making local calls. Clients simply invoke a method using the programming language of their choice, and similarly services can be implemented as if they were invoked by a local method. A simple visual representation of the above concepts is provided in Figure 6.2 that, as the reader will notice, is similar to Figure 2.10, which depicts IDL compilation in CORBA. The most striking difference is the absence of a common middleware platform.

Finally, once services can be described and invoked, the only missing piece for a basic middleware infrastructure for Web services is a name and directory service. Being able to use Web services in a pervasive manner and at a global scale requires a standard way to publish and locate services. In this way, requesters can look for services of interest and understand their properties (e.g., their interfaces and the URI at which they are made available). Hence, a basic step toward having a functional Web services architecture is to standardize the Web services registry. Such a standardization is taking place as part of the *Universal Description, Discovery, and Integration* (UDDI) project. This effort comprises two parts: the UDDI registry and the UDDI APIs. The registry is the equivalent of the name and directory server found on any middleware plat-

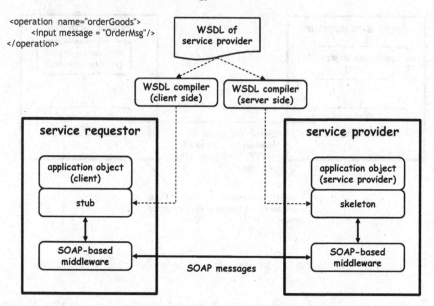

Fig. 6.2. WSDL specifications can be compiled into stubs and skeletons, analogously to IDL in conventional middleware. Dashed lines denote steps performed at development time, solid lines refer to run-time

form. It is the place where service descriptions are published in catalogs that can be searched by users. The UDDI APIs (Figure 6.3) determines how to publish services, what information needs to be provided to register a service, and how to query the registry.

Web services, of course, encompass many more aspects than those covered by SOAP, WSDL, and UDDI. Keep in mind, however, that Web services represent the first concerted effort that has gathered wide support for standardizing interactions across information systems. In many ways, Web services are at the same stage that RPC was when it was first proposed. RPC initially was no more than a mapping to the underlying communication protocols (TCP/IP at the time), a standardized syntax to build the stubs and skeletons (IDL), and a basic name server for dynamic binding. Web services are following the same path although at a faster pace, so fast that today there are already many products supporting these three relatively new standards. They represent basic concepts that will be enriched with countless ideas and functionality in the same way RPC was enriched to create the wide variety of middleware platforms available today. In what follows, we will describe the basics of SOAP, WSDL, and UDDI. The extensions to these basic specifications are discussed in Section 6.7 and in the next chapter.

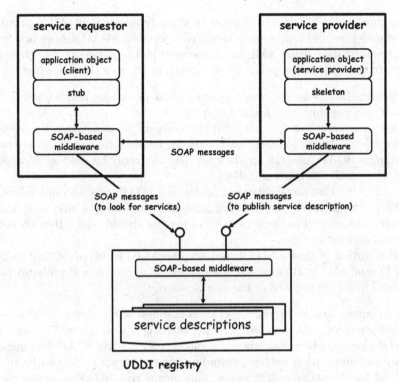

Fig. 6.3. Providers advertise their services in a UDDI registry. Clients (at development time or run-time) look for services in the registry, thereby statically or dynamically binding to a service. Then, clients can invoke the service

6.2 SOAP: Simple Object Access Protocol

The World Wide Web Consortium (W3C) started working on SOAP in 1999. In the first version (1.0) of the specification, SOAP was entirely based on HTTP. In the next revision of the specification (SOAP 1.1, May 2000 [32]) this was changed to make SOAP a generic conveyor of information on top of a variety of transport protocols. In May 2003, the W3C proposed SOAP 1.2, its next revision. SOAP 1.2 clarifies and adds additional semantics over SOAP 1.1 in terms of protocol bindings and XML encoding [87]. SOAP 1.2 is a joint effort from Canon, IBM, Microsoft, and Sun. At the time of writing, SOAP 1.2 was in the review phase.

6.2.1 Goals of SOAP

In the previous chapters, we discussed the difficulties of integrating applications across the Internet: firewalls, lack of standardized protocols, need for loosely-coupled interactions, etc. Obviously, this is the first problem that Web services must face. The current answer to these problems is SOAP, a protocol that underlies all interactions among Web services. SOAP defines how to organize information using XML in a structured and typed manner so that it can be exchanged between peers. In particular, it specifies the following:

- A message format for one-way communication, describing how information can be packaged into an XML document.
- A set of conventions for using SOAP messages to implement the RPC interaction pattern, defining how clients can invoke a remote procedure by sending a SOAP message and how services can reply by sending another SOAP message back to the caller.
- A set of rules that any entity that processes a SOAP message must follow, defining in particular the XML elements that an entity should read and understand, as well as the actions these entities should take if they do not understand the content.
- A description of how a SOAP message should be transported on top of HTTP and SMTP. Bindings to other transport protocols will probably be defined in future versions of the specification.

As a communication protocol, SOAP is stateless and one-way. It also ignores the semantics of the messages being exchanged through it. The actual interaction between two sites has to be encoded within the SOAP document and any communication pattern, including request-response, has to be implemented by the underlying systems. This means that SOAP is created by design to support loosely-coupled applications that interact by exchanging one-way asynchronous messages with each other. Any further complexity in the communication pattern such as two-way synchronous messaging or RPC-style interaction requires SOAP to be combined with an underlying protocol or middleware that has some additional properties. For example, to implement a conventional RPC call that takes input parameters and returns some output using SOAP, one has to first encode the input parameters and the call to the procedure into one SOAP message. The response of the procedure should also be encoded into another SOAP message. Finally a synchronous transport protocol such as HTTP (as opposed to an asynchronous one such as SMTP) should be used to transport the two messages. This allows the first message to be transported in the HTTP request while allowing the response message to be returned in the HTTP reply. The SOAP specification deals with such an exchange. It describes how such documents are to be written and organized so that they capture the interaction (e.g., RPC), and how to map the documents to underlying protocols (e.g., HTTP).

To define document types, SOAP 1.2 uses the W3C XML Schema recommendation. XML Schema [211] is a schema definition language for defining the structure of XML documents. This interdependency with other specifications is typical of Web services standards and results in added complexity when trying to understand their evolution. In what follows, we try to identify the key aspects of the specification and ignore details that are likely to change from version to version.

6.2.2 Structure and Contents of a SOAP Message

SOAP exchanges information using *messages*. These messages are used as an *envelope* where the application encloses whatever information needs to be sent. Each envelope contains two parts: a *header* and a *body* (Figure 6.4). The header is optional, that is, it may or may not be present in a SOAP message. The body is mandatory, i.e., all SOAP messages must have a body. Both header and body can have multiple sub-parts in the form of *header blocks* or *body blocks*. A header (body) block is any first-level child of the header (body) element of a message.

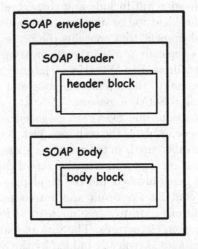

Fig. 6.4. Schematic representation of a SOAP message

SOAP assumes that every message has a sender, an ultimate receiver, and an arbitrary number of *intermediaries* (called *nodes*) that process the message and route it to the receiver. The core of the information the sender wants to transmit to the receiver should be in the body of the message. Any additional information necessary for intermediate processing or added value services (like transactional interaction, security, etc.) goes into the header. The idea follows the approach of standard communication protocols. The header contains information that can be processed by intermediate nodes. The *payload* or body is the actual message being conveyed. This is the reason why the header is optional. If there are no intermediaries in a SOAP transmission, the header might not be necessary at all. If there are intermediaries, they will work with the information in the headers as the need dictates (processing the header, adding new headers, keeping track of the message, etc.). The need for such intermediaries is obvious if we keep in mind that the actual procedure being invoked is probably part of a multi-tier architecture.

SOAP does not require any further structure within the content placed in header or body blocks. Nevertheless, there are a few common ways in which the header and body are constructed, and these are likely to become accepted forms. Typically, there are two aspects that influence how the header and body of a SOAP message are constructed: *interaction style* and *encoding rules*. Broadly speaking, SOAP can be used in two interaction styles: *document-style* and *RPC-style*. In document-style interaction, the two interacting applications agree upon the structure of documents exchanged between them. SOAP messages are used to transport these documents from one application to the other. For instance, a client that has to order goods from a supplier creates a *PurchaseOrder* document as a SOAP message. The body of the SOAP message will then consist of all the items requested as well as their quantities. The header will include any contextual information that is necessary to identify the client to the supplier. In response, the supplier sends an *Acknowledgement* document that contains the order ID of the confirmed order. This response is typically sent to the client asynchronously, although it could be also sent synchronously. Whether an interaction is synchronous or asynchronous is orthogonal to the interaction style and does not impact the structure of the exchanged SOAP messages.

In RPC-style interaction, one SOAP message encapsulates the request while another message encapsulates the response, just as in document-style interaction. However, the difference is in the way these messages are constructed. The body of the request message contains the actual call. This includes the name of the procedure being invoked and the input parameters. The body of the response message contains the result and output parameters. Thus, the two interacting applications have to agree upon the RPC method signature as opposed to the document structures. The task of translating the method signature in SOAP messages is typically hidden by the SOAP middleware.

If there are additional properties associated with the RPC call, they are expressed in the header. Thus, if the RPC is going to be transactional, the header would include the necessary transactional context for the receiving site to process the request transactionally. To illustrate how goods in the procurement example discussed in the previous chapter are ordered using RPC-style interaction, the client creates a SOAP message with *orderGoods*, which is the method name, as the immediate child of the SOAP body element. Parameters to the method are represented as sub-elements of the *orderGoods* element. Figure 6.5 summarizes how the interaction style influences the structure of a SOAP message. It shows two sets of sample SOAP messages used for ordering goods and for returning an acknowledgement—one using document-style interaction and the other using RPC-style interaction. It is assumed that the order itself has only two parameters—the product item and the quantity. It should be noted that SOAP does not impose any particular interaction style. However, it does define a convention for representing RPC requests and responses in SOAP messages.

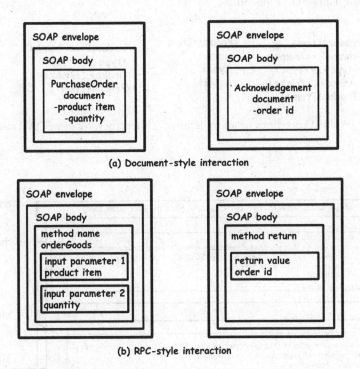

(a) Document-style interaction

(b) RPC-style interaction

Fig. 6.5. The document-style interaction involves the client sending a *Purchase-Order* document and the supplier responding with an *Acknowledgement* document. The RPC-style interaction involves the client making a *orderGoods* method call using a SOAP message and the supplier responding with a order id as the return value in another SOAP message

The structure of a SOAP message is also influenced by encoding rules, which define how a particular entity or data structure is represented in XML. For example, a product item can be represented in several ways, some of which are shown in Figure 6.6. In order for the client and server to interoperate, it is essential that they agree on how the contents of a SOAP message are encoded. SOAP 1.2 defines a particular form of encoding called *SOAP encoding*. This defines how data structures including basic types such as integers and strings as well as complex types such as arrays and structures can be serialized into XML.

Once again, it should be noted that SOAP 1.2 does not impose any specific form of encoding. In other words, applications are free to ignore SOAP encoding and choose a different one instead. For instance, two applications can simply agree upon an XML Schema representation of a data structure as the serialization format for that data structure. This is commonly referred to as *literal encoding*. Figure 6.7 shows a complete SOAP message in RPC-style interaction using SOAP encoding.

```
<ProductItem>              <ProductItem
   <name>...</name>          name="..."        <ProductItem name="..."
   <type>...</type>          type="..."           <type>...</type>
   <make>...</make>          make="..."           <make>...</make>
</ProductItem>            />                  </ProductItem>
```

Fig. 6.6. Different encodings result in different XML structures in a SOAP message

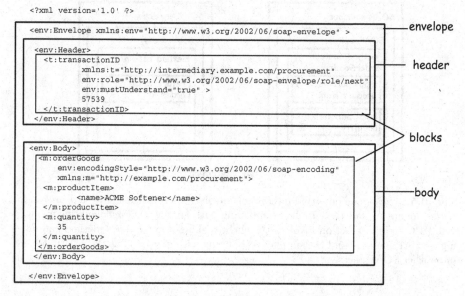

```
<?xml version='1.0' ?>
<env:Envelope xmlns:env="http://www.w3.org/2002/06/soap-envelope" >        ──── envelope
   <env:Header>
      <t:transactionID                                                     ──── header
            xmlns:t="http://intermediary.example.com/procurement"
            env:role="http://www.w3.org/2002/06/soap-envelope/role/next"
            env:mustUnderstand="true" >
            57539
      </t:transactionID>
   </env:Header>
                                                                           ──── blocks
   <env:Body>
      <m:orderGoods
            env:encodingStyle="http://www.w3.org/2002/06/soap-encoding"
            xmlns:m="http://example.com/procurement">
         <m:productItem>
               <name>ACME Softener</name>                                  ──── body
         </m:productItem>
         <m:quantity>
            35
         </m:quantity>
      </m:orderGoods>
   </env:Body>
</env:Envelope>
```

Fig. 6.7. An example of a SOAP message with a header block that is intended for processing by an intermediary

6.2.3 Processing a SOAP Message

The division between header and body already provides some indication of how SOAP expects messages to be processed by the different nodes along the message path. These nodes will, in most cases, constitute the different tiers of the Web services middleware. In the SOAP model, nodes processing a message can play one or more *roles*. Each block in a SOAP header may include the definition of the role for which it is intended. The SOAP specification defines three roles, informally called *none*, *next*, and *ultimateReceiver*.

- If a block is assigned to a *none* role, it means that such a block should not be processed by any node receiving the message (although the block might be read if it contains information important for processing other blocks).
- If a block is assigned to the ultimateReceiver role, that block is solely intended for the recipient of the message, not for any intermediate node.
- If a block is assigned to the *next* role, every node receiving the message can process that block. This is because every node receiving a message is the "next" one in the chain of nodes processing the message. The ultimateReceiver is also included in the set of *next* nodes.

The body of the message does not have a role associated to it. Its role defaults to *ultimateReceiver*.

Processing a block may encompass very different operations, and each node involved in the processing could do something different. For example, processing can involve removing blocks from the header, performing some action (such as logging the message), extending the header with additional information, removing the header and introducing a new one, and more. A block may contain a *mustUnderstand* flag, indicating that a node playing the role indicated by the block *must* process the block. If the flag is set and, for some reason, the node cannot process the block as needed, any further processing of that message stops and a fault is generated. The message is not forwarded to any other node. If the mustUnderstand flag is not set or is absent, a node is free to decide whether to process or ignore the block (assuming it has the corresponding role). The body does not have a mustUnderstand flag, but the ultimateReceiver must process the body or generate a fault. Figure 6.7 shows a SOAP message with a header block that includes a transaction identifier intended to be read by an intermediary, for example for tracking purposes.

6.2.4 Binding SOAP to a Transport Protocol

The final step to having a functional protocol is defining how a SOAP message is going to be transported through the network. SOAP does not impose any transport protocol. Typically, it is associated with HTTP but it can also be used with other protocols such as SMTP (e-mail). The specification of which protocol to use is called a *binding*, a term not to be confused with the notion of (static or dynamic) binding in service discovery. In this context, bindings define how a message is wrapped within a transport protocol and how the message has to be treated using the primitives of the transport protocol used.

For instance, when SOAP is used over HTTP, what is being sent is the SOAP envelope within an HTTP request. Depending on what needs to be done, SOAP can use GET, POST or other HTTP primitives. POST, for instance, can be used to implement the RPC invocation we have used as an example in this section. As shown in Figure 6.8, the RPC request is sent as part of an HTTP POST request. As part of the HTTP protocol, the receiving node has to acknowledge the POST request, indicating whether it received the request and whether it could appropriately process the request. As part of this response, the receiving site includes the RPC response or the corresponding fault message.

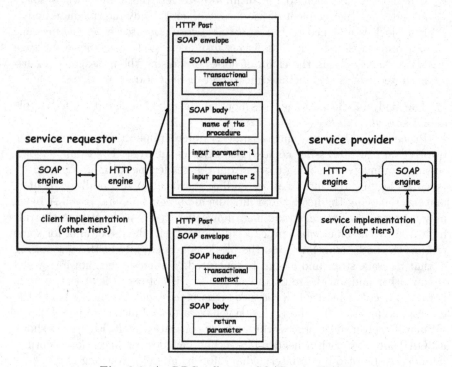

Fig. 6.8. An RPC call using SOAP over HTTP

In addition to describing how a SOAP message gets transported on an underlying protocol, SOAP transport bindings have another implicit functionality: *addressing*. The reader may note that the identification of the ultimate receiver's address is not part of a SOAP message. This is resolved by including the SOAP message as part of an HTTP request or as part of an SMTP message. In the case of HTTP, the URL of the target resource describes the receiver of the SOAP message. Similarly, in SMTP, the "to" address in the e-mail header also describes the SOAP receiver.

A closely related problem is that of *routing*. Though SOAP describes the notion of a SOAP path as comprising of a set of nodes, there is no mechanism for describing a SOAP path as part of a SOAP message. The path of a SOAP message is essentially the same as the route taken by the underlying protocol message. In Section 6.7 we examine some emerging Web services standards that propose alternative solutions to addressing and routing.

6.2.5 A Simple Implementation of SOAP

Figure 6.9 shows a simple approach to implementing a SOAP-based interaction. It follows the same principles as the implementation of RPC. The client (e.g., a Java object) makes a procedure call that looks like a local call. The call is in reality an invocation of a proxy procedure located in a stub appended to the client at compile time. The client stub re-routes the call to a SOAP subsystem (which can be an independent module or a part of the stub) that will transform the call into an XML document formatted according to the SOAP message specifications. It will also wrap the resulting SOAP message into HTTP format. Once this is done, the HTTP document is passed to an HTTP module (which again can be independent, e.g., a Web server, or a part of the stub) that will forward the request to the remote location.

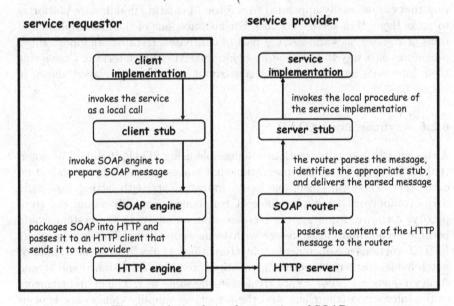

Fig. 6.9. A simple implementation of SOAP

At the remote location this procedure is reversed. An HTTP module receives the request and passes it along to a SOAP subsystem. There, the HTTP wrap is removed and the XML document is extracted and analyzed to retrieve its contents. These contents are then forwarded to the server stub that will call the corresponding procedure. The return parameters of the call are treated in a similar manner. Again, the SOAP engine and the stub can be combined or they can be independent modules. If the SOAP related part is independent, then it is often referred to as *SOAP router*, since one of its tasks is to route the call to the appropriate object.

Although implementations may differ, the mechanisms just described reflects what is being done today. The main differences across implementations are in the specific instances of middleware being adopted, in whether the SOAP system is an independent module provided by a Web services middleware infrastructure or attached to the client and server as a library (dynamic or static), and in whether the HTTP support is provided by a library or a complete Web or application server.

Readers surprised by the simplicity of the whole approach should be reminded that simplicity is one of the main goals of SOAP. After all, it was initially called *Simple* Object Access Protocol. Recall also that Web services appeared as a way to solve the problem of connecting conventional middleware platforms across the Internet. As we saw in previous chapters, conventional middleware is strongly tied to RPC and it is therefore only natural for SOAP to build upon this tradition. Doing so leads to a straightforward implementation that can be easily appended to the top of existing middleware platforms to make them *Web service enabled*. For instance, one of the first implementations of Web services appeared as part of databases. Databases support *stored procedures* as a way to hide queries behind an RPC-like interface. Converting these interfaces into Web services is as simple as adding the layers shown in Figure 6.9.

6.2.6 Asynchronous SOAP

Although RPC-style interactions are possible using SOAP, it should be noted that RPC results in a tight integration that makes components dependent on each other. This is unacceptable in any industrial-strength setting, especially if the components belong to different companies. Not only would the complexity of the resulting system increase, but maintaining the system would become a coordination challenge with tremendous costs. This is why many B2B interactions use document-style interactions, typically in asynchronous or batch mode. Rather than direct invocations, requests are batched and routed through queues. Responses are treated in the same way. The actual elements of the interaction (the client and the server, to simplify things) are kept as decoupled as possible so that they can be designed, maintained, and evolved independently of each other. Systems based on EDI [66] and SWIFT [182] are, again, good examples of the typical loosely coupled architectures of B2B systems.

There is a strong trend toward using SOAP asynchronously in B2B interactions. One way to achieve this is to rely on an asychronous transport protocol such as SMTP for exchanging SOAP messages. Another way of achieving asynchronous SOAP interactions involves setting separate threads, one with the main logic and another in charge of making each SOAP call. In this way, the main thread can make the request by passing the data to the second thread and then continue processing. The second thread places the call and waits for the response. When the response arrives, a *callback* occurs and the main thread is notified of the arrival of the response. Alternatively, the response can be placed in a buffer until the main thread decides to act upon it. There are no technical difficulties involved as the mechanisms are identical to those used for implementing asynchronous RPC. In fact, many message oriented middleware platforms are implemented on top of RPC. A message is placed in a queue and a daemon makes an RPC call to another remote daemon, which takes the message and places it on the receiving queue. SOAP can be used in exactly the same way.

6.2.7 Binary Data and SOAP

XML is a blessing as a syntax standard. It allows one to build generic parsers that can be used in a multitude of applications, thereby ensuring robustness and low cost for the technology. The downside is that the data transformations to and from XML as well as the associated XML parsing can result in a significant performance overhead, a typical price paid for generality. In addition, XML does not always gracefully support the necessary data types, such as binary data (e.g., an image) or nested XML documents [177]. In many cases, even if it is possible, there may be no reason to format application data into an XML document. For example, a Web service implemented as a queue expecting EDIFACT e-mail messages does not gain much by having the message encoded in XML. In fact, it only loses performance and introduces unnecessary software layers.

XML encoding makes sense when linking completely heterogeneous systems or passing around data that cannot be immediately interpreted. It also makes sense when there is no other standard syntax and designers must choose one. When Web services are built based on already agreed upon data formats, then the role of XML is reduced to being the syntax of the SOAP messages involved. This is why there is such a strong demand for SOAP to support a binary or *blob* type. There are several ways of doing this [177]: using URLs as pointers, as an attachment, or with the recently proposed Direct Internet Message Encapsulation (DIME) protocol [150]. Whatever mechanism becomes the norm, expect a considerable amount of Web services traffic to contain binary data rather than explicit XML.

6.3 WSDL: Web Services Description Language

WSDL was originally created by IBM, Microsoft, and Ariba by merging three previous proposals: Microsoft's SOAP Contract Language (SCL) and Service Description Language (SDL), together with IBM's Network Accessible Service Specification Language (NASSL). At the time of this writing, a working draft of WSDL 1.2 is available [49].

6.3.1 Goals of WSDL

The Web Services Description Language (WSDL) [49] has a role and purpose similar to that of IDLs in conventional middleware platforms. In WSDL, specifications are XML documents that describe Web services, and in particular describe service interfaces. In a nutshell, this is what WSDL is about. However, from an IDL perspective, the problems in Web services are more complex than in conventional middleware.

A significant difference with respect to conventional IDLs is that, in addition to specifying the operations offered by a service, WSDL also needs to define the mechanisms to access the serviceWeb service!access mechanism. In fact, since existing IDLs are tied to a concrete middleware platform, they are only concerned with the description of the service interface in terms of service name and signature (input and output parameters). The rest of the information is implicit, as the access mechanisms are identical for all services available on that middleware platform. In the context of Web services, each service can be made accessible using different protocols, and it is therefore crucial that such information is provided as part of the service description (note the correlation with the fact that SOAP supports bindings to different transport protocols).

Another difference caused by the lack of a common middleware platform is the need for defining the location at which the service is available. In fact, in conventional middleware the service provider could simply implement an interface and register the implemented object with the middleware, which would take care of activating the object as needed. The location of the object would be transparent and unknown to the client. The absence of a centralized platform in Web services means that the client (or, rather, the Web services middleware at the client's site) should be able to identify the location at which the service is made available, so that it knows where to send SOAP messages. Therefore, service providers should have a standardized means for specifying this information.

The separation of interfaces and bindings to protocols, and the need for address information, also make the case for modular specifications: in fact, we can imagine that different services will want to implement the same interface, but provide the service at different addresses and be able to interact with different transport protocols.

In addition to the problems caused by the lack of a centralized middleware, WSDL also needs to cope with the higher complexity of Web services, and in particular with the fact that interactions are often asynchronous. Conventional IDLs are typically used to describe a single entry point to a service (a single RPC interaction). As we have seen in the previous chapter, the invocation of a Web service typically involves the exchange of several asynchronous messages between requesters and providers. To support these needs, WSDL includes a collection of different interaction paradigms, along with the ability to combine operations or groups of operations within an interface.

6.3.2 Structure of a WSDL Interface

To address the above-mentioned problems, WSDL specifications are often characterized by an *abstract* part, conceptually analogous to conventional IDL, and a *concrete* part, that defines protocol binding and other information (Figure 6.10). The abstract part is made of *port type* definitions, which are analogous to interfaces in traditional middleware IDLs. Each port type is a logical collection of related *operations*. Each operation defines a simple exchange of *messages*. As described in the previous section, a message is a unit of communication with a Web service, representing the data exchanged in a single logical transmission. As in the case of other Web services standards, these constructs are all defined in XML.

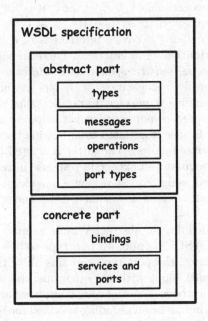

Fig. 6.10. A WSDL service specification

As with any IDL, WSDL needs a type system so that the data being exchanged can be correctly interpreted at both ends of the communication. By default, WSDL uses the same type system as XML Schemas, although the WSDL document can specify a different type system if necessary. Note that this is different from IDLs in conventional middleware, where the type system was imposed by the underlying platform (e.g., CORBA or J2EE). XML Schemas have built-in basic data types and allow users to define more complex data types such as structures. So, the first step in defining a WSDL interface is to identify and define all the data structures that will be exchanged as parts of messages between applications.

The second step is to define messages that build on such data structures. In WSDL, each message is a typed document divided into *parts*. Each part is characterized by a name and by a type, referring to a type typically defined in XML schema. As an example, to invoke a procedure that takes one integer and one floating point number as parameters, we can define a message that has two parts. One will contain the integer and the other will contain the floating point number. In this case, new data types need not be defined since both the integer and floating point data types are part of the standard XML Schema specification. On the other hand, if we define a message that requires exchanging purchase orders, then data structures that represent product items and purchase orders have to be defined. The concrete relationship between the message and its parts is dependent on the interaction style of the operation in which the message is exchanged. But, for now, it is sufficient to regard the message as an abstract aggregate of its parts.

The third step in defining a WSDL interface is to define operations, also called transmission primitives or interactions. There are four basic operations: *one-way*, *request-response*, *solicit-response*, and *notification*. One-way and notification operations involve a single message. In one-way interaction, the client invokes a service by sending a message. In notifications, it is the service that sends the message. Request-response and solicit-response involve the exchange of two messages. The former is initiated from outside the service (the service is invoked and a response follows). The latter is started by the service itself (the service makes a request and expects a response in return). Synchronous interactions are defined using request-response or solicit-response operations, while asynchronous interactions are defined using one-way and notification operations.

The final step in defining an abstract WSDL interface is to group operations into port types. WSDL 1.2 allows a port type to be extended from other port types. In such cases, the port type contains all of the operations from the port types it extends, along with any other operations it defines.

The reason why the above definitions are considered abstract is that there is neither a concrete binding or an encoding specified for these constructs nor a definition of a service that implements a set of port types. For example, in defining a real instance of a service, one has to define the exact set of port types that it implements, the transport bindings used in implementing such port types, and the addresses at which those implementations are made accessible to clients. The lack of these descriptions makes the port type definitions abstract. The same port type can be implemented using multiple bindings and can be combined with other port type implementations in different combinations to form different services. Similarly, the above definition of messages is abstract since information about their XML encoding and protocol binding is absent. The same data type can be encoded into a message using different rules and the same message can be exchanged using different protocol bindings. The second part of a WSDL interface definition is to define a concrete service by specifying all of these aspects.

The concrete part of a WSDL interface is defined using the following three constructs (Figure 6.10):

- **InterfaceBindings.** The binding specifies the message encoding and protocol bindings for all operations and messages defined in a given port type. For instance, it could specify that an operation is an RPC-style operation or a document-style operation. In an RPC-style operation, the input and output messages carry input and output parameters of the procedure call. In a document style operation, the input and output messages carry documents that are agreed upon by the two applications. An InterfaceBinding could also specify that the messages of an operation have to be communicated using the SOAP protocol and HTTP transport bindings. WSDL allows communications protocols other than SOAP to be used as well, although this is rarely the case in reality. Given that the communications protocol is SOAP, the main available transport binding options are HTTP and SMTP. Finally, an InterfaceBinding also specifies the encoding rules that should be used in serializing the parts of a message into XML. As described in Section 6.2, there are usually two possible encodings–literal and SOAP . Literal encoding takes the WSDL types defined in XML Schemas and "literally" uses those definitions to represent the XML content of messages. In other words, the abstract WSDL types also become concrete types. SOAP encoding, on the other hand, takes the XML Schema definitions as abstract entities, and translates them into XML using SOAP encoding rules defined as part of SOAP 1.2. Typically, literal encoding is used for document-style interactions whereas SOAP encoding is used for RPC-style interactions.
- **Ports.** Also known as *EndPoints*, ports combine the InterfaceBinding information with a network address (specified by a URI) at which the implementation of the port type can be accessed. Again, this is not needed in conventional middleware due to the presence of a centralized infrastructure that manages addresses in a transparent manner.
- **Services.** Services are logical grouping of ports. Note that, at least in principle, this also means that a specific WSDL service could be available at different Web addresses (for example, different URIs corresponding to different server machines, maybe one in Europe and one in Australia). It could also combine very different port types. In practice, however, it is likely that a WSDL service will group related ports, typically available at the same address. Another common grouping is the one in which the different ports represent different bindings for the same port type. This allows the same functionality to be accessible via multiple transport protocols and interaction styles.

As each of the above constructs are added to WSDL, the interface definition of a Web service becomes more concrete. With the binding information, users know what protocols to use, how to structure XML messages to interact with a service, and what to expect when contacting the service. WSDL

1.1 currently defines binding extensions for SOAP, HTTP GET and POST, and MIME. With the port information, users know the network address at which the functionality of a port type is implemented. Finally, with the service definition, users know all the ports that are implemented as a group.

The combination of these elements in a WSDL document is shown in Figure 6.11.

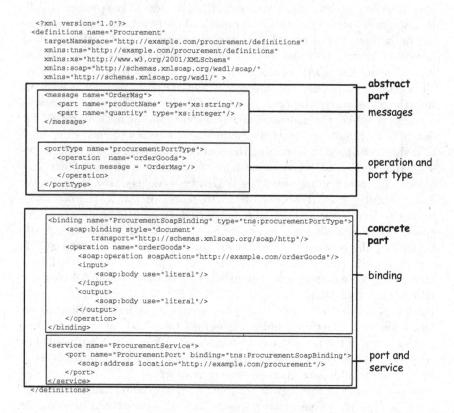

Fig. 6.11. A WSDL service specification

6.3.3 Implications of the WSDL Model

The WSDL data structure has interesting implications on how services are described and how they interact. One of them is related to the different operation types. In fact, the interaction modes that can be associated with a WSDL operation show that, unlike IDLs in conventional middleware, a service can proactively initiate the interaction. In other words, it not only exposes operations that can be invoked, but also operations that invoke, meaning that a service can also behave like a client. This leads to a further blurring of the notion of clients and service providers (something we have already seen when speaking about messaging in conventional middleware), which is natural when the interaction tends to be more asynchronous in nature. Indeed, in the Web services domain, it is quite common to model every interacting entity as a WSDL service.

Another implication of the data structure specification is that WSDL does not presume that exchanges will take place using a particular form of communication. This is why WSDL can be used to describe two aspects of a Web service, as depicted in Figure 6.11. The first is the abstract interface of the service, without specifying the location or the protocol to be used. The second is the actual location of the service and the communication protocol to be used.

The advantage of this separation is that WSDL specifications that describe abstract interfaces are reusable: different services could combine different interfaces using different bindings, and could make them available at different addresses. Reuse is also facilitated by the fact that WSDL documents may import other WSDL documents. This allows for modular WSDL specifications, where typically some documents define abstract interfaces, while other documents import those definitions and make them concrete by defining bindings and addresses.

Note also the correlation of the WSDL description with SOAP. If the messages defined in WSDL are exchanged using SOAP, then the InterfaceBindings contain all the information needed to infer or automatically construct the SOAP messages. In this case, the interaction style, XML encoding, and transport bindings specified in WSDL translate to those used for constructing SOAP messages. For example, if the interaction style is RPC, then the input message of an operation in WSDL determines the procedure name and input parameters of the RPC call. The ability of both SOAP and WSDL to be able to use multiple transport bindings and XML encodings is a crucial aspect of the standardization efforts around Web services. SOAP is a generic envelope to wrap invocations that the applications may make using other tools. WSDL is a generic service description that may correspond to services actually built using other languages (e.g., stored procedures in databases that are automatically converted into Web services). In both cases, the idea is to standardize interactions through an additional tier and therefore facilitate the development of tools that will translate existing interoperability mechanisms into Web services mechanisms. Eventually, middleware platforms may directly use SOAP or WSDL but, at this stage and for probably quite a while, SOAP and WSDL will act as wrappers over existing protocols and description languages. Hence the need to accommodate multiple communication protocols.

Following this idea, the W3C working group has documented a number of different services that can be represented using WSDL [175]. Some of the examples include simple service semantics, although the enforcement of these semantics and their actual meaning will necessarily be part of other specifications. These examples (which include synchronous and asynchronous operations, multiple faults scenarios, versioning, and the use of events) show that WSDL needs to evolve much more to adapt to changes in SOAP and in many other specifications that cover aspects such as security, delivery guarantees, transactional interaction, coordination, etc.

6.3.4 Using WSDL

As with any interface definition language, WSDL can be used in different ways and for different purposes. There are also many aspects not covered by WSDL that system designers need to resolve outside its specification. To clarify the use of WSDL, the W3C Web Services Description Working Group has documented and published use cases that illustrate how a Web service could be described in WSDL. The Working Group has identified three potential uses of WSDL descriptions [175]:

1. The first use is as a traditional service description language (see the abstract part of Figure 6.11). Thus, a WSDL description can be seen as a contract that a Web service implements. This contract indicates how to interact with the service, what data needs to be sent, what data is to be expected in return, what operations are involved, and the format and protocol necessary to invoke the service.
2. The second use is as input to stub compilers and other tools that, given a WSDL description, will generate the required stubs and additional information for developing both the service and the clients that invoke the service. Figure 6.2, presented earlier in this chapter, describes this usage. As with IDLs in conventional middleware platforms, the use of automated tools for generating stubs facilitates development and ensures that the service is invoked properly.
3. The third use proposed by the Working Group is rather vague, and it concerns semantics. The proposal is for a WSDL description to capture information that will eventually allow designers to reason about the semantics of a Web service. Nevertheless, it is important to keep in mind that semantics are outside the scope of the current WSDL specification (version 1.2) and it is likely that they will remain outside the specification even in future versions. Currently, each Web service must use a separate specification to pin down the actual semantics or use some other mechanism outside the WSDL description to establish the necessary conventions.

The obvious conclusion to draw from this list of potential uses is that WSDL should not be understood as being anything more than a form of advanced IDL for Web services, with the differences already mentioned in access mechanisms and groupings of ports. Of the three listed potential uses, the first two are identical to those of IDL languages. The advantage of WSDL over previous solutions is the reliance on XML and the potential for widespread acceptance, which can lead to a level of automation that was not possible before. Stub compilers and tools that help in developing interfaces have existed for a long time. However, they are tied to the underlying middleware platform and cannot be made generic. If WSDL is widely adopted, such tools will become pervasive and much more sophisticated than existing ones.

It is quite interesting to observe that, in most scenarios, the WSDL itself is automatically generated. In fact, as observed in Chapter 5, Web services are a way of exposing internal operations. Therefore, in many cases, the application implementing the service is pre-existing. Based on the API of the application, a WSDL document can be automatically generated. From the WSDL, stubs and skeletons can also be derived, as discussed above. This scenario is shown in Figure 6.12. As an example, commercial databases have started to provide functionality that automatically generates the WSDL description for a given stored procedure. Analogously, application servers provide facilities both for generating stubs from WSDL documents and for generating WSDL documents from classes (e.g., Java classes).

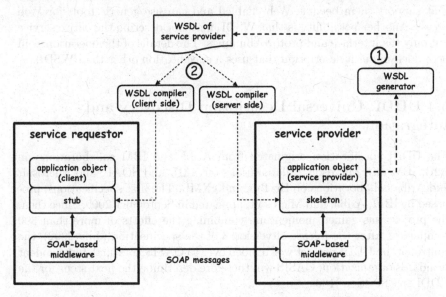

Fig. 6.12. WSDL documents can be generated from APIs. Dashed lines represent compile-time activities. First, WSDL is generated. Next, stubs and skeletons are created

6.3.5 WSDL and Other Standards

WSDL is a horizontal standard in the sense that it can be used in a wide variety of settings and does not contain any specifics of particular domains.

It has been designed as a generic service description language that can be used for many services independently of what the service does. Useful as it is, this is clearly not enough in the context of Web services. In fact, it has been pointed out that "standard" no longer means "globally unique" in the B2B world. In addition to WSDL, a few hundred competing B2B standards may coexist [38]. Examples of such established standards (that will simply not go away because of WSDL) are the Electronic Data Interchange (EDI) [66], used in manufacturing, and SWIFT [182], used in the financial world.

The advantage of such standards over WSDL is that they are specifically designed for a concrete application and capture many semantic aspects that WSDL will never be able to capture. It is possible that some of these standards will converge toward WSDL and produce hybrids that will be used for concrete application areas. It is also possible that some of these standards will survive and remain independent of WSDL. Given the heavy investments on infrastructures based on these standards, it is unlikely that such standards will be immediately discarded to take up WSDL. Hence, in many cases, WSDL will act only as a wrapper over these standards so that the systems that support them become Web enabled and can use generic tools for Web access. Another possibility is that WSDL may not describe the entire service but only the interface and protocol bindings. The details of the operations will be hidden under a description that uses a specification other than WSDL.

6.4 UDDI: Universal Description Discovery and Integration

The UDDI specification originated from Ariba and IBM collaborations on B2B, IBM and Microsoft collaborations on XML and SOAP, and Microsoft and Ariba collaborations on BizTalk and cXML. The first specifications, proposed by IBM, Ariba, and Microsoft, appeared in September 2000. Since then, the project has gained momentum, combining the efforts of more than 300 companies. After the release of version 3 of the specification (July 2002), the control of the UDDI project was handed over to OASIS, a formal, independent standards organization. OASIS will therefore determine the next steps for the UDDI specification [180].

6.4.1 Goals of UDDI

The primary goal of UDDI is the specification of a framework for describing and discovering Web services. The core of UDDI revolves around the notion of *business registry*, which is essentially a sophisticated naming and directory service. In particular, UDDI defines data structures and APIs for publishing service descriptions in the registry and for querying the registry to look for published descriptions. Being about Web services, UDDI APIs are also specified in WSDL with SOAP binding, so that the registry can itself be accessed as a Web service (and, consequently, its characteristics can be described in the registry itself, just like any other Web service).

The UDDI registry specifications have two main goals with respect to service discovery: first, to support developers in finding information about services, so that they know how to write clients that interact with those services. Second, to enable dynamic binding, by allowing clients to query the registry and obtain references to services of interest. This dual nature is clearly reflected in UDDI, which leaves room for both structured and unstructured information.

In addition to defining a Web services registry, UDDI also addresses the notion of *Universal Business Registry* (UBR). In fact, the initial goal of the consortium was supporting worldwide directories where everybody could publish service descriptions (essentially for free) and where everybody could query these directories to find services of interest. The idea was that UBRs could contain every service ever deployed in the world. With time, the specifications evolved in the direction of also supporting private registry implementations, in conjunction with the interaction of private and public implementations [180].

6.4.2 Information in a UDDI Registry

A simple way of categorizing the information contained in a UDDI registry is in terms of what each type of information is used for. This categorization is best understood by means of an analogy with the telephone directory:

- **White pages.** They are listings of organizations, of contact information (e.g., telephone or e-mail address), and of the services these organizations provide. Using the registry as a white pages catalogue, UDDI clients can find Web services provided by a given business.
- **Yellow pages.** They are classifications of both companies and Web services according to taxonomies that can be either standardized or user-defined. Through yellow pages, it is possible to search for services based on the category they belong to, according to a given classification scheme.
- **Green pages.** This information describes how a given Web service can be invoked. It is provided by means of pointers to service description documents, typically stored outside the registry (e.g., at the service provider's site).

6.4.3 UDDI Data Structures

In the UDDI registry, Web services descriptions contain four types of information: business information, service information, binding information, and information about specifications of services, described by several entities. The four main entities of the registry (Figure 6.13) are described below:

- **businessEntity.** It describes an organization that provides Web services. It lists the company's name, address, and other contact information.

- **businessService.** This element describes a group of related Web services offered by a businessEntity. Typically, a businessService will correspond actually to one kind of service (such as a procurement or a travel reservation service), but provided at different addresses, in multiple versions, and through different technologies (e.g., different protocol bindings). Business services, like business entities, can also include classification information. A businessEntity entry can include multiple businessService elements, but a businessService belongs to one and only one businessEntity (Figure 6.13).
- **bindingTemplate.** This element describes the technical information necessary to use a particular Web service. Essentially, it defines the address at which the Web service is made available along with a set of detailed information, such as references to documents (called *tModels*) describing the Web service interface or other service properties. It also defines how operation parameters should be set and the default values for such parameters. A businessService entry can include multiple bindingTemplate elements (one for each interface or address), but a bindingTemplate belongs to one and only one businessService (Figure 6.13).
- **tModel.** The cryptic name stands for "technical model", and it is a generic container for any kind of specification. For example, it could represent a WSDL service interface, a classification, or an interaction protocol, or it could describe the semantics of an operation. Unlike the previous entities, tModels are not subject to parent-child relationships, and can be referred to by other entities to denote conformance to an interface, or to classify businesses or services.

In summary, if we want to publish one or more services in a UDDI registry, we first need to define a set of tModels describing the different characteristics of the services (such as the WSDL service interface or an informal description of what the service does). Note that some of tModels may be pre-existing, for example in those cases where our services implement standardized interfaces, and the corresponding tModels have been defined and published by the corresponding standardization consortium. We then publish our company information (a businessEntity), general information about the services we provide (a set of businessServices), and a set of detailed technical information for each different implementation and access point we make available for the service (a bindingTemplate). The technical descriptions will contain references to the previously published tModels.

6.4.4 Understanding tModels

The tModel and the way it is used by the businessEntity, businessService, and bindingTemplate elements, is really at the heart of the UDDI specification. It is important to understand how it works, as it unveils the philosophy of UDDI. In fact, the key information about a service is specified as a reference to a tModel.

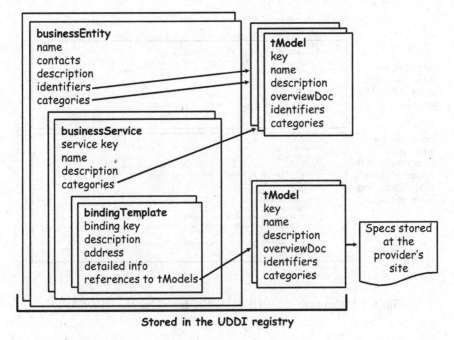

Stored in the UDDI registry

Fig. 6.13. A schematic view of a UDDI registry entry

The structure of a tModel is very simple, as shown in the example of Figure 6.14. The example presents a tModel describing the UDDI API, and specifically the operations provided to publishers in order to advertise their services (remember that UDDI is itself a Web service, and as such it can be described in a UDDI registry and has a WSDL interface). The actual content (the service description) resides within a document (the *overviewDoc*) to which the tModel points, but that is stored outside the registry, typically at the publisher's site (Figure 6.13).

In principle, a tModel (or, rather, the overviewDoc it refers to) can represent anything and can be written in any language. For example, one could define a tModel that describes an interface for a procurement service, and could do so by referring to an overviewDoc that contains specifications in natural language, WSDL, or in any other language for describing interfaces. In the context of Web services, of course, the idea is that the service description is done in WSDL. The tModel of Figure 6.14 includes two overviewDocs, one referring to the WSDL specifications and another containing a textual description of the API.

The content of the overviewDoc, being unstructured, is typically meant to be read by human beings, and not by an automated system. The important point is that, once a tModel is published with a UDDI registry, it is assigned a unique key. This simple feature, together with the fact that many UDDI

```
<tModel tModelKey="uddi:uddi.org:v3_publication">
    <name>uddi-org:publication_v3</name>
    <description>UDDI Publication API V3.0</description>
    <overviewDoc>
        <overviewURL useType="wsdlInterface">
http://uddi.org/wsdl/uddi_api_v3_binding.wsdl#UDDI_Publication_SoapBinding
        </overviewURL>
    </overviewDoc>
    <overviewDoc>
        <overviewURL useType="text">
            http://uddi.org/pubs/uddi_v3.htm#PubV3
        </overviewURL>
    </overviewDoc>
```

overviewDoc
(refer to WSDL
specs and to API
specs)

classification
information
(specifies that this
tModel is about
XML, WSDL, and
SOAP specs)

```
    <categoryBag>
        <keyedReference keyName="uddi-org:types:wsdl"
            keyValue="wsdlSpec"
            tModelKey="uddi:uddi.org:categorization:types"/>
        <keyedReference keyName="uddi-org:types:soap"
            keyValue="soapSpec"
            tModelKey="uddi:uddi.org:categorization:types"/>
        <keyedReference keyName="uddi-org:types:xml"
            keyValue="xmlSpec"
            tModelKey="uddi:uddi.org:categorization:types"/>
        <keyedReference keyName="uddi-org:types:specification"
            keyValue="specification"
            tModelKey="uddi:uddi.org:categorization:types"/>
    </categoryBag>
</tModel>
```

Fig. 6.14. Example of a UDDI tModel, describing the UDDI API

entries, possibly belonging to different services or businesses, may refer to the same tModel, is crucial to supporting both developers (design-time discovery) and clients (run-time binding). In fact, users can browse a UDDI registry, find services, examine the references to tModels (expressed through the unique keys embedded into bindingTemplate elements), read the tModels, and gain insights on what the service does, what is the interface, and whatever other information is included in the tModel. In this way, developers can understand how to develop client applications.

In addition, assume now that a developer knows that a certain tModel, say tModel number 327, describes an interface for supply chain services, as defined by a supply chain standardization consortium. Then, not only can the developer read the tModel to figure out how to write the client application, but he or she can also program the client so that it dynamically binds to a service that supports this standard interface; all that is needed is to program the client so that it searches a UDDI registry for services whose bindingTemplate references tModel 327.

The discussion above shows that UDDI does not impose languages for describing interfaces, properties, or semantics. This is left to other standardization consortia, and is considered irrelevant from a discovery and binding perspective. UDDI simply provides the means for publishing and finding such descriptions. Such an open approach enables flexibility and makes UDDI robust to evolution in the Web services scenario. It would simply be impossible to "hardcode" into the UDDI structure a collection of different standards: there are too many and they keep evolving.

Note that tModels can be used for more than just interfaces and protocols. For example, they are also used in UDDI for identification and classification. In fact, trying to come up with a limited set of classifications or identification schemes (e.g., assuming that everybody has a taxpayer number as unique identifier) would be too inflexible. A number of different schemes are used in different industries and in different countries. However, once again, this kind of agreement is not needed. Anyone can define a classification scheme in a tModel (say, a geographical classification scheme that divides the world into Europe, AustralAsia, the Americas, and Africa). A full description of the classification would be contained in the overviewDoc pointed to by the tModel. Then, entries in the registry can refer to this tModel and state that, with respect to it, they are classified as "Europe", for example. Again, if the unique key of the tModel defining the classification is known (say, key number 441), then clients can programmatically search for all businesses or services that, with respect to tModel 441, are classified as "Europe" or "Africa" or something else.

We also observe that, just like businesses and services, tModels can themselves reference other tModels, for example for classification purposes. This is also the case of the tModel in Figure 6.14, which refers to other tModels for classifying the information it is providing.

In addition to allowing custom taxonomies, UDDI also defines a categorization scheme (a specific tModel) that can be used to classify other tModels. This predefined classification scheme is defined by a tModel called *uddi-org:types*, and allows a developer to state, for example, that a tModel defines a WSDL interface or a SOAP message. In this way, clients can search for all tModels that are about WSDL descriptions or SOAP message specifications.

6.4.5 UDDI Registry API

UDDI registries have three main types of users to whom they expose their API: service providers that publish services, requesters that look for services, and other registries that need to exchange information. These clients can access the registry through six sets of APIs:

- The **UDDI Inquiry API** includes operations to find registry entries that satisfy search criteria and to get overview information about those entities (*find_business, find_service, find_binding, find_tModel*),   and operations that provide details about a specific entity (*get_businessDetail, get_serviceDetail, get_bindingDetail, get_tModelDetail*).   This API is meant to be used by UDDI browser tools that help developers find information and by clients at run-time, for dynamic binding.
- The **UDDI Publishers API** is directed to service providers. It enables them to add, modify, and delete entries in the registry. Examples of operations it supports are *save_business, save_service, save_binding* and *save_tModel*   for creating or modifying entries, and *delete_business,*

delete_service, delete_binding, and *delete_tModel*   for removing entries. Upon publication, the registry also assigns unique keys to the newly added entries.

- The **UDDI Security API** allows UDDI users to get and discard authentication tokens to be used in further communication with the registry (*get_authToken, discard_authToken*).
- The **UDDI Custody and Ownership Transfer API** enable registries to transfer the "custody" of information among themselves and to transfer ownership of these structures from one publisher to another. Messages exchanged in this API include *get_transferToken, transfer_entities*, and *transfer_custody*.
- The **UDDI Subscription API** enables the monitoring of changes in a registry by subscribing to track new, modified, and deleted entries. The Subscription API includes the following operations: *delete_subscription, get_subscriptionResults, get_subscriptions*, and *save_subscriptions*.
- The **UDDI Replication API** supports replication of information between registries, so that different registries can be kept synchronized.

UDDI registries maintain different access points (URIs) for requesters, publishers, and other registries. For example, Figure 6.15 depicts two UDDI registries (UDDI registry A and UDDI registry B). Each of these registries exposes an Inquiry API and a Publishers API for service requestors and providers to use, and Subscription, Replication, and Custody Transfer APIs for communicating with other UDDI registries. One reason for access point separation is that inquiries do not require authentication (they use standard HTTP) while other invocations require users to authenticate themselves with the registry (the interaction takes place through HTTPS).

Interaction with a UDDI registry takes place as a series of exchanges of XML documents, typically using SOAP. UDDI specifies the possible message exchanges in terms of requests and responses. It also specifies the structure of the XML documents included in the messages. Note that these details are hidden from the developer and user of Web services. Indeed, application servers today provide facilities both for publishing services in a UDDI registry and for searching the registry.

Interaction between registries is needed essentially for two purposes: transferring the custody of an entry and replicating information. Replication occurs according to protocols defined by UDDI, and it is used to keep registries synchronized on either a local or a global scale, depending on the nature of the registry. Although the information is replicated, each entry is "owned" by a single registry that, using UDDI terminology, has the *custody* of the entry. The registry that has the custody is the one the publisher has contacted when creating the new entry. Modifications to an entry can only be made at the registry that has the custody. In some cases, publishers may request to transfer the custody to another registry, perhaps because the previous custodian

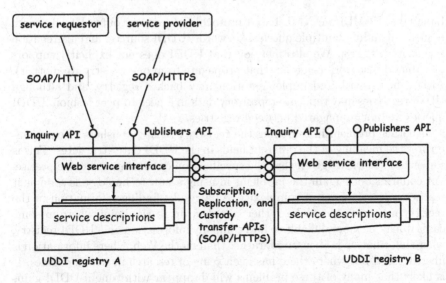

Fig. 6.15. Interaction with and between UDDI registries

is ceasing operations or because of contractual agreements. This triggers an inter-registry communication that occurs through the Custody Transfer API.

6.4.6 Searching the UDDI Registry

From a user's perspective, the most important of these APIs is the Inquiry API. It is quite interesting to observe that this API is intentionally kept simple. Only a few types of queries are allowed, as opposed to a more powerful and general query language (such as SQL). As such, the process to be followed for searching information is rather cumbersome. In principle, UDDI could have defined more complex APIs, allowing sophisticated searches. However, complex specifications also mean complex implementations. We have also seen that simple standards tend to be accepted much more easily than complex ones. This is especially true for new technologies such as Web services. A simple API is therefore a good compromise between functionality and ease of implementation. In addition, this approach leaves room for registry providers that offer additional query facilities, perhaps by charging a fee. In other words, it enables differentiation and competition while standardizing the basics.

Recently, several proposals for more sophisticated query capabilities have appeared, although they are outside the specification of the standards [3]. They include mechanisms that would extend UDDI to support discovery of resources according to characteristics that can change frequently and that are maintained by the service provider, as opposed to being maintained in the registry. An example of such characteristics could be the expected response time. Furthermore, an initial proposal has been made for the UDDI Search Markup

Language (USML), an XML-based protocol for carrying out a UDDI search request, including multiple queries, keywords, UDDI sources, and aggregation operators [22, 118]. We also mention that UDDI does not explicitly support distributed discovery (searches that propagate from one registry to another). Although a distributed implementation may back a registry, and although UDDI registries may replicate repository data in a peer-to-peer fashion, UDDI queries are not propagated between registries.

Another problem in searching the registry is that publishers often misinterpret the meaning of the different fields in the UDDI data structures. This is somewhat surprising given that the specification documents are quite precise, but confirms once again the problems in using a new technology as soon as it reaches a certain level of complexity. As a result, finding information in the registry may turn out to be rather complex, up to the point where in some cases it may be more difficult to find company information on a UDDI registry, where information is structured, rather than on the Web, where information is unstructured but where there has been years of research in search engines. It is likely that many of these problems will disappear with time if UDDI gains acceptance.

6.4.7 Storing WSDL Interfaces in a UDDI Registry

We have said earlier that UDDI does not impose any restriction on the languages used to describe interfaces or other properties of a service. It only provides a framework for publishing and searching such descriptions. This is important because it makes UDDI robust to changes in standards. Indeed, the very same mechanism can be used even as interface and service description languages continue to evolve. As such, WSDL and UDDI do not overlap. Instead, they complement each other. The adoption of WSDL is indeed so widespread (relative to the other Web services standards) that the UDDI consortium has released guidelines on how to use WSDL to describe service interfaces and store them in UDDI registries [55]. Note that these are only guidelines or, as they are called in UDDI, they are "best practices".

The suggested way of combining WSDL and UDDI is no different from what we would expect and what we have hinted to throughout this section. Essentially, WSDL interface definitions (specifically, port types and protocol bindings, but not ports and addresses) are registered as tModels, whose *overviewDoc* field will point to the corresponding WSDL document (Figure 6.16). Multiple services can then refer to the same tModel to state that they implement that WSDL interface and support that binding. The address at which the service is provided can be defined in a UDDI bindingTemplate. As we have seen, UDDI also recommends that tModels referring to WSDL specifications be classified as *wsdlSpec* in the *uddi-org:types* taxonomy. Thanks to this convention, clients can easily search for WSDL tModels in a UDDI registry. This is also the case for the example tModel shown in Figure 6.14.

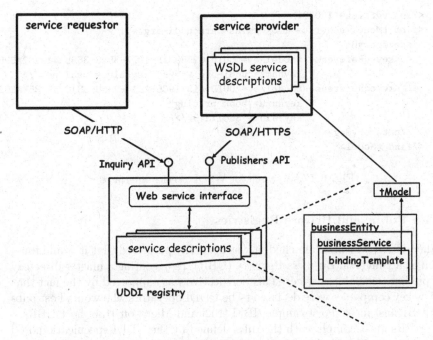

Fig. 6.16. A schematic view of the relation between UDDI and WSDL

Once such a tModel has been published, say by some industry consortium, programmers can retrieve this tModel description and implement a service that supports the published service interface definition. For example, a user could find WSDL service interface descriptions as follows:

1. Use the find_tModel message to retrieve a list of tModel keys corresponding to wsdlSpec entries. Additional qualifiers can be added to the find_tModel message in order to refine the search by limiting the set of tModels that are returned in the response to this find request. For example, the find_tModel message in Figure 6.17 can be used to locate all of the book pricing services that are defined using WSDL [36]. Note that the message contains two key values. The first specifies that desired service type should be classified as a "wsdlSpec" type in the *uddi-org:types* taxonomy. The second indicates that the service is classified as a "book pricing" service (in a custom taxonomy).
2. Use the get_tModelDetail message to retrieve the tModels for specific service interface descriptions.
3. Examine the overviewDoc field of a retrieved tModel in order to retrieve the contents of the WSDL service interface document.

```
<?xml version="1.0"?>
<find_tModel generic="1.0" xmlns="urn:uddi-org:api">
  <categoryBag>
    <keyedReference tModelKey="UUID:C25893AF-1977-3528-36B5-4192C2AB9E2C"
                    keyName="uddi-org:types" keyValue="wsdlSpec"/>
    <keyedReference tModelKey="UUID:A15019C5-AE14-236C-331C-650857AE0221"
                    keyName="book pricing"
                    keyValue="36611349"/>
  </categoryBag>
</find_tModel>
```

Fig. 6.17. A search for WSDL service interfaces

6.4.8 Public and Private Registries

When UDDI was first launched, it was generally perceived that it would function as a Universal Business Registry (UBR), representing a master directory of publicly available services. This perspective was supported by the fact that a few key companies were declared to be UDDI operators who would host public UBR instances. For example, IBM [102] and Microsoft [136] host UBRs.

UBRs must comply with the rules defined by the UDDI specification, and are supervised by OASIS. Being a UBR means in particular that the content of the registry must be kept consistent with the content of other UBRs, and changes in publications must be propagated to the other registries.

However, most of today's Web services applications are either intra-enterprise or shared between established and trusted business partners. Thus, UDDI has evolved in version 3.0 to support private UDDI registries in addition to the UBR model. UDDI Version 3 enables a variety of registry interaction models by supporting mechanisms such as publish/subscribe and replication among registries, which in turn enables the following types of architectures, identified by the Stencil Group [180]:

- A **public** registry, which provides open and public access to registry data. For example, a UBR is available as a well-known published Web site, and is a specific type of public UDDI registry. A public registry does not necessarily have to be a UBR and comply with the UDDI regulations for UBRs.
- A **private** registry, which is an internal registry isolated behind a firewall of a private intranet. For example, an enterprise might use such a registry to support the integration of its own internal applications.
- A **shared** or **semi-private** registry, which is deployed within a controlled environment and is shared with trusted partners. For example, a trading partner network might use a shared UDDI registry to support interoperability in a decentralized manner while ensuring the security of information about the systems in the network.

The reader interested in viewing a UDDI registry can browse the content of the UBRs hosted by IBM [102] and Microsoft [136]. A simple Web application placed on top of the registries enables access to their content via an ordinary browser, so that it is easy to look at these registries and get a feel for the kind of information stored in them.

6.5 Web Services at Work

Based on the discussions so far on SOAP, UDDI, and WSDL, it is possible to present some basic examples of how these specifications are being used. As we have done throughout the book, we will concentrate on concepts rather than on low level details.

To show how existing services can be made available as Web services, we discuss the case of *stored procedures*. A similar approach is used for a wide variety of conventional middleware services such as EJBs, CORBA objects, and COM objects. The process is graphically summarized by Figure 6.18, which combines the concepts presented throughout the chapter.

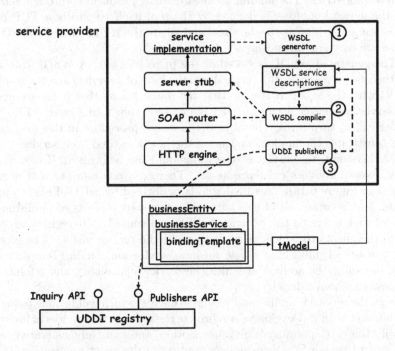

Fig. 6.18. Exposing an internal service as a Web service

Stored procedures allow the implementation of application logic to reside close to the database engine rather than within an external middleware layer.

They have the advantage of running within the scope of the database and, therefore, are in principle more efficient than similar code running outside the database. Using stored procedures it is possible to create an RPC-like interface to a database so that users do not need to worry about SQL, database schemas, or details of the data organization. They simply call the stored procedure that runs the corresponding query and returns the results as output parameters of the call. In a way, stored procedures are how services are implemented directly on a database. One of the first commercially available implementations of Web services has been in the form of tools that automatically transform a stored procedure into a Web service, a feature that is already available in many database management systems. These tools are either independent or part of XML extensions to database engines.

This process is conceptually very simple. The stored procedure already has a defined interface that specifies the name of the procedure, the parameters it takes, and the output it generates. This information can be automatically translated into a description of the Web service by mapping the information into the corresponding WSDL structures (step 1 in Figure 6.18). The mapping is obvious in all cases and it is not substantially different from the examples discussed for RPCs. The binding in most existing products is through SOAP, and the network address is defined by the tool itself (typically a TCP port on the same machine as the database and where the HTTP server and SOAP router are listening for messages).

The generated WSDL is stored at the provider's site. A WSDL compiler can then create a server stub (typically in the form of a servlet) and register the servlet with the SOAP router, so that the router knows that it has to invoke the servlet whenever a certain URI is invoked (step 2 in Figure 6.18). The servlet will in turn invoke the object (the stored procedure in this example). This constitutes the implementation of the newly created Web service.

At this point, the service is operational and can be invoked. However, nobody knows about its existence as yet. Therefore, one more step is needed (step 3 in Figure 6.18). This final step is performed by a UDDI client application, and is composed of two parts. The first part consists of publishing a tModel that refers to the generated WSDL in some UDDI registry accessible to the clients to which we want to make the service visible. The second part consists of publishing a new businessService and bindingTemplate entries, providing the address at which the service is available, and referencing the newly created tModel.

Now the service is on line and visible to clients, which will be able to find it and interact with it. Developers can browse the registry for services of interest, identify the corresponding WSDL description, automatically generate client-side stubs through WSDL compilers, and write the client application. Once the application has been developed, the next step consists of binding to a specific endpoint. Binding can occur either statically or dynamically, and in both cases it can occur through the UDDI registry.

The entire process illustrates how Web services are meant to be used in a completely transparent and highly automated manner. SOAP engines, WSDL compilers, and other development tools make the whole process transparent to developers of both clients and Web services, which can write applications as if they were making local calls. XML, SOAP, and WSDL are completely hidden from the programmers. Most application servers offer these and many more features (e.g., message tracking).

In the above discussion we have taken the perspective of the service provider exposing an existing service as a Web service. Another typical scenario is the one in which a WSDL specification has been defined by some standardization consortium, and a provider wants to offer a service compliant with the standardized interface. The process is similar to the one described above. The only difference is that now the WSDL is retrieved from the UDDI registry, following the pointer in the tModel up to the appropriate overviewDoc. Then, a WSDL compiler generates the code required on the server side. In the Java world, this consists of a servlet to be registered with the SOAP router and a Java interface that service implementations must extend. Once the service has been implemented and the object has been registered with the SOAP router, the Web service is again online and ready to be invoked. Its publication on the UDDI registry will occur as described above, with the exception that now there is no need to register the tModel, since it has been already registered by the consortium.

6.6 Interactions Between the Specifications

XML, SOAP, UDDI, and WSDL are heavily interrelated. They are being developed in parallel but changes in one have marked effects on the others. It is important to keep in mind the implications that certain features in one specification have on how the others are used.

6.6.1 Proliferation of Standards

As pointed out earlier, Web services will need to accommodate a large collection of already existing standards that specify how to exchange information in concrete application areas. As a result, Web services specifications need to be kept as generic as possible. We have already seen that SOAP and WSDL can support bindings to different communication protocols. In addition, specific application domains are likely to come up with their own specifications, possibly (but not necessarily) on top of WSDL, SOAP, and UDDI. The risk in this scenario is ending up with too many standards, which is analogous to having no standard at all.

Generality is certainly a solution to the lack of standardization. If no standard dominates, a generic architecture can be easily adapted to whatever specification comes along. Unfortunately, generality comes at a price. The reason is that, in practice, Web services are not being built from scratch. They are being built on top of existing multi-tier systems that are all but general. Hence, many Web services are biased from the start toward specific protocols, representations, and standards, i.e., those already supported by the underlying middleware. The necessary generality will only be achieved, if at all, by yet additional software layers. Even the WSDL specification has allowed for such generalization by providing alternative entry points to a given Web service (the *port types* in WSDL jargon).

What is then wrong with this picture? It has been argued that there is already too much middleware with competing and overlapping functionality [185]. The solution is to integrate middleware functionality into just a few system types, namely data federation systems, EAI, and application servers. Otherwise, the sheer complexity of the IT infrastructure becomes unmanageable. This is an argument often repeated in the middleware arena [26, 6], where real convergence was starting to take place. Web services, however, add new tiers to the already overly complex multi-tier architecture typical of B2B interactions. Translation to and from XML, tunneling of RPC through SOAP, clients embedded in Web servers, alternative port types, and many of the technologies typical of Web services do not come for free. They add significant performance overheads and increase the complexity of developing, tuning, maintaining, and evolving multi-tier systems.

Taken together, these two concerns (the proliferation of standards and the need for less heterogeneous middleware) create a difficult dilemma for Web services. The proliferation of competing standards, whether based on the same syntax (such as XML) or not, will require additional software layers to address interoperability problems. Even in the cases where a single set of standards can be used, Web services are almost universally being built as additional tiers over existing middleware platforms. Unfortunately, multi-tier architectures are already too complex and cumbersome. Adding more tiers will not make them any better and the sheer complexity and cost of such systems may prevent the widespread use of the technology. If technology instead consolidates around a few standards, at least as far as the basic abstractions are concerned, and all application vendors and developers start building around these standards, then it is possible to have middleware systems that are simpler to develop, deploy, and manage.

6.6.2 Advanced SOAP: Effects on Service Description and Discovery

The two most relevant trends affecting SOAP are its use in document-style interactions and the inclusion of attachments with binary data (or, more generally, non-XML data) as part of the specification. Both are unavoidable as they reduce overhead and make SOAP much more flexible when used for application integration (regardless of whether it occurs across the Internet or across a LAN). These new features, however, will have a significant impact on service description and discovery.

For instance, the use of binary data rather than XML for formatting application data has a wide range of implications. First, it will provide a vehicle for vertical (i.e., domain specific) B2B standards to survive even if Web services-related specifications become dominant. In practice, Web services will be used as a mechanism to tunnel interactions through the Internet. The actual interaction semantics will be supported by other standards, those used to encode the data in binary form (e.g., EDI). Similarly, Web services specifications that involve binary data will describe only the interaction; they will not describe the binary data. Such Web services cannot specify the actual programming interface of a service as this is hidden in the binary document and, therefore, cannot be controlled by the Web services infrastructure. This will reduce even further the chances of having tightly coupled architectures built around Web services. Finally, as related to service discovery, Web services based on binary formats will increase the dependency on human beings for binding to services, as much of the information needed to bind to a service might not be expressed according to widespread, horizontal Web services standards.

In a similar vein, using SOAP for exchanging documents, especially in batch mode, reinforces all these effects. Descriptions of Web services in these cases may have more to do with the interaction mechanism (the queues) than with the service interface. In fact, in many cases, the actual service interface will not necessarily be made explicit. A service may, for instance, simply indicate that it is a queue that accepts EDIFACT purchase order messages without describing them (since their format is already known to those using them, and documents are likely sent as binary data). Such interface descriptions drastically separate the mechanism for interaction (Web services) from the contents of the interaction (e.g., EDIFACT messages). Automation will happen bottom up: a middleware platform that for example supports EDIFACT messages will provide tools that will automatically generate and publish the WSDL description and registry entry for the corresponding Web service. However, consulting the UDDI registry will provide information only about the access channel. Building the corresponding messages requires in this case knowledge of EDIFACT and the appropriate support for it. Since information is encoded according to vertical standards, not common across Web services, the possibility for automation in service discovery is reduced.

6.6.3 UDDI and Dynamic Binding

The richness of the UDDI model may lead one to believe that dynamic binding will be a very common way of working with Web services. This is far from being the case, and there are several arguments against this assumption.

There are two main types of dynamic binding, that differ in the specificity of the client. The most generic one follows a model analogous to CORBA clients using the dynamic invocation interface (DII), where an object could actually query for a service it has never heard of and build on the fly a call to that service. Such level of dynamism makes sense (if at all) only in the very concrete, low level scenarios that appear almost exclusively when writing system software. Application designers have no use for such dynamic binding capabilities. How can one write a solid application without knowing which components will be called? It is nearly impossible to write sensible, reliable application logic without knowing which exceptions might be raised, which components will be used, which parameters these components take, etc. In this form, dynamic binding does not make sense at the application level, and this also holds true for Web services.

The second type of dynamic binding, more realistic and easier to implement, involves client applications searching for services supporting a specific set of interfaces and protocols. In UDDI, this can be done through tModels, as we have seen. The only "dynamic" aspects here are the provider and the location of the service. Everything else is hardcoded in the client application, which is written assuming a detailed knowledge of the service that will be invoked at run-time.

Even in this case, dynamic binding is only applicable in restricted contexts. In fact, in business-critical applications, interactions between different companies are regulated by contracts and business agreements. Without a proper contract, not many companies will interact with others. To think that companies will (or can) invoke the first Web service they find on the network is unrealistic. Web services-based B2B systems are therefore likely to be built by specialists who locate the necessary services, identify the interfaces, draw the necessary business agreements, and then design and build the actual applications.

With regard to dynamic binding as a fault-tolerance and load-balancing mechanism in the context of Web services, the UDDI registry is only applicable where performance is not a primary concern. In fact, UDDI has been designed neither with the response time capabilities not the facilities necessary to support these kinds of dynamic binding. Moreover, the UDDI registry can do neither any load balancing nor any automatic failover to a different URI in case of failures. Such problems are to be solved at the level of individual Web service providers using known techniques like replication, server clustering, and hot-backup.

Besides being directed to applications and being used for dynamic binding, UDDI can be also leveraged for design-time discovery. Users can browse or search the content of a registry for services of interest, read the service descriptions, and subsequently write clients that can interact with the discovered services. This is indeed the main usage mode of UDDI today.

Even design-time discovery, however, is not exempt from problems. First of all, as mentioned above, contracts or agreements are required before the interaction can take place. Secondly, even if it is a human being that reads the service description, understanding what a service does and how to configure a client to interact with it is not trivial. It is quite hard to define the semantics of a Web service in a manner that is unambiguous. Each operation, each parameter, each interaction should be completely and clearly defined for developers to write clients that can use the service in a correct way. Clearly, unless the Web service is trivial, this is a very challenging task.

6.7 Related Standards

There are many related proposals for standards that build upon the basic ones described in this chapter. In what follows we discuss some of them.

6.7.1 WS-Addressing

In Section 6.2 we have noted that SOAP relies on transport bindings to indicate the address of the receiver. WS-Addressing [30] proposes a protocol-neutral mechanism for specifying endpoint references of services within SOAP messages. It defines an endpoint reference as consisting of an address (a URI) and a set of reference properties that uniquely identify the target instance. The URI typically points to an application that dispatches the message correctly, based on the reference properties. For example, consider a service defined in WSDL that takes purchase orders from clients and returns confirmation IDs. An implementation of this service may be done by creating one stateful persistent object for each new client, which manages all the interactions with that client. In this case, when a purchase order request is received from a client at the URI specified in WSDL, it has to be directed to the service instance object which handles that client. Implementing such a dispatch mechanism requires the identity of the client to be present in the SOAP header as well. This is what WS-Addressing enables. Using WS-Addressing endpoint references, a client can specify both the URI of the receiver and *reference properties* that uniquely identify which service instance object will handle a request. In our example, where a different service instance handles each client, the reference properties would contain a *client-id* property, which uniquely identifies a client, which in turn uniquely identifies the target service instance object.

The specification describes how service instance endpoints are described and how SOAP messages should carry standardized header blocks that help in identifying a single service instance. WS-Addressing relies on a protocol-neutral mechanism to describe these header blocks because the mechanisms provided by the underlying transport protocol may be insufficient to specify the reference properties. For instance, the URI of a service's port can be described as an SMTP "to" address. But there is no place in the header of a standard SMTP message for including reference properties such as client-id from the above example.

6.7.2 WS-Routing

Another related problem in SOAP messages is that of routing. The intermediaries in a SOAP path are essentially the same as (or a subset of) the intermediaries in the underlying transport protocol. This means that there is no way of specifying which intermediaries should be visited by a SOAP message en route to its destination. Being able to specify such a path has its advantages. It allows pipeline architectures to be built, where a client forwards the SOAP message to a sequence of nodes, which in turn can further change the path to be taken by that SOAP message. This is also useful for systematically adding functionality to the processing of a SOAP message by adding and removing headers. For instance, a set of nodes along a SOAP path can gradually add more header blocks that include security, tracking, and other information. Similarly, on the receiver's side, a series of SOAP nodes can parse and remove each of those headers. Without a standardized approach to defining a path, none of the SOAP nodes have any control on how the message actually travels.

WS-Routing is a proposal for specifying a SOAP path as part of a SOAP message header [138]. Simply put, it is a sequence of references to SOAP nodes. The message travels from one node to another in the order specified by this sequence. When a node reads the message, it removes its own reference from the sequence, does the necessary processing, and forwards the message to the next node. Each node can also update the path in the header to include new nodes or to remove existing ones.

6.7.3 WS-Security

When SOAP first appeared, it was heavily criticized for lacking what many considered fundamental properties of any middleware infrastructure: security, reliable messaging, and transactions. Such criticism is somewhat unjustified. It is true that without support for some of these properties the practical value of any middleware platform is rather questionable. This also applies to SOAP. However, SOAP was not intended as the security or transaction mechanism for Web services. As its name implies, SOAP was intended as a simple mechanism for turning service invocations into XML messages, exchanging such messages across the Internet, and unfolding the XML message into a service invocation at the receiving site. Properties such as transactions or security were meant to be built on top of the SOAP specification. In the next chapter we will discuss in detail some of these properties. Here, we will briefly describe how SOAP can be enhanced for secure interactions between two Web services.

WS-Security is an extension to SOAP that can be used to implement integrity and confidentiality [13]. Important as it is from the point of view of Web services middleware, the only thing that WS-Security does is to define a SOAP header block (called *Security*) which can carry a signature; this is where security information is to be included. It also indicates how the Security block must be processed by nodes receiving the message. The specification also defines what elements can be found within the block and how they must be processed. Examples of the elements defined are *Username Token* (used to provide user name and password information) and *BinarySecurityToken* (used to include security certificates and keys).

WS-Security addresses a fundamental need for end-to-end application-level security that is otherwise ignored by underlying protocols such as HTTPS. HTTPS allows an entire payload (including the SOAP message) to be encrypted. However, there are a few drawbacks to this approach that necessitate the need for a higher-level security standard. First, HTTPS is a hop-by-hop security mechanism and not an end-to-end security mechanism. For instance, if an HTTPS message flows between two endpoints while flowing through multiple HTTPS intermediaries, each intermediary can decrypt and re-encrypt the message. There is no way to encrypt the SOAP message from the initiating application to the ultimate receiver.

Second, application-level security enables portions of a SOAP message to be encrypted rather than the entire transport message payload. For example, it should be possible to encrypt just the body of a SOAP message (so that SOAP intermediaries can process the headers) or even just a block within a body. The latter is needed, for instance, to encrypt just the credit card information in a SOAP message for ordering goods, while leaving the rest of the message un-encrypted. WS-Security is aimed at solving these problems.

WS-Security illustrates how much of the ongoing work around Web services middleware is now focused on agreeing on message formats and protocols rather than on overall external architectures. SOAP provides the basic vehicle for exchanging information. Once in place, additional standards are needed for the contents of the information being exchanged within SOAP messages.

6.7.4 WS-Policy

There are a number of factors that a client has to consider before interacting with a service. Similarly, there are a number of factors that a service has to consider before it accepts a client. We have already seen some examples in the standards discussed so far. For instance, WSDL defines the methods, data encoding formats, and protocols supported by a service. For a client and a Web service to communicate, they should agree on all these definitions. Similarly, the security mechanisms supported by a service are described in WS-Security. Only clients that adhere to or are satisfied by these mechanisms will use the service.

WS-Policy is a proposal for a framework through which clients and services can express their requirements, capabilities, and preferences (commonly referred to as *policies*) to each other in an interoperable manner [34]. It defines a set of generic constructs for defining and grouping *policy assertions*. An assertion is a representation of a single preference, capability, or requirement. For example, an assertion may state that a service requires a certain authentication mechanism.

A complex policy often has a number of such assertions, some of which should be applied together as a set, some of which are alternatives to others, and some of which are mutually exclusive. For instance, a service may require one of two supported authentication mechanisms. In addition, it may further specify that an audit trail will be taken whenever the first mechanism is used. For these purposes, assertions in WS-Policy are grouped using operators such as *All* or *ExactlyOne*. An All operator implies that all assertions within the group should hold while ExactlyOne implies that only one assertion within the group should hold. The latter is used to express that a choice has to be made between two sets of assertions (for e.g., between two authentication mechanisms). Multiple levels of grouping (for e.g., an All operator nested within an ExactlyOne operator) allow flexible combinations of assertions.

WS-Policy does not define how policies are attached to services. Instead, it describes an abstract entity called *policy subject* to which a policy is bound. An endpoint defined in WSDL is one particular example of a policy subject. In fact, there is another proposal called WS-PolicyAttachment that describes how to attach policies to WSDL endpoints, WSDL type definitions, and UDDI entities [33].

Further, WS-Policy does not define any domain-specific policies. It only provides a framework through which domain-specific policies can be described. The task of describing the actual policies is left to other standards. For example, WS-Policy does not define a language for specifying authentication policies. It just defines a way to group them. Thus, we can anticipate other standards to build on the WS-Policy framework, just like they use WSDL for defining interfaces.

6.7.5 Web Services Invocation Framework (WSIF)

Although Web services specifications are general in spirit, in most cases SOAP has taken a dominant role in terms of bindings for services described in WSDL. Hence, when working with a tool that supports WSDL, it is likely that the design will be based on SOAP because that will probably be the only binding supported by the tool. Thus, even if WSDL is generic and allows the specification of many different bindings, using a binding other than SOAP usually means that the development will no longer be supported by most tools.

Following the idea that Web services should be truly transparent and with the intention of making WSDL specifications truly generic, IBM proposed in October 2001 the *Web Services Invocation Framework* (WSIF) [145], which has been now donated to the Apache Software Foundation for inclusion in the set of tools under that name. WSIF is a pluggable framework that allows *providers* to be added to an existing Web services infrastructure. A provider is an implementation of a WSDL binding that allows a service to be invoked through this binding. In other words, WSIF is used to hide from the developer the type of binding used by a Web service. The idea is to use a standard description of the binding and to let the Web service infrastructure automatically do the rest.

By using providers, the user of a Web service needs to only worry about the abstract service descriptions (i.e., messages, operations, and PortTypes). The binding information can be ignored as it is now the responsibility of the infrastructure to take care of selecting the appropriate protocols to contact a Web service. In WSIF, the port and binding to be used can be determined at either deployment or configuration time by using the corresponding provider. These WSIF providers can function as stubs or as dynamic link libraries (DLLs). In both cases, the client or service requester must obtain a port (in DLLs) or a stub (in stub-based providers) before invoking the service. This way, the service is invoked in exactly the same way independently of the bindings used.

WSIF reinforces the trend toward hiding the details of Web services specifications. In an ideal case, the WSIF provider could even be made available by the service itself when it is advertised so that potential users need only to pay attention to the abstract interface description of the Web service and leave the details of the binding to the provider. WSIF also opens the door to a more efficient use of Web services within conventional middleware and EAI settings. The vendor of a concrete middleware platform needs only to develop the corresponding WSIF provider. Using the techniques described in the previous section, services can be posted as Web services and used by linking to the WSIF provider, either from the same middleware platform or another one. Together with WSDL, WSIF constitutes an excellent vehicle for standardizing the interfaces of different middleware platforms.

6.8 Summary

In this chapter we have discussed SOAP, WSDL, and UDDI as the basic Web services technologies.

Interactions between Web services happen through SOAP. SOAP specifies messages as documents encoded in XML, and defines bindings to actual transport protocols. A binding specifies how a SOAP message is transmitted using protocols such as HTTP or SMTP. SOAP can be best understood when it is considered as the specification of a protocol wrapper rather than a communication protocol itself. Its main purpose is to provide a standardized way to encode different interaction mechanisms into XML documents. As such, each concrete interaction mechanism needs a SOAP specification. An example is the specification of how to use RPC over HTTP. The specification describes how to encode an RPC invocation into an XML document and how to transmit the XML document using HTTP.

The interface to a Web service is defined using WSDL. This language enables designers to specify the type system used in the interface definition, the operations offered by the service along with the messages necessary to invoke them, and the binding to the actual protocol to be used to invoke the operations (e.g., SOAP). What is known as *service* in WSDL is a logical unit encompassing several interfaces, typically aimed at providing the same logical service (e.g., flight reservations), but through different access mechanisms or interaction paradigm (e.g., asynchronous messaging or RPC).

Service discovery in Web services is based on the UDDI specification. UDDI defines the structure of a Web services registry and a set of APIs to interact with the registry. Entries in the registry contain information about the service provider (e.g., address, contact person), categorization information, and information about the service interface and pointers to the service provider (where the actual WSDL interface definition can be found). The APIs essentially enable providers to publish descriptions of their services and allow requesters to look for services of interest. There are already several UDDI registries that are publicly accessible, and that are maintained by software vendors such as IBM and Microsoft. These public registries are meant as low-level, generic systems supporting only the most basic interactions. The underlying idea is that more sophisticated repositories (e.g., with advanced querying capabilities) will be built on top of UDDI repositories. Such *Web service databases*, however, are not part of the UDDI specification. For obvious reasons, industrial-strength Web service implementations are likely to be based on private repositories rather than on public ones. It remains to be seen to what extent private repositories will use UDDI, since much of its functionality is not needed for private use.

The syntax for all these specifications is based on XML. However, WSDL and SOAP support alternative type systems. UDDI may contain pointers to service descriptions written in languages other than WSDL. In any case, UDDI, WSDL, and SOAP should be seen as templates rather than strict standards. The fact that two Web services use WSDL and SOAP does not necessarily make them compatible. One of them could be an RPC service accessible through HTTP. The other could be a batch service accessible through e-mail and using EDIFACT. Both are Web services compliant with accepted specifications and yet perfectly incompatible.

These three specifications are becoming increasingly complex and their interactions are all but simple. Developments in one area may affect what can be done in others. The take-home message is that all these specifications are still evolving and it is still early to identify all of their crucial elements. Designers of the specifications are trying to generalize them as much as possible but the jury is still out on the extent to which this generic approach will prevail over more efficient, narrower specifications covering a few widely used cases.

7

Service coordination protocols

The basic Web services infrastructure presented in the previous chapter suffices to implement simple interactions. In particular, it supports interactions where the client invokes a single operation on a Web service. When the interaction involves coordinated sequences of operations, additional abstractions and tools are needed to ensure the correctness and consistency of the interactions. This is no different from how conventional middleware evolved. RPCs support simple, one-call-at-a-time interactions between clients and servers. Adding guarantees to the interactions (e.g., transactions), requires additional protocols (e.g. two-phase commit) and an infrastructure that supports the necessary abstractions and the corresponding protocols (e.g., a TP monitor). The same applies to Web services. Once we go beyond simple, independent service invocations, new protocols, abstractions, and infrastructures are needed.

This chapter focuses on such infrastructures for Web services. More precisely, it deals with the extensions necessary to support *coordination* among Web services. Thus, we discuss how complex interactions among Web services can be modeled, which abstractions can be provided to simplify Web services development, and how the middleware infrastructure can support such abstractions and enforce the properties assigned to the coordination. As we will see, the need for modeling and supporting coordination has led to many different standardization efforts, not always coordinated and sometimes even competing. Hence, the material covered in this chapter must be taken with a grain of salt in that, although Web services will certainly incorporate such features, the final form that these features will take is not yet clear.

In the following we discuss coordination protocols (Section 7.1) and the infrastructure needed to support their execution (Section 7.2). We also present concrete specifications that add coordination support to the technologies presented earlier: WS-Coordination (Section 7.3), defining a coordination protocol infrastructure; WS-Transaction (Section 7.4), aiming to provide transactional semantics to coordination protocols; and RosettaNet (Section 7.5), a relatively successful example of coordination protocols. Finally, Section 7.6 briefly describes other standardization proposals for coordination protocols.

7.1 An Introduction to Coordination Protocols

7.1.1 The Need for Coordination

In real applications, interactions are typically more complex than single, independent invocations. Using a particular service typically involves performing sequences of operations in a particular order. Sometimes, these sequences of operations might even involve more than one Web service. For example, consider a *supplier* Web service where clients can connect to buy certain items. As part of the purchasing procedure, clients typically have to identify themselves, request a quote for prices and delivery time, place the order according to the quote received, and submit the payment (Figure 7.1). All of these operations are necessary and they must be performed in a given order.

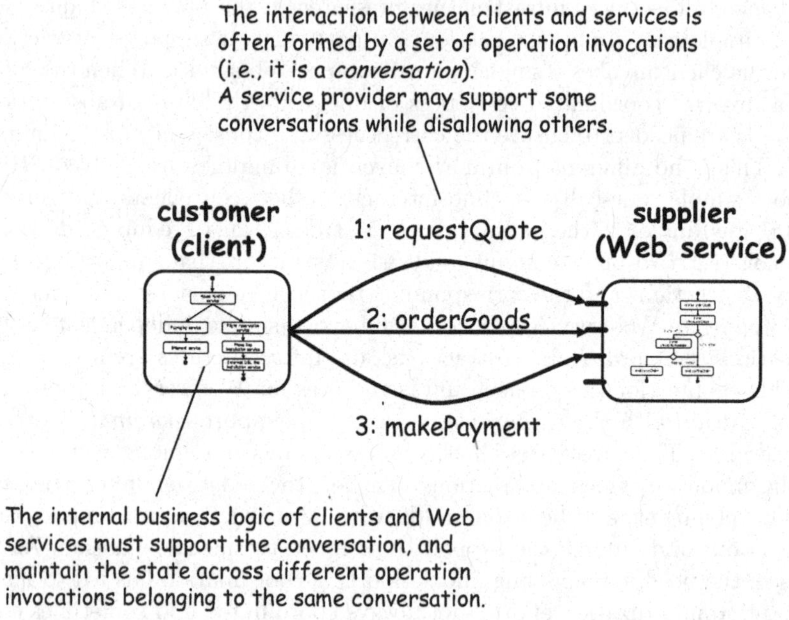

The interaction between clients and services is often formed by a set of operation invocations (i.e., it is a *conversation*).
A service provider may support some conversations while disallowing others.

customer (client)   1: requestQuote   **supplier (Web service)**

2: orderGoods

3: makePayment

The internal business logic of clients and Web services must support the conversation, and maintain the state across different operation invocations belonging to the same conversation.

Fig. 7.1. A sample conversation between a client and a Web service

Moving from simple, independent invocations to sequences of operations where their order matters has important implications from both an internal (implementation) and an external (interaction) perspective. From an internal perspective, the client must be able to execute relatively complex procedures to perform the different operations in the appropriate order. The client must also be capable of maintaining context information (e.g., the purchase order number) that needs to be forwarded from one operation to the next. As a result, the internal logic at the client is necessarily more complex. This logic can be developed using conventional programming languages. A better approach, however, is to use *service composition*, typically in the form of a workflow system tailored to Web services.

From an external perspective, the implication is that the interaction between the client and the server has to obey certain constraints. As already mentioned, a Web service may allow its operations to be invoked only in a specified order. In the example above, the supplier allows the *requestQuote*, *orderGoods*, and *makePayment* operations to be executed only in that order. Clients should always request a quote before they submit an order, and should always submit an order before they make a payment. If these constraints are not followed, the Web service will be unable to process the messages and will return an error to the client.

In what follows, we will use the term *conversation* to refer to the sequences of operations (i.e., message exchanges) that could occur between a client and a service as part of the invocation of a Web service. We will use the term *coordination protocol* to refer to the specification of the set of correct and accepted conversations.

Conversations and coordination, although related to each other, present different problems and require different abstractions. On the internal side, the problem is how to make it easy for developers to specify complex procedures that can implement the logic required to conduct a conversation. This is an implementation problem. Possible solutions will involve developing models, abstractions, and tools that facilitate the effort of implementing a given conversation. Being about implementation, the abstractions and tools used internally and the details of the business logic are private and are not disclosed to the other parties, just as the implementation of an interface is private.

On the interaction side, the problem is how a Web service can describe the set of coordination protocols it supports and make the clients aware of this information. In fact, just like WSDL interfaces, the description of coordination protocols supported by a service should be advertised in Web services registries, so that programmers can discover how to develop clients that can interact correctly with a Web service.

In this chapter we focus on the external interactions among Web services, specifically on coordination protocols and related middleware. The internal implementations of clients and Web services (and specifically the implementation by means of service composition techniques) is discussed at length in the following chapter, along with the relation between external interactions and internal implementations.

7.1.2 Modeling Conversations between a Client and a Web Service

We start by focusing on conversations between two parties, e.g., a client and a Web service. We will later extend the discussion to conversations among multiple services. Specifically, the problem we address here is how a Web service can specify the set of correct conversations that a client should support to interact with it.

A common way to describe the set of correct conversations is by means of a state machine. In such a state machine, the states define each possible stage of a correct conversation (Figure 7.2). For example, the procurement conversation described above can be in the *quote requested, goods ordered, order completed*, or *order canceled* state. A conversation is in one and only one state at any time.

Each state can have one or more output transitions, each labeled with a different operation name corresponding to one of the operations offered by the Web service interface. The semantics are such that when the conversation is in state S, only operations associated with output transitions of S can be invoked. Upon the invocation of one of these operations, the conversation changes state according to the operation executed (following the output transition corresponding to the operation that took place). In the figure, state *goods ordered* has two possible operations: *cancelOrder* and *makePayments*. The next state to which the conversation will transition after *goods ordered* depends on which one of the two possible operations is executed. If the operation invoked is not among those associated with the output transitions of S, then an error is returned to the client (in the procurement example, this can happen if, for example, the *orderGoods* operation is invoked while the conversation is in the *goods ordered* state). Therefore, given the set of operations provided by a Web service interface, such a specification determines the set of correct conversations by defining which interface operation can be invoked, based on the conversation state. This specification becomes then the coordination protocol for that particular Web service.

Although simple, the example in the figure illustrates well how a provider can specify how to correctly interact with its services, complementing the information available from the WSDL interface description. A number of specifications have been proposed that enhance this basic idea in various ways. However, what is important is having a standardized way to specify coordination protocols. Such standardization could eventually lead to tools that automatically support and control the conversations involving Web services. As long as such standardization does not occur, each Web service will specify coordination protocols in a different manner, thereby making it difficult to come up with generic solutions for building correct conversations and enforcing them. Current attempts at standardization, such as the *Web Services Conversation Language* (WSCL) [14], have had only limited success at this stage.

7.1.3 Modeling Conversations among Multiple Web Services

The previous discussion assumed a single client interacting with a Web service. Hence, it only addressed the problem of how the Web service can tell the client which sequences of operations are valid. In reality, the problem is often more

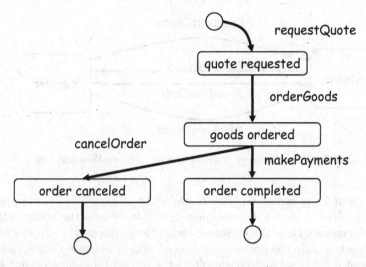

Fig. 7.2. Specification of a conversation using a state machine model. The rounded boxes are states, while the labels on the edges denote operations associated with the state where the edge originates

complex, since the client may not just be code that follows the conversation specification but it may itself be a Web service. The problem then becomes how to specify conversations between Web services (also called *multi-party conversations*), as both sides impose constraints on how the conversation must proceed.

The need for conversations between Web services is not a far-fetched idea. In fact, it is implicit in the more asynchronous nature of Web services interactions with respect to what happened in conventional middleware, meaning that replies to a request are often modeled and implemented as other operations, this time invoked by the provider on the requestor. Furthermore, as discussed in the previous chapter, WSDL operation invocations are modeled, on the requestor's side, by out/in (solicit/response) operations that in turn correspond to the invocation of in/out (request/reply) operations on the provider's side. The obvious consequence of this coupling is that the requestor is also acting as a Web service, and it also expects its operations to take place in certain order. Consider for example the message exchange of Figure 7.3, describing a procurement conversation between two Web services. The customer would be very confused if it received a *confirmOrder* message before actually placing the order.

The problem of expressing valid conversations among Web services is independent of the number of Web services involved. To illustrate the problem in its full generality, consider again the procurement example. Assume that when the Web service acting as a supplier receives an order, it contacts a warehouse to check whether the material is in stock and whether it can be shipped

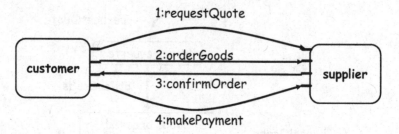

Fig. 7.3. A procurement conversation among two Web services

on the requested day before replying to the client (Figure 7.4). The supplier delivers a positive reply to the customer only if it receives the confirmation from the warehouse. Once the customer makes the payment, the supplier asks the warehouse to ship the goods as requested. The warehouse then arranges the shipment directly with the client. Once the physical shipment occurs, the customer confirms the receipt of the goods to the warehouse, and the warehouse in turn confirms the delivery to the supplier, thereby completing the conversation.

Although apparently convoluted, the example in Figure 7.4 is much simplified with respect to a real procurement procedure. For example, we have not considered exceptions, the possibility of executing alternative conversations depending on run-time conditions, the fact that service providers may play different roles in a multi-party conversation (and therefore behave differently depending on the role they assume), etc.

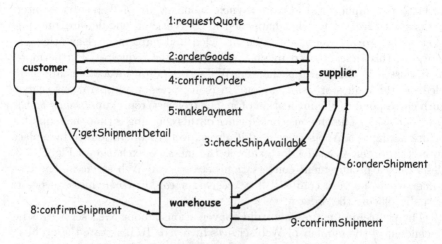

Fig. 7.4. The *procurement* protocol

The notation of Figure 7.4 shows one of the possible ways to describe coordination protocols. As in the client/server case, there is no agreed upon way on how to do this. However, the basic philosophy is the same in all approaches: protocol languages allow the definition of a protocol in terms of *roles* (e.g., supplier, customer, warehouse) and of message exchanges among entities playing those roles, along with constraints on the order in which such exchanges should occur.

For example, one possible technique consists of using state machines analogous to the one of Figure 7.2, although extensions are needed so that they can cope with multi-party conversations. In fact, in Figure 7.2 transitions were simply labeled with operation names, which was acceptable in client/server conversations since the assumption was that a client was invoking an operation offered by the service (in other words, the roles were implicitly defined). In multi-party settings we can still use state machines in the same way, as long as we associate with each transaction not just an operation name, but a triplet *<invoker, operation, provider>* (e.g., <customer, orderGoods, supplier>), meaning that the state transition occurs when the *invoker* calls the specified *operation* offered by the *provider*. If we do not specify the roles, then it is not clear if and when the transition should occur, since multiple parties may in principle offer the same operation, and multiple parties may invoke that operation. Otherwise, the semantics of the state machine and the way it constrains the set of correct conversations is analogous to the client/server case, and is not discussed further.

Another common model for describing protocols is that of *sequence diagrams* (Figure 7.5), that once again emphasize the presence of roles and message exchanges among roles as the basic ingredients of a protocol description. As the reader can appreciate, sequence diagrams are widely used for their simplicity and intuitiveness: by looking at such a diagram it is very easy to understand the protocol. However, their limitation is that when the protocol becomes complex, one sequence diagram does not suffice. In fact, most protocols are much more convoluted than the one shown in Figure 7.5. In particular, rather than modeling just a single conversation, it is common to describe alternative conversations to be executed depending on run-time conditions.

Consider again the procurement scenario described above. In Figures 7.4 and 7.5 we assumed that the warehouse always has goods in stock and is always available for shipping at the desired date. In practice this is not always true, and therefore a procurement coordination protocol typically includes the description of additional (or alternative) message exchanges to cover this situation. For example, such messages could include negotiations with the customer about an alternative delivery date, or interactions among warehouses to verify whether it is possible to supply and ship the goods through a different warehouse.

There are many ways in which alternative conversations can be modeled. One approach is that of using multiple sequence diagrams. This is a common

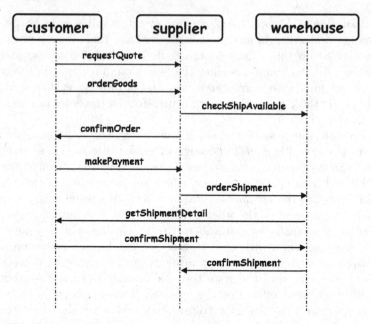

Fig. 7.5. The procurement protocol modeled as a sequence diagram

approach when describing protocols such as TCP, and is applicable only when there are few alternatives, otherwise too many diagrams are required.

Another approach is to use *activity diagrams* [154], or some other variations of flow chart models, re-interpreted and modified to make them suitable for defining protocols. As an example, Figure 7.6 shows the procurement protocol modeled with this technique. The "activities" (rounded boxes) in the figure correspond to messages sent by a Web service playing a certain role to another Web service, playing a different role. As such, they represent the invocation of synchronous or asynchronous operations. The figure shows that the protocol defines two possible, alternative scenarios, depending on whether the supplier decides to accept or reject the order. This is modeled by the condition following the invocation of the operation checkShipAvailable, graphically depicted by a diamond. In this way, activity diagrams can model alternative executions within a single figure. Analogous constructs are provided to model *parallel* executions, to specify protocols in which, at some point in the conversation, two or more operations need to be invoked and there are no particular ordering constraints among them. As we will see in this and in the following chapter, activity diagrams (or variations thereof) seem to be quickly becoming the preferred approach to describing protocols, due to their intuitiveness and their ability to easily model alternative and parallel executions.

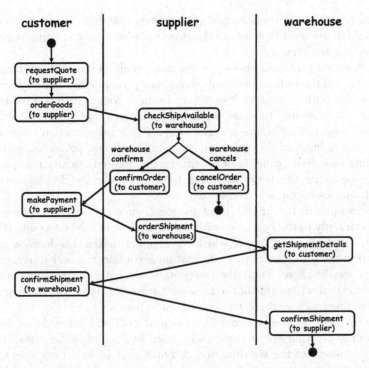

Fig. 7.6. The procurement protocol modeled as an activity diagram

7.1.4 Service Interfaces and Coordination Protocols

There is a clear similarity between service interfaces and coordination protocols: both of them describe how to interact with Web services. Indeed, as for interfaces, the ultimate goal of coordination protocols is to facilitate design-time discovery and run-time binding. Design-time discovery is possible since, by knowing the coordination protocol supported and the role the service plays in that protocol, programmers can develop applications to interact with the Web service. Dynamic binding is also possible since applications (e.g., customers) designed to understand a certain protocol (e.g., the procurement protocol) can restrict their search for Web services to those supporting some other role (e.g., supplier) in the same protocol. How to technically publish and make this information known is clear. Coordination protocols can be published as tModels (assuming that a UDDI-compliant registry is used). The fact that a Web service plays a certain role can be described as bindingTemplate elements referring to the tModels containing the coordination protocol. Again, this is analogous to how interfaces are published and discovered. In the next chapter, once we have introduced service composition (which can be seen as an implementation technique for complex Web services), we will also show that protocol descriptions can be used to generate skeletons that support the implementation of a service playing a certain role, much like interfaces in CORBA/IDL are used to generate skeletons to be used as a starting point for implementing the service.

Coordination protocols also share the same goals as interfaces in terms of information hiding. In fact, protocols should not reveal details of how they are implemented, both to protect proprietary business logic which companies do not want to expose and to make the interaction more robust to changes. For interfaces, information hiding consists of specifying an operation's signature without describing how the operation is implemented. For protocols, information hiding essentially consists of describing the allowed operation sequences without specifying the logic according to which a service decides between different options within a conversation.

For example, in the procurement protocol, once the supplier receives an order it can reply to the customer with either a *confirmOrder* or a *cancelOrder* message. The logic according to which the supplier makes this decision is not described in the protocol, as this information is confidential and is technically irrelevant for the client. Similarly, the protocol does not describe how a Web service determines the value of the message parameters (e.g., the price quoted to the customer as a reply to the *quoteRequest* message).

Another issue related to coordination protocols and information hiding consists of generating *role-specific views* from protocol specifications. These views are subsets of the coordination protocol that include only operations and messages involving a service playing a given role. Such views can be either explicitly specified or automatically derived from the global specification of the protocol. To understand the need for role-specific views, consider again the procurement protocol. In this protocol, Web services playing the customer role are not interested in the interactions between the supplier and the warehouse, but only in message exchanges that involve the customer. The rest is not relevant to them, and there is no reason for customers to be concerned with message exchanges among other parties, both in terms of design-time discovery and run-time binding. Therefore, consistent with the principles of information hiding, each role should only be concerned with its role-specific view of the protocol, and not with the whole protocol. As an example, Figure 7.7 shows the procurement protocol seen from a customer perspective, i.e., including only message exchanges involving the customer.

Assuming that a UDDI registry is used to advertise protocol descriptions, the different views will be registered as different tModels. If the customer view of the procurement protocol is, say, tModel 681, then all customers need is to find Web services playing the supplier role in the protocol represented by tModel 681. Even if the interaction between a supplier and a warehouse changes, the supplier is still playing the supplier role in the protocol represented by tModel 681, and therefore customers will still be able to bind to it and interact correctly with it.

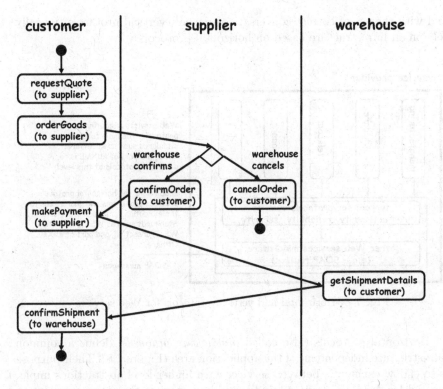

customer   **supplier**   **warehouse**

Fig. 7.7. The "customer view" of the procurement protocol. Only message exchanges involving the customer are described

7.1.5 Classifying Web Services Protocols

Web services protocols can be classified into *vertical* and *horizontal* protocols. Vertical protocols are specific to business areas, and are applicable only within those domains (which is why they are also called *business protocols*). Typically, they specify in great detail how to conduct concrete business transactions, the documents involved, the format of these documents, and the semantics of both the contents of the documents and the operations involved in sending and receiving them. Many such vertical protocols are related to previous B2B protocols, like EDI, that are now being extended to support XML and the notion of Web services. Examples of vertical protocols are xCBL and RosettaNet (discussed later in his chapter). The procurement protocol described in the previous sections is also an example of a vertical protocol.

In the big picture of Web service protocols, vertical protocols are domain-specific modules, typically depicted as vertical pillars in protocol infrastructure diagrams (Figure 7.8). Vertical protocols, however, do not necessarily include all low level details of, for example, how to exchange messages. They concern themselves much more with the semantic aspects of the exchanges and with the set of correct conversations. Hence, vertical protocols typically rely on an infrastructure based on horizontal protocols.

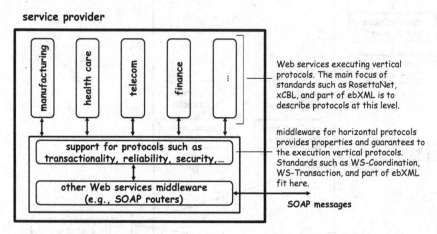

Fig. 7.8. Horizontal and vertical protocols for Web services

Horizontal protocols (also called *middleware protocols*) define a common infrastructure independent of the application area (Figure 7.8). Their purpose is to endow exchanges between services with higher-level abstractions implemented by the Web services middleware in a manner that is transparent to Web services developers. This is analogous to what happened in conventional middleware, where abstractions and protocols (such as Transactional RPC and 2PC) were developed to extend basic interoperability technologies (such as RPC). Other examples of important properties provided by conventional middleware are reliability and service management functionality.

Although the desired properties are similar, the issues are more complex in Web services, especially due to their cross-enterprise nature and to the lack of trust between parties when interactions occur across enterprise boundaries. Therefore, many of the assumptions behind existing technologies no longer hold in the context of Web services. For example, as also mentioned in Chapter 5, keeping resources locked for the entire duration of a 2PC protocol is no longer an appropriate solution for long-running business transactions across trust domains. Therefore, protocols providing transactional support will have to take these additional challenges into considerations. In this chapter we will examine in detail two important examples of horizontal protocols: *WS-Coordination* and *WS-Transaction*.

Vertical and horizontal protocols are often combined, with horizontal protocols being executed by the middleware to provide properties to the execution of vertical protocols. In a typical scenario, Web services implement and execute vertical protocols, such as the procurement one described above. To guarantee properties to the different messages of a procurement conversation, the middleware executes horizontal protocols. For example, the middleware can ensure guaranteed delivery or transactional semantics to the procurement conversations executed by the Web services.

7.2 Infrastructure for Coordination Protocols

The execution of a conversation compliant with a vertical or horizontal protocol can be supported by the middleware, with varying degrees of automation.

7.2.1 Conversation Controllers

Tools facilitating the execution of conversations are called *conversation controllers*. They provide two kinds of functionality: *conversation routing* and *protocol compliance verification*.

Conversation routing refers to the problem of dispatching messages to the appropriate internal object. To understand the problem and the need for conversation routing, consider a Web service that is engaged in several different executions of a coordination protocol P (named P_1, P_2, ..., P_5 in Figure 7.9). If all clients invoke operations provided by the same port, then they are sending messages to the same Web address.

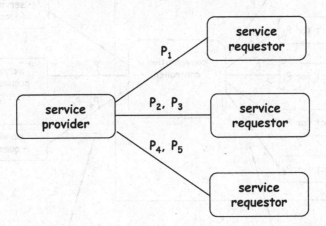

Fig. 7.9. Many clients can interact with the same Web service, each client executing a conversation compliant with a protocol P

When the Web service receives the message, it must determine to which conversation the message belongs, as each conversation has a state (that possibly includes variables that are holding information from previous messages, such as the delivery date or the product ordered), and the way each message is processed depends on the conversation state. If the Web service is implemented by means of a single object, and this object handles all conversations, then the object implementation must take care of maintaining the different states and must contain the logic necessary to understand to which conversation a message belongs. This is quite a burden in terms of implementation effort, and must be repeated in more or less the same way for every implementation of any Web service.

An alternative solution, that avoids the need for implementing this logic in each Web service, consists of creating one object for each conversation and of letting the infrastructure handle the routing of messages to the appropriate object, as shown in Figure 7.10. For example, whenever an operation is invoked by a client, causing the start of a new conversation, the conversation controller could contact a factory object and create, say, an Enterprise JavaBean (EJB) that manages the conversation. If a Web service has n ongoing conversations with its clients, then there will be n objects, each supporting a different conversation. Furthermore, the controller can handle the dispatching of messages pertaining to each conversation instance to the appropriate EJB.

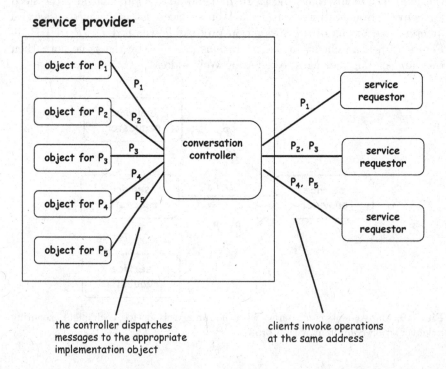

Fig. 7.10. The conversation controller routes messages to the appropriate objects

The conversation controller can accomplish this by including a unique identifier in the header of all messages exchanged within a conversation. The identifier can be generated by the controller each time a message that starts a new conversation (and has no such identifier already included) is received. From that point on, the identifier is included in all message exchanges related to that conversation. When a message is received by the controller, the infrastructure looks at the identifier and determines the object that should receive the message. Figure 7.11 shows in more detail how this can be achieved: SOAP messages are received by the SOAP router, which embeds a conversation controller. The controller, based on a <conversation identifier, object reference> mapping, determines the EJB to which the message should be delivered. Observe that the EJB may not even be aware of the fact that it is being exposed as a Web service.

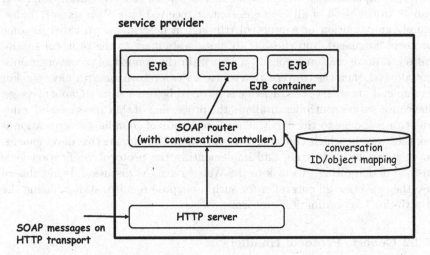

Fig. 7.11. The conversation controller can be part of a SOAP router, as the access point to the internal services implementing the Web service

This approach works for all protocols–horizontal and vertical–as long the messages have the right identifier in their header. However, it requires standardization, as all interacting parties are expected to know how the conversation identifier is embedded into the messages and to insert it in every message they send. Note that if such a standardized infrastructure is in place, conversation routing is transparent to both a Web service description and its implementation. In fact, there is no need to define data items within WSDL messages for the purpose of correlating messages, and there is no need for a Web service to implement any correlation detection code. It is all taken care of by the infrastructure.

Observe that conversation identifiers are also useful for Web services implemented by a single object. Although the controller would not be able to perform routing (all messages go to the same object, regardless of the conversation they belong to), the identifier would still provide an easy way for the object implementation to determine the conversation to which a message belongs and to process it accordingly.

Not all existing approaches rely only on an infrastructure, though. Many vertical protocols include well defined ways to correlate messages. For instance, xCBL defines in great detail how a *ChangeOrder* message should refer to the original order that it is supposed to modify, based on protocol-specific information (rather than being based on generic conversation identifiers). This is because some vertical protocols do not assume that the infrastructure handles correlations in a manner transparent to applications.

Another function of conversation controllers is verifying that a conversation is compliant with the protocol specifications. A conversation controller can sit in the path of all messages sent or received by a Web service, understand the definition of a protocol (through a description provided in some protocol language), and check if all messages adhere to the protocol specification. If an operation invoked by a client in the context of a conversation is not allowed, then the conversation controller can return an error message. For example, if an *orderGoods* message is received before a *requestQuote* message, the conversation controller disallows the processing of that message and sends an error response to the client. Therefore, protocol compliance verification is another way in which conversation controllers simplify service development, in this case by factorizing and implementing the protocol verification logic instead of delegating this task to the Web service. As discussed, being able to use the conversation controller for such a purpose requires standardizing the description of coordination protocols.

7.2.2 Generic Protocol Handlers

Conversation controllers constitute a generic protocol infrastructure that can support all kinds of protocol. In addition to this generic component, the Web services middleware may contain modules that implement a specific coordination protocol, i.e., include protocol-specific logic to act and generate messages in accordance with the rules defined by the protocol. We refer to these modules as *protocol handlers*.

In principle, protocol handlers can be deployed for any kind of protocols. However, they are most applicable to horizontal ones. In fact, such protocols are needed by many Web services, and their purpose is to enforce generic properties of a conversation, such as transactional guarantees. Consider again the example of a protocol supporting distributed transactions based on 2PC. The messages to be exchanged to coordinate the parties and to achieve atomicity are standardized (see WS-Transaction later on in the chapter), and most of the implementation logic is the same regardless of the conversation to which such property is provided. Therefore, it is both possible and useful to develop modules (the protocol handlers) that are generally applicable and can provide this functionality in a generic manner, as part of the Web services middleware infrastructure. Vertical protocols are instead typically implemented by the Web services, not by the Web services middleware. In fact, each party (requester or provider) will have its own internal logic that, as we have stressed earlier in this chapter, is not part of the protocol definition, and that each party wants to keep confidential. Therefore, it is not possible to provide generic implementations for it, but only to support its execution by means of conversation controllers, possibly coupled with protocol handlers that provide properties such as transactions, reliability, and security. For this reason, in the remainder of this section we focus our discussion on handlers for horizontal protocols.

The protocol handler can support protocol execution in two forms:

1. The handler receives, interprets, and sends protocols messages automatically, without intervention by the Web service. The implementation of the protocol is transparent to the Web service in this case. For example, reliable message delivery and the associated protocols can be implemented in this manner. It is the task of the underlying infrastructure, once configured, to ensure that messages are delivered to the target reliably. The logic for storing messages until they are delivered, for re-trying, and for sending and receiving acknowledgments is handled within the infrastructure.
2. The handler and the Web service share the burden of implementing the protocol. For instance, in the case of the 2PC protocol, the logic for coordinating the delivery/receipt of prepare, commit, and abort messages is usually handled by the infrastructure. This is only a framework, since the actual decision of whether to commit or abort a transaction and the logic for implementing these operations (e.g., what "commit" exactly means) is left to the participating Web services, which need to understand what it is being done.

Figure 7.12 shows the interaction among conversation controllers, protocol handlers for horizontal protocols, and Web services implementations. The conversation controller routes business protocol messages to the appropriate Web services implementation, which contains the business logic implementing the protocol. Messages related to horizontal protocols are instead routed to the protocol handlers, since that is where the protocol implementation resides. In principle, the conversation controller could be unaware of whether it is routing messages to a Web services implementation or to a protocol handler: they all look alike to the controller, and they all provide protocol implementations. Conversation controllers and protocol handlers could also be combined; their separation in the figure is mostly to highlight different functionality, not how the components are packaged within the Web services middleware.

Implementing horizontal protocols in the infrastructure instead of the Web services poses some challenges. To exchange protocol messages, the Web services must know each other's ports. They can discover these ports in the binding process (e.g., through UDDI). However, if the task of implementing

service provider

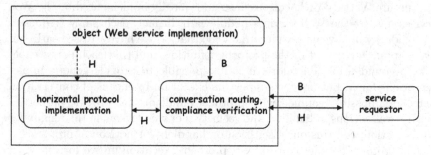

B: conversation compliant with a business protocol
H: conversation compliant with an horizontal protocol

Fig. 7.12. Infrastructure support for implementing horizontal protocols. The dashed line denotes communication needed if the protocol handlers implement the protocol logic only in part, and therefore require decisions from the Web service implementation

a protocol is delegated to the infrastructure, then the protocol handler is responsible for knowing the ports of the entities to which it must send messages. Therefore, this information must somehow be communicated to the handler on which the Web services that need to interact are based.

In addition, as we have seen, each Web service can potentially assume a different role in executing a protocol. If the infrastructure handles the protocol implementation automatically, it should be told the role it has to take in implementing that protocol. Figure 7.13 shows two Web services, W1 and W2, both delegating the execution of a protocol to the protocol handlers A and B in their infrastructure. Before A and B can exchange protocol messages with each other, A needs to know the port reference of B and vice-versa. This can be accomplished by passing them to the infrastructure through the Web services, as shown in the figure.

7.2.3 Standardization Requirements for Coordination Protocols

The above discussion shows that regardless of whether it is conversation routing, protocol verification, or implementation of horizontal protocols, the Web services infrastructure relies on certain standards to be adopted. First, it requires a way to generate and transport unique conversation identifiers in the headers of SOAP messages. This is needed to map messages to conversations, and eventually to the objects handling the conversations. A first effort in this direction has taken place as part of ebXML (see Section 7.6 in this chapter). Second, it requires a framework and a set of protocols (that we call *meta-protocols*) whose purpose is to agree on such aspects as which protocol should

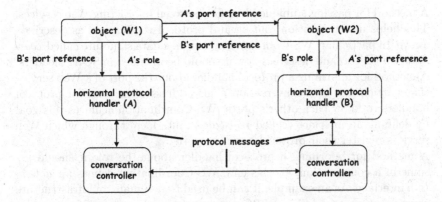

Fig. 7.13. Web services must communicate port references and role information to the infrastructure

be executed and how it is coordinated, since otherwise the Web services cannot agree on how to talk to each other. Third, it requires horizontal protocols to be standardized, so that additional properties can be provided by the middleware. Without standards, the burden of implementing these tasks will be left to the Web services, leading to much more complex development and to increased heterogeneity of the Web services middleware. Finally, it requires standard protocol languages, so that conversation controllers can interpret protocol specifications and verify protocol compliance. These and many other facilities are missing from the current versions of SOAP, WSDL, and UDDI, and are being addressed by other specifications, some of which are described in the remainder of this chapter.

7.3 WS-coordination

In the previous section we have introduced the notion of coordination protocols and have seen what kind of support can be provided by the middleware. In the following sections we introduce a concrete proposal for a protocol infrastructure and present examples of a horizontal protocol and a vertical protocol. We start with WS-Coordination, a specification initially proposed by IBM, Microsoft, and BEA in August 2002 [41].

7.3.1 Goals of WS-Coordination

The primary goal of WS-Coordination is to create a framework for supporting coordination protocols. In this regard, it is intended as a meta-specification that will govern specifications that implement concrete forms of coordination (e.g., transactional coordination). This is accomplished by standardizing the following:

- A method for passing a unique identifier between interacting Web services. This helps in conversation routing and protocol verification, as described above. In particular, WS-Coordination defines a data structure called *coordination context* and describes how it should be included in SOAP headers.
- A method for informing a protocol handler about the port of a Web service that participates in a conversation. This addresses the need for protocol handlers to know each other's ports. WS-Coordination achieves this goal by defining an interface (called *registration* interface) through which Web services register their protocol-handling ports.
- A method for informing a protocol handler about the role it should assume in a conversation. To this end, WS-Coordination defines an *activation* interface. As an example, it can be used to designate an infrastructure component as a "slave" in a 2PC conversation and another infrastructure component as a "master".

7.3.2 Components of WS-Coordination

The basic entities of the WS-Coordination framework are *coordinators* and *participants* that wish to be coordinated in the execution of a conversation. They can interact according to two kinds of architectures (Figure 7.14): all participants can talk to the same coordinator (central coordination) or each participant can talk to its own coordinator (distributed coordination).

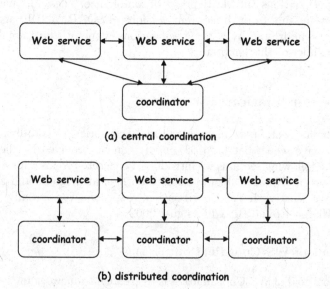

Fig. 7.14. Central or distributed coordination in WS-Coordination

WS-Coordination uses three abstractions to describe the interactions between a coordinator and its participants: *coordination type*, *coordination protocol*, and *coordination context*.

- A **coordination protocol** is a set of rules governing conversations between a coordinator and its participants. 2PC is an example of a coordination protocol.
- A **coordination type** represents a set of coordination protocols, logically related to each other. For example, we can think of an *atomic transaction* coordination type, logically grouping a two phase commit and an outcome notification protocol (the latter is executed by participants who want to be informed about the outcome of a 2PC). An instance of a coordination type may involve the execution of several instances of the same or of different protocols. For example, executing an instance of the coordination type *atomic transaction* may include the execution of a 2PC conversation and one or more *outcome notification* conversations, depending on the number of parties interested in the outcome.
- A **coordination context** is a data structure used to mark messages belonging to the same conversation (called *coordination* in WS-coordination). All SOAP messages exchanged between participants in the scope of a single conversation include the corresponding coordination context in their headers. Among other elements, the data structure contains a field that identifies the coordination type and a field that uniquely identifies the instance of that coordination type. The notion of conversation refers therefore to an instance (execution) of a coordination type, not to an instance of a coordination protocol.

WS-Coordination defines three forms of interactions between a coordinator and its participants:

- **Activation.** A participant requests a coordinator to create a new coordination context. New contexts are created whenever a participant initiates an instance of coordination type (a conversation). This happens, for example, when a Web service initiates an atomic transaction.
- **Registration.** A participant registers as a coordination protocol participant with a coordinator. By registering, a Web service declares that it is participating in the execution of the protocol and that it should be notified when the corresponding steps of the coordination protocol are executed. For example, a Web service can register as a participant in an atomic transaction, thereby providing information about its role and its port.
- **Protocol-specific interactions.** The coordinator and its participants exchange messages that are specific to a coordination protocol. For example, the coordinator can send commit or abort messages to the participants, and specifically to the ports they have indicated in the registration phase.

Interactions for activation and registration are independent of the type of coordination, i.e., they are horizontal. In other words, they do not change from one coordination type to another. Hence, the interfaces that should be implemented by coordinators and participants for these two types of interactions are part of the WS-Coordination specification. On the other hand, interfaces needed for protocol-specific interactions vary from protocol to protocol. As a result, WS-Coordination does not specify those interfaces.

Two port types are defined for the activation: *ActivationCoordinatorPortType*, to be implemented by the coordinator, and *ActivationRequestorPortType*, to be implemented by a participant (Figure 7.15). A Web service that initiates a new coordination sends a *CreateCoordinationContextRequest* message to the *ActivationCoordinatorPortType* of the coordinator. As part of this request, the Web service specifies the type of coordination it wants to initiate (e.g., atomic transaction) as well as a reference to (the address of) its own *ActivationRequestorPortType*. The latter is needed so that the coordinator knows where to send its response. The coordinator creates a new context and sends it back to the Web service in a *CreateCoordinationContextResponse* message.

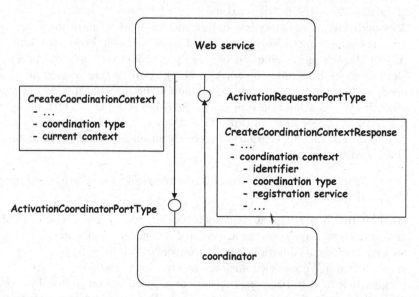

Fig. 7.15. Activation or creation of a coordination context in WS-Coordination

The registration phase is necessary so that the coordinator and the participant exchange information about each other's protocol-specific interfaces. Each participant that wants to take part in a coordination (i.e., execute one of the coordination type's protocols) must register with a coordinator. As for activation, two port types are defined for registration: *RegistrationCoordinatorPortType* and *RegistrationRequestorPortType*. The former is implemented by the coordinator while the latter is implemented by the participant (Figure 7.16). To register as a participant in a protocol, a Web service sends a

Register message to the *RegistrationCoordinatorPortType*. As part of this request, the Web service specifies the name of the protocol, a reference to its *RegistrationRequestorPortType*, and a reference to its protocol-specific participant interface. In response, the coordinator provides a reference to its own protocol-specific coordinator interface. After activation and registration have been executed, the coordinator is aware of who is taking part in a coordination and of their protocol-specific ports. Protocol-specific messages can therefore be exchanged.

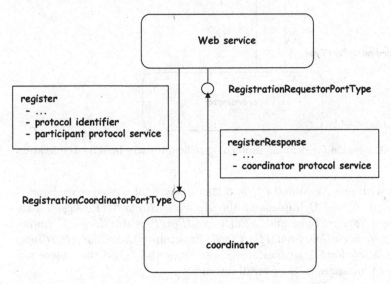

Fig. 7.16. Registration in WS-Coordination

Although protocol-specific interfaces are not defined in WS-Coordination since they vary from protocol to protocol, it is assumed that these too will come in pairs. For each protocol (say X), there will be a participant port type (usually named *XParticipantPortType*) as well as a coordinator port type (*XCoordinatorPortType*), as shown in Figure 7.17. The exact references to these ports are exchanged between the coordinator and the participant through the registration process described above. To simplify the discussion, we use the notation *XCoordinatorPortType* to denote the coordinator's protocol specific interfaces and *XParticipantPortType* to denote the participant's protocol specific interfaces.

7.3.3 Central Coordination

We now examine how all the components of WS-Coordination can be put to use in a central coordination scenario. Consider two Web services A and B that participate in a coordination protocol X. Figure 7.18 shows A and B

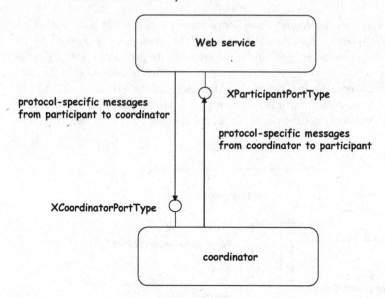

Fig. 7.17. Convention for defining protocol-specific interfaces in WS-Coordination

interacting with one coordinator C and the sequence of messages exchanged between them. A and B implement the *ActivationRequestorPortType*, *RegistrationRequestorPortType*, and *XParticipantPortType* interfaces. C implements the *ActivationCoordinatorPortType*, *RegistrationCoordinatorPortType*, and *XCoordinatorPortType* interfaces. Note from the figure that there are three types of messages in the overall interaction:

1. **Operational messages.** These are messages exchanged between A and B, such as orderGoods or requestQuote. Operational messages are shown as dotted lines in Figure 7.18.
2. **WS-Coordination messages.** These are messages between a Web service (A or B) and the coordinator (C) that are exchanged either for activation or registration. Their structure is defined by WS-Coordination. WS-Coordination messages are shown as solid lines in Figure 7.18.
3. **Protocol-specific messages.** These are messages between a Web service (A or B) and the coordinator (C) that are exchanged as part of protocol X. Protocol-specific messages are shown as dashed lines in Figure 7.18.

Among these three types, WS-Coordination specifies only the second type of message. The others are dependent on the Web services and on the coordination protocol between them. It is assumed that the coordinator C is aware of protocol X and knows how to support it. The sequence of messages is as follows:

1. A initiates a coordination instance by asking C to create a new coordination context.

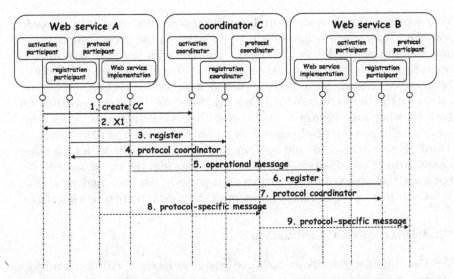

Fig. 7.18. Messages exchanged in the execution of a conversation with a central coordinator

2. C returns a coordination context X1 to A. The coordination context contains a reference to C's *RegistrationCoordinatorPortType*.
3. A registers itself as a participant of protocol X with C by passing a reference to its *XParticipantPortType*.
4. C returns a reference to its *XCoordinatorPortType* to A.
5. A sends a message to B within the scope of the coordination. To indicate the scope, it includes the coordination context X1 it obtained in step 2 as part of the SOAP header.
6. B retrieves C's *RegistrationCoordinatorPortType* reference from the coordination context X1 and uses it to register with C as a participant of protocol X. B also passes its own *XParticipantPortType* to C as part of the registration.
7. C returns a reference to its *XCoordinatorPortType* to B.

At this point, all the parties involved are aware of who the coordinator is, and the coordinator knows who the participants are. Furthermore, the coordinator also knows all the ports of the participants, and the coordination context has been generated. Therefore, the Web services can interact as prescribed by protocol X. The figure shows two (arbitrarily chosen) protocol specific messages (steps 8 and 9).

By looking at this example, it becomes clear how WS-Coordination enables the implementation of different types of coordination. First, all the participating Web services need to agree on who the coordinator for a particular conversation is. WS-Coordination solves this problem by describing a data structure for the coordination context and by specifying a method of passing it between

Web services. The data structure has a reference to the *RegistrationCoordinatorPortType*, which is how all the participants in the above example were able to register their interest in the conversation with the same coordinator. Second, many types of coordination require a unique identifier to be passed between participants for automatic conversation routing and protocol verification by the infrastructure. WS-Coordination defines a generic mechanism both to define such identifiers and to pass them between Web services. This is once again accomplished through the coordination context data structure. Third, there is a need to bind coordinators and participants with each other in any form of coordination. Without such a binding, the coordinator would not know the reference to the participant's protocol interface, and vice-versa. WS-Coordination solves this problem using the generic registration interfaces.

7.3.4 Distributed Coordination

WS-Coordination also allows each participant to interact with its own coordinator, instead of using the same central coordinator. This is likely to be a common scenario in Web services, where interactions occur in a peer-to-peer fashion.

To understand how this works, consider two Web services A and B interacting with coordinators C_a and C_b respectively (Figure 7.19). The sequence of messages exchanged is as follows:

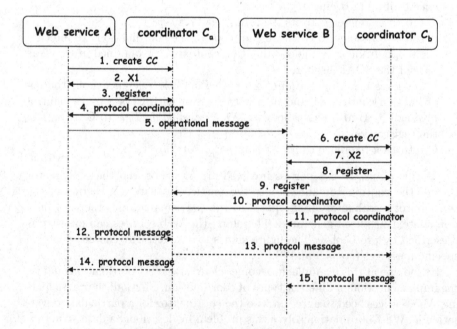

Fig. 7.19. Messages for distributed coordination

1. A initiates a coordination instance by asking C_a to create a new coordination context.
2. C_a returns a coordination context X1 to A. The coordination context contains a reference to C_a's *RegistrationCoordinatorPortType*.
3. A registers itself as a participant of protocol X with C_a by passing a reference to its *XParticipantPortType*.
4. C_a returns a reference to its *XCoordinatorPortType* to A.
5. A sends a message to B within the scope of the coordination. To indicate the scope, it includes the coordination context X1 it obtained in step 2 as part of the SOAP header.
6. B notices a coordination context X1 in the SOAP message it receives. It asks C_b to create a new coordination context. It also indicates that the new context should be a sub-context of X1.
7. C_b returns a coordination context X2 to B. X2 contains a reference to C_b's *RegistrationCoordinatorPortType*.
8. B registers with C_b as a participant of protocol X. B also passes the coordination context and its own *XParticipantPortType* to C_b as part of the registration.
9. C_b registers as a participant of protocol X with C_a. By doing so, C_b informs C_a about who its counterpart is with respect to protocol X1, and can receive and forward all protocol messages from C_a to B.
10. C_a returns to C_b with a reference to its *XCoordinatorPortType*. C_b uses it to forward protocol messages from B to C_a.
11. C_b returns to B with a reference to its *XCoordinatorPortType*.

Again, at this point the coordinators know who the participants are. Furthermore, they also know all the ports of the participants, and the coordination context has been generated. They can therefore interact among them as prescribed by protocol X. The last few protocol-specific messages were chosen arbitrarily to demonstrate the overall flow.

To summarize, distributed coordination is achieved by chaining coordinators. One coordinator (C_b) acted as a proxy to another coordinator (C_a). All the messages between C_a and B passed through C_b. There are two mechanisms at work in the above example that made such distributed coordination possible. First, C_b has to know that its role in the protocol is to act as a proxy coordinator to C_a. Second, C_b has to be able to forward messages both ways: from B to C_a as well as from C_a to B. We now examine how these two mechanisms are realized in WS-Coordination.

Activation, or creation of coordination context, has two purposes: for the *participant* to get a new context and for the *coordinator* to know its role in the overall protocol. If an existing coordination context is passed as part of the *CreateCoordinationContextRequest* message, then the coordinator realizes that it is a proxy to some other coordinator. The reference to the *RegistrationCoordinatorPortType* of the other coordinator is already included in the passed coordination context. This is how a proxy coordinator knows the reference to its primary coordinator. On the other hand, if the *CreateCo-ordinationContextRequest* message does not include an existing coordination context, then the coordinator acts as if it is the primary coordinator.

As a result of the activation process, a proxy coordinator knows the *RegistrationCoordinatorPortType* of the primary coordinator. Whenever a participant registers with the proxy coordinator for a protocol, the proxy coordinator can register with the primary coordinator for the same protocol. In order to be able to do this, the proxy coordinator should also implement *XParticipantPortType* in addition to *XCoordinatorPortType* (Figure 7.20). In fact, the proxy coordinator appears to the primary coordinator as the participant. By chaining registrations, whenever the primary coordinator sends a protocol message to its participants, the proxy coordinator can receive and forward the message to its own participants. Similarly, whenever a participant sends a protocol message to its *XCoordinatorPortType*, the proxy coordinator can forward the message to the primary coordinator.

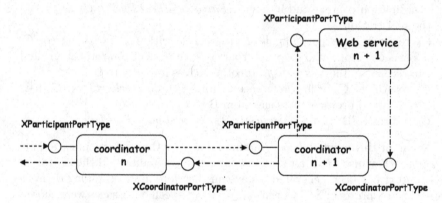

Fig. 7.20. Coordinator chaining for distributed coordination

Arbitrary levels of nesting can be achieved by chaining coordinators. Furthermore, coordinator chaining is only one form of distributed coordination that is supported by WS-Coordination. Other forms of distributed coordination, where a coordinator translates one protocol message from its participants into another protocol message on a different coordinator (and vice-versa), can also be implemented using WS-Coordination. However, this requires a protocol-specific implementation of the Activation and Registration components.

7.3.5 Summary of WS-Coordination

WS-Coordination addresses several fundamental issues in coordination among Web services:

1. It defines *SOAP extensions* that are necessary to achieve coordination.
2. It defines *meta-protocols* for creating coordination contexts (Activation) and for binding coordinators and participants to each other (Registration). Recall that we define a meta-protocol as a protocol supporting the execution of other protocols.
3. It defines a basic set of *middleware components* as well as their interfaces for implementing central or distributed coordination.

WS-Coordination includes, therefore, some of the ingredients needed by a conversation controller, such as a mechanism for transporting conversation identifiers. However, there are several aspects of coordination that still remain to be addressed. Specifically, WS-Coordination is not a language for describing coordination protocols. Although it assumes that such protocols will be implemented through a pair of coordinator and participant interfaces (described in WSDL), there is no way to describe a sequence of messages in a coordination protocol. Such a definition becomes useful in enabling the development of general (protocol-independent) logic for protocol compliance verification. Otherwise, ad hoc logic must be developed for each protocol and embedded into the protocol handlers.

Similar forms of coordination are specified in traditional middleware systems such as CORBA. For example, the coordination scheme in WS-Coordination is very similar to the one described for CORBA's OTS (which can be seen as a transactional coordinator). This is not by accident. The mechanisms are virtually the same. CORBA, however, assumes that there is a single object transaction manager (OTM) and all services interact with this OTM. WS-Coordination allows each Web service to have a local coordinator, thereby giving rise to a peer-to-peer mechanism for enforcing coordination.

Furthermore, traditional middleware systems have not addressed coordination as a generic building block. Specific forms of coordination (such as transactions and reliability) were addressed directly without building on a common foundation, such as coordination context, activation, and registration as described in WS-Coordination.

7.4 WS-Transaction

WS-Coordination provides a framework for implementing Web services protocols. Indeed, it is clear that automation in Web services interactions requires several protocols. As we have learned from conventional middleware, one of the main protocols needed by most application integration efforts are those enabling transaction support. In the context of Web services, such protocols are defined by *WS-Transaction*, a set of specifications built on top of the WS-Coordination framework described in the previous section. WS-Transaction was proposed in August 2002 by IBM, Microsoft, and BEA [42].

7.4.1 Transactions in Web Services

In this and in the previous chapters we have often used the 2PC example to explain the differences between protocols in conventional middleware and their counterparts in Web services. We have specifically underlined the implications of the lack of a centralized middleware platform, which calls for a redesign of the protocols so that they can work in a distributed setting.

For transactions, however, this is not the only difference. In fact, transactions implemented through Web services are often long-running. Since Web services implement business applications, completing a transaction may involve manual intervention or executing lengthy business processes. For example, validating an order by checking that goods are in stock may require several hours. This is different from a database insertion, that is likely to take a much shorter time. As a consequence, it may not always be possible (or even desirable) to preserve ACID properties using 2PC. In fact, this requires locking resources for the duration of the entire transaction.

Another important difference is related to the lack of a fixed resource and operation model. In database transactions, there is a clear definition of what concepts such as "resource," "lock," "commit," and "rollback" mean. The database transaction model is very precise with respect to what exactly is locked and what happens at commit. There is a defined (meta-)data structure and a fixed set of operations that can be executed on these data, essentially creations, insertions, updates, and deletions. In Web services there is no such thing. WSDL operations can represent anything, from database insertions to sending a letter to a customer. Rolling back a transaction can mean very different things based on what the transaction was about. For example, rolling back the delivery of a letter to a customer may involve making a telephone call to the same customer, asking him or her to disregard the letter. This generality makes it difficult to characterize the notion of resources, locks, and rollback.

The approach adopted by Web services to solving these issues is to relax the rigidity of ACID properties and to leverage *compensation* mechanisms, in a similar fashion to what has been proposed by *sagas* [78]. The basic idea underlying the approach is that each of the participating Web services can update its persistent storage (or state) after each step of the transaction, thereby making the effects of the step durable and visible outside the scope of the transaction, analogously to a commit. Since the results of a task are visible before the completion of the overall transaction, the atomicity and isolation constraints are relaxed. If, for some reason, the transaction must abort, then the Web services execute a compensation operation that semantically undoes the effects of the (partial) transaction execution. The task of canceling the effects of a previous step is considered business logic and is left to the implementation of the compensation operation. Each operation may have a different compensation logic, and each provider may have a different opinion about the exact meaning and the appropriate way of compensating an operation. For example, in a travel reservation Web service, compensating a reservation may involve canceling the reservation already made. Furthermore, providers may or may not impose a time limit for cancellation or impose cancellation fees.

Regardless of how each Web service internally implements transactions and compensations, standardized protocols are required to enable all participating Web services to determine if any of them has failed in executing its step, and ask all other participants to execute compensation operations. To cater to this need, WS-Transaction specifies a standard protocol for long-running transactions, called *business activities*.

Having said that, there is still a need for Web services executing short-duration transactions within limited trust domains to preserve ACID properties in the strict sense, analogously to what happens in EAI. To this end, WS-Transaction also provides a set of specifications for short-duration transactions, called *atomic transactions*.

Other proposals for defining and implementing transactions also exist, typically based on tagging WSDL specifications or vertical protocols with transactional information (e.g., to state that a certain operation is compensatable, or that operation O_c can compensate the execution of operation O). We refer the interested reader to [141, 75, 21] for details. In the following, we focus instead on the approach proposed by WS-Transaction.

7.4.2 Relationship with WS-Coordination

WS-Transaction defines a set of protocols that require coordination among multiple parties. Therefore, it naturally builds upon the framework described in WS-Coordination (Section 7.3). In particular, WS-Transaction assumes the existence of a set of Web services that participate in a transaction and of one or more coordinators that coordinate the transaction, either in a centralized or a peer-to-peer fashion. WS-Transaction also details the structure of the coordination context and defines standard WSDL interfaces to be implemented by coordinators and participants. Transactional semantics are then achieved through a combination of WS-Coordination and WS-Transaction protocols, executed with the support of the coordinators.

WS-Coordination protocols are used by the following parties and for the following reasons:

1. By the initiating Web service, to create a new coordination context.
2. By a participating Web service, to pass the coordination context to another Web service.
3. By a participating Web service, to register for a transaction protocol with a central transaction coordinator or with its own coordinator.
4. By a proxy coordinator, to chain with a primary coordinator.

7.4.3 Atomic Transactions

The first coordination type defined by WS-Transaction is *Atomic Transaction*. This coordination type is composed of several coordination protocols, executed in sequence or in alternative by the participating Web services or by the coordinator, depending on what must be done during the different phases of a distributed transaction.

Five protocols make up this coordination type: *Completion, 2PC, CompletionWithAck, PhaseZero,* and *OutcomeNotification.* When a Web service wishes to complete a transaction, it executes a Completion protocol with the coordinator. Its purpose is to inform the coordinator that it should start a 2PC protocol to verify the outcome of the transaction and ask the participants to either commit or abort. 2PC is the standard two-phase commit protocol with a prepare phase and a commit or abort phase. Once 2PC is executed and the transaction is completed, the outcome is returned to the Web service. In some cases, before actually starting the 2PC protocol, the coordinator may execute a PhaseZero protocol with the other participants. The intention is to let all participants know that a 2PC protocol is about to commence[1]. At any point during or after the execution of a 2PC protocol, a participant can query the coordinator about the outcome of the transaction (whether it has been committed or not) using the OutcomeNotification protocol. Finally, the CompletionWithAck protocol can be initiated by a Web service as an alternative to the Completion protocol. The difference is that in the CompletionWithAck protocol the coordinator has to remember the outcome of a transaction without discarding it, until the requesting Web service sends an acknowledgment that it has received the outcome. Corresponding to these protocols, the standard specifies the following port types to be implemented by the coordinator (in addition to those specified in WS-Coordination):

- CompletionParticipantPortType and CompletionCoordinatorPortType
- CompletionWithAckParticipantPortType and CompletionWithAckCoordinatorPortType
- PhaseZeroParticipantPortType and PhaseZeroCoordinatorPortType
- 2PCParticipantPortType and 2PCCoordinatorPortType
- OutcomeNotificationParticipantPortType and OutcomeNotificationCoordinatorPortType

The reason for having coordinators implement the participant port types is that in this way coordinator chaining can be accomplished. The Web services should also implement the participant port types, depending on their role in the transaction (Figure 7.21). For example, a Web service that initiates a

---

[1] This is useful in case the participant needs to perform some actions (such as flushing a memory cache to the database). It caters to situations in which the 2PC implementation is such that the database cannot be updated after the 2PC is started.

transaction also typically requests the coordinator to commit or rollback the transaction. Therefore, it implements either the CompletionParticipantPort-Type or the CompletionWithAckParticipantPortType. A Web service executing database state changes that must be either committed or rolled back at the end of a transaction implements the 2PCParticipantPortType. A Web service that executes other forms of state changes (e.g., in-memory or cache changes for performance reasons) and wishes to be notified before commencement of a 2PC protocol implements the PhaseZeroParticipantPortType. The reason for this interface is to let the Web service write those changes to a database before the start of 2PC protocol. (Some implementations of 2PC prevent any further updates to a database while the protocol is being executed.) Finally, any Web service that would like to check the outcome of a transaction implements the OutcomeNotificationParticipantPortType.

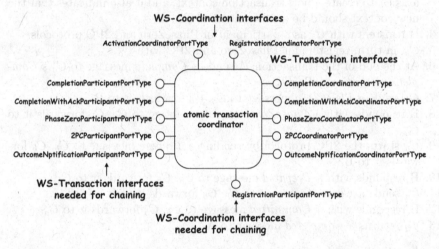

Fig. 7.21. Port types used in atomic transactions

In addition to defining the five protocols, WS-Transaction also defines a structure for the transaction coordination context. Recall that this data structure is returned by the coordinator in response to a CreateCoordination-Context request and is passed between Web services as part of the SOAP header, to indicate that a message is being exchanged within the scope of a conversation. The value of the coordination type entry in the context (set to *http://schemas.xmlsoap.org/ws/2002/08/wstx*) indicates that the context is a transaction context. This value is the URI of the location where the WS-Transaction specification for atomic transactions can be found.

We now describe a typical scenario that shows how WS-Coordination and WS-Transaction protocols are combined to execute a distributed transaction (Figure 7.22). The scenario has two Web services, A and B, participating in a transaction. Each of them has its own coordinator (C_a and C_b respectively).

Let us assume that A initiates the transaction and B executes steps in the transaction that involve uncommitted state changes. Let us further assume that some of the state changes in B are made directly over a database, while others are in memory and not stored in a database until the end of the transaction. This means that a PhaseZero protocol must be executed, in addition to the 2PC and the Completion protocols, necessary to perform a two-phase commit. The series of messages are as follows:

1. A initiates a transaction instance by asking C_a to create a new transaction context T1. A also registers for the Completion protocol with C_a.
2. A sends a message to B within the scope of the transaction. To indicate the scope, it includes the transaction context T1 as part of the SOAP header.
3. B notices the transaction context T1 in the SOAP message it receives. It asks C_b to create a new transaction context, and it also indicates that the new context should be a sub-context of T1.
4. B registers with C_b as a participant of PhaseZero and 2PC protocols.
5. C_b, in turn, registers for PhaseZero and 2PC with C_a.
6. At the end of the transaction, A sends a *Complete* message to C_a's *CompletionCoordinatorPortType*.
7. C_a sends a *PhaseZero* message to C_b. C_b forwards it to B.
8. B responds with a *PhaseZeroComplete* message to C_b. C_b forwards it to C_a.
9. C_a starts the 2PC protocol by sending a *Prepare* message to C_b. C_b forwards it to B.
10. B responds with a *Prepared* message to C_b. C_b forwards it to C_a.
11. C_a sends a *Commit* message to C_b. C_b forwards it to B.
12. B responds with a *Committed* message to C_b. C_b forwards it to C_a.
13. C_a returns a *Completed* message to A.

As a final consideration on these sets of protocols, we observe again that WS-Transaction only specifies part of the business logic. For example, the semantics of commit and abort are only informally defined, and while their general meaning is commonly understood, the behavior of different Web services upon a commit or an abort may differ considerably.

7.4.4 Business Activities

To handle long-running business transactions across Web services without having to lock resources using 2PC, WS-Transaction also defines another coordination type, called *Business Activity*. Two protocols make up this coordination type: *BusinessAgreement* and *BusinessAgreementWithComplete*. The BusinessAgreement protocol is initiated by a participating Web service to inform the coordinator about the status of its execution (Exited, Completed, or Faulted). After reaching a consensus on whether to go forward with the

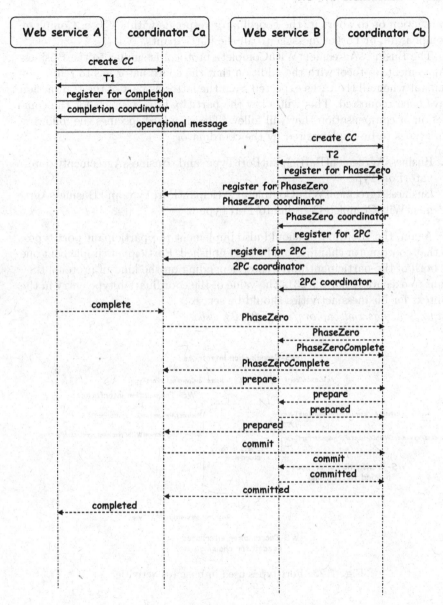

Fig. 7.22. Example for Atomic Transaction

transaction or to abort it, the coordinator responds with a Close, Complete, Compensate, or Forget message to all the participants.

The BusinessAgreementWithComplete protocol is similar to the BusinessAgreement protocol with the addition that the coordinator has to tell a participant when all the tasks expected from the latter as part of the transaction have been requested. This will allow the participant to prepare for the completion or compensation that will follow. The standard specifies the following port types to be implemented by the coordinator:

- BusinessAgreementParticipantPortType and BusinessAgreementCoordinatorPortType
- BusinessAgreementWithCompleteParticipantPortType and BusinessAgreementWithCompleteCoordinatorPortType

Again, the coordinator should also implement the participant port types, so that coordinator chaining can be accomplished. Participants implement one or both of the participant port types, depending on the kind of protocol they want to execute (Figure 7.23). The value of the coordination type entry in the context for business activities should be set to *http://schemas.xmlsoap.org/ws/2002/08/wsba*.

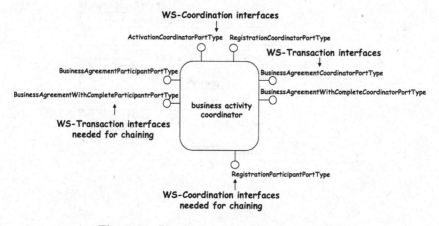

Fig. 7.23. Port types used in business activities

To see an example of how the business activity protocol is used, consider a scenario with three Web services, A, B, and C, and with one coordinator R (this example can also be extended to multiple coordinators). We assume that A initiates the protocol while B and C participate in the protocol (Figure 7.24). The series of messages are as follows:

1. A initiates a business activity conversation and passes the context to B and C. B and C register for the BusinessAgreement protocol with R.

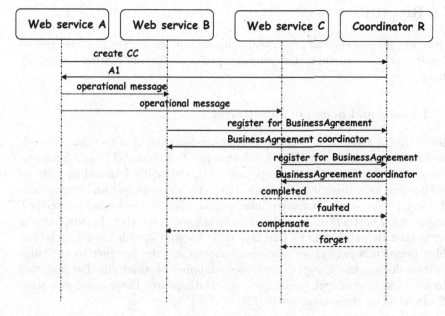

Fig. 7.24. An execution of the Business Activity protocol

2. B successfully finishes its tasks, but C encounters a failure. So, it sends a Faulted message to R.
3. By the time R receives the Faulted message from C, it may or may not have received the Completed message from B. If it has received the Completed message from B, R sends a Compensate message to B. If not, it sends a Cancel message to B.
4. R also sends a Forget message to C, thereby denoting that the protocol is terminated and no further actions are required from C.

As mentioned earlier, the implementation of compensation operations are specific to the Web services and are considered part of the business logic. Furthermore, there is only one compensation operation defined per business activity and per Web service. Hence, if a Web service executes a series of tasks as part of a single business activity in a particular order, all of those tasks must be nullified at once. There is no support for rolling back the series of tasks in the reverse order, for example by sending a series of Compensate messages, one for each task. Doing so would require a coordinator to be familiar with the order in which operational messages were exchanged between the Web services. These issues will be addressed in the following chapter, when speaking about service composition.

7.5 RosettaNet

As an example of vertical protocol, in this section we discuss the approach of RosettaNet, a consortium that proposes protocols for automating the supply chain.

7.5.1 Goals and Scope of RosettaNet

RosettaNet is a global, non-profit, business consortium of more than 400 leading Electronic Components (EC), Information Technology (IT) and Semiconductor Manufacturing (SM) companies [171]. Originally founded in 1998 by 40 IT companies, RosettaNet is dedicated to the development and deployment of standard electronic commerce interfaces to align the processes between IT supply chain partners so that they can leverage the Internet. In other words, the goal of RosettaNet is to facilitate dynamic and flexible trading relationships between supply chain partners who can use the Internet to exchange business documents. RosettaNet defines a number of standards that facilitate the establishment of such trading partner relationships. These standardization efforts focus on three main areas [224]:

- **Business processes.** The most visible aspect of RosettaNet is probably the specification of coordination protocols (which RosettaNet refers to as "business processes") for trading partners. *RosettaNet Partner Interface Processes* (PIPs) define horizontal and vertical protocols to be executed between partners. Each PIP specifies the business documents, vocabulary, and the choreography of the message dialog needed to achieve a particular business goal. PIPs are collected and published by RosettaNet in a *PIP Directory*.

- **Data format.** Every company inevitably develops its own terminology and reference codes that it uses in its day-to-day business. One of the most critical aspects of integrating trading partners is thus the establishment of a common vocabulary. Like its namesake [2], RosettaNet provides a means to overcome such language barriers. To this end, RosettaNet specifies two kinds of dictionaries that publish common sets of properties for PIPs, as well as product and partner codes. The *RosettaNet Business Dictionary* designates the properties used in basic business activities between trading partners. The *RosettaNet Technical Dictionary* lists common terminology used to define products and services.

- **Messaging services.** Once a PIP specification has been defined, the RosettaNet Implementation Framework (RNIF) defines how it may be executed. At the time the RosettaNet effort started, no universal horizontal standard existed for the transfer, routing, and packaging of messages. Therefore, RNIF was defined to enable the reliable and secure execution

---

[2] The Rosetta Stone, which was inscribed with the same message in three languages, was the key to deciphering the hieroglyphics of ancient Egypt.

of PIP specifications by delineating how to package, transfer, and route encrypted and authenticated business messages between trading partners and networks. In particular, RNIF defines the container structure, message header format, protocol bindings, and choreographic patterns (including both synchronous and asynchronous interactions) for the exchange of business data.

7.5.2 Partner Interface Process (PIP) Specifications

A RosettaNet PIP specification describes how to implement a collaborative coordination protocol. Each PIP specification includes a Technical Dictionary (that describes the components that are exchanged as part of the process) and a Message Guideline document that includes a PIP-specific version of the Business Dictionary (specifying the business properties and the PIP protocols) for communicating properties between networked applications [172]. RosettaNet distinguishes between two categories of messages involved in PIP business document exchanges: "business action" messages and "business signal" messages. Business actions are messages that contain business documents, such as a *Purchase Order* or a *Billing Statement*. Business signals are messages that indicate a positive or negative response to acknowledge the receipt of a business action message.

RosettaNet follows a four-step methodology to develop PIP specifications:

1. Develop an "as-is" business model that describes how *partner types* (supply chain business entities) do business today.
2. Re-engineer this model to specify how partner types will use Web-based interactions to do business.
3. Create a *PIP Blueprint* document from the re-engineered process that describes how the *partner roles* (roles that business partners play in the supply chain) will achieve a business objective. The RosettaNet members vote to approve this blueprint.
4. Create a PIP protocol that dictates to system architects and software engineers how networked applications will interoperate.

The first two steps of this process are not published formally; artifacts of the latter three are reflected in the three major sections of a PIP Specification [173, 172], which can be viewed as a drill-down from the high-level vision of how the entities will interact, to a low-level functional view of the coordination protocols:

- **Business Operational View.** Also known as the Action Layer [172], this section describes the flow of the business interactions between business entities (as identified by business analysts). It includes information from the PIP Blueprint, such as the partner roles in the supply chain, the partner role interactions, and a PIP-specific version of the Business

Dictionary (specifying the business properties as well as their permissible values used to create the PIP blueprint),

- **Functional Service View.** Also known as the Transaction Layer [172], this section, which is derived from the Business Operational View, specifies the business transactions between entities in terms of message exchanges between RosettaNet "services." The Functional Service View defines coordination protocols that correspond to the Business Operational View, as well as message exchange control information for the actions and signals involved in the conversations. For example a Functional Service View might specify the interactions that implement the flow described by a given PIP, the time within which an Acknowledgment of Receipt signal should be sent for a given step in the flow, and whether a secure transport should be used for the transmission of that signal. This view includes the PIP protocol transaction dialogs that are developed for the PIP Blueprint.

- **Implementation Framework View.** Also known as the Service Layer, this section defines communication protocol and message format requirements (based on Business Operational and Functional Service views) [172]. For example, this view might specify whether or not a secure transport protocol, such as SSL, or digital signatures are required, as well as XML DTDs or Message Guidelines that describe the messages exchanged when the PIP is executed.

Messages and coordination protocols are specified using RosettaNet's protocol specification patterns. PIP Blueprints use UML activity diagrams to create *PIP Business Process Flow Diagrams*[3] that specify how business documents will flow among the business activities executed by the partner roles. Roles in the diagram can be associated either with an organization or with a person (employee of an organization).

The Business Process Flow Diagram is a role-based diagram that represents the messages exchanged and protocol interfaces. Each role involved in the flow is represented using a vertical "swimlane" in the diagram. Each diagram contains a single Start State, which indicates where the process begins, and multiple End States that correspond to the activity's success and failure states as defined in the corresponding PIP Blueprint. Rectangles with straight sides and rounded corners represent the Business Documents that are exchanged when the Activities of two different partner roles interact. The rectangle is labeled with the name of the Business Document. The label <<Secure Flow>> indicates that the interaction takes place using point-to-point security, implemented using digital certificates and Secure Sockets Layer (SSL) technology. (Although it is not shown in this example, the rectangle may also be labeled with the name of the activity that generates the document.) Rectangles with rounded sides represent Activities. Each Activity has a name shown in the center of the rectangle, as well as an Activity type, enclosed in angle brackets.

---

[3] Despite the misleading name, these are in fact coordination protocols.

For example, Figure 7.25 depicts the legal interactions between a buyer role and a role, as defined by RosettaNet PIP3A2, Request Price and Availability (Release 02.01.00B). The documents "Price and Availability Request" and "Price and Availability Response" correspond to message exchanges between business processes fronted by independent trading partners. The activities "Request Price and Availability" and "Process Price and Availability Request" represent the internal activities of the trading partners.

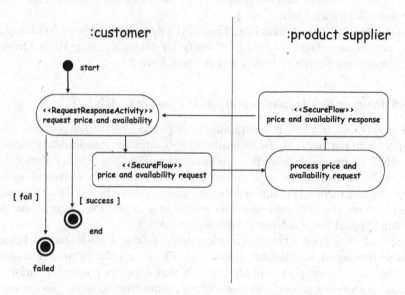

Fig. 7.25. RosettaNet PIP 3A2 (Request Price and Availability)

RosettaNet arranges its PIP definitions into seven clusters of core business processes, which are in turn broken down into segments. These clusters are:

1. **Cluster 0: RosettaNet Support.** These PIPs support administrative functionality (e.g., "Notification of Failure," "Asynchronous Test Notification," etc.).
2. **Cluster 1: Partner Product and Service Review.** These PIPs support the collection, maintenance, and distribution of information related to trading-partner products and services (e.g., "Request Account Setup," "Manage Product Information Subscriptions," etc.).
3. **Cluster 2: Product Information.** These PIPs support the distribution and update of product information (e.g., "Distribute New Product Information," "Query Technical Product Information," etc.).
4. **Cluster 3: Order Management.** These PIPs support order management processes (e.g., "Request Quote," "Query Order Status," etc.).

5. **Cluster 4: Inventory Management.** These PIPs enable inventory management (e.g., "Notify of Forecast Reply," "Distribute Inventory Report," etc.).
6. **Cluster 5: Marketing Information Management.** These PIPs support the exchange of marketing information (e.g., "Distribute Product List," "Query Registration Status," etc.).
7. **Cluster 6: Service and Support.** These PIPs describe processes for technical services and support (e.g., "Query Service Entitlement," "Request Warranty Claim," etc.).
8. **Cluster 7: Manufacturing.** These PIPs describe processes that support "virtual manufacturing" (e.g., "Notify Of Manufacturing Work Order," "Distribute Product Quality Event Data," etc.).

7.5.3 RosettaNet Implementation Framework (RNIF)

The RosettaNet Implementation Framework (RNIF) 2.0 defines protocols that supply chain partners can use to implement RosettaNet standards. In particular, RNIF addresses three main areas of functionality [224]. First, it defines the RosettaNet Business Message, a standardized, protocol-independent means for packaging payload documents, header components, digital signatures, and other entities that are exchanged as a unit in a RosettaNet interaction (including support for third-party service content).

Second, it defines a transport-independent protocol stack that specifies a reliable messaging mechanism supporting HTTP and SMTP (other transfer protocols will be supported in the future), that captures contextual information in header documents, and that defines standard models for the exchange of action and signal messages that can be used to compose PIP specifications. As an example of the last, RNIF defines an "asynchronous single-action PIP activity" where a single action message is sent from Partner A to Partner B, and a Receipt Acknowledgment is then sent from Partner B to Partner A. This pattern is used to define simple PIPs such as *PIP2A1: Distribute New Product Information*. Finally, RNIF includes a security mechanism for the digital signature and/or encryption of messages that meets the requirements of authentication, authorization, encryption (of both the payload and the service header), and *non-repudiation* (i.e., provide proofs that a client has sent a certain message and that a server has received the message).

As an example, Figure 7.26 depicts the components of a transport protocol-independent RosettaNet business message from the perspective of the network application protocol stack. The RNIF 2.0 specification defines schemas for the preamble, delivery, and Service header components; instances of these components are contained in all RosettaNet business messages. The MIME envelope and the business process payload may be secured using Secure Multipurpose Internet Mail Extensions (S/MIME) and optional digital signatures.

As this section has shown, RosettaNet specifications are quite detailed and cover several levels of the protocol stack. This is because RosettaNet was

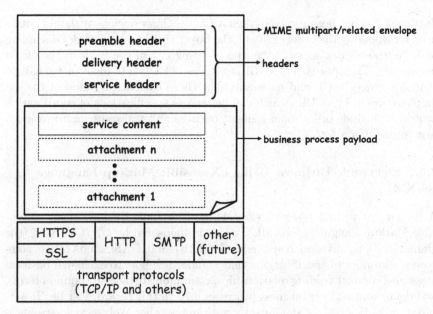

Fig. 7.26. RosettaNet business message components and RosettaNet protocol stack

designed before protocols such as SOAP become widely adopted. In time, it is likely that RosettaNet and analogous efforts will focus on vertical protocols, and rely on existing standards for the horizontal protocols.

7.6 Other Standards Related to Coordination Protocols

For completeness of presentation, this section briefly describes other standardization proposals related to coordination protocols.

7.6.1 XML Common Business Library (xCBL)

The XML Common Business Library (xCBL) [50] from CommerceOne combines an XML version of the standardized documents available in EDI along with predefined business protocols. For instance, xCBL specifies in detail how to do order management [51]. It not only prescribes which documents need to be exchanged as part of the order management protocols, but also the contents and semantics of those messages (like EDI, but using XML). The specification includes roles (e.g., buyer and seller), who initiates what exchange and what document is involved (e.g., ChangeOrder document is a buyer initiated document used to change an existing order), and ordering constraints on when each document should be used (e.g., ChangeOrder can only be used to change an order already received and responded to by a reseller; if an OrderResponse document has not been received, then a *ChangeOrder* document should not be used for changing the order; instead, the buyer should use an *Order* document with "purpose" *Replacement*, "purpose" being one of the fields of the Order document). The approach of xCBL, as it was in EDI, is to focus on exchanges that are widely used, and to standardize those exchanges. Some of the examples covered by xCBL (which can be seen as specifications of coordination protocols) include order management, package and transport, and invoicing, just to mention a few.

7.6.2 Electronic Business Using eXtensible Markup Language (ebXML)

A similar but further reaching effort is the Electronic Business using eXtensible Markup Language (ebXML), which is sponsored by UN/CEFACT (the United Nations division responsible for EDI) and OASIS. ebXML encompasses a number of specifications that standardize how to exchange business messages, conduct trading relationships, communicate data in common terms, and define and register business processes [61]. In this regard, just like RosettaNet, ebXML overlaps significantly with many other Web services specifications. The expectation is that many of these efforts will slowly converge, e.g., that xCBL will evolve toward compliance with ebXML. ebXML can be seen as the framework that defines how efforts like xCBL should be formulated. Even more, ebXML acts in many ways as the specification of how electronic commerce exchanges should be specified, documented, and conducted. In this regard, the interpretation of Web services provided by ebXML is more complete and detailed than what discussed in the previous chapters and gives a better perspective on what is involved when using Web services. In many ways, ebXML describes what is still missing in the specifications we have discussed so far (mainly UDDI, SOAP, and WSDL). These missing parts are mostly related to conversations and coordination protocols.

In the ebXML world [63], a company that wants to make its services available through the Internet uses an ebXML Registry, which is similar in spirit to a UDDI registry but contains much more detailed information about the service being provided. Current suggestions for combining UDDI and the ebXML registry involve finding services in UDDI and looking up the details in an ebXML registry [62]. To use the registry to advertise its services, the company must provide an ebXML-compliant application. To do this, it submits to the registry a *Business Profile* (including implementation details and reference links) that describes the company's ebXML capabilities and constraints, as well as the *business scenarios* it supports. The notion of business scenario in ebXML is similar to the notion of Web service as described in WSDL, but includes much more information, particularly coordination protocol information. The ebXML registry verifies that the format and usage of a business scenario is correct and makes the business scenario available as part of the registry. Potential users of the business scenario find information about the scenario by querying the registry. If they decide to use the business scenario, they send a request to its provider. In ebXML, the actual linking between service requester and provider is regulated by additional specifications. For instance, before engaging in the business scenario, a *business arrangement* must be exchanged between the companies. In fact, one of the interfaces a company must support to have an ebXML-compliant business scenario is the one supporting business arrangements. The business arrangement describes the mutually agreed upon business scenarios, agreements about the interaction, and information about messaging, transactions, contingency plans, and security-related requirements. Once the business agreement is accepted, the two companies can proceed to use the business scenario.

The parallel with what has been discussed so far is obvious. The difference is that ebXML has gone a step beyond specifying generic protocols like SOAP, UDDI or WSDL to include the logic behind electronic commerce exchanges such as business arrangements. In this regard, ebXML shows how all the different protocols and initiatives relate to each other and how they should be combined. It also shows what is missing in these basic protocols. For instance, in terms of coordination protocols, ebXML addresses the problem right from the beginning. ebXML considers the participants in an exchange as *trading partners* rather than as service requester and service provider. A trading partner publishes information about its business processes using a Collaboration Protocol Profile (CPP). The CPP includes contact information, industry classification, supported business processes, interface requirements, and messaging service requirements (and it is thus similar to a UDDI registry entry for a Web service). The CPP also includes information on the roles assumed by the trading partner in the interaction and error-handling and failure scenarios (making it more complete than a UDDI or WSDL description by incorporating coordination protocol information). The business agreements that govern the interaction between business partners (Collaboration Protocol Agreements, or CPAs) are built from the intersection of two or more CPPs. The CPA is used to narrow the CPP of each trading partner until what each trading partner will do as part of the business process is completely defined. This business process defined in the CPA is what we call a coordination protocol.

Finally, the CPA is also used to govern the exchange of messages between partners (as a coordination protocol should do). It is for this reason that ebXML uses its own *messaging service*. This messaging service builds upon SOAP and HTTP but is more complete than SOAP (e.g. it allows the inclusion of attachments) and, more importantly, ties the messages to the rules declared in the CPA, thereby directly incorporating the notion of coordination protocol in the implementation of the exchanges. In many ways, the messaging service of ebXML is an indication of what is missing in SOAP. The ebXML specification, for instance, includes standard headers that cover the use of unique ids, mapping to conversations, duplicate elimination, etc. It also covers many aspects of exchanging messages over an unreliable medium. As part of this, ebXML includes a reliable messaging module, a message status service to inquire the status of a given message, a ping service, a message order module to enforce delivery ordering, and a multi-hop module for sending messages through a chain of intermediaries (and still achieving reliability).

ebXML illustrates very well the actual complexity of business-to-business interactions and the importance of conversations and coordination protocols. SOAP, UDDI and WSDL, as they are today, can hardly be used for anything but the simplest Web services. It is only within the context of efforts like ebXML and others described in this and in the following chapter that they will be able to develop their full potential as tools for implementing complex interactions between companies.

7.6.3 Web Service Choreography Interface (WSCI)

The *Web Service Choreography Interface* (WSCI) is a specification introduced in 2002 by Intalio, SAP, BEA, and Sun [11] that proposes a language for defining coordination protocols. It does not introduce specific (vertical or horizontal) protocols, and it does not define how protocols are implemented internally. Therefore, unlike RosettaNet or ebXML, WSCI focuses solely on coordination and does not attempt to define lower level protocols. This is because WSCI is fairly recent, and was designed after specifications such as SOAP and WSDL become widely adopted. Therefore, WSCI builds on top of existing specifications, and in particular on top of WSDL.

In essence, WSCI proposes a way to extend a WSDL interface definition with constraints about the order in which WSDL operations can be executed, thereby adding protocol information to the interface. Several WSCI protocol specifications (called *WSCI interfaces*) can be coupled with the same WSDL interface, since a Web service can support several different protocols.

The objectives of WSCI, and the ways they are achieved, are exactly as described in the first two sections of this chapter, where we provided an introduction to coordination protocol languages and discussed why they are needed. In particular, a WSCI description is conceptually analogous to a role-specific view of a protocol, described with a model essentially similar to that of activity diagrams (Section 7.1). However, WSCI extends this model in several ways. As such, the WSCI specification represents an interesting complement to this chapter for the reader interested in more details about coordination protocols. We now review the main extensions introduced by WSCI.

- **Exception handling.** WSCI allows the definition of parts of a protocol to be executed upon the occurrence of some exceptional situation, such as the receipt of a message not compliant with the protocol or of a fault message by one of the parties in response to an operation invocation.
- **Transactions.** WSCI allows the definition of portions of the protocol that are atomic or that can be compensated once they have been completed. This specification has the only purpose of informing clients about the atomic nature of the message exchange, about the exceptions that will

initiate the rollback or the compensation, and about the (externally visible) operations that the service will execute when performing the rollback or the compensation. WSCI does not define how atomicity is to be implemented by the Web service and does not define protocols such as 2PC to support atomicity. Hence, it is complementary to WS-Transaction.

- **Correlators.** We have seen earlier in this chapter that WS-Coordination uses conversation identifiers to match messages to conversations. WSCI uses a different approach. Specifically, WSCI interfaces can denote that certain data items of messages exchanged in the conversation (e.g., an orderID) are unique identifiers of the conversation. It is through these data items that conversation controllers (or the Web services themselves) can associate messages to conversations.
- **Time constraints.** WSCI interfaces can include time constraints, to specify that a certain time interval should elapse between the invocation of two operations.

WSCI represents an interesting approach to protocol descriptions. It remains, however, to be seen how it relates to competing specifications such as BPEL (described at length in the next chapter).

7.7 Summary

This chapter has discussed how to extend Web services beyond basic interoperability. In terms of abstractions, the extensions presented revolve around the notion of coordination protocols: from vertical protocols, specific to a given industry sector, to horizontal protocols, whose purpose is essentially that of providing Web services with properties similar to those of conventional middleware.

Regardless of their nature, coordination protocols require languages for their definition as well as frameworks and infrastructures for supporting their execution. A standardized protocol language enables providers to describe the kind of interactions they support, and consequently allow requesters to identify how client applications should be developed to interact with the service. They will eventually also enable automated support in the form of *conversation controllers*. A controller provides two main benefits: the first is the ability to verify that a sequence of message exchanges taking place between two parties is compliant with the protocol specification; the second is sophisticated message routing, with the ability to deliver messages related to different conversations to different implementation objects (e.g., different EJBs).

Standardization in this important area is still in the early stages although several, sometimes conflicting, proposals have appeared, some of which are rapidly gaining momentum. ebXML is one of the most complete specifications in this regard. RosettaNet is quite popular, especially as an interoperability standard between suppliers and vendors in the IT industry. In both cases, these efforts predate to a certain extent the appearance of SOAP, UDDI, and WSDL. They are also tied to the EDI world, which is both an advantage (as they can leverage all the semantics associated with EDI specifications) and a disadvantage (since EDI implementations are legacy systems that impose many constraints on what can be done at the Web service level). Specifications like WS-Coordination and WS-Transaction are more recent and address horizontal protocols that build upon SOAP, WSDL, and UDDI. It remains to be seen which of these specifications will be eventually adopted and how the different parallel and competing efforts will be combined to provide a coherent set of standards. It will certainly be the case, as basic Web services standards gain acceptance, that they will be leveraged by efforts such as ebXML and RosettaNet, thereby resulting in specifications that are both simpler and easier to adopt.

8

Service Composition

The previous chapter has shown that interactions among Web services can consist of several operation invocations, to be executed in accordance with certain ordering constraints. We have discussed one of two implications of that observation: the need for coordination protocols and for middleware that helps define and enforce protocols. This chapter tackles the other implication, which is related to the *implementation* of Web services whose business logic involves the invocation of operations offered by other Web services. We refer to a service implemented by combining the functionality provided by other Web services as a *composite service*, and the process of developing a composite Web service as *service composition*.

As we have seen in Chapter 3, the implementation effort required to develop complex applications from other applications is far from trivial, and this is also true for service composition. To support developers in this effort, the *Web services composition middleware* provides abstractions and infrastructures facilitating the definition and execution of a composite service. The concepts and technologies that underline such middleware are the focus of this chapter. As in other chapters, we start by clarifying the need for service composition (Section 8.1). We then discuss why Web services have a chance of making composition a viable proposition, overcoming the problems encountered in EAI and workflows (Section 8.2). Next, we go into the details of service composition by examining the different issues to be addressed in developing a composite service and by showing different kinds of service composition models (Section 8.3). At that point, once the reader is familiar with the basic concepts of service composition, we examine the relationship between composition and coordination protocols, showing how protocol definitions pose requirements on how the composition should look (Section 8.4). Finally, as in the previous chapters, we present a recent standardization effort for composition: the Business Process Execution Language for Web Services, or BPEL (Section 8.5). Unlike previous chapters, however, we do not review other standardization proposals, as this language has managed to become the convergence point for all other analogous proposals.

8.1 Basics of Service Composition

8.1.1 Composition as a Way to Master Complexity

To understand the need for service composition technologies, and their purpose, we start again from our procurement example introduced in Section 7.1. We assume that the procurement procedure followed by the customer involves requesting quotes from multiple suppliers, selecting the supplier that offers the best deal, requesting approval for the purchase amount, and finally ordering the goods from the selected supplier (Figure 8.1). The suppliers are implemented as Web services, as is the internal application that manages approvals.

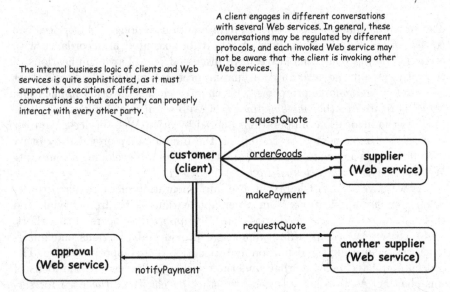

Fig. 8.1. The client is engaged in multiple conversations with different Web services to achieve its goals

Hence, the business logic of the client in this case is realized by composing multiple services, and by executing a different conversation with each of them. This is analogous to what happened in workflow management, where the business logic of an application was implemented composing other autonomous, coarse-grained applications [1]. Note that, in general, different Web services may support different protocols, and it is therefore the responsibility of the client to implement all the protocols needed to communicate with the invoked services.

---

[1] We will often use the term *service* composition, consistent with practice, although it is the *operations* offered by the service that are being combined.

One of the most interesting properties of service composition is that it can be iterated, allowing the definition of increasingly complex applications by progressively aggregating components, at increasingly higher levels of abstraction. In fact, as we have seen in the previous chapter, a client can itself be exposed as a Web service, and as such it can be used as a component by other, higher-level (composite) services. For example, the client of Figure 8.1 can be exposed as a procurement Web service that is used internally by the customer to implement a supply-chain Web service involving procurement and other functions, such as the managing of receipts and the internal distribution of the goods once they are delivered or the performing of internal accounting operations (Figure 8.2). Hence, composition can be seen as a way to master complexity, where complex services are incrementally built out of services at a lower abstraction level.

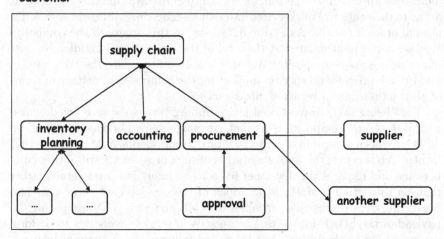

Fig. 8.2. Composite services are themselves Web services, and can be used as components for creating other composite services, at higher levels of abstraction

Observe that unlike traditional composition (both in software engineering and manufacturing), composition of Web services is not based on the physical integration of all components. Web services are not application libraries to be compiled and linked as part of an application. Instead, they are interfaces that can be used to invoke them. As in EAI, composition of Web services equates to specifying which services need to be invoked, in what order, and how to handle exceptional situations. The basic components remain separated from the composite service.

8.1.2 The Need for Service Composition Middleware

Today, the most widely used approach to composition is to code the composite Web service by means of conventional programming languages such as Java or C#. The reason is simple. Composite Web services are still being used mostly in single enterprise settings as a way to bridge heterogeneous middleware platforms. In those environments, service development and composition is traditionally done through programming languages, as this is the dominant approach in conventional middleware. For instance, TP monitors extend programming languages for composition in a transactional RPC setting (e.g., Encina's *Transactional-C* and *Transactional-C++* [101]). Such extensions, typically in the form of libraries and procedure stubs, provide the additional logic necessary to perform composition directly at the programming language level. It is a natural and obvious step to use the same approach for Web services. The way Web services standards are being designed even promotes this approach to a certain extent, since SOAP was initially intended as a way to turn calls to Web services into remote procedure calls, which look like normal procedure calls. As Figure 8.3 shows, in this approach the composite Web service is implemented at the level of the conventional middleware, just like basic (i.e., non-composite) Web services. In other words, the Web services middleware provides no specific support for the composition, neither in terms of abstractions nor in terms of infrastructure.

That being said, conventional programming languages were not designed with Web service composition in mind. Although many libraries and standard APIs have been defined in order to facilitate the development of programs that invoke Web services, the implementation of such programs is still rather cumbersome and requires the developer to focus on many low-level details rather than on the actual business logic. Much of the development effort goes into converting data from scalar variables to XML and vice versa, preparing the payload of the SOAP messages, accessing Web services registries to perform dynamic binding, handling persistence and failures, managing multiple concurrent conversations, and the like. Furthermore, the business logic and these low-level details are intermingled in the code, meaning that not only the development of the composition, but also its maintenance, can prove to be very complex. We have encountered similar problems when discussing application integration in Chapter 3, and we have shown that they lead to the need for higher-level programming models, such as those of workflows. This need exists for Web services as well, and the proof lies in the many languages proposed for Web services composition (e.g., XL [74], WSFL [119], and BPML [10]) and in the many composition systems provided by most major software vendors. These different approaches share many similarities and have converged into the BPEL language [7], discussed later in this chapter.

In the following discussion, we underline the main characteristics shared by virtually any kind of service composition middleware.

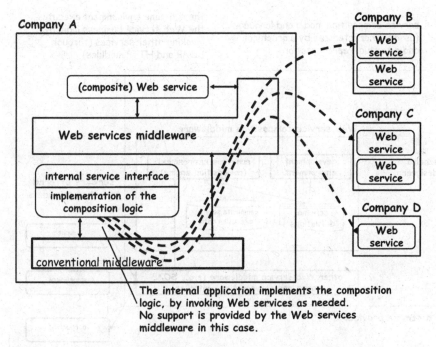

Fig. 8.3. In the absence of Web service composition middleware, the implementation of a composite Web service resides in the conventional middleware

8.1.3 Main Elements of Web Services Composition Middleware

To understand the nature of Web services composition middleware, it should be noted that service composition is an implementation technology. Service composition defines how to implement a Web service by composing other services. Correspondingly, the Web services composition middleware comprises abstractions and tools that facilitate the definition and execution of a composite service by allowing developers to focus on the business logic rather than on low-level details. This middleware (Figure 8.4) includes:

- a **composition model and language**, enabling the specification of the services to be combined, the order in which the different services are to be invoked (based possibly on run-time conditions), and the way in which service invocation parameters are determined (i.e., the way in which messages are built). The specification of a composite service expressed through a composition language is called *composition schema*. The schema therefore defines the business logic of a composite Web service, and can be seen as a program written in a language designed specifically for composing Web services rather than in a conventional programming language.
- a **development environment**, typically characterized by a graphical user interface, through which designers can specify a composition schema by

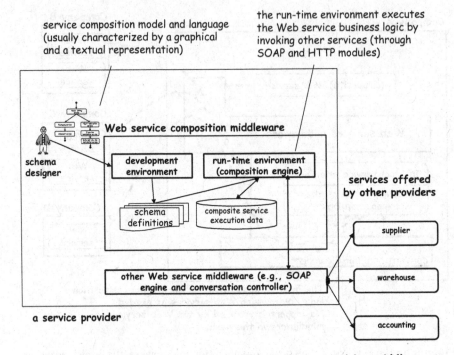

service composition model and language
(usually characterized by a graphical
and a textual representation)

the run-time environment executes
the Web service business logic by
invoking other services (through
SOAP and HTTP modules)

Fig. 8.4. Fundamental elements of a Web service composition middleware

dragging and dropping Web services into a canvas and by then designing
graphs denoting the order in which the services are to be invoked. The
graphs and other descriptive information are then translated into textual
specifications (the composition schema).

- a **run-time environment**, often called *composition engine*, that executes
  the business logic of the composite Web service by invoking component
  services as defined in the schema. Each execution of a composite service is
  called a *composition instance*.

Note that when service composition middleware is used, the implementation of the composite service is done at the Web services middleware level and
not within the conventional middleware, as shown in Figure 8.5.

8.1.4 Composition Versus Coordination Middleware

Now that we have described what composition middleware is about, we summarize the key differences between composition and coordination middleware.
This is a difficult but important issue to understand how Web services are implemented in practice, and is often source of confusion when speaking about
Web services middleware.

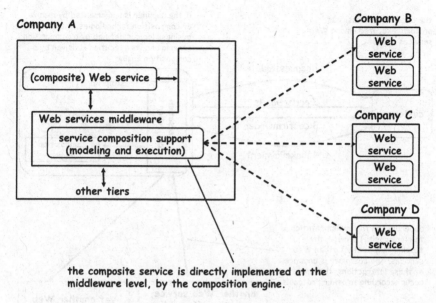

the composite service is directly implemented at the
middleware level, by the composition engine.

Fig. 8.5. By using Web service composition middleware, the implementation of a
composite Web service resides in the Web services middleware

As we have seen, service composition is about the internal implementation
of operations in a Web service. The specification of a composite service is
done by a company and is kept private, i.e., it is not typically advertised
to clients through Web services registries. This is because companies do not
want to expose how they implement their operations. The specification of the
composition is for the consumption of the Web services middleware, which
automates the *execution* of the composition by invoking operations offered by
other Web services as specified in the composition schema (Figure 8.6).

Being about implementation, whether a service is basic or composite is
irrelevant from the client's perspective. A client does not need to be aware of
how a service is implemented–whether it is implemented using a conventional
programming language or through service composition technologies.

The scope and purpose of composition are therefore in sharp contrast
with those of coordination protocols, described in the previous chapter. Coordination protocols are in fact public documents, described by standardization
consortia and by means of standard languages (or at least this will be the
case once standard languages become available and widely accepted). These
documents are meant to be advertised in Web services registries, and their
purpose is to support design-time discovery and run-time binding. There is no
point in keeping the specifications private, as otherwise binding is not possible.
Conversations compliant with a coordination protocol are supported by conversation controllers, whose purpose is not to execute any business logic, but
to dispatch messages to internal objects and to *verify* protocol compliance.

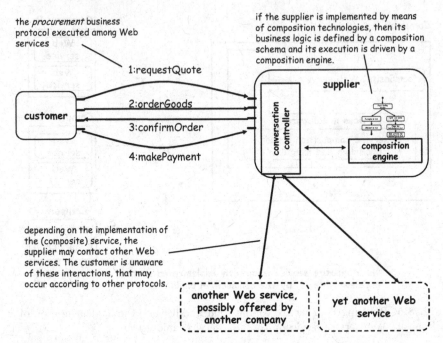

the *procurement* business
protocol executed among Web
services

if the supplier is implemented by means
of composition technologies, then its
business logic is defined by a composition
schema and its execution is driven by a
composition engine.

depending on the implementation of
the (composite) service, the
supplier may contact other Web
services. The customer is unaware
of these interactions, that may
occur according to other protocols.

Fig. 8.6. Composition and coordination protocols have a different scope: external interaction versus external implementation

The conversation controller could be unaware of whether it is dispatching messages to a basic or a composite service.

Part of the confusion between these concepts arises from the fact that a process that describes a Web service A that invokes another Web service B must reflect the coordination protocol that governs the conversations with Web service B. In fact, the coordination protocol imposes requirements on how the composition is to take place, since the order in which operations are invoked has to be compliant with the protocol definition. On the other hand, the composition logic determines the conversations that a composite service is able to execute. Thus, there is a clear relationship between a Web service's *internal* composition and *external* coordination.

We will revisit the subtle relationships between composition and protocols later in this chapter, once the reader is more familiar with the details of service composition. For now, it will suffice to keep in mind the above-mentioned differences between the two.

8.2 A New Chance of Success for Composition?

Composition is hardly a new idea. It has been proposed many times and is in fact what EAI and workflows are about. Indeed, service composition has many similarities with workflow technology, the main difference being that some of the actions in the business process happen to be the invocation of Web services operations rather than conventional applications. However, when discussing traditional application integration technology in Chapter 3, we commented that such systems had only limited success and, to a certain extent, proved to be a disappointment from the point of view of composition. There were several reasons for this. Systems supporting composition were complex, difficult to deploy and maintain, had a very steep learning curve, and still required a significant development effort, especially when the integration logic involved heterogeneous and distributed systems. Now we are back to composition, but in the context of Web services. Will Web services composition suffer from the same limitations and drawbacks of workflow management systems? Before we start discussing Web services composition, we need to find an answer to this question.

8.2.1 Limitations of Conventional Composition Middleware

The success of composition as a technique for building complex systems depends on the availability of adequate components and adequate component interoperability models. This requires a precise description of their functionality (what the components do) as well as of the interfaces and protocols they support (how they can be interconnected with the other components). To make these descriptions universally understandable and easily implementable, they must follow a standard notation and syntax. This is precisely what is missing in conventional middleware. One of the trademarks of conventional middleware is to make as few assumptions as possible about the nature of the components. Indeed, WfMS and EAI systems are very flexible and generic, enabling the integration of all sorts of applications, typically through the development of application-specific adapters (wrappers). There is no need for a standard way of describing components. However, this gain in flexibility has a price in complexity and cost. Incorporating a new component always requires considerable development effort.

As an example, consider a workflow system: its basic function is to place work items in the appropriate work queue at the appropriate time. It is up to the component (or, more likely, to an adapter providing the linkage between the component and the WfMS) to pick up the work from the queue and execute it. This approach requires that the component (or the adapter acting on its behalf) be aware of the WfMS API and interact with it according to the WfMS-specific protocols and data formats. Hence, composition requires ad hoc development for every type of component.

Some of this work can be avoided by using message brokers to interact with external applications. In this case, the integration work consists in either configuring the adapter connecting the broker to the application or in developing the adapter if none is available (Section 3.3). In any case, the end effect is that conventional middleware requires additional development for composition, as components cannot be simply plugged together. To make matters worse, this development is largely system and vendor specific. There is very little hope of being able to port solutions from one system to another, thereby increasing the cost of development and making it very difficult to evolve the resulting systems.

Another important problem in conventional middleware is the lack of a standard composition model. There has been no lack of ideas on how such models should look like as process models have been produced by the dozen [68, 106]. However, consolidation was never achieved. Thus, creating a component that provided an interface according to a given composition model and system often meant that such component could not be used anywhere else. Of course, there have been several attempts at standardization. For instance, the Workflow Management Coalition (WfMC) [221], a consortium of workflow vendors, has tried to make some progress in this direction. It is only fair to say, however, that the WfMC efforts have had limited success. Only a handful of vendors actually implement the proposed standards, and the standards themselves are too generic to serve as useful references for composition. Another example of standardization are the efforts around CORBA. The drawback of CORBA, however, is that its composition model is too low level to be useful at the granularity of EAI or Web services.

8.2.2 Opportunities for Web Service Composition Middleware

What makes Web services different from the point of view of composition? The main difference is that Web services appear to be adequate components. They have well-defined interfaces, and their behavior is specified as part of the information provided in Web services registries. In addition, they have been standardized: they are described using the same language (WSDL) and invoked by sending XML documents packaged into SOAP messages. All this suggests that Web services may be well suited to composition. To see this more concretely, consider a conventional and a Web service workflow management system. The former will be continuously hampered by the heterogeneity of the components and by the need for manual integration at every turn. The latter can work on standard interfaces and protocols to provide a much faster and efficient integration, since the composition system can natively support the interaction protocols of the component.

Note that standardization does not immediately resolve all interoperability problems. An RPC-based service is still incompatible with a queue-based service, regardless of whether they are Web services. If these two services need to be connected, integration efforts are needed regardless of whether the components use conventional or Web services middleware. An advantage of Web services standards is that they advocate a common language for components that can be used across all platforms. Although components may still be incompatible, we at least do not need to worry about the dialect of IDL used in each component or about how to carry an invocation to a remote system.

In addition to the standardization of component representation, a big part of the effort in Web services is also being devoted to the standardization of composition models. For instance, BPEL [7] has been proposed as a way to model and program the composition by combining services whose interfaces are specified in WSDL. WS-Transaction (discussed in the previous chapter) is a similar attempt to agree on how to perform transaction-based composition. As with conventional middleware, it is likely that different composition models will appear. This is not necessarily a bad thing, as long as their number remains relatively small, since different applications need different composition models (e.g., not all applications need transactions). One important characteristic of Web services is that such composition models will be standard and, therefore, tools that automatically support such models will be developed. This will also result in less steep learning curves (there being no need to learn a new language when a new composition model is used).

Web services also promise to reduce significantly the cost and complexity of developing such systems, as many system modules will be similar for all platforms. For instance, Web services offer standardized directory and service selection mechanisms (e.g., UDDI) that can be easily adopted (and adapted if necessary) by any composition system. Hence, service composition can be provided by a relatively lightweight component with respect to workflows. The hope is for simpler, less expensive, and more standardized Web services composition tools.

The standardization efforts described above have the potential for focusing research and development efforts on common requirements. A good comparison is the effect that the relational model had on databases. Once the relational model became widely adopted, developing algorithms, optimizations, and mechanisms for storing and manipulating data became a much more attractive endeavor. Students and professionals could develop skills that were system-independent and applicable across a wide market. A generic database architecture emerged and a shared understanding of complex problems quickly evolved among developers and researchers. Web services can play a similar role in the area of middleware and service composition, a development that can only result in better systems.

Collectively, it would seem that service composition has higher chances of succeeding than workflow management. Service composition systems, still in their infancy (since the area of Web services itself is quite young), promise to be lightweight and easy to use, enabling the rapid design and development of services by composing other services. Indeed, it looks like the "dream" of workflow management. Creating new, complex applications quickly by almost literally drawing boxes and arrows on a screen could finally become reality thanks to Web services.

8.3 Service Composition Models

Service composition models can be quite complex. In the following we discuss the different dimensions of a service composition model and analyze each one in detail. This presentation will be instrumental in understanding in more detail what composition is about. Throughout this section we will often use terminology borrowed from the workflow domain. In particular, we use the term *process definition* (or simply *process*) to refer to a composition schema, while *process instance* refers to a specific, individual execution of a process definition. The term *orchestration schema* (or simply *orchestration*) refers to the part of the composition schema that specifies the order in which the different component services should be invoked.

8.3.1 Dimensions of a Web Service Composition Model

As a first step toward characterizing service composition, we consider six different *dimensions* of a composition model:

- **Component model**. It defines the nature of the elements to be composed in terms of the assumptions that the model makes on such components.
- **Orchestration model**. It defines abstractions and languages used to define the order in which services are to be invoked. We consider several possibilities: activity diagrams, Petri-nets, π-calculus, statecharts, activity hierarchies, and rule-based orchestration.
- **Data and data access model**. It defines how data is specified and how it is exchanged between components.
- **Service selection model**. It defines how static or dynamic binding takes place, i.e., how a specific service is selected as a component.
- **Transactions**. It defines which transactional semantics can be associated to the composition, and how this is done.
- **Exception handling**. It defines how exceptional situations occurring during the execution of the composite service can be handled, without resulting in the composite service being aborted.

8.3.2 Component Model

A key difference between composition models is the type of components they consider and what is assumed about them. At one extreme, a model can assume that components implement a specific set of Web services standards, such as HTTP, SOAP, WSDL, and WS-Transaction. Making such assumptions makes composition easier, since it limits heterogeneity. At the other extreme, a composition model may make only very basic assumptions about components. For example, it may only assume that components interact by exchanging XML messages in either a synchronous (RPC-like) or asynchronous fashion. The advantages of doing so are obvious: the model is more general.

The disadvantages are also clear: making composition work is much more involved because of the heterogeneity of the components.

An interesting intermediate solution is to simultaneously support different models and offer additional facilities for components that do not fall into any of the supported models. However, this openness results in languages that are more complex (too much choice is often equivalent to no choice!) and in heavier systems, due to the need to support multiple formats and protocols.

As with component granularity, the jury is still out on which one will be the winning approach. Currently, the leading composition language (BPEL) assumes that components are WSDL services, and relies as well on other standards, such as XPath and WS-Addressing. Future versions are likely to be integrated with WS-Transaction.

8.3.3 Orchestration Model

Orchestration deals with how different services are composed into a coherent whole. In particular, it specifies the order in which services are invoked, and the conditions under which a certain service may or may not be invoked. Many orchestration models have been proposed in the literature (see, e.g., [139, 7, 119, 47, 178, 1]). However, they are all variations of a few, basic models, discussed next.

To introduce these models we refer again to our procurement example, although in a slightly simplified version for ease of presentation. We assume that a supplier Web service allows customers to place orders, by invoking an *orderGoods* operation. The supplier, implemented using service composition technologies, executes this operation by invoking other services. Therefore, its business logic is defined by a composition schema. The orchestration of the composition schema is illustrated in Figure 8.7, where it is modeled by means of a UML activity diagram [154]. Activity diagrams (and, in general, techniques based on flow charts or variations thereof) are the most widely used process modeling paradigm, both in conventional middleware (workflows) and in Web services. The reason for their success is that, in this paradigm, orchestrations are defined by specifying which operations should be invoked, from the beginning of the execution to the end. This seems to be the most natural way in which people think of a process, and it is analogous to how developers code their applications. The reader should not be confused by the fact that, in some cases, simplified versions of activity diagrams are also used to model coordination protocols. While the paradigm is similar, its use has different purposes, as we have seen.

The business logic of the Web service is as follows: when the orderGoods operation is invoked by a customer, a new composite service instance is started. The composite Web service invokes operation *checkLocalStock*, offered by a local Web service and used by the supplier to determine whether the requested goods are in stock. If so, the supplier confirms the order to the customer, by invoking the *confirmOrder* operation offered by the customer's

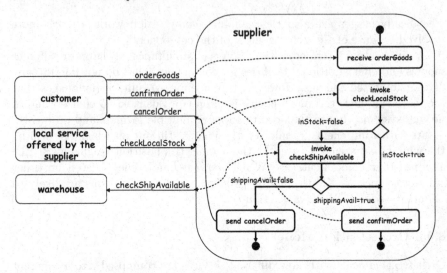

Fig. 8.7. The supplier Web service modeled as an activity diagram. Dashed lines depict the relation between (internal) activities and (external) protocol messages

Web service. Otherwise, the supplier contacts a warehouse to verify whether the goods are available at that location. If so, the supplier again confirms the availability to the customer, otherwise the order is canceled. Note that the *checkLocalStock* operation was not present in the description of the procurement protocol, emphasizing again that a composite service may indeed implement different protocols and that some aspects of the behavior of a service are not exposed as part of a protocol. This example is quite simple and does not involve any sophisticated control or information flow. It suffices, nevertheless, for the purposes of illustrating the different orchestration models we will consider. It is also a good starting point to understand the complexities of service composition. Different variations of the activity diagram paradigm assign slightly different semantics to the activities.

In the diagram of Figure 8.7, we assume that activities always model the notification (or the receipt) of a message to (from) a Web service:

- Notifications of messages to other Web services (invocations of one-way operations offered by the component Web services) are modeled by means of *send* activities, such as the *send cancelOrder* in the example. Send activities are non blocking.
- Invocations of synchronous (request/reply) operations offered by another Web service are modeled by means of *invoke* activities, such as the *invoke checkLocalStock* in the example. This activity is blocking, since it waits for a reply from the invoked service.
- Receipts of messages, corresponding to component services invoking one-way or request/reply operations offered by the composite service, are modeled by *receive* activities, such as the *receive orderGoods* in the example.

They are also blocking, since the execution of the composite Web service does not proceed until the message is received.

- If the received message is invoking a request/reply operation, then the composition schema will also include a *reply* activity, that will send a response to the invoking client.

In addition to messages sent and received, activity definitions typically include many more details, depending again on the specifics of a model. These may include the definition of the service (URL) to which the message should be sent, of how the message should be constructed based on the execution of previous activities, or of how exceptions that may occur during activity executions should be handled. We will examine these later in this section. Note that, unlike activity diagrams for protocol description, conditions and data items are fully specified here, as there are no confidentiality issues (specifications are private) and as the specifications must include all the information necessary to execute them (no room for non-determinism).

Although activity diagrams are the most popular orchestration paradigm, a number of alternative models, each emphasizing different aspects of the orchestration, also exist. We briefly examine them below.

Statecharts

Statecharts are formalisms based on state machines. However, they extend state machines to enable the definition of the activities to be performed while entering a state, while exiting a state, or while within a state. They also allow events, conditions, and actions to be associated to a transition, such as to define a transition to be fired at the occurrence of an event if an associated Boolean condition is true. In this case, the specified action is also performed. A number of other extensions are also provided, including composite states, composite transitions, parallel states, synchronization after the execution of parallel composite states, and many more. The extensions are so rich that we have probably reached the point at which the distinction between statecharts and activity-oriented models is blurred. Indeed, according to the Unified Modeling Language (UML) specification document [154], activity graphs are "a variation of a state machine in which the states represent performance of actions or subactivities and the transitions are triggered by the completion of the actions of subactivities."

As an example, Figure 8.8 models the orchestration of the supplier service by means of a statechart. As the figure shows, the emphasis is on states, while activities are almost "hidden." Although this is a limitation, the interesting aspect is that we now have an explicit notion of state that was missing from activity diagrams. This enables the development of tools that provide state information. If we assign meaningful names to states, we are able to quickly get useful information on the progress of an instance. In contrast, with activity-oriented models, a tool would only be able to tell us which activity is in execution. Since activity names tend to be cryptic and implementation-specific, once processes become complex (e.g., "get user data from database XYZ") they are not typically useful to provide monitoring and tracking information. One of the most relevant contributions in orchestration modeling by means of statecharts is provided by Mentor [219, 218].

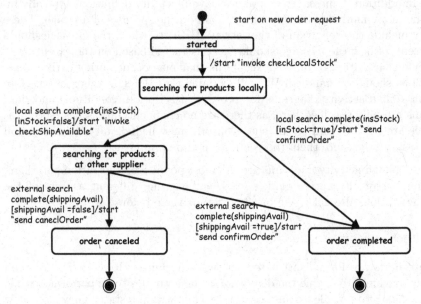

Fig. 8.8. The supplier process specified by means of a statechart

Petri Nets

Orchestration models based on *Petri nets* [169] combine an activity-oriented paradigm (like activity diagrams) with the definition of process states (like statecharts). In addition, the properties of Petri nets have defined and well-known semantics, and have been thoroughly studied. This is precisely the advantage of Petri net-based models. They can leverage this huge body of work as well as benefit from many existing automated analysis tools. These tools help users in assessing the properties of the specification and can detect deadlocks or other potentially erroneous conditions.

Figure 8.9 shows the supplier service described as a Petri net. Some transitions are labeled with Boolean predicates denoting when they are triggered. Examples of Petri net-based models for defining orchestrations are *WorkFlow nets* [204] and *Orchestration nets* [132] A thorough discussion on Petri net-based process modeling is provided in [205]. Several commercial applications as well as research prototypes are currently available for the design and analy-

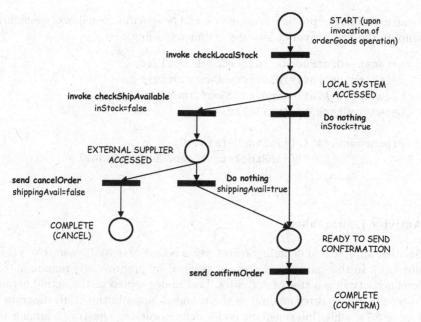

Fig. 8.9. The supplier process specified by means of a Petri net

sis of processes using Petri net-based models. Examples are Promatis process designer by Promatis [168], and Woflan [207].

π-calculus

π-calculus [143] is a process algebra that has inspired modern composition languages such as XLANG [139] and, subsequently, BPEL. It descends from *Communicating Sequential Processes* (CSP) [95], from the *Algebra of Communicating Processes with Abstractions* (ACP) [107] and from the *Calculus of Concurrent Systems* (CCS) [142]. π-calculus can be seen as an attempt at developing a formal theory of process models, analogous to what relational algebra did for the relational model. As with Petri nets, the rationale behind using π-calculus for describing processes lies in the advantages that a precise and well-studied formalism can provide for the verification of its properties.

There are several variants of π-calculus. They are all based, however, on the same basic principles. From an orchestration perspective, π-calculus offers constructs to compose activities in terms of sequential, parallel, or conditional execution. Specifically, the notation $A.B$ denotes that activity A happens before activity B, $A|B$ denotes that A and B occur in parallel, $A + B$ denotes that either A or B is executed (the choice is non-deterministic), while $[var = value]A$ denotes that A is executed if and only if var equals $value$. These notations can be combined to define orchestrations of arbitrary complexity.

As an example, the procurement process can be specified as follows (we slightly simplify the actual syntax for ease of understanding):

```
A=receiveOrderGoods.invokeCheckLocalStock
B=[shippingAvail=false]sendCancelOrder+
  [shippingAvail=true]sendConfirmOrder
C=invokeCheckShipAvailable.B

Procurement=A.( ([inStock=false]C) +
                ([inStock=true]sendConfirmOrder)
              )
```

Activity Hierarchies

Another approach to defining orchestration is that of *activity hierarchies* (Figure 8.10). In this model, a process is specified by progressively refining a top-level activity into a tree of activities. Leaf nodes represent the actual actions to be executed (corresponding to the rounded boxes in the UML diagram of Figure 8.7), while intermediate nodes define ordering constraint among the child activities.

This formalism tends to be less practical and intuitive for designers, both because of the need to introduce "artificial" steps and because of the need to think in terms of the chronological ordering of the steps (which is equivalent to designing the hierarchy depth-first, by expanding the left subtrees). These are the reasons why most commercial systems are based on activity diagrams, at least at the GUI level.

However, models based on activity hierarchies have several advantages. The structure that they impose makes it possible to look at the orchestration from different levels of abstraction: higher abstraction levels are toward the root of the tree, while more details can be progressively uncovered by traversing the tree toward the leaves. They also naturally modularize the definitions, making it easier to modularize the schema and delegate the specification of different modules to different designers.

An example of orchestration model based on activity hierarchies is *Little-JIL* [48, 217].

Rule-based Orchestration

An orchestration schema can also be specified by means of a set of *rules*. Rule-based specifications are often used in reactive systems, i.e., systems that monitor one or more applications for the occurrence of *events* of interest, in particular for events signaling some critical conditions. Once the event is detected, a specified *action* is performed to handle the situation. As such, rules in software systems are typically specified by <event-action> pairs. In

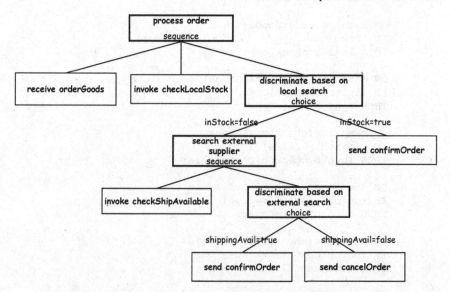

Fig. 8.10. The supplier process specified by an activity hierarchy

some models, a rule specification can also include a *condition*, i.e., a Boolean predicate over event parameters, evaluated when the event is detected, that defines whether the action should be executed. When the rule language allows the specification of conditions, the rule model is said to follow the so-called *event-condition-action* (ECA) paradigm.

The analogy with service composition lies in the observation that a composition engine can be considered a kind of reactive system. In fact, it reacts to messages received by clients or other services (events) by progressing through the orchestration schema (which may include conditions), and by eventually sending other messages (actions).

Figure 8.11 shows a rule-based specification for the supplier service. Note that, although rules are written in a sequence to make it easier for the reader to understand the semantics, there is no ordering between them. Each rule is "triggerable" as the service is invoked.

Unlike activity hierarchies, rule-based models are inherently less structured and less amenable to imposing an order in the flow. They are well suited to model orchestrations that have few constraints among activities and where a few rules can therefore specify the entire schema.

In addition, since rules are always triggerable, they can model activities that are to be started at the occurrence of asynchronous events, i.e., events that can happen at any stage during process execution. This characteristic makes them suitable for defining exception-handling logic that, just like rules, is asynchronous and reactive in nature.

Despite their applicability in some contexts, rules have had limited success in orchestration models and languages. Their problem is that, unless the

```
ON receive orderGoods
IF true
THEN invoke checkLocalStock;

ON complete(checkLocalStock)
IF (inStock==true)
THEN send confirmOrder;

ON complete(checkLocalStock)
IF (inStock==false)
THEN invoke checkShipAvailable;

ON complete(checkShipAvailable)
IF (shippingAvail ==true)
THEN send confirmOrder;

ON complete(checkShipAvailable)
IF (shippingAvail ==true)
THEN send cancelOrder;
```

Fig. 8.11. The supplier process specified by means of rules

orchestration is very simple, specifications become difficult to understand and maintain. Imagine having to go through 50 or 100 rules, trying to figure out the behavior that they describe. In the best case it will be very time-consuming; in the worst case it will lead to erroneous interpretations.

Examples of rule-based orchestration languages exist, but they are mainly confined to research prototypes of process management systems developed on top of DBMSs (database management systems) [59, 46, 113].

8.3.4 Data and Data Transfer Model

Like programming languages, service composition models need explicit ways to define and access data. We first examine the different kinds of data involved in service composition and how to define them, and then show how data can be passed among the different Web services being composed.

Data Types

At a very general level, data used during composition can be divided into *application-specific* data and *control flow* data. Application specific data are the parameters sent or received as part of message exchanges. For example, when the operation *checkShipAvailable* is invoked on the warehouse, data items such as the product needed and the desired delivery date are passed to the Web service of the warehouse, typically as part of an XML message transported through SOAP. Control flow relevant data are essentially the ones used to evaluate branching conditions, and in general those accessed by the composition engine to determine how the execution should proceed. They are often referred to as *process variables*. For example, in the supplier service, variables *inStock* and *shippingAvail* are used to determine which branches of the flow should be followed (orchestration schema of Figure 8.7).

In most systems, application data is richer than control flow data. This makes sense, since control flow can generally be done using a few selected data items. Application data, on the other hand, can be more complex and involve more sophisticated data types. Control flow data is usually restricted to a few basic types such as string, integer, or real, although a few models also include complex types such as structures or arrays. The value of control flow data is typically derived from messages received by the Web services that are part of the composition, according to some user-defined mapping.

There are two approaches for application specific data. One approach treats the data as a black box and concerns itself only with forwarding pointers from one activity to the next. This means that instead of exchanging textual documents or image files, the Web services only exchange URLs or other kind of pointers to the location where the data resides. From the perspective of the composition schema, the URL is the application data, while the actual data is hidden from the schema. The other approach tries to make all the application data explicit by including appropriate data definitions as part of the composition schema, similar to what is done for control flow data.

Treating application data as a black box has several advantages. One is that the composition model can ignore complex data exchanges between the activities. Early workflow systems adopted this approach for very pragmatic reasons: if all the data exchanged is part of the process, the engine has to deal with large volumes of data [120]. Many processes involve complex documents that are sent back and forth with minimal modifications after each step. Making the document an intrinsic part of the process, and therefore under the control of the system, resulted in processes of such enormous size that the system quickly collapsed. The black box approach forces developers to write additional wrappers since most applications expect to receive the actual data and not just a pointer.

In terms of data types for variables and application specific data, many systems today support a generic *XML* type that may or may not be associated with a certain XML schema (see, e.g., [92]). In *puristic* models everything is XML, including control flow data (as in XL [74]). An XML data type makes perfect sense for application specific data as this is the standard representation used in Web services. Unfortunately, XML documents are a very inefficient way to represent information, requiring lots of parsing and data conversions. Many applications have no reason at all to work in XML. This is recognized by the attempts to include binary attachments in SOAP messages, attachments that may or may not correspond to Multi-Purpose Internet Mail Extensions (MIME) types. Once this practice is generalized, XML documents may become simple containers for application specific information that can only be treated as a black box.

Data Transfer

Data transfer refers to how data is passed from one operation invocation to the next. There are essentially two types of approaches to data transfer: the *blackboard* approach and the *explicit data flow*.

The blackboard approach is analogous to conventional programming languages. It is based on the principle that all data involved in the execution of the composite service is explicitly named and listed. The blackboard is a collection of variables where activities (operation invocations) deposit their output and gather their input. When an operation is invoked, the message to be sent as input takes its values from the variables in the blackboard, according to a mapping defined as part of the composition schema. Similarly, whenever a message is received as output of an operation, the data in the message is mapped back to variables in the blackboard. Modifications to variables are performed "atomically" as the message is received, and changes due to the receipt of previous messages are overwritten. Activities may have different access rights to the variables (e.g., read-write or read-only). Each composition instance has its own blackboard, just like every execution of a program has its own set of values for the program variables. Many models and systems are based on this approach (see, e.g., [92, 7]).

The explicit data flow approach is based on making the data flow between activities (in addition to the control flow) an explicit part of the composition. By using data flow connectors between activities, the designer may specify that the input data of an activity (such as the data to be used for building messages that constitute the operation invocation) should be taken from the output data of other, previously executed activities. Consider, for instance, the simple sequential process depicted in Figure 8.12: the control flow specifies that activities A,B, and C should be executed in sequence. However, in the data flow approach it is possible to specify that activity C will take the version of data item *quantity* returned by the execution of A instead of that returned by B. The explicit data flow approach has been used in several workflow engines like MQSeries Workflow [104] and BioOpera [15], and has been adopted as part of the WSFL specification [119] in the context of Web services.

Which of these two approaches works best depends on many factors. Data flow approaches are more flexible and richer than blackboard approaches. However, they also introduce more complexity in the design. In fact, they create implicit control dependencies, as activities that are the source of a data flow must be completed for the destination activity to commence, since data must be available before the activity can start. Furthermore, data flow approaches could cause race conditions in cases where the same input data item can be provided by different data flows. We also observe that the black-

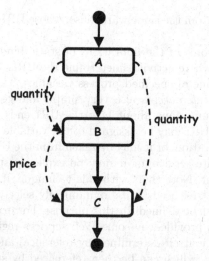

Fig. 8.12. Data flow approach for data transfer between components

board approach is more natural for programmers, as this is the way most programming languages work for data transfer.

8.3.5 Service Selection

We have seen that a composition schema enables the specification of messages to be sent and received and the order in which message exchanges should occur. To execute the composition logic, the engine must also be informed which specific service (e.g., which URL) is to be the target of a message. Typically, this information is specified in abstract terms in the composition schema (e.g., the message is sent to a service supporting a certain port type or playing a certain role and not to an actual endpoint). Hence, composition languages typically compose port types rather than actual ports. However, at run-time, before the message is sent, the port type needs to be resolved to a specific service so that the engine knows who is to be the recipient. In other words, the composite service must select (bind to) specific services. There are at least four ways in which this can be done: static binding, dynamic binding by reference, dynamic binding by lookup, and dynamic operation selection.

The easiest approach to service selection is to hardcode the URL as part of the composite service specification. This is equivalent to *static binding*. The simplicity inherent in this technique makes it the most widely used service selection mechanism, and it is particularly useful when prototyping and testing the composition. The obvious drawbacks are that it is not robust to changes of the service URI (the process definition needs to be modified and re-deployed when this happens), and that all instances always invoke the same service, so there is actually no "selection." For example, we are always forced to check availability from the same warehouse, whose URI is hardcoded in the specifications.

A way to avoid some of the limitations of static binding is to follow the *reference* approach, where activities determine the URIs of the services to be invoked from the value of specified process variables. This technique, called *dynamic binding by reference*, is also very simple and generic, in that it actually makes no assumptions about how the URI ends up in the variable. Typically, a specific URI may be assigned to the variable as a result of a previously executed operation, or it may be taken from the URI of the client that invoked the composite service, or it may be explicitly specified at the time of service deployment. Note that, with this technique, if the process semantics are such that a URI needs to be dynamically selected from a directory, then an activity must be defined for this purpose. For example, the invoking of an API operation provided by some Web services registry (whose URI is statically defined or is itself determined by reference) and the storing of the result into a variable, which can be then referenced by subsequent activities to determine the URI to be used (see Figure 8.13). The reference approach is a natural extension of the static one previously defined, retaining the same simplicity but adding the possibility of dynamically selecting the URI. Indeed, the majority of composition models and languages offer this approach to service selection.

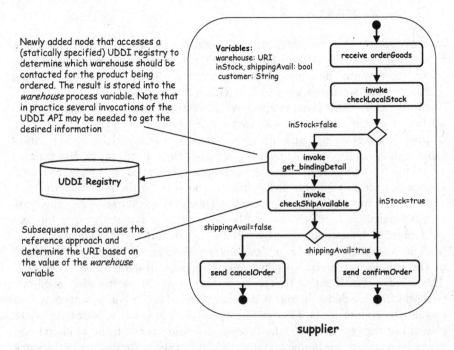

Fig. 8.13. Combining service selection by reference with access to a service directory

In *dynamic binding by lookup*, the composition middleware allows the definition, for each activity, of a query whose result will be used to determine the service to be invoked, to be executed on some directory. For example, the composition language WSFL [119] (one of the predecessors of BPEL) enables the definition, within an activity specification, of a service selection query to be executed on top of a UDDI registry. In this case, the specification of the service selection criteria is to be done according to the UDDI API format. In general, this approach may cause multiple URIs to be returned, since many services may satisfy the selection criterion. Therefore, this selection criterion is usually endowed with logic that enables the identification of one specific URI within a list. For example, the first taken or a randomly selected. URI.

As in CORBA and other conventional middleware, service composition models may allow forms of dynamic binding where not only the service, but also the operation to be invoked on the service, are determined dynamically. This gives us another approach to service selection called *dynamic operation selection*. For example, in a travel reservation process, an activity "book trip" may invoke different operations (and, of course, different services) depending on whether the customer wants to travel by boat, plane, or car. The choice can be modeled at the orchestration level, for example by introducing a condition that discriminates between the traveler's preferences by activating one of three different activities, as depicted in Figure 8.14. However, this approach makes the orchestration more complex and difficult to manage, especially as the number of possible choices grows. A more manageable and flexible solution consists of allowing the definition of *abstract* activities [80] (sometimes also called *generic* activities [47]), that do not explicitly specify the operation to be invoked. Instead, the operation is selected at run-time, along with the service. The choices available for selecting the operations are analogous to those described above for selecting the service URI, and are therefore not repeated here.

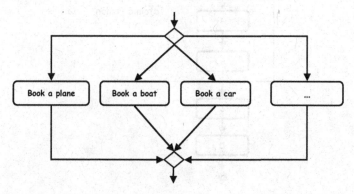

Fig. 8.14. Dynamic binding: the orchestration schema can become complex and difficult to maintain as the number of options grow

Dynamic operation selection can be also useful in those cases where the signature of the operation to be invoked varies with the selected service. In an ideal scenario, and wherever business interests converge, operation signatures will be standardized by some domain-specific consortium (as done by RosettaNet), and each service provider will support the same signature, thereby facilitating interoperability. However, in practice, there may be cases in which different service providers may offer the same (or similar) functionality but through different operations. For example, two different warehouses may offer two different operations to allow clients to determine whether products are in stock. Therefore, the operation to be invoked by the composite service depends on which service has been selected.

We must however observe that although dynamic operation selection is conceptually possible, it is also very difficult to implement, since as we already observed when speaking about CORBA and the Dynamic Invocation Interface, or DII (Chapter 3), it is very difficult to develop robust applications without knowing which particular operation will be invoked.

8.3.6 Transactions

The approach taken to provide transactional behavior to composite services consists of enabling the definition of *atomic regions* within an orchestration schema. The atomic region typically surrounds a set of activities that should exhibit the all-or-nothing property, i.e., either all or none of them should be executed (Figure 8.15). Atomicity can be achieved by executing 2PC protocols with the involved services, possibly based on the WS-Transaction specifications. This behavior can be fully implemented by the middleware, without requiring the designer to do any coding.

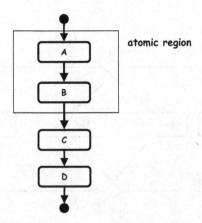

Fig. 8.15. A simple example of atomic region

The previous chapter has, however, motivated the need for looser transactional semantics, where ACID properties are relaxed, mainly due to the fact that it is impractical to lock resources for the long period of time often required to execute a composite service. In this case, the services invoked in the atomic region would actually commit, and therefore the 2PC approach is not applicable to guaranteeing atomicity. As we have seen, the solution adopted in this case relies on *compensation*, where committed service executions are semantically undone by executing other operations. From a service composition perspective this means that if a failure occurs, the Web services middleware will have to initiate and execute protocols to compensate for committed activities in order to roll back the partial execution of an atomic region. The compensation may be transparently handled by the engine that, in cooperation with the Web services middleware implementing the WS-Transaction specifications (particularly the business activity protocol), executes the compensation protocols to inform the invoked services of the need for compensation.

However, not all services support WS-Transaction. Furthermore, even when the invoked services do support WS-Transaction, the designer of the composite service may want to explicitly define the business logic executed to perform compensation. To cater to these situations, most composition models and languages that include transactional semantics (such as BPEL and its predecessors XLANG and BPML) provide abstractions borrowed from those of *sagas* [78]. The saga model allows long-lived transactions to be broken down into a set of sub-transactions to be executed in some predefined order, as shown in Figure 8.16. The sub-transactions have the "traditional" ACID properties. At their completion they commit, thereby releasing the locks and making the results visible to other (possibly concurrent) transactions. Each sub-transaction S_k is associated with a compensating transaction CS_k, whose execution semantically undoes the effect of the sub-transaction. A rollback of a saga is performed by aborting all active sub-transactions, and by then compensating for committed sub-transactions in the reverse order of execution. Many variations on the saga theme exist, such as *flexible transactions* [174] or *polytransactions* [179].

Many composition models today allow the designer to explicitly define the compensation logic, in the form of an orchestration schema that describes how the atomic region should be compensated. In this case, when a failure occurs, the composition engine aborts the active operations and executes the user-defined compensation logic.

At this point, another comparison between workflow and service composition is in order. The integration of process models with extended transaction models has been studied for years within the workflow research community. Approaches in this direction have been proposed by Meteor [220], by the *ConTracts* framework [170], and by the *WAMO* [64, 65], *Crew* [112], *Exotica* [4, 5], and *Changengine* projects [116]. A summary of the work done in workflow transactions during the past decade, both in the research world and

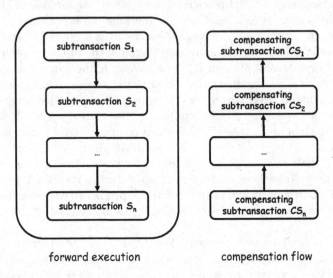

long-lived transaction T (saga)

forward execution   compensation flow

Fig. 8.16. A saga can be broken into ACID subtransactions, each associated to a compensating subtransaction

in commercial systems, is presented in [56]. Surprisingly, this large body of research translated into very few commercial products supporting transactions. Furthermore, even when transactional features are made available as part of the WfMS, they are not widely used.

The reason lies in the complexity of the design and development of the compensation logic. In conventional middleware, components do not provide compensation features out of the box and, even when they do, the heterogeneity problems discussed earlier in the chapter make them complex and difficult to leverage. Furthermore, there are no standard and commonly accepted compensation protocols. Therefore, the development of the compensation logic is left entirely to the designer of the composition. This can be a very difficult effort, requiring intimate knowledge of how each component works in order to properly compensate for its execution.

The situation in Web services appears to be different. First of all, standard transaction protocols are emerging. Along with them, several techniques for extending Web services interfaces and protocol languages with transaction and compensation information have been recently proposed [7, 141, 11, 21]. Collectively, these techniques share a trend toward placing the burden for implementing the compensation on the Web services developer, i.e., on the component side instead of on the composition side. If a component includes the definition of the transaction and compensation logic (e.g., states that operation o can be compensated for by operation c), then the designer of the composition is relieved, for the most part, from having to implement the compensation logic. That is, composition designers can simply invoke operation c whenever they need to compensate for o. If, in addition, the component supports standard compensation protocols, then we could eventually have a scenario where transactions (from a service composition perspective) are automatically supported without any effort from the designer, since not only could the description of each invoked component provide the information required to trigger its compensation, but the Web services composition middleware could also interpret this information (thanks to these standard descriptions and protocols) and perform the compensation in an automated fashion.

8.3.7 Exception Handling

In the context of Web services composition, the term *exception* refers to a deviation from the expected or desired execution of the composition. Exceptions can typically be caused by a failure in the system or in the invoked applications (e.g., the server goes down or an invoked service returns a fail message instead of the expected reply), or they can be situations that, although contemplated by the semantics of a Web service, are infrequent, such as when the customer cancels an order previously entered. Transactions are one possible way to handle exceptions, although they are sometimes a rather crude way to address the problem, since they essentially cause the partially completed work to be undone (i.e., to be lost). There are several other ways in which exceptions can be modeled and handled within a composition, possibly to be used in conjunction with transactions, that aim at providing more flexibility. We next examine the main techniques.

Flow-based Approaches

When no specific exception-handling constructs are available, developers can handle exceptions by using the *flow-based* approach. This technique is analogous to the one adopted when coding application logic in a third-generation language that does not have exception support: basically, at the end of each operation invocation, the result is tested for errors, and appropriate actions are taken if an error has been detected. An analogous behavior can be implemented in service composition, by properly placing conditional branches after the activities to be tested for failures, as shown in Figure 8.17. We observe that an important kind of exceptional situation, present in service composition but not so important in conventional computer programs, is one in which the invoked operation does not return a result at all. This case can be handled with the same technique, but requires the definition of timeouts associated with activities, so that when the timeout expires the activity is terminated by the engine and the execution proceeds.

Note that exceptions can also be explicitly thrown by the composition engine or by a Web service, and in contexts other than for signaling a failure

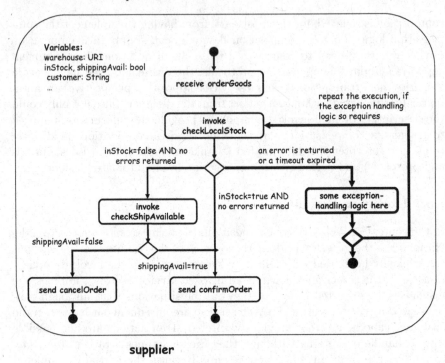

supplier

Fig. 8.17. Failures can be handled analogously to what is done in many programming languages, when no ad hoc support is available. The exception-handling part of the flow is depicted in bold

in response to an operation invoked by the composite service. In this case, the exception is captured by activities associated with one-way or request-reply operations, which are instantiated as a message is received. For example, a designer may define exception-handling logic by defining an activity that "listens" to (is instantiated upon) messages such as a customer cancellation request, and that invokes an exception-handling part of the orchestration.

Try-catch-throw Approaches

This technique is conceptually very similar to what is done in Java through the try, catch, and throw instructions (hence the name), although adapted to service composition. The idea here is to associate exception-handling logic to an activity (or to a group of activities). The exception is sensitive to some Boolean condition expressed over service composition data, typically on the output (return) message of the operation invoked by activities in the group. If the condition is verified, then an exception-handling portion of the code is executed. After the exception has been handled, and depending on the exception specification (and on the expressive power of the language), process execution can proceed with the next activity, or the failed activity can be retried, or the process can be terminated. This technique is particularly useful if the orchestration model includes the possibility of defining groups of activities and of associating properties to each group or, better yet, if the orchestration can be structured into hierarchies, either by means of sub-processes or by means of a decomposition tree as in the activity hierarchies model described earlier. In fact, when a hierarchy is available, it is possible to define exception handlers at the different levels of abstraction. As in Java, exception handlers defined within the activity or group of activities in which the exception occurs are invoked first. At their completion, they have the choice of throwing the exception again so that it is handled also by the parent activity, according to the specified hierarchy. If no exception handler is found within the activity, then a suitable handler is searched by going up the hierarchy, until one is found. Otherwise, the process is terminated. This kind of approach is used by the process management system Little-JIL [48, 217], and a similar technique is adopted by BPEL. In both these languages, the choice of the exception-handling technique is naturally driven by the choice of the orchestration model that, being based on activity hierarchies, lends itself to a hierarchical exception-handling mechanism.

The *try-catch-throw* mechanism has several advantages. First, it enables the clear separation of the normal and exceptional logic. This helps structuring the composition so that it is easier to design and maintain, similar to the way it helps structuring the code in programming languages. Second, when the composition is structured according to a decomposition tree, then exception definitions can be similarly factored. Third, it includes the definition of a *continuation strategy*, i.e., it provides a way to specify what happens to the composition instance, and in particular to the "exceptional" activity, after the exception has been handled.

Rule-based Approaches

In these approaches the exception-handling logic is specified by means of ECA rules, where the event defines the exceptional event (e.g., customer cancellation) to be captured in the form of messages sent by a client to the composite service or in the form of timeouts. The condition is a Boolean expression over the message that verifies whether the event actually corresponds to an exceptional situation that must be handled (for example, it verifies whether a certain customer is allowed to have a negative account balance). The action then reacts to the exception, by invoking operations or aborting transactions. Rules are typically defined in some textual language, endowing the graphical notation that is used to define the normal orchestration. Their expressive power depends on the language for defining events, conditions, and actions, which can indeed be rich and complex. We refer the reader to [45, 59] for examples of rule-based languages for exception handling.

The rule-based approach provides for the clear separation of the normal and exceptional behaviors of a process. However, the system has one more language to interpret, and the developer has one more language to learn. In addition, the approach is applicable only if the number of rules is very small. Otherwise, as mentioned earlier, it becomes very difficult to analyze and understand the collective behavior of the ruleset, and the (possibly unexpected and undesired) interactions within the ruleset and between rules and flows. For these reasons, rule-based approaches have seen limited applicability up to now.

8.4 Dependencies between Coordination and Composition

In Section 8.1.4 we have outlined the differences between composition and coordination protocols, stating in particular that coordination protocols are public documents focusing on external interactions, while composition schemas are private documents that define the internal implementation of a Web service. We have also said that there are dependencies between the two that caused a certain confusion in how the topics are often presented. In the following discussion, we elaborate on such dependencies.

8.4.1 Coordination Protocols and Composition Schemas

The main relation between coordination protocols and composition stems from the fact that the definition of a protocol imposes constraints on the composition schema of Web services implementing the protocol logic. In fact, if a Web service plays a role in a certain coordination protocol, and the implementation is done through composition technologies, then the composition schema must, as a minimum, include activities that receive and send messages as prescribed by the protocol, and in the appropriate order. We rely once again on the procurement example to demonstrate this dependency in a concrete scenario. We also show how protocol definitions can be used to drive the design of composition schemas that send and receive messages in a way that is compliant with the protocol.

Figure 8.18 shows the procurement protocol modeled as an activity diagram. It is the same as Figure 7.6 of Section 7.1, and is repeated here for convenience. Assume now that we want to develop a (composite) Web service that can play the supplier role. The first step we need to take is to create the role-specific view of the protocol, shown in Figure 8.19. As discussed in Section 7.1, the role-specific view of a protocol includes all the message exchanges that involve a certain role (the supplier, in this case), and is therefore all the supplier should care about to build composition schemas that generate correct procurement conversations.

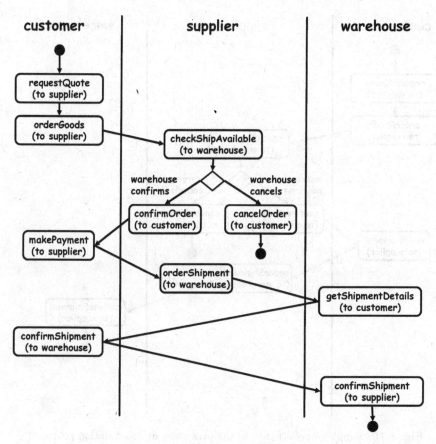

Fig. 8.18. The procurement coordination protocol

The next step consists of going from the role-specific view of the protocol to the definition of a process that exchanges messages as prescribed by the role-specific view. The aim here is to build a skeleton of a process that includes all the activities that send and receive messages as prescribed by the protocol. The skeleton will represent the starting point for service developers, who will then extend it with proprietary business logic to obtain a composition schema that can play the supplier role in the procurement protocol.

We now show how process skeletons can be built from the role-specific view when the process is modeled using activity diagrams. We do this by showing how each operation invocation in the role-specific view is mapped into an activity (or into a pair of activities) in the process skeleton. The principles are the same regardless of the modeling paradigm used to specify the process.

1. Request/reply operations invoked by a role R on the supplier are mapped into a *receive* and a *reply* activity. An arc connects the receive activity to the reply activity, to denote that receive is executed before reply. For

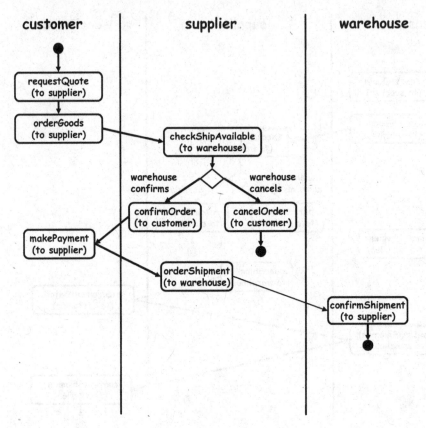

Fig. 8.19. Supplier-specific view of the procurement coordination protocol

example, the protocol activity *requestQuote (to supplier)* of Figure 8.19
is mapped to the pair of activities *receive requestQuote* and *reply requestQuote* in the process skeleton of Figure 8.20. Additional information
associated with activity definitions will denote that these receive and reply
activities exchange messages with role R.

2. One-way operations invoked by another role on the supplier are modeled
   as receive activities. For example, the protocol activity *orderGoods (to
   supplier)* of Figure 8.19 is mapped to activity *receive orderGoods* in the
   process skeleton of Figure 8.20.

3. One-way operations invoked by the supplier are modeled as send activities. For example, the protocol activity *confirmOrder (to customer)* of
   Figure 8.19 is mapped to activity *send confirmOrder* in the process skeleton of Figure 8.20.

4. Request/reply operations initiated by the supplier are modeled as invoke
   activities. For example, the protocol activity *checkShipAvailable (to ware-*

house) of Figure 8.19 is mapped to'activity *invoke checkShipAvailable* in the process skeleton of Figure 8.20.

5. The other constructs (e.g., arcs and symbols denoting conditional or parallel executions) are mapped as is into the process skeleton.

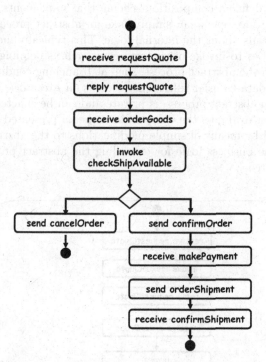

Fig. 8.20. An abstract process defining the behavior of the supplier role in the procurement coordination protocol

The process skeleton (also called *abstract process* or *public process*) is essentially a dual representation of the role-specific protocol view, described with a slightly different perspective. Instead of saying that at a certain point role *customer* sends a message to role *supplier*, in the abstract process everything is expressed in terms of what the supplier has to receive, send, invoke, or reply to.

The reader should therefore realize that, despite the name, the abstract process describes a protocol. The information it provides is the same as the role-specific view of the protocol. It does not include any internal and confidential business logic (such as branching conditions or the definition of how message parameters are determined). Instead, it only defines the externally visible behavior of a Web service, and this is why it is also called a *public* process in the literature [39, 206]. This also means that the abstract process is not executable. Its definition can be consumed by a conversation controller, to verify that message exchanges occur in compliance with a protocol, but not by a composition engine, as the engine would not know how to construct messages or how to evaluate branching conditions.

The advantage of representations done in terms of abstract processes is that they make it easy to understand how composition is constrained by the protocol and to define a composition schema that implements a protocol. In fact, to do this, developers can simply take an abstract process and extend it by adding details about the internal logic. This typically includes specifying other activities to invoke other services as well as defining anything left undetermined in the abstract process, such as branching conditions, data assignments, and data transfer rules. The result is an *executable* process which, in contrast to an abstract process, is private and can be enacted by a composition engine. For example, the composition schema presented in Figure 8.21 can be obtained by means of simple modifications to the abstract process of Figure 8.20. The business logic for extending the abstract process has been arbitrarily selected.

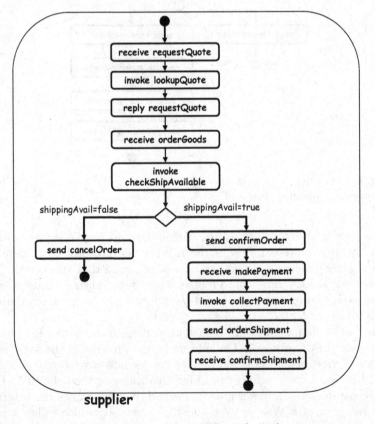

Fig. 8.21. Sample implementation of the supplier role in the procurement protocol

Observe that in the discussion above we have conveniently simplified the problem instead of considering it in its full generality. In fact, we have silently assumed that a Web service supports only one protocol. In reality, a Web service may need to support several protocols and carry on many concurrent conversations. For example, a supplier may actually interact with multiple warehouses, or may want to contact a manufacturer to see if a certain product requested by the customer can be produced and shipped in time. This case has no easy solution as, in general, the different protocols are independent of each other and it is up to the implementation (the business logic of the Web service) to establish dependencies (e.g., to define that a manufacturer is to be contacted whenever the order comes from premium customers and the warehouse does not have goods in stock). The research community has not yet fully addressed this scenario, although we envision that this will be a hot topic of research in the very near future.

The discussion above has outlined a path that goes from protocol specifications to role-specific views of the protocol, to abstract processes for each of the roles involved, to concrete implementations of these abstract processes. This is a common route, since very often the external behavior is designed before the internal one. As done in ebXML or xCBL, one can pick a given coordination protocol which will constrain the appearance of the internal implementation. However, the inverse route can also be taken: in fact, whether the internal implementation or the coordination protocol comes first is a matter of how a Web service is built. For instance, one can first design the internal process and then generate the corresponding abstract process and role-specific protocol.

Process-oriented languages and standardization proposals take different stands with respect to how they address composition, protocols, and the relationships between the two. For example, workflow languages have traditionally focused on the internal implementation, and do not provide support for abstract processes. This is also true for languages that include service composition among their main goals, such as XLANG. BPEL (discussed later in this chapter) is also a language designed with service composition in mind: its basic idea consists of modeling a composite service by means of a business process description language analogous to those of conventional workflow systems, but where the workflow activities represent the invocation of Web services rather than representing the invocation of conventional applications [122]. Unlike workflow languages, however, BPEL can specify both the external behavior (abstract process) and the internal implementation (executable process). Therefore, even when describing protocols, BPEL takes a process-centric perspective and focuses on the interactions supported by a specific service.

ebXML also addresses both protocols and composition. A protocol is seen as the interplay between peer-to-peer business processes implementing the Web services. The interaction among Web services is defined in terms of a business agreement that describes what messages need to be exchanged between the business processes implementing each side of the interaction (one of the business processes being the implementation of the Web service, the other being either another Web service or a client process that enacts the business protocol for the Web service being accessed). In this model, the specification focuses more on the implementation of the coordination protocol rather than on the implementation of a single Web service. The protocol is meant to be enforced in a distributed manner as the collaboration agreement will be used directly by the messaging system of each participant to control its side of the conversation.

The reader interested in more in-depth analysis of the relationships between coordination protocols, abstract processes, and executable processes, is referred to [39, 40, 206, 132].

8.4.2 Conversation Controllers and Composition Engines

The attentive reader will have observed that service composition architectures following an engine-based approach are faced with a conversation routing problem of their own. In fact, Web services middleware that includes both a conversation controller and a composition engine works as shown in Figure 8.22, where the conversation controller verifies protocol compliance and routes messages to the composition engine. From the perspective of the controller, the composition engine is the internal object that implements the conversation. Since a single engine executes many composition instances, to which all messages related to these instances go, the engine has to figure out the composition instance to which a message is directed, a problem analogous to that of conversation routing.

The way this can be done depends on the details of how the conversation controller and the composition engine operate, and on the composition model. If the conversation controller and the SOAP router leave header information in the message when routing it to the engine, then the coordination context can be used to determine the target instance, in a way analogous to what the conversation controller does to route messages to object instances. If, instead, the conversation controller strips header information from the SOAP message and just delivers the payload (i.e., the operation parameters), then the engine has to find some other way to correlate messages with instances.

A possible solution is to have the composition schema explicitly include correlation information by defining the logic by which messages can be associated with composition instances, based on the message parameters. For example, assume that the supplier's composition schema includes a variable called *orderID*. If each message in a conversation carries an order identifier as one of its parameters, and if each conversation is characterized by a unique order number, then the composite schema designer may state that the correlation is performed by delivering messages to instances whose orderID variable matches the order number contained in the message. This, of course, means that routing is not transparent any more to the developers, and that its applicability depends on whether the protocol messages actually include information that can be used to uniquely identify a conversation.

As technologies mature, it is likely that conversation controllers and composition engines will be integrated or will interact by means of standard interfaces, in a way that makes it possible to hide the routing problem from the developers of the composite service.

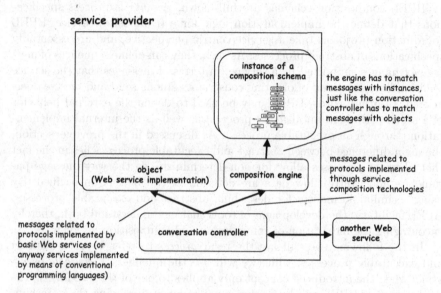

Fig. 8.22. The composition engine is faced with a conversation routing problem similar to the one addressed by the conversation controller

8.5 BPEL: Business Process Execution Language for Web Services

Although several standardization proposals have appeared in the service composition space (such as BPML [10] and WSFL [119]), attention seems to be focusing on a language initially proposed in July 2002 by BEA, Microsoft, and IBM, called Business Process Execution Language for Web Services (BPEL[2]) [7]. Not surprisingly, the language reflects in many ways the characteristics of earlier proposals by the same vendors, such as WSFL and XLANG. The 2002 specifications have been subsequently revised (May 2003) and have gained the support of many other vendors, such as SAP and Siebel systems. BPEL is now being transferred to OASIS for standardization.

---

[2] We will use this acronym, as opposed to the lengthy *BPEL4WS* that appears in the BPEL specification document.

8.5.1 Overview

BPEL is a language that can support the specifications of both composition schemas as well as coordination protocols. As seen earlier in this chapter, coordination protocols and compositions are specified with similar techniques. BPEL takes advantage of these similarities and provides a single framework for defining both of them.

BPEL composition schemas are full-blown, *executable* process specifications that define the implementation logic for a (composite) service. BPEL coordination protocols take a service-centric perspective, and are essentially specifications of abstract processes. As such, they can define sequences of message exchanges supported by a service (in terms of messages that the service sends and receives) and of ordering constraints among send and receive operations). In other words, BPEL may be used to define the external behavior of a service (through an abstract process) as well as the internal implementation (through an executable process). As discussed in the previous section, the main difference between abstract and executable processes lies in the fact that abstract processes allow for non-determinism, so the way message parameters and control flow data are determined can be left unspecified. By using a similar formalism for describing abstract and executable processes, BPEL facilitates the development of tools that can understand both, thereby encouraging the integration of conversation and composition middleware.

In the following, we will use the term *process* to refer to both abstract and executable processes, while we will use the qualifiers *executable* or *abstract* when the introduced concept only applies to one of the two forms. The dual nature of BPEL will be further detailed when discussing the data handling part, since that is where most of the differences between abstract and executable processes reside.

In a nutshell, BPEL specifications are XML documents that define the following aspects of a process (Figure 8.23):

- The different roles that take part in the message exchanges with the process.
- The port types that must be supported by the different roles and by the process itself.
- The orchestration and the other different aspects that are part of a process definition, as discussed in Section 8.3.
- Correlation information, defining how messages can be routed to the correct composition instances.

The above discussion shows that BPEL assumes that both the process and the partners that interact with it are described as WSDL abstract services (port types and operations). As we will see, no reference to specific endpoints is hardcoded in the specification. This information is assumed to be specified at deployment time or at run-time, possibly in a manner that is implementation-specific.

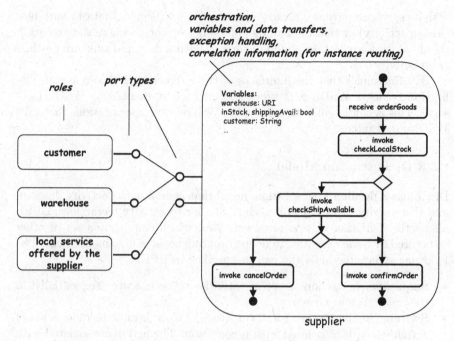

Fig. 8.23. Scope of the BPEL specifications

In this section we show how these aspects are defined in BPEL. The structure of this section will mirror that of Section 8.3, with the addition of the definition of correlation information, present in BPEL but absent in most service composition models. As Figure 8.23 shows, we will use once again the supplier service as an example throughout this section. As customary, we will focus on the concepts rather than on the details, for which we refer the reader to the BPEL specification [7].

8.5.2 Component Model

BPEL has a fine-grained component model, consisting of *activities*, which can be *basic* or *structured*. Structured activities, as in the activity hierarchy approach, are used for defining the orchestration. Basic activities represent the actual "components," and correspond to the invocation of a WSDL operation performed by a service playing a role onto a service playing a different role. BPEL offers *invoke* activities representing the invocation of a request/reply or a one-way operation offered by a service; *receive* activities, corresponding to the receipt of a message from a client; and *reply* activities, which model a message sent by the process in response to an operation invoked by a client. These are analogous to the types of activities defined in Section 8.3. In addition to operation invocations, BPEL processes may include other types of activities, whose purpose, for example, is that of assigning data to variables (*assign* activity) or that of defining points in the process where the execution should block for a certain period of time or until a date and time are reached (*wait* activity).

BPEL assumes that the interfaces of the interacting Web services are defined in terms of WSDL port types and interact by exchanging WSDL messages. This is consistent with most other Web services specifications that take WSDL for granted.

8.5.3 Orchestration Model

BPEL has a peculiar orchestration model that combines the activity diagram and the activity hierarchy approaches. Similar to activity hierarchies, BPEL allows the definition of *structured activities*, which can group a set of other structured or basic activities to define ordering constraints among them. The following structured activities can be specified in BPEL:

- **Sequence.** It contains a set of activities to be executed sequentially, in the order they are listed.
- **Switch.** Similar to the switch construct in C or Java, it includes a set of activities, each associated with a condition. The activity associated with the first true condition is executed, while the others are skipped. It is also possible to specify an *otherwise* activity, executed if no condition is true.
- **Pick.** It includes a set of *events* (such as the receipt of a message or the expiration of a time alarm), each associated with an activity. When one of the events occurs, the associated activity is executed and the pick is considered completed. Note that race conditions (caused by concurrent events) are handled in an implementation-specific manner.
- **While.** It includes exactly one (basic or structured) activity, which is executed repeatedly while a specified condition is true.
- **Flow.** It groups a set of activities to be started in parallel, and it is considered completed when all the included activities are completed.

Figure 8.24 provides a pictorial representation of the supplier composite service, specified in BPEL by using structured activities. The graphical notation we adopt is arbitrary, as BPEL does not propose one. Note that this figure is similar to Figure 8.10 shown earlier, the only difference being that in this one we use BPEL terminology.

The flow construct is where the "activity diagram" nature of BPEL (largely borrowed from WSFL) comes in and blends with the "activity hierarchy" aspect. In fact, a flow activity can include the specification of *links*. Like an arc in an activity diagram, a link l can be used to connect one and only one source activity S to one and only one target activity T; the target activity T cannot be started until the source activity S has been completed. An activity can have multiple incoming and outgoing links. Links can also be

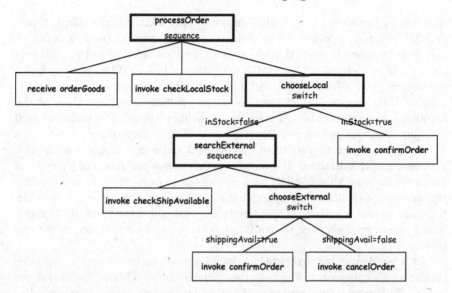

Fig. 8.24. Orchestration in BPEL. Structured activities have a thicker border

associated with a transition condition, evaluated when the link's source activity completes. The condition evaluation determines whether the link must be followed and the target activity must be started. The set of links can only generate acyclic graphs, i.e., defining cycles through links are not allowed (they are modeled by means of the *while* structured activity).

Link semantics are actually more complex than this. Links may require the definition of *join conditions* (to further define when an activity should be executed in case it has multiple incoming links) and of attributes denoting the behavior when a transition condition is false (e.g., the raising of an exception or the continuing of the execution normally). While an in-depth description of links and of their many subtle implications is outside our scope, we observe that a rather unique peculiarity of the BPEL orchestration model is the possibility it affords of specifying the same orchestration logic in two different ways: through activity hierarchies (i.e., through constructs such as *sequence* and *switch*) and through links (as in activity diagrams). This is also the case for our supplier process example. The sequence of invocations of activities A, B, and C, for instance, can be defined either as a *sequence* of the three or as a *flow* including the three basic activities and links between A and B and between B and C.

8.5.4 Data Types and Data Transfer

BPEL maintains the state of the process and manipulates control data by means of variables. BPEL variables are analogous to variables in conventional programming languages. They are characterized by a name and by a type, specified as a reference to a WSDL message type, XML schema simple types, or XML schema elements. Once defined, variables can be used as input or output parameters in operation invocations, and are referred to by conditions (such as those defined within switch activities or links). When used as input parameters, the values of the variables form the message data sent to the invoked Web service. When used as output parameters, the values of the variables are set to the data of the message being received. The variables used as input or output parameters must be of WSDL message types.

At the time a composite service is invoked and a new instance is created, variables are not initialized. If a variable is the output parameter of a receive or an invoke activity, then initialization occurs upon completion of such activity. Initialization can also occur by explicit assignment of a value to the variable, through the *assign* activity. This activity allows defining the value of a variable based on expressions over the value of other containers and over constants (literals).

As a particular but frequently occurring case, variables can be updated through an expression defined on the variable itself. This is useful, for example, for incrementing counters. If within assignments there is the need to identify a particular value in the variable (to assign, for example, the desired delivery date to a variable called *delivery*, which is one of the elements of *orderMessage*), then some XML query language can be used. While BPEL enables the use of any query language as long as the implementation can support its execution, it does prescribe that any BPEL-compliant implementation support XPath 1.0.

The discussion above shows that BPEL follows a blackboard approach. Finally, we mention that concurrent access to variables can be controlled by means of serialization: if two activities access the same set of variables and the activities state that their execution should be serialized, then the BPEL semantics ensure that the end result of the concurrent execution is equivalent to a serial execution of the two activities.

As mentioned earlier in this section, data handling and assignments constitute the main difference between abstract and executable processes. In fact, in abstract processes, assignments may be opaque. An opaque assignment is an assignment where the source of the data is left unspecified. Referring once again to our procurement scenario, an executable process must specify how values are assigned to each data item. For example, the process specification defines that variable *inStock* takes its value from the output result of the *checkLocalStock* activity. In contrast, in opaque assignments, the designer needs only to specify that variable *inStock* will be assigned some value, without specifying what the source of this value is. In other words, in an abstract process it is possible to specify that a variable will change value without defining how the new value is determined. Since variables are used to control the orchestration and to form message parameters, opaque assignments enable non-deterministic specifications both in the orchestration and in the data transfer between activities. This is how abstract processes hide implementation details from the clients, and specify only the external behavior of a service.

8.5.5 Service Selection

Service selection in BPEL revolves around the notion of *partner link types*, *partner links*, and *endpoint references*. Partner link types identify a pair of roles that exchange messages during process execution and the WSDL port types that the services playing these roles are required to implement. For example, a partner link type *orderLT* can specify that a process will involve interactions between a customer and a supplier, that Web services implementing suppliers should support a *supplierPT* port type, and that Web services implementing customers should support a *customerPT* port type. Note that, per se, partner link types are not directly related to service composition: they could be used to define relationships among any pair of (abstract) Web services.

Once roles, relationships, and port types have been defined by means of partner link types, the next step consists of specifying partner links. While partner link types identify roles, partner links identify services invoked during the execution of a process, and are therefore meant to be (statically or dynamically) bound to specific endpoints.

The definition of a partner link references a partner link type, and then states the role played by the process and the one played by the partner with respect to that link. For example, designers can specify a partner link identifying a specific customer. The partner link refers to partner link type *orderLT*, and further states that the role played by the composite service is *supplier*, while the one played by the other interacting party is *customer* (Figure 8.25).

A specific endpoint reference can be then associated to the partner link, thereby identifying a specific customer[3]. Such an association can be done at composite service deployment time, in a manner that is dependent on the specific BPEL implementation, and is therefore not part of the specification. In addition, references can also be discovered and assigned dynamically to partner links: indeed, just as it is possible to assign values to variables, it is also possible to assign endpoint references to a partner link. The assignment can be done several times during the execution, so that the endpoint to which the partner link refers changes as the execution proceeds. This is useful, for instance, if several different warehouses are contacted, one after the other. The partner link types and the roles involved would always be the same (the warehouse), but the actual Web service being invoked would be different at each invocation.

Activity definitions can then refer to partner links, so that the composition engine is aware of the specific service to which messages have to be delivered while executing the activity.

---

[3] The notion of endpoint reference in BPEL is as defined by WS-Addressing.

partner link definition: it further qualifies the interactions occurring through a partner link type. Its definition refers to a partner link type and specifies the role played by the composite service as well as the one played by the other partner

```
<partnerLink name="customerP"
  partnerLinkType="orderLT"
  myRole="supplier"
  partnerRole="customer">
</partner>
```

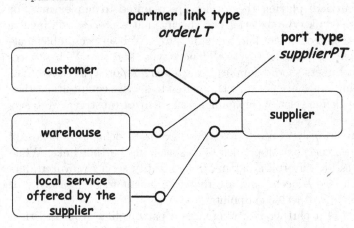

Fig. 8.25. Definition of partners in BPEL

8.5.6 Exceptions and Transactions

With respect to exception handling, BPEL essentially follows a try-catch-throw approach. This is consistent with the fact that BPEL has a structured orchestration model where activities can be nested into each other, as discussed in Section 8.3.

In BPEL, each (basic or structured) activity implicitly defines a *scope* (Figure 8.26). In addition, scopes can be explicitly declared. Any scope-defining element can include the specification of one or more *fault handlers*, dictating how a certain exception should be managed. A fault handler is characterized by a *catch* element, defining the fault it manages and the (basic or structured) activity to be executed as the fault occurs.

Faults can be generated during the execution of an activity within the scope, either by the invoked operation (returning a WSDL fault message) or by the execution engine (due to run-time errors). Faults can also be explicitly thrown within the orchestration schema, through the throw activity. When a fault occurs within a given scope, a BPEL engine will terminate all running activities in that scope and execute the activity specified in the fault handler

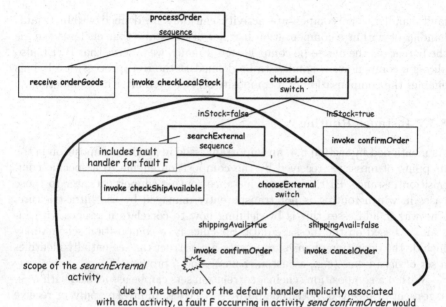

Fig. 8.26. Exception handling in BPEL

for that scope. If no handler exists for a given fault, then a default handler is executed (see below).

In addition to the try-catch-throw approach, another construct useful for handling exceptions is the *event handler*, which enables continuous monitoring for a certain event (such as a message received by the process or a deadline expiration) and executes an activity in response to the event. Unlike the pick activity, an event handler is always active when the scope in which it is declared is active, and it can be triggered several times.

BPEL combines exception handling approaches with transactional techniques. It is possible to define, for each scope, the logic required to semantically undo the execution of activities in that scope. The compensation logic is specified by a *compensation handler*, consisting of a single (basic or structured) activity, that will take care of performing whatever actions are needed to compensate for the execution.

Every scope has a default compensation handler, whose behavior consists of invoking the compensation handler for each enclosed scope in the reverse order of execution. Similarly, every scope also has a default fault handler, whose behavior also consists in compensating enclosed scopes. The default fault handler, in addition, re-throws the fault to the enclosing scope.

The compensation handler for a given scope can only be invoked once the scope execution has completed normally. Its invocation can either be explicitly initiated by a *compensate* activity or occur automatically as part of the default

fault handler. The compensate activity can only be defined within a fault handler or within a compensation handler of the scope that encloses (i.e., is the parent of) the one to be compensated. Finally, we observe that BPEL also allows a compensation handler to be defined at the top (process) level. This enables the compensation of a composite service even after its completion.

8.5.7 Instance Routing

As mentioned in Section 8.4, an important issue in service composition is the mapping of messages received by the composition engine to a specific composition instance. BPEL includes instance routing support to cater to those cases in which routing is not transparently managed by the infrastructure. The way it addresses this is by defining how to correlate messages with instances, based on the message data. Specifically, a composition schema may include the definition of *correlation sets*, a construct that essentially identifies a set of data items (e.g., a customer name and a product ID).

Within a composition schema, correlation sets can be associated with messages sent or received by the composite service within invoke, reply, or receive activities. By associating a pair of messages to the same correlation set, the designer specifies that if these messages have the same value for the correlation set, they belong to the same instance. For example, assume that in the invoke checkShipAvailable activity, the supplier sends a checkAvailability message to the warehouse and receives an availability message in reply (Figure 8.27). These messages need to be correlated, since when the composition engine receives the reply, it needs to know the instance to which the message should be delivered. To this end, the designer may specify a correlation set that refers to the orderID data item (present in both the sent and received messages), uniquely identifying a composition instance (since different orders are assigned different orderIDs), and associate the correlation set to both the outgoing and the incoming message. Thanks to this specification, a composition engine will correlate the incoming availability messages based on the orderID, and route them accordingly.

Observe that the BPEL approach allows for multiple correlation sets to be defined. This is needed because the characteristics that enable the identification of an instance from the message data may change based on the messages being exchanged and on the service provider being invoked. For example, assume that, at some point in the supplier process, the supplier invokes a payment service to collect the money paid by the customer. The interface offered by the payment service may not provide for an order ID. Correlation can instead be made on the payment ID, or any other data item that uniquely identifies the message exchange. Different correlation sets are needed for this purpose.

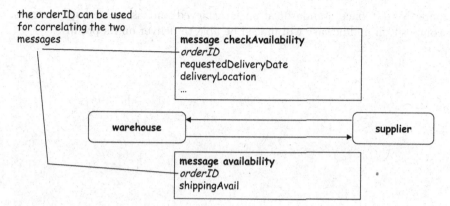

Fig. 8.27. A correlation set referring to the orderID data item can be associated to the messages exchanged with the warehouse

8.6 Summary

The two previous chapters have considered Web services from an external perspective: SOAP, WSDL, UDDI, and the different coordination protocols are all about enabling binding and interactions among Web services. This chapter has focused on the implementation of a Web service. It has shown how a Web service can be implemented by combining other Web services. Services developed in this way are called *composite*, to distinguish them from the ones implemented though conventional programming languages and invoking conventional services, which are called *basic*. We have also emphasized that whether a service is basic or composite is transparent to clients. They all are Web services.

The execution of a composite service is supported by a set of techniques, collectively known as Web services composition middleware. The promise of Web services composition middleware is to make composition quick and easy, up to the point where new services can be implemented without writing any code, by using a simple graphical user interface (GUI). The same promise was made by conventional composition middleware but, in that context, it failed to deliver. Web services composition middleware has higher chances for success, due to the standardization efforts taking place, which reduces heterogeneity and therefore makes integration easier.

Standardization is not only happening in the components, but also in the composition language. Indeed, several languages have recently been proposed in an attempt to establish a commonly accepted way of defining a composite service. The most credible proposal to date is BPEL, since it is backed by the main players in the Web services space. If this and other standardization efforts succeed, they will foster the availability of low-cost, robust middleware and, more importantly, create a shared set of concepts and terminology that will at last allow the widespread adoption of composition technologies. The hope is that once standardization is achieved and as technology matures, composition middleware will indeed be able to deliver on its promise.

9

Outlook

Throughout this book we have tried to balance two conflicting perspectives. One sees Web services as a revolutionary technology triggering radical changes in the way we think about middleware, application integration, or the way we use the Internet. The other sees Web services as yet another step in the evolution of middleware and EAI. In the revolutionary camp, the assumption seems to be that once applications speak XML, systems support SOAP, and providers describe services using WSDL and advertise them in UDDI registries, then Web services will facilitate the development of infrastructures that support programmatic application integration, dynamic B2B marketplaces, and the seamless integration of IT infrastructures from different corporations. In the evolutionary side, Web services are just an additional layer on top of existing middleware and EAI platforms that provides a set of simple, lowest common denominator interfaces for interactions across the Internet.

Enthusiastic as we are about Web services, we must acknowledge that Web services today are not as revolutionary as some may think. For instance, Web services are mostly used today for conventional EAI. Of course, it is possible that Web services will trigger yet unforeseen changes but, in their current state and with the exception of the standardization efforts, today's Web services technology essentially extends conventional middleware to enable integration across the Web. With time, it is likely that Web services will lead to new computing paradigms and to dynamic B2B interactions, but it remains to be seen whether this "revolutionary" power can be unleashed.

In this chapter we revisit the ideas discussed in previous chapters and analyze their potential as revolutionary and/or evolutionary technologies. We start with a critical overview of the current state of the art (Section 9.1) in Web services, describing which technologies are used in practice, why, and what is their likely evolution. Next, we address the applicability of Web services. We show that, despite the many benefits they provide, there are complexities in B2B interactions that remain hard to address (Section 9.2). Finally, we demonstrate a concrete and important application area of Web services, to give an idea of the problems and opportunities that they bring (Section 9.3).

9.1 State of the Art in Web Services

In Web services there is a wide gap between what is being proposed or desired
and what is actually available. In this section, we briefly review many of the
technologies discussed in the previous chapters and point out the ones that
are a reality today.

9.1.1 Available Technology

At the time of this writing, Web services are essentially SOAP and WSDL,
notwithstanding early prototypes, proposals, and attempts to position companies and products within a given market. Some specifications are already
implemented or could be quickly implemented, but most of them are still at
very early stages in the standardization process and it will take a while for
them to become widely used, despite some convergence (such as the consolidation of efforts around BPEL).

In this regard, UDDI deserves special mention. Unlike SOAP and WSDL,
UDDI has changed its goals in a significant manner from version to version.
The initial claims of universal repositories and fully automated electronic commerce have been markedly downplayed or completely eliminated. The initial
versions (1 and 2) viewed a UDDI repository as a universal repository of business information that would contain all information necessary for electronic
commerce activities. Version 3 of the specification clearly shifts emphasis toward private repositories. UDDI implemented in private repositories could
play an important role in many Web service installations but this is not yet
the case today. Part of the problem is that, unlike SOAP and WSDL, UDDI
does not naturally fit with the way conventional middleware platforms work
today. As such, it will take a while before UDDI repositories find their place
in the architecture of Web services. Today, most of the systems that provide
support for SOAP and WSDL either ignore UDDI or provide only minimal
support (like publishing a WSDL document in a UDDI repository). Even when
UDDI directories are deployed, they are mainly used for design-time discovery
rather than run-time binding. This is only natural, considering that advanced
forms of dynamic binding (such as dynamic interface invocations in CORBA)
were rarely used in EAI, and are much more challenging in B2B as we will
see later in this chapter.

9.1.2 Current Architecture of Web Services

The architecture of Web services as pursued today and as supported by SOAP
and WSDL has a very strong client/server flavor. The architecture is, of
course, much more complex than in a conventional client/server system, but
for all intents and purposes, the pattern of interaction is similar. In fact, the
model quite closely follows that of conventional middleware: a service is offered
by a server (service provider) and invoked by a client (a service requester).

Service information for search and possibly even binding is stored in an intermediate entity such as a name and directory service (the UDDI registry). The resulting external architecture of Web services is thus an extension to the conventional, RPC-based middleware platforms discussed in Chapter 2.

The client/server flavor in the external architecture of Web services is mainly due to the way SOAP works and is being used today. Support for SOAP is nowadays widely available in many languages and systems. In almost all cases, however, the support amounts to using SOAP as a tunneling mechanism for synchronous invocations. This predominant use of SOAP does not change the nature of the invocations, it just allows calls to take place over the Internet. In this regard, SOAP has become the protocol for implementing some of the most basic extensions to conventional middleware that were discussed in Chapter 4, mainly remote clients. This use is very much in agreement with the initial idea of what SOAP was supposed to be when it was first designed: a simplified, Web-enabled version of the mechanisms already explored in CORBA's IIOP and GIOP.

Similarly, WSDL is an obvious extension of conventional IDL concepts that adapt it to the needs of wide-area integration. This adaptation mainly involves transforming the procedural interfaces used in conventional middleware platforms into message interfaces so that the procedure call that is being mapped to a SOAP exchange can take place as an HTTP interaction. Since procedure calls specify the input and the output together, WSDL adds the notion of operations to tie together the messages that provide the input and the messages that return the output of an invocation. The transformation from conventional IDL and procedural interactions into the simple message exchanges supported by SOAP is straightforward, and many conventional middleware platforms today support the automatic generation of WSDL documents that describe services. Together with the widely available support for SOAP, this functionality allows conventional middleware platforms to publish and invoke existing middleware services as Web services. As with SOAP, the big advantage of WSDL is that it does not change the model or pattern of interaction already used in existing middleware platforms and, therefore, can be used as a simple extension to these platforms.

In fact, the specifications of Web services standards are often formulated in a way to make a reader suspect that their primary goal is to ensure that conventional middleware platforms can be easily adapted to support Web services. This makes sense from a practical point of view as it offers a clear evolutionary path to many existing products and vendors and greatly lowers the learning curve for developers. This has been, for example, true for service composition, where early proposals strongly resembled what existing workflow products could offer.

The downside of such an approach is that, as extensions to an already existing interaction model (i.e., the RPC model), they do not provide the functionality necessary to implement applications that might need a completely different interaction model. Also, in order to provide a smooth evolution path for existing platforms, the change in technology cannot be too large. Yet, by adopting a lowest common denominator approach (as indeed WSDL and SOAP do), much of the important functionality must remain unspecified and outside the current standards. In practice, as an obvious example, this is a good reason for SOAP not to consider asynchronous interaction, even though it is a more natural interaction model for SOAP messages than for RPC calls. Asynchronous interaction is not the way the vast majority of middleware platforms work today. Tying asynchronous interaction to the SOAP specification would have required some major changes in many middleware platforms to make them SOAP-compliant. By ignoring asynchronous interactions, SOAP can be quickly adopted by existing platforms. The price for this is that SOAP is not well suited for B2B interactions that, as discussed in Chapter 4, are mostly based on the asynchronous exchange of messages.

Of course, it is not just the evolution of existing platforms that plays a role in determining the nature of Web service specifications. When RPC was first proposed, it was mostly implemented as a set of libraries. SOAP and WSDL are no different and are at a very similar stage. Some current implementations of SOAP are in fact remarkably similar to that of early RPC systems. It took a while before RPC was enriched with the functionality that eventually led to the many different middleware platforms discussed in Chapter 2. It will also probably take some time before SOAP and WSDL are enriched with properties that need much more infrastructure to be properly supported (e.g., security, transactions, coordination, etc.). As this additional functionality increases in complexity and becomes more application specific, the standardization process also becomes much more complex, and may never in fact converge to a single specification. This will likely lead to several flavors of the same basic mechanisms (i.e., SOAP and WSDL) to be implemented in systems that are tailored to concrete applications, much as the RPC concept is employed in different forms of middleware.

An alternative to the client/server view of Web services is a peer-to-peer view. We have seen that much of the complexity in Web services is due to the cross-organizational environment for which they have been designed, and the consequent lack of a central location for the middleware. This, in turn, raises the need for peer-to-peer interactions and for achieving middleware properties through protocols to be cooperatively executed by the interacting parties. Furthermore, we have also seen that interaction among Web services is often much more complex than simply executing an RPC call through the Internet. As we have seen in standardization proposals such as WS-Coordination, ebXML, and RosettaNet, the emphasis is on the coordination among services, which in turn often translates into coordination among the business processes of different partners, as opposed to between a requester and a provider. Peer-to-peer interactions are likely to be the accepted interoperability paradigm in the future, but they are not commonly used in practice as yet.

9.1.3 EAI as a Natural Fit for Today's Web Services

The close relationship between the concepts used in SOAP and WSDL and the programming and service models used in conventional middleware has been a determining factor in how SOAP and WSDL are being used today. The current leading applications for Web services are in conventional EAI [57] and in restricted B2B settings that have characteristics similar to those of EAI due to cooperation among the interacting companies.

In hindsight, it seems natural that this should be the case. First, as pointed out above, SOAP and WSDL are so close to conventional middleware that they seem to have been designed with mainly that purpose in mind. Extending middleware platforms so that their services become Web services is trivial in most cases, even for those platforms that had not already evolved toward application servers. The process can be made completely transparent, without changing the applications already running on the middleware platform.

Second, Web services are indeed a natural solution to the standardization problems that have plagued EAI in the past. As discussed in Chapter 3, one of the biggest limitations in EAI is the manual and ad hoc implementation of the wrappers that allow different platforms and applications to interact with the EAI system (be it a message broker, a workflow management system, or any other form of middleware). Web services immediately eliminate this huge effort for all those platforms that can be extended with Web services. As just discussed, this is indeed the case today for most middleware platforms and can be applied to existing application logic.

Third, Web services enable a company to open its IT infrastructure to external partners. This is in fact what Web services are all about. Yet, Web services do not help with the many legal and contractual issues involved in B2B interactions. There is also a clear lack of support for the more advanced aspects of Web services involved in realistic B2B settings (e.g., conversations, enforcement of business protocols, delivery guarantees, etc.) although, as mentioned above, the many disparate standardization efforts in these areas are starting to converge. At this stage in the evolution of Web services, it is much easier to use them for internal EAI than for implementing complete B2B systems.

For all these reasons, particularly the minimal infrastructure involved, we expect that conventional EAI will remain the main application area for Web services in the short term.

To summarize, the current state of the art is that the most basic Web services technology (i.e., SOAP and WSDL at this stage) is slowly becoming a standardized, low level mechanism for interconnecting platforms and software services. What we have today is the most basic plumbing: a standard way to exchange messages (SOAP) and a standard way to define interfaces for message exchanges (WSDL). Both have been designed to be a natural extension to existing middleware platforms which is how they are being used today. Other standards are emerging, but they are neither mature nor widely adopted. Whether from this state of the art a universal platform for fully automatic B2B interactions eventually emerges depends on many factors that we will discuss in Section 9.2.

9.1.4 Emerging Trends

The rapidly increasing number of proposals around Web services makes it difficult to get an overall and precise picture of how Web services might evolve. In this chapter we discuss some of the most important trends and their effect on basic Web services technology, focusing primarily on SOAP and WSDL.

Regardless of whether B2B interactions take place using a client/server model or are based on asynchronous messages, the most important steps in the evolution of Web services will probably be extensions to SOAP. SOAP does not cover many important parts of realistic message exchanges such as message identifiers and general message information. It also ignores properties of typical communication protocols such as reliable delivery or error handling. Of course, nothing prevents an additional specification from establishing how to add such information and functionality. Because realistic B2B applications cannot be implemented without this extra functionality, we expect that many of the extensions that will be most relevant in the near future will be those related to issues such as reliable delivery or standardization of message headers.

These extensions should help make SOAP more flexible and better suited for B2B applications than it is today. Given the rate at which some of these extensions are being proposed, it is clear that everybody involved believes that such extensions are necessary. A different matter is how these extensions should be developed, whether as part of a single messaging specification or as an optional extension to SOAP. For our purposes here, such extensions are interesting not only by themselves, but also because they illustrate how the interaction model needs to change to adapt Web services to B2B settings.

9.2 Applicability of Web Services

The ultimate goal of Web services is to provide the infrastructure for B2B interactions. In this section we discuss how far we are from this goal.

9.2.1 The Holy Grail

Dynamic interaction in a completely open community of businesses is seen by many to be the Holy Grail of Web services. The goal that early Web services visionaries had in mind is for automated clients to browse UDDI registries, find adequate services and service providers, automatically discover how to interact with the service, and finally invoke the service, all programmatically, without manual intervention. SOAP, UDDI, and WSDL should form the basic infrastructure. Through successive layers of extensions and enhancements,

Web services should become a reliable platform offering all the necessary functionality for electronic commerce. Finally, through a rich and structured description language, the use of ontologies, and yet additional layers of software it should be possible to entirely automate the discovery and interaction among Web services.

Of these successive steps, as discussed at the beginning of this chapter, the only one really in place is the first one, and even then only in part (i.e., SOAP and WSDL). UDDI is also relatively mature, but its use is by far much less widespread than that of SOAP and WSDL. The layers of extensions and enhancements are, for the most part, being designed and it will take quite a while before they are sufficiently established. It can be considered a matter of faith whether it will ever be possible to solve the problems that need to be solved to reach such an automated level of integration.

It is only fair to say that today we are still very far from this ultimate goal of full automation. The difficulties involved in getting there should be obvious to anyone who has ever been involved in a B2B integration project. The challenges that arise are enormous even in cases where the interaction is static and, in principle, guided by well-defined and well-known standards, as we will show later on. Full dynamism and complete automation, as some Web services preachers advocate, will require a real revolution in technology. Yet there are many people working toward such a goal. In what follows, we discuss some of these efforts and the problems they are trying to address.

9.2.2 The Complexity of B2B Interactions

To put the problem into perspective and appreciate why, even using Web services, B2B interactions can be quite challenging, let us consider a simple case. Let us examine specifically the problem of developing Web services that enable two business partners to interoperate by following the RosettaNet standard [171] (see Section 7.5). As a test case, the example is very humble and far from the most extreme ideas pursued around Web services. Yet, the example illustrates very well why Web services in their current state do not, by themselves, solve all the problems that need to be tackled.

Suppose that two business partners decide to engage in a business transaction with each other according to a well-known, thoroughly designed, and well documented set of specifications. Assume as well that all legal issues (contracts, responsibilities, etc.) and security requirements have been discussed and agreed upon beforehand. Even under these assumptions, the work required to enable this interaction will be far from easy.

More than any other problem, no exchange between the partners will be possible until they agree on the semantics of the documents involved. In fact, no matter how precise the specifications are, there is always room for ambiguity and misunderstandings, and Web services technology does not currently offer any solution to this most important problem. As an example, take the simple case of a price field within an XML document, describing the price of a product requested by a customer. First of all, the content of the field may be expressed in different currency units. Does the specification assume a given currency, or does it allow users to qualify the price by explicitly stating the currency unit? And how should the currency unit be specified? In addition, different countries have different conventions on the decimal symbol: some use the dot, others use the comma. Depending on the domain, there may be a number of additional semantic issues that, if left undefined, may lead different partners to make different assumptions, thereby generating errors and inconsistencies. For example, the price may be interpreted as being inclusive or exclusive of sales tax; the same applies to value-added taxes. Different countries may have different taxation rules, thereby requiring further details in the specifications.

The number and types of details that must be specified is, in principle, boundless, and we could go on for several pages mentioning more sources for misinterpretations related to the price element. As the number of elements in an XML document grows, the challenges in the specifications and the risks of misinterpretations grow as well. This is a problem common to most vertical standards, which are often inherently complex. Indeed, these observations reinforce the well-known principle that only simple languages and protocols can be easily and rapidly adopted by users.

Besides imprecise specifications, another problem is that all practical situations have their own peculiarities, and may therefore require the exchange of information for which there is no room in the XML schema defined by the standardization body. Therefore, despite the adoption of a specific standard, meetings and discussions among the interested parties are required before two companies can interoperate, to agree not only on the exact meaning of each data item, but also on how to exchange additional information for which there is no room in the standard specification.

Given all the challenges that must be faced in such a simple scenario, it is easy to imagine that B2B integration becomes very hard to achieve if the problem is more complex than the one mentioned above. For example, consider the case in which the interaction is again based on vertical standards, but where business partners are dynamically selected and invoked, without prior meetings or agreements between companies. Web services technology facilitates this kind of interaction since, in addition to standard interface and conversation languages as well as basic interaction protocols, it also provides Web directories that can be used for the dynamic discovery of service providers that are able to provide a given service. In addition, thanks to UDDI tModels, client applications can even restrict their searches to those providers that implement a given vertical standard, such as RosettaNet. However, there is no way of automatically addressing the problems of the different semantic interpretations of the XML document elements and of exchanging additional information not contemplated by the standard.

Even if we assume that these issues do not exist or have somehow been solved (as it could indeed be for very simple cases or for mature standards), doing business with previously unknown partners is something that many companies, both clients and service providers, tend to avoid for many reasons: the quality of the provider's service may be unknown, the provider may not be trusted, or there may be no legal agreements or trust relationships to help manage disputes.

Indeed, even in the "traditional" Internet and e-commerce, when we purchase goods online, we tend to go to Web sites that we know or that are at least referred to by some portal we trust, perhaps *Yahoo!* or *altavista*, rather than buy from some random vendor we never heard of before. Furthermore, even when there is no such middleman to give us advice, we can use our own judgment, maybe based on how professional the Web site looks, or by reading the terms and conditions written on the Web site. In any case, we would very likely only be willing to pay very small amounts when buying from an unknown seller.

In Web services the situation is much more complex because human beings are outside the picture. The interaction is between applications. Of course, one can think of hybrid approaches, where Web services technology facilitates the interaction, but where human beings are still involved in the service selection phase. This is the main reason why it is widely accepted at this stage that UDDI registries will be used mostly by human beings to find information rather than by programs to perform dynamic binding to Web services. But this would mean giving up many of the benefits promised by Web services, i.e., those of going from a "do-it-yourself" to a "do-it for-me" Internet.

9.2.3 Bypassing Complexity in Closed Communities

Severe and difficult as these problems are, there are ways to address them when the interaction can be confined to within a very well-defined domain, such as those encountered in closed business communities (Figure 9.1), possibly operating on a private UDDI registry. In these settings, many of the limitations of the current technology can be overcome "by hand," so to speak, through joint development teams that cover issues such as business protocols, semantics of the operations and their parameters, as well as contracts and legal issues. In those cases, Web services (even at their current stage of development) can be effectively used to build a B2B platform, but not without a significant manual effort.

The sobering aspect about closed community settings is that they are no different from an EAI scenario. There is the added complication that the systems to be integrated belong to different organizations, but this is exactly what SOAP and WSDL help to solve. Because of this, most B2B implementations with Web services will be of this kind, at least in the short and medium terms.

An effect similar to closed communities can be achieved when there is a dominant entity in the community (e.g., a company leader in its market) that simply prescribes what to do to invoke its Web services to anybody

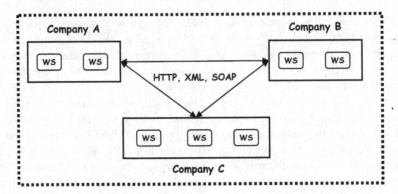

Fig. 9.1. Small closed community, direct interaction, static binding

wanting to do business with it (e.g., a collection of small suppliers). In such scenarios it is possible to compensate for the lack of functionality in current Web services systems by simply making public any additional information necessary to interact with the Web services. It will be in the interest of clients to interact with the market leader as it prescribes in order to obtain the services it provides. Once again, this setting reduces the problem to one very similar in nature and scope to that of EAI. As a matter of fact, once EAI platforms and middleware platforms support Web services, they can be used immediately to implement these two types of scenarios. For instance, in these scenarios, a private UDDI registry will act very much like a name and directory service to provide dynamic binding, and to decouple to a certain extent the service requesters and the service provider.

In both scenarios, there is a good chance to find solutions to the problems of semantics and of contractual relationships, but these solutions will be ad hoc for quite a while until existing vertical standards are adapted to Web services and become widely accepted.

9.2.4 Toward Open Communities

A generalization of the scenarios discussed above can be achieved by introducing intermediate entities that take care of some of the problems. Many software vendors and providers interested in Web services have an eye on this possibility, as the potential gains by acting as an intermediary in Web services-based exchanges are very large.

For instance, trust and quality of service problems could be solved by introducing rating services, i.e., entities that give information about the quality and reliability of the services offered by a provider, usually based on feedback from previous customers. Such a service would make it easier to trust a provider that has been automatically discovered by an application by enquiring at a UDDI registry. Rating systems are used today in online auction sites to address the quality of service issue in a consumer-to-consumer (C2C) context (such as the auctions on eBay): buyers in an auction can rate the speed at which the seller delivers the goods as well as the correspondence between the promised and the actual state of the goods. To some extent this also happens in B2C contexts, where many companies evaluate products and services offered by different businesses, although this is done mainly to compare prices and aggregate information rather than to asses the reliability of the provider [127].

In addition to rating, these "middleman" entities may also verify and certify compliances to the specifications involved in the exchange. One of the problems with vertical standards is the different choices and interpretations that can be made both in the implementation of the standard by different software vendors and in the deployment within a given application. Certification services can provide benchmark implementations, which can be used as references with which all other services must be able to interact before they can be certified as being compliant with a given standard. Note that this can be in addition to official certification mechanisms, if they exist, defined by the standardization body, and it may be specialized for a given industry.

The next step toward providing some degree of control in an otherwise unstructured environment is represented by *market makers*. These are entities that create and control an electronic marketplace, where customers and service providers meet to conduct business online. Besides rating service providers, market makers may define rules, constraints, legal bindings and, in general, offer a "protected" environment that makes electronic business, or e-business, more reliable. This scenario is somewhat in between a completely open and a completely closed community: on the one hand, customers do not have contracts, agreements, or even knowledge of a certain service provider before it is dynamically discovered during the service selection process; on the other hand, the community is controlled by an entity that is trusted by different parties, and that is typically free to accept or reject additions to the community.

Rating and certification services as well as market makers facilitate the dynamic service selection phase. The actual service is directly invoked by calling the methods offered by the selected service provider. However, in some cases, these entities can also play a role in the interaction phase. For example, they can provide a hub through which all messages exchanged when executing conversations according to given standard must be sent (see Figure 9.2). The hub can mediate among possible differences in the implementation and deployment of the standard (such as different transport protocols or security requirements), and provide robustness to changes (such as the transport protocols and security requirements supported by a provider).

That being said, it is still to be seen whether such intermediary entities become a reality by virtue of a good business model, or if confidentiality issues prevail, thereby ruling out any form of "middleman" entity.

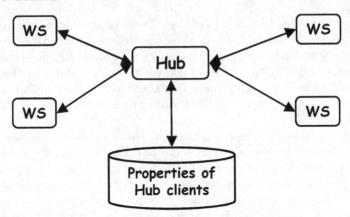

Fig. 9.2. Interactions may be mediated by a hub

9.2.5 The Semantic Web

The Semantic Web efforts [222], especially with respect to the recent trend toward Semantic Web Services [131], aim at fully automating all the stages of the Web services lifecycle. The idea is to standardize the representation and handling of the semantic metadata used to describe Web services and all aspects of using them. Based on such standardization, one can develop tools that take advantage of the standard representation to automate the use of Web services, especially to automate service discovery by including, for instance, capabilities for searching for services that are semantically equivalent to each other (therefore going beyond the support for searching for services that support a given interface or a given protocol). Work on Semantic Web services tend to revolve around the following specifications: *RDF* and *RDF Schema*, *DAML+OIL*, *OWL*, and *DAML-S*.

RDF and RDF Schema

The Resource Description Framework (RDF) is designed for the representation and processing of metadata about information (resources) on the Web. RDF defines a model for describing relationships among resources in terms of uniquely identified properties and values. RDF-Schema (RDFS) extends RDF by defining a class and property system similar to an object-oriented system. Using RDF and RDFS, it is possible to describe complex properties of resources (such as Web services), and complex relations between these resources, using a notation that resembles that used in an object-oriented system. Since the rules for writing such descriptions are well defined, the descriptions can be parsed automatically to extract information about the resources.

DAML+OIL

An ontology is a formal definition of a common set of terms used to describe and represent a domain of knowledge [58]. Ontologies make knowledge reusable by encoding formal definitions of basic concepts and the relationships among them. Ontologies are usually expressed in a logic-based language so as to support automated reasoning upon them. In the Semantic Web, ontologies provide a means for representing the semantics of documents and for structuring and defining the meaning of standardized metadata terms. DAML+OIL combines two previous efforts: the DARPA Agent Markup Language (DAML), which extends XML, RDF, and RDFS to enable the creation and instantiation of ontologies that describe Web resources, and the Ontology Inference Layer (OIL), a proposal for a Web-based representation and an inference layer for ontologies. As such, DAML+OIL is a semantic markup language for Web resources that extends RDF and RDFS with richer modeling primitives, such as those commonly found in frame-based languages [53].

OWL

The Ontology Web Language (OWL) is a revision of the DAML+OIL Web ontology language currently being designed by the W3C Web Ontology Working Group as a successor to DAML+OIL. OWL's goal is to facilitate greater machine readability of Web content than XML, RDF, and RDFS by providing an additional vocabulary for term descriptions [130]. OWL is intended to address DAML+OIL shortcomings, by allowing, for example, untyped literals (e.g, it does not distinguish between strings and integers, which are incompatible with XML Schema datatypes) and by providing a better data typecasting solution that is compatible with XML Schema and RDFS [96]. Because one criticism of OWL is that it is too complicated, OWL provides three increasingly expressive sublanguages: OWL-Lite, which attempts to capture many of the commonly used features of OWL and DAML+OIL, such as a classification hierarchy and simple constraint features; OWL-DL, which supports users who need computational completeness and decidability as well as expressiveness (DL is short for "description logic"); and OWL-Full, which provides the rich expressiveness and syntactic freedom of RDF without any computational guarantees [223].

DAML-S

DAML-S is a DAML+OIL language for Web services that represents a collaborative effort by BBN Technologies, Carnegie Mellon University, Nokia, Stanford University, and SRI International. DAML-S complements current Web services specification languages such as WSDL and BPEL. Like other service specification languages, DAML-S provides a means to create descriptions of Web services that can be interpreted programmatically. The distinguishing characteristic of DAML-S is that, while current Web services specification standards focus on service syntax, its goal is to facilitate the description of the semantics of services, their interfaces, and their behavior [8].

In addition to the DAML-S work, a number of other efforts also explore the use of Semantic Web technologies in the context of Web services. [157]

proposes a mapping that allows the translation of WSDL into RDF, and an RDFS representation of the WSDL specification. Representing WSDL service descriptions in RDF would enable RDF-aware applications such as search engines to utilize the WSDL descriptions automatically. [200] presents a prototype that uses RDF to perform service matchmaking. Similarly, [201] transforms RosettaNet PIP XML Schemas into DAML+OIL and RosettaNet PIP XML documents into RDF format in order to facilitate the programmatic discovery of relationships between business documents and processes.

9.2.6 How Far Are We from the Holy Grail?

As we discussed, the most futuristic Web services visions always involve automated interactions among applications that support different interfaces and protocols previously unknown to the clients. Basically, the hope is that clients will be able to search the available services for one that best fits their needs (based on functionality, quality of service, and cost), read the associated specification that describes how to interact with the service, and, based on this information, invoke the service. All without any human intervention.

Rating services, certification services, market makers, and B2B hubs are essential toward achieving (at least in part) this vision, despite all the disadvantages, in terms of confidentiality, caused by having intermediaries in the interaction. Semantic Web services efforts here have largely (but not entirely) taken place in the research and academic communities. It remains to be seen when and if this technology will be adopted for commercial purposes. Furthermore, this work has yet to gain wide acceptance outside of the artificial intelligence and agent communities, although recent standardization efforts tend to be much more cross-disciplinary. In order for Semantic Web services technologies to be adopted, they must mature and advance beyond description languages to deal with the practical details of service advertisement and discovery. In particular, the tools and enabling technology must be developed so that it becomes more practical for commercial service implementors to create, manage, and use semantic metadata. Once this obstacle has been overcome, Semantic Web solutions could be developed to address other areas of the service lifecycle, such as naming, security, negotiation, and contract formation. Even then, it remains to be seen whether the problems related to semantic interpretations of documents can be solved in the full generality needed for real-life interactions between corporations.

9.3 Web Services as a Problem and a Solution: an Example

Even with only SOAP and WSDL in place, Web services create problems of their own as they add a new layer that needs to be taken into consideration when designing, maintaining, and tuning multi-tier systems. These problems will need to be solved in the short and medium term to allow designers to use Web services efficiently and with the same confidence with which they use today's middleware platforms. In this section we use service management to illustrate this new class of problems, re-introduced or aggravated by the use of Web services. Service management is particularly interesting because it illustrates very well how Web services both create a new problem and become part of the solution for that same problem.

9.3.1 Management in Conventional Middleware

Enterprise application management can be seen as the task of monitoring and controlling applications in an enterprise so that they can be made resilient to failures, configurable to changing needs of the business, accountable for billing and auditing, capable of performing under varying workloads, and secure to intended or unintended attacks [1] (FCAPS) [186].

There have been several attempts at standardizing such tasks in the context of conventional middleware. For example, CORBA specifies lifecycle interfaces for configuration management [153], Java Management eXtensions (JMX) from Sun [193] specifies a framework for defining management interfaces on Java objects, the Simple Network Management Protocol (SNMP) defines a set of objects called application Management Information Bases (MIBs) for managing applications [111], the Common Information Model (CIM) from Desktop Management Task Force (DMTF) defines a standard information model for managing applications among various other systems [60], and Application Response Measurement (ARM) is a standard for notifying performance events from applications [159]. All the management standards described aim at defining interfaces between the management system and managed applications. Some of these interfaces are useful in sending data from the application to the management system (e.g., SNMP, CIM, ARM). These are called *data collection interfaces* or *instrumentation interfaces*. Others are used by the management system to execute control actions on the application (e.g., JMX, CORBA lifecycle interfaces, SNMP, CIM). These are called *control interfaces*.

The infrastructure that manages applications using these abstractions is called an *enterprise application management system*. Examples of commonly used application management systems are HP OpenView [93], Computer Associates Unicenter [52], and Tivoli [103].

9.3.2 Management in Web Services

Web services management is an extension of enterprise application management and has two sides: management of applications within an enterprise and

---

[1] This definition is derived from the ISO definition of network management, which consists of Fault management, Configuration management, Accounting, Performance management, and Security management

management of relationships with other Web services across enterprises. The challenges in and approaches to dealing with the first part of Web services management are very similar to those in traditional application management. However, Web services simplify certain aspects of application management through their standardized abstractions. The second part of Web services management (i.e., managing relationships with other Web services) raises a completely new set of challenges, since cross-enterprise interactions were not dealt with before in application management.

Web services act as an additional tier in a middleware platform. The impact of adding such an additional tier to an application is that management has to be expanded to cover the new tier as well. The new tier becomes another source of failures, configuration problems, and performance problems. It also becomes another source of instrumentation to collect data and another control point to correct or optimize the overall system. In the case of Web services, the additional tier is usually implemented using SOAP routers, conversation controllers, horizontal protocol handlers, and composition engines. All these components must be instrumented to provide data about themselves and about the objects they wrap.

Figure 9.3 shows the architecture of a typical Web services management system. In addition to interacting with other tiers of the information system, the Web services management system also collects data and executes control actions on the Web services middleware components.

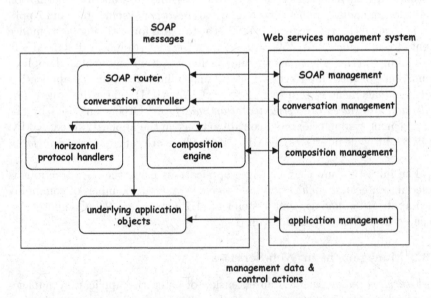

Fig. 9.3. Instrumentation and control of middleware components by a Web services management system

Typically, operation invocations on a Web service happen through a SOAP router. The SOAP router has information about all the invocations, their timing, and whether they complete successfully or not. This information can be communicated to a management system using standards such as ARM. With that information, a management system (labeled as SOAP management in Figure 9.3) can monitor the performance of a Web service. As an application management system, one can set response time thresholds and policies to automatically instantiate new objects when the response time of an operation goes beyond a threshold. Note that this functionality can also be physically embedded into the SOAP router instead of having a separate management system.

A conversation controller dispatches incoming messages to the right conversation instance. It has information about the state of ongoing conversations, their timing, and their accuracy. A management system (labeled conversation management in Figure 9.3) that receives this information can analyze conversation bottlenecks, manage their performance, and perform lifecycle operations, such as suspend and resume, on ongoing conversations. Once again, this management functionality can be physically embedded into the conversation controller.

A composition engine implements the business logic of Web services operations by invoking them in a particular order. It has information about the component Web services that should be invoked, the order in which they should be invoked (expressed as a graph or workflow), and the timings of the invocations in progress and of past invocations. Using this data, a management system (labeled composition management in Figure 9.3) can correlate the response times of a Web service's operations with the response times of its component Web services. One can then make a judgment on whether a performance degradation in a Web service is caused by an internal failure or by a performance degradation in another Web services. A composition management system should also be able to analyze the composition model for bottlenecks, compare two alternative service providers for executing a step in the composition, or automatically select one of the service providers depending on historical data analysis.

In addition to collecting data from the Web services tier, a Web services management system should also correlate that data with data collected from other tiers of the underlying application. Correlation techniques have been used in the past to parse end-to-end response times into response times of individual tiers [43, 77]. Similar techniques can be extended to the Web services tier as well. With these extensions, a Web services management system will not only be able to report on metrics collected at the interface of the Web services, but also to drill-down into lower tiers to analyze failures or diagnose performance, security, and configuration problems.

With the exception of additional components to instrument, monitor, and control, management of the internal aspects of a Web services is very similar to that of the internal aspects of any other distributed application. But, in certain ways, managing Web services is simpler than managing conventional applications that are not wrapped into Web services. This is because many aspects of Web services, including their operational interfaces, horizontal protocol interfaces, business protocols, structures of exchanged messages, and composition models, are all specified in XML and are being standardized. This makes collecting and processing the information much simpler than when the management system has to deal with heterogeneous representations.

Another advantage of Web services is that they enable service-level and business-level management in ways that were not possible before. SOAP operations and conversations are the externally visible aspects of a Web service. In other words, clients of a Web service use SOAP and conversation protocols to interact with it. The term Service Level Management (SLM) is used in management literature to refer to management done at the interface of an application, as opposed to it being done at the level of application internals [187]. SLM provides a better gauge of how clients perceive the performance or availability of an application. The SOAP and conversation management described above thus implement such SLM. An advantage of SLM is that it can be used to set, monitor, and enforce performance thresholds or other kinds of service level agreements (SLAs) on the operations of a Web service [176]. The use of SLM in the context of Web services is made easier due to the separation between internal and external architectures of a Web service. The service level management can be done on the external architecture of the Web services without having to deal with the (possibly legacy) underlying application.

Finally, Web services may help bridge the gap between business management and application management. Business management involves managing business metrics (e.g., revenue, number of completed orders, etc.) and business objectives (e.g., revenue targets, order targets, etc.). Application management involves managing the data collected from instrumenting the software and hardware that constitute the application. Mapping these two domains has never been easy, as application management data is too low-level to be directly translated into information relevant at the business management level. The increasing use of business processes to implement and orchestrate Web services makes this gap smaller. Service level measurements such as operation response times, SLA violations, and comparisons between two supplier Web services are all much closer to business-level metrics than traditional application measurements. This advantage of Web services is often overlooked but it might play a crucial role in practice. Business protocols such as those specified through ebXML, RosettaNet, or BPEL may eventually include quality of service information that will need to be enforced through the appropriate support for systems management.

9.3.3 Cross-Enterprise Management

The instrumentation just described corresponds to the *internal management architecture* of a Web services. The internal management architecture identifies how a Web services has to be managed within an enterprise boundary. Clients and other interacting Web services are not aware of the existence of an internal management system. What we discuss next is the *external management architecture* of a Web service. This arises out of the need to manage relationships with Web services across enterprise boundaries and requires additional Web services protocols to be standardized.

The use of Web services to integrate applications across enterprises resulted in a whole new set of management challenges that did not exist while managing enterprise applications. These challenges are caused by limited visibility and control over portions of the application that are not owned by the same enterprise and by the lack of trust between communicating Web services [126].

When a Web service composes other Web services, it is not only the functional but also the non-functional attributes such as performance, availability, and security that get composed. Using a Web service whose performance is bad impacts the performance of the composite service as well. Similarly, a security problem with one of the component services implies a security problem in the overall service. When both the composite Web service and the component Web service are within the same enterprise, there is no issue in understanding whether a problem is caused by one or the other. A management system can get data and events from both the Web services, analyze problems, and control one or both of the Web services. Instrumentation and control interfaces such as the ones mentioned in Section 9.3.1 are sufficient to accomplish these tasks.

But, as discussed in previous chapter, Web services are generally not just invoked from a simple client but involve multi-party conversations among sets of Web services. To support a minimal infrastructure for management in the presence of multi-party conversations, Web services need to support:

- **Measurements or states.** Web services interfaces such as WSDL expose the operations offered by a Web service to its clients. However, they are not used to expose state information or measurements to clients. The state of a Web service can be considered a set of attributes, some of which are static and some of which are dynamic. Static attributes are those whose values do not change over time. For example, the port reference at which operations are made available is a static attribute. Other attributes are dynamic and their values change every time they are queried. For example, the anticipated response time of an operation or the state of a conversation change from time to time and from client to client. In either case, a client would benefit from querying these attributes both before composition and during execution to get a better understanding of a Web service's quality of service.
- **Events.** When two or more Web services interact, a problem in one can affect the other. For example, if the execution of an operation in one Web service depends on the results of an operation in a different Web service,

then the performance of the latter has an effect on the performance of the former. In traditional distributed applications, unanticipated problems are notified by application components through events. A management system that listens to these events takes decisions on how to isolate the problems without propagating its effects to other components. Similar mechanisms are needed for Web services. It should be possible for one Web service to generate events that are intended for another Web service (or for another Web service's management system).

- **Policies.** Policies are a convenient mechanism to change the behavior of a system. Policies have been used to indicate what a management system may or may not do (authorization policies) and must or must not do (obligation policies) [181]. For example, a policy can be used to establish that no more than five unsuccessful login attempts should be permitted on a system. Policies are also useful between interacting Web services. They can be used by a Web service to inform clients about the constraints under which it operates (for e.g., that operations will not be accessible during a particular set of maintenance hours or that all messages exchanged should be encrypted in a certain manner). Similarly, clients can indicate their preferences and constraints to a Web service using policies.
- **Service level agreements (SLAs).** Another mechanism for expressing constraints (or desired quality guarantees) between Web services is through the use of SLAs. SLA monitoring and enforcement requires the SLAs, the measurements needed to measure the SLAs [91], and their outcomes to be exchanged between interacting clients and Web services. To a certain extent, this is what the CPA in ebXML is intended to do, although ebXML does not explicitly mention non-functional properties. To cover the entire range of constraints on multi-party conversations, the SLAs must have the facility for including quality-of-service information.

Standards such as ARM and SNMP that have been traditionally used for intra-enterprise application management are insufficient to define the above interfaces and protocols. The reasons are as follows:

- These standards have been designed primarily with the assumption that all the available management information and controls can be exposed between an application and its management system. This is not true in the case of Web services that work across enterprise boundaries. Web services management standards have to deal with multi-party interactions while resolving the limited end-to-end visibility and control one has over the other's services.
- These standards haven't been developed to work over the Internet or to manage applications as complex as Web services. For example, ARM is a simple Java/C API and requires both the sender and the receiver of events to be within the same process. SNMP is a management protocol that lacks security and can only handle exchange of simple attributes.

None of these standards are built on the top of Internet protocols or Web services standards.

- Since there are a large number of management standards and systems, every Web service in a collection of interacting Web services can potentially use different standards and management systems. However, for the purpose of interoperability, Web services should be capable of managing their relationships with each other by exchanging measurements, events, policies, and SLAs in a standardized manner that hides the heterogeneity of internal management systems. This requires a richer set of Web services management standards.

Even if management information is exchanged between Web services through standardized interfaces and protocols, there is another challenge to be resolved in Web services management: the data exchanged cannot be trusted. For example, there are no simple mechanisms for all the parties to agree on in the outcome of an SLA if everyone blames the other for a problem. One solution to this issue is to use trusted third parties who have better visibility and control over each of the participants and hence can mediate between interacting Web services. The other possibility is to leave issues of trust to be resolved by manual mechanisms (such as auditing) without incorporating them into the management infrastructure.

Figure 9.4 shows a high-level architecture for managing multi-party conversations among Web services. It consists of yet-to-be-defined management interfaces and protocols for exchanging management data between interacting Web services. There is also a possible role for centralized and trusted third parties to mediate management between multiple Web services.

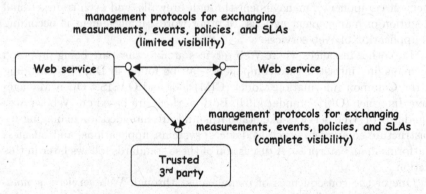

Fig. 9.4. External architecture for Web services management

9.3.4 Management through Web Services

In the previous two sections, we have discussed the management *of* Web services. There is another evolving trend in the industry, which is to use Web services as a mechanism for managing infrastructure within or across enterprises. This results in management *through* Web services. The infrastructure that is managed includes servers, data, and other forms of physical and logical IT resources.

The key distinction here is that the role of Web services standards in this case is only to define interfaces for the purposes of management. Web services standards are not being used to wrap a resource's functionality. Existing modes of accessing the primary functionality of resources are still left intact. As an example, the Global Grid Forum (GGF) is defining Open Grid Services Infrastructure (OGSI) [81] using which distributed applications could be created over the Internet. One such application has to do with being able to find and reserve global resources for computationally-intensive jobs (for example, to find and reserve a sufficient number of powerful servers to run a big simulation). The primary use case here is that of resource management. For this purpose, resources and clusters of resources are being wrapped with Web services interfaces defined in WSDL. The resulting Web services execute resource allocation protocols among themselves. Once the allocation is done, the tasks of deploying jobs onto those resources, executing the jobs, and collecting the results are done using basic protocols, such as FTP.

This is not a surprising trend given the fact that management is by itself a complex application that suffers from the same kinds of challenges that Web services are supposed to address–distribution, interoperability between components developed by different vendors, registration and discovery of management components, management through firewalls, and even transactional execution of management actions. In other words, management is becoming an application of Web services.

Two other instances where Web services architectures are being proposed for managing infrastructure components can be found in DMTF's encoding of the Common Information Model (CIM) [60] and OASIS's Open Management Interface (OMI) standard [94]. Both of them are based on Web services standards or Web services-like standards and are intended for managing infrastructure components such as devices, systems, applications, and business platforms in an enterprise. A discussion of these standards follows later in this section.

One of the consequences of management through Web services is *management outsourcing*. When interactions between a managed system and a management system occur through WSDL interfaces and SOAP messages, it becomes possible to move the management system out of the enterprise (Figure 9.5). A service provider who provides management outsourcing is known as Management Service Provider (MSP). In this case, both the managed system and the management system are wrapped as Web services. This is a highly desirable outcome for enterprises that would like to outsource their IT management. Even today, some of the IT management tasks such as backup and recovery, email management, Web site throughput analysis, and trouble ticket management are being outsourced to MSPs. Web services will simplify and enable the creation of many more such remote management applications.

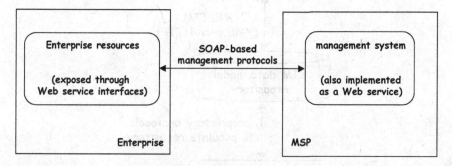

Fig. 9.5. Management outsourcing

9.3.5 Web Services Management Standards

Web services management standards are just beginning to emerge. Some of them are aimed at enabling interoperability between management systems and managed resources wrapped as Web services, as described in Section 9.3.4. Others are aimed at solving the challenges related to management of cross-enterprise Web services, as discussed in the Section 9.3.3. We highlight three standards in this section:

1. XMLCIM from DMTF,
2. OMI from OASIS, and
3. Grid services from GGF [81]

Since it is premature to discuss syntactic details of these standards, we will just talk about their motivations, the problems they solve, and the approaches they take.

In Section 9.3.3, we have mentioned CIM as a data model standard for managing applications. The data model consists of a number of object-oriented classes and instances that model managed systems and their properties, events, methods, and relationships. CIM, by itself, does not specify a concrete representation for these objects. It does not specify interfaces to access these objects or an encoding for transporting these objects using a communication protocol. XMLCIM, on the other hand, is an additional standard from DMTF that is aimed at addressing exactly that. It is an encoding of CIM data models in XML and a way of transporting that information using HTTP. XMLCIM has been designed to enable interoperability between applications, repositories that store the CIM data model, and management systems that manage applications using the data model (Figure 9.6).

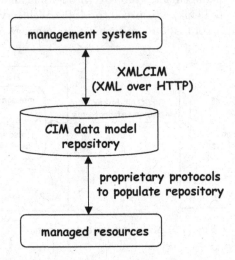

Fig. 9.6. Interoperability between managed systems and management systems using XMLCIM .

The part of XMLCIM that deals with encoding CIM data in XML is currently in version 2.1, whereas the part that deals with mapping CIM operations over HTTP is in version 1.1. When XMLCIM was originally conceived in 1999, Web services standards were nonexistent and XML was in its inception. But, since then, XMLCIM has lagged behind the developments in the Web services world. This is evident in the fact that it still uses DTDs as opposed to XML Schemas for representing CIM data encodings, and proposes additional HTTP headers instead of WSDL interfaces to represent CIM operations. Still, XMLCIM is one of the first efforts aimed at transporting management information using XML over HTTP between applications and management systems that are distributed across enterprise boundaries.

Figure 9.6 showed how XMLCIM can be used for managing enterprise infrastructure. Since the management system can potentially be across enterprise boundaries, the same standard can also be used to facilitate cross-enterprise Web services management. As shown in Figure 9.7, every Web service exposes a set of CIM classes and instances that are accessible to the management systems of the other Web services through XMLCIM. For example, CIM defines a class called UnitOfWork, instances of which can be used to represent an operation in progress or already completed. Properties such as the completion status of an operation or the elapsed time since the operation has begun execution are part of this object. XMLCIM defines how UnitOf-Work instances can be encoded in XML and how a management system can query them using methods such as GetInstance, ExecQuery, or GetProperty that are encoded in HTTP. In Figure 9.7, the management system associated with the first Web service sends an HTTP request querying for instances of UnitOfWork to the CIM repository associated with the second Web service. The instances are returned in the HTTP response.

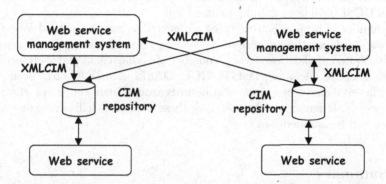

Fig. 9.7. Exchanging management data between Web services using XMLCIM

An emerging standard that relies on SOAP and HTTP to exchange management information is OMI. The purpose of OMI is to propose standardized SOAP messages through which management data and controls can be exchanged between applications and management systems. In spirit, it is similar to XMLCIM. However, the focus of OMI is to manage business applications whereas CIM defines data models for managing all kinds of resources.

Another standard that comes much closer to using Web services for management is the Open Grid Services Infrastructure (OGSI) from GGF. OGSI is a distributed computing infrastructure that builds on Web services standards and protocols. Services created using OGSI concepts are known as Grid services. Grid services are different from Web services in two ways. First, the WSDL used for defining port types in Grid services is an extension of WSDL 1.1 defined by W3C. Second, OGSI defines a set of standard port types that have to be implemented to call a Web service a Grid service. Both WSDL extensions and pre-defined port types have to do with enabling the communication of states and events between Web services, as pointed out in Section 9.3.3. Recall that WSDL 1.1 defines operations and groups them into ports. The only way in which the state of a Web service can be exposed to clients currently through WSDL is by defining a new set of operations. This is not very convenient for several reasons. The number of attributes that comprise the state of a Web service can be potentially very large. Defining an operation for each of these attributes is quite cumbersome and requires multiple invocations to retrieve the entire state of a Web service. Also, it becomes difficult to support query mechanisms for selecting a subset of attributes or to subscribe to notifications when the value of an attribute changes. Hence,

GGF proposes extensions to attach attributes (called service data) to port types in WSDL.

OGSI extensions enable Web services across enterprise boundaries to exchange management information either about themselves or about the managed resources they represent. At the time of this writing, GGF and its efforts around OGSI have been gaining momentum.

A number of proposals were being submitted to use and extend Web services standards for the purpose of developing resource management systems and distributed applications. Also, a number of management and Web services standards bodies including DMTF, GGF, OASIS, and W3C have been collaborating to define a new wave of standards around management of/through Web services. It remains to be seen how these standards will evolve or which of them will be adopted and used.

9.4 Summary

This chapter has presented an outlook on Web services, putting them into perspective and discussing the contexts in which they can be applied. We have stressed the evolutionary nature of Web services, presenting them as extensions to conventional middleware that enable interaction across the Web. These extensions make Web-based integration possible at least in simple scenarios (such as EAI or closed communities of business partners), although more is needed before Web services technology can be used to support dynamic business interaction among casual business partners, which was indeed the original intent of many visionaries in this area.

This is in contrast with a revolutionary view, which sees Web services as radically changing the way integration is achieved. While it may well be that in the future such a view is finally realized, it is quite far from the current state of affairs. This is not meant to belittle the impact or underestimate the potential of Web services: indeed, we believe that Web services will be a successful technology that will be heavily applied. Their evolutionary nature may actually facilitate their adoption, since the paradigms are essentially analogous to those found in conventional middleware.

Regardless of the specific direction that Web services technology will take, it is clear that it will have a very concrete impact on how integration is achieved, both within and across enterprises. Web services are already being used, and the applicability of this technology is likely to grow as extensions are added and as standardization efforts in areas such as reliability, security, and management finally converge and become generally accepted. Once completed, this process will generate a robust framework for taking the Internet to the next level, from a Web of unstructured information to a Web of services through which customers and providers can conduct business in a seamless manner.

Bibliography

1. M. Aiello, M. P. Papazoglou, J. Yang, M. Carman, M. Pistore, L. Serafini, and P. Traverso. A request language for Web-services based on planning and constraint satisfaction. In *Proceedings of the International VLDB Workshop on Technologies for E-Services*, pages 76–85, Hong Kong, China, 2002.
2. E. Akarsu, G. C. Fox, W. Furmanski, and T. Haupt. WebFlow - high-level programming environment and visual authoring toolkit for high performance distributed computing. In *Proceedings of the ACM Conference on Supercomputing*, Orlando, FL, Nov. 1998. ACM SIGARCH.
3. A. S. Ali and O. Rana. *UDDI extensions.* Cardiff University. http://www.cs.cf.ac.uk/user/A.Shaikhali/uddie/.
4. G. Alonso, D. Agrawal, A. E. Abbadi, M. Kamath, R. Gunthor, and C. Mohan. Advanced transaction model in workflow context. In *Proceedings of the International Conference on Data Engineering (ICDE)*, New Orleans, LA, USA, Feb. 1996.
5. G. Alonso, M. Kamath, D. Agrawal, A. E. Abbadi, R. Gunthor, and C. Mohan. Failure handling in large scale workflow management systems. Technical Report RJ9913, IBM Almaden Research Center, Nov. 1994.
6. G. Alonso and C. Mohan. WFMS: The next generation of distributed processing tools. *Advanced Transaction Models and Architectures*, 1997. S. Jajodia and L. Kerschberg (Eds.). Kluwer Academic Publishers, 1997.
7. T. Andrews et al. *Business Process Execution Language for Web Services. Version 1.1.*
8. A. Ankolekar, M. Burstein, J. Hobbs, O. Lassila, D. Martin, S. McIlraith, S. Narayanan, M. Paolucci, T. Payne, K. Sycara, and H. Zeng. DAML-S: Web service description for the Semantic Web. In *Proceedings of the International Semantic Web Conference (ISWC)*, Sardinia, Italy, June 2002.
9. ANSA. The Advanced Network Systems Architecture. Technical report, Castle Hill, Cambridge, England: Architecture Project Management, 1989.
10. A. Arkin. Business process modeling language 1.0. Technical report, BPMI Consortium, June 2002. http://www.bpmi.org/.
11. A. Arkin et al. *Web Service Choreography Interface 1.0*, 2002. http://www.w3.org/TR/wsci/.
12. ATG. *ATG Dynamo Personalization Programming Guide*, 2002. http://www.atg.com/en/support/product_resources/.

322   Bibliography

13. B. Atkinson et al. *Web Services Security (WS-Security), Version 1.0 April 2002.* http://www.ibm.com/developerworks/library/ws-secure/.

14. A. Banerji et al. Web Services Conversation Language (WSCL) 1.0. W3C technical note, Mar. 2002. http://www.w3.org/TR/wscl10/.

15. W. Bausch, C. Pautasso, and G. Alonso. Programming for dependability in a service-based grid. In *Proceedings of the International Symposium on Cluster Computing and the Grid (CCGrid)*, Tokyo, Japan, May 2003.

16. W. Bausch, C. Pautasso, R. Schaeppi, and G. Alonso. Bioopera: Cluster-aware computing. In *Proceedings of the 4th IEEE International Conference on Cluster Computing*, 2002.

17. BEA Systems Inc. *BEA Tuxedo: The Programming Model*, 1996. http://edocs.bea.com/wle/tuxedo/main/stref.htm.

18. BEA Systems Inc. *BEA WebLogic Integration: Application Intergration*, 2002. http://bea.com/products/weblogic/server/index.shtml.

19. BEA Systems Inc. *BEA WebLogic Server 7.0 Overview*, Apr. 2002. http://bea.com/products/weblogic/server.

20. T. Bellwood et al. UDDI version 3.0, July 2002. This version is available at http://uddi.org/pubs/uddi-v3.00-published-20020719.htm. The latest version is available at http://uddi.org/pubs/uddi_v3.htm.

21. B. Benatallah, F. Casati, F. Toumain, and R. Hamadi. Conceptual modeling of Web services conversations. In *Proceedings of the International Conference on Advanced information Systems Engineering (CAiSE)*, Klagenfurt/Velden, Austria, June 2003.

22. K. H. Bennett et al. Prototype implementations of an architectural model for service-based flexible software. In *Proceedings of the Thirty-Fifth Hawaii International Conference on System Sciences (HICSS-35)*, Jan. 2002.

23. T. Berners-Lee and R. Cailliau. *WorldWideWeb: Proposal for a HyperText Project.* European Laboratory for Particle Physics (CERN).

24. T. Berners-Lee, R. Cailliau, J.-F. Groff, and B. Pollermann. World-Wide Web: The information universe. *Electronic Networking: Research, Applications and Policy*, 1(2):74–82, 1992.

25. P. Bernstein and E. Newcomer. *Principles of Transaction Processing for the Systems Professional.* Morgan Kaufmann, 1997.

26. P. A. Bernstein. Middleware: A model for distributed system services. *Communications of the ACM*, 39(2):86–98, 1996.

27. P. A. Bernstein, M. Hsu, and B. Mann. Implementing recoverable requests using queues. In *Proceedings of the Association for Computing Machinery Special Interest Group on Management of Data (SIGMOD)*, pages 112–122, Atlantic City, NJ, USA, 1990.

28. A. D. Birrell and B. J. Nelson. Implementing remote procedure calls. *ACM Transactons on Computer Systems*, 2(1):39–59, Feb. 1984.

29. S. Bodoff et al. *The J2EE tutorial.* Addison Wesley, 2002.

30. Bosworth et al. *Web Services Addressing (WS-Addressing)*, Mar. 2003. http://msdn.microsoft.com/ws/2003/03/ws-addressing/.

31. K. Boucher and F. Katz. *Essential guide to object monitors.* John Wiley & Sons, 1999.

32. D. Box et al. *Simple Object Access Protocol (SOAP) 1.1*, May 2000. This version is available at http://www.w3.org/TR/2000/NOTE-SOAP-20000508/. The latest version is available at http://www.w3.org/TR/SOAP/.

33. D. Box et al. *Web Services Policy Attachment (WS-PolicyAttachment)*, Dec. 2002. http://msdn.microsoft.com/webservices.

34. D. Box et al. *Web Services Policy Framework (WS-Policy)*, Dec. 2002. http://msdn.microsoft.com/webservices/default.aspx?pull=/library/en-us/dnglobspec/html/ws-policy.asp.

35. G. Bracchi and B. Pernici. The Design Requirements of Office Systems. *ACM Transactions on Office Information Systems*, 2(2):151–170, Apr. 1985.

36. P. Brittenham, F. Cubera, D. Ehnebuske, and S. Graham. *Understanding WSDL in a UDDI Registry*, September 2001. http://www.ibm.com/developerworks/webservices/library/ws-wsdl/.

37. BroadVision, Inc. *BroadVision*. http://www.broadvision.com/.

38. C. Bussler. B2B protocol standards and their role in semantic B2B integration engines. *IEEE Data Engineering Bulletin*, 24(1), Mar. 2001.

39. C. Bussler. Process inheritance. In *Proceedings of the International Conference on Advanced information Systems Engineering (CAiSE)*, pages 701–705, Toronto, Canada, 2002.

40. C. Bussler. Public process inheritance for business-to-business integration. In *Proceedings of the International VLDB Workshop on Technologies for E-Services*, pages 19–28, Hong Kong, China, 2002.

41. F. Cabrera et al. *Web Services Coordination (WS-Coordination), 9 August 2002*. http://www.ibm.com/developerworks/library/ws-coor/.

42. F. Cabrera et al. *Web Services Transactions (WS-Transaction), 9 August 2002*. IBM, Microsoft, BEA. http://www.ibm.com/developerworks/library/ws-transpec/.

43. Candle. *ETEWatch: End-to-end Response Time Monitoring*. http://www.candle.com.

44. H. Casanova and J. Dongarra. NetSolve: A Network Server for Solving Computational Science Problems. In *Proceedings of the 1996 ACM/IEEE Supercomputing Conference*, 1996. http://www.cs.utk.edu/netsolve.

45. F. Casati, S. Ceri, S. Paraboschi, and G. Pozzi. Specification and implementation of exceptions in workflow management systems. *ACM Transactions on Database Systems*, 24(3):405–451, 1999.

46. F. Casati, S. Ceri, B. Pernici, and G. Pozzi. Deriving active rules for workflow enactment. In *Proceedings of the International Conference on Database and Expert Systems Administration(DEXA'96)*, Lecture Notes in Computer Science, Springer Verlag, Zurich, Switzerland, Sept. 1996. Springer-Verlag.

47. F. Casati and M.-C. Shan. Dynamic and adaptive composition of e-services. *Infosystems*, 24(3):211–238, Jan. 2001.

48. A. Cass, B. Lernerand, E. McCall, L. Osterweil, S. Sutton Jr., and A. Wise. Little-JIL/Juliette: A process definition language and interpreter. In *Proceedings of the International Conference on Software Engineering (ICSE)*, Limerick, Ireland, June 2000.

49. R. Chinnici, M. Gudgin, J.-J. Moreau, and S. Weerawarana. *Web Services Description Language (WSDL) Version 1.2*, July 2002. http://www.w3.org/TR/wsdl12.

50. Commerce One, Inc. *XML Common Business Library*. http://www.xcbl.org.

51. Commerce One, Inc. *Order Management Recommended Use: xCBL 3.5, version 1.0*, November 2001. http://www.xcbl.org.

52. Computer Associates, Inc. *CA Unicenter*. http://www.ca.com.

53. Connolly et al. DAML+OIL (March 2001) Reference Description. W3C note, World Wide Web Consortium (W3C), Dec. 2001. http://www.w3.org/TR/daml+oil-reference.

54. G. Coulouris, J. Dollimore, and T. Kindberg. *Distributed Systems: Concepts and Design.* Addison-Wesley, 3rd Edition, 2000.

55. F. Curbera, D. Ehnebuske, and D. Rogers. *Using WSDL in a UDDI Registry, Version 1.07 UDDI Best Practice*, May 2002. This version is available at http://www.uddi.org/pubs/wsdlbestpractices-V1.07-Open-20020521.pdf The latest version is available at http://www.uddi.org/pubs/wsdlbestpractices.pdf.

56. U. Dayal, M. Hsu, and R. Ladin. Business process coordination: State of the art, trends, and open issues. In *Proceedings of the International Conference on Very Large Data Bases (VLDB)*, Rome, Italy, Sept. 2001.

57. Delphi Group. *BPM 2002. Market Milestone Report*, 2002.

58. M. Denny. Ontology building: A survey of editing tools. *XML.com*, November 2002.

59. K. K. Dickson Chiu, Qing Li. ADOME-WFMS: Towards cooperative handling of workflow exceptions. In A. Romanovsky, C. Dony, J. L. Knudsen, and A. Tripathi, editors, *Advances in Exception Handling Techniques*, pages 271–288. Springer-Verlag, LNCS-20022, 2001.

60. Distributed Management Task Force (DMTF). *Common Information Model.* http://www.dmtf.org.

61. ebXML (Electronic Business using eXtensible Markup Language. *ebXML–Enabling a Global Electronic Market.* http://www.ebxml.org/geninfo.htm.

62. ebXML Registry Project Team. Using UDDI to Find ebXML RegReps. Technical report, http://www.ebxml.org/specs/rrUDDI.pdf, May 2001.

63. ebXML Technical Architecture Team. The Advanced Network Systems Architecture, v1.0.4. Technical report, http://www.ebxml.org/specs/ebTA_print.pdf, February 2001.

64. J. Eder and W. Liebhart. The Workflow Activity Model WAMO. In *Proceedings of the International Conference on Cooperative Information Systems (CoopIs)*, Wien, Austria, May 1995.

65. J. Eder and W. Liebhart. Contributions to exception handling in workflow management. In *Proceedings of the EDBT Workshop on Workflow Management Systems*, Valencia, Spain, Mar. 1998.

66. EDIFACT. *United Nations Directories for Electronic Data Interchange for Administration, Commerce and Transport.* http://www.unece.org/trade/untdid/welcome.htm.

67. J. Edwards. *3-Tier Server/Client at Work.* John Wiley & Sons, 1999.

68. A. Elmagarmid. *Database Transaction Models.* Morgan Kaufmannn, 1992.

69. A. Emtage and P. Deutsch. Archie: An electronic directory service for the internet. In *Proceedings of the Winter 1992 USENIX Conference*, pages 93–110, San Francisco, California, 1991.

70. R. Fielding, J. Gettys, J. Mogul, H. Frystyk, and T. Berners-Lee. RFC 2068: Hypertext Transfer Protocol — HTTP/1.1, Jan. 1997.

71. Fiorano. *FioranoMQ Enterprise Messaging Server.* http://www.fiorano.com/.

72. M. Fisher. Introduction to web services. part of the java web services tutorial, Aug. 2002. http://java.sun.com/webservices/docs/1.0/tutorial/.

73. Flashline Inc. *Application Server Comparison Matrix.*
    http://www.flashline.com/components/appservermatrix.jsp.
74. D. Florescu, A. Grunhagen, and D. Kossman. XL: an XML Programming
    Language for Web Service Specification and Composition. In *Proceedings of
    the 11th International World Wide Web Conference (WWW02)*, Honolulu,
    Hawaii, USA, May 2002.
75. S. Frolund and K. Govindarajan. Transactional conversations. In *Proceedings
    of the W3C workshop on Web services*, San Jose, CA, USA, Apr. 2001.
76. C. Frye. Move to Workflow Provokes Business Process Scrutiny. *Software
    Magazine*, pages 77–89, Apr. 1994.
77. Y. Fu, L. Cherkasova, W. Tang, and A. Vahdat. Ete: Passive end-to-end
    internet service performance monitoring. In *Proceedings of the USENIX
    Annual Technical Conference*, Monterey, CA, U.S.A, June 2002.
78. H. Garcia-Molina and K. Salem. Sagas. In *Proceedings of the Association for
    Computing Machinery Special Interest Group on Management of Data
    (SIGMOD)*, San Francisco, CA, USA, Dec. 1987.
79. D. Georgakopoulos, M. F. Hornick, and A. P. Sheth. An overview of workflow
    management: From process modeling to workflow automation infrastructure.
    Distributed and Parallel Databases, 3(2):119–153, Apr. 1995.
80. D. Georgakopoulos, H. Schuster, D. Baker, and A. Cichocki. Managing
    escalation of collaboration processes in crisis mitigation situations. In
    Proceedings of the International Conference on Data Engineering (ICDE),
    San Diego, CA, USA, Feb. 2000.
81. Global Grid Forum. *OSGI Working Group.*
    http://www.gridforum.org/ogsi-wg/.
82. Y. Goldberg, M. Safran, and E. Shapiro. Active Mail - A Framework for
    Implementing Groupware. In *Proceedings of the Conference on
    Computer-Supported Cooperative Work (CSCW)*, pages 281–288, Toronto,
    Canada, October 31 - November 4 1992.
83. K. Gottschalk, S. Graham, H. Kreger, and J. Snell. Introduction to Web
    services architecture. *IBM Systems Journal, vol 41, No 2.*, pages 170–177,
    2002.
84. J. Gray. Notes on data base operating systems. In *Operating Systems, An
    Advanced Course*, volume 60 of *Lecture Notes in Computer Science*, pages
    393–481. Springer, 1978.
85. J. Gray. Why TP-Lite will dominate the TP market. In *Proceedings of the
    1993 Asilomar Conference on High Performance Transaction Processing
    (HPTS)*, 1993.
86. J. Gray and A. Reuter. *Transaction Processing: Concepts and Techniques.*
    Morgan Kaufmann Publishers, 1993.
87. M. Gudgin, M. Hadley, J.-J. Moreau, and H. Frystyk. *SOAP version 1.2*,
    July 2001. This version is available at
    http://www.w3.org/TR/2001/WD-soap12-20010709/. The latest version is
    available at http://www.w3.or/TR/soap12/.
88. C. Hagen and G. Alonso. Flexible exception handling in the OPERA process
    support system. In *Proceedings of the International Conference on Distributed
    Computing Systems (ICDCS)*, Amsterdam, The Netherlands, May 1998.
89. C. Hall. *Building Client/Server Applications Using Tuxedo*. John Wiley &
    Sons, 1996.

90. M. Hammer and J. Champy. *Reengineering the Corporation: A Manifesto for Business Revolution.* HarperBusiness, New York, 1993.

91. R. Hauck and H. Reiser. Monitoring Quality of Service across Organizational Boundaries. In *Trends in Distributed Systems: Towards a Universal Service Market. Proceedings of the third International IFIP/GI Working Conference, USM 2000*, Sept. 2000.

92. Hewlett-Packard Company. *HP OpenView.* http://www.openview.hp.com.

93. Hewlett-Packard Company. *HP Agile Business Infrastructure Solution*, 2002. http://www.hoffmanmarcom.com/IT_ebusiness/Examples/agile_infrastructure.pdf.

94. Hewlett-Packard Company and webMethods. *Open Management Interface Specification.* http://www.oasis-open.org/committees/ mgmtprotocol/Docs/ OMISpecification_1.0rev1_OASIS.pdf.

95. C. Hoare. *Communicating Sequential Processes.* Prentice Hall, 1985.

96. I. Horrocks, P. Patel-Schneider, and F. van Harmelen. Reviewing the design of DAML+OIL: An ontology language for the Semantic Web. *AAAI 2002*, 2002.

97. J. Horswill and S. Miller. *Designing and Programming CICS Applications.* O'Reilly & Associates, 2000.

98. P. J. Houston. Introduction to DCE and Encina. Whitepaper, Transarc Corp., Nov. 1996. http:// www.transarc.com/afs/transarc.com/public/www/Public/ ProdServ/Product/Whitepapers/.

99. IBM. *Getting Started with WebSphere Application Server*, 2001. http://www-3.ibm.com/software/webservers/.

100. IBM. *WebSphere MQ Integrator Broker: Introduction and Planning*, June 2002.

101. IBM Pittsburgh Lab. *Encina online documentation.* http://www.transarc.ibm.com/Library/documentation/encina/unix/2.5/.

102. International Business Machines Corporation (IBM). *IBM UDDI Business Registry Version 2.* https://uddi.ibm.com/ubr/registry.html.

103. International Business Machines Corporation (IBM). *Tivoli Software.* http://www.tivoli.com.

104. International Business Machines Corporation (IBM). *MQ Series Workflow for Business Integration*, 1999. http://www.ibm.com.

105. S. Jablonski and C. Bussler. *Workflow Management.* International Thomson Computer Press, 1996.

106. S. Jajodia and L. Kerschberg. *Advanced Transaction Models and Architectures.* Kluwer Academic Publishers, 1997.

107. J.Bergstra and J. Klop. Algebra of communicating processes with abstractions. *Journal of Theoretical Computer Science*, 33:77–121, 1985.

108. JBoss. *JBossMQ.* http://www.jboss.org/developers/projects/jboss/jbossmq.jsp.

109. JORAM. *Java Open Reliable Asynchronous Messaging.* ObjectWeb Consortium. http://www.objectweb.org/joram/.

110. Jupitermedia Corporation. *Webopedia: Online Dictionary for Computer and Internet Terms.* http://www.webopedia.com/.

111. C. Kalbfleisch, C. Krupczak, R. Presuhn, and J. Saperia. *RFC 2564: Application Management MIB*, May 1999. http://www.ietf.org/rfc/rfc2564.txt.

112. M. Kamath and K. Ramamritham. Failure handling and coordinated execution of concurrent workflows. In *Proceedings of the International Conference on Data Engineering (ICDE)*, Orlando, FL, USA, Feb. 1998.

113. G. Kappel, P.Lang, S. Rausch-Schott, and W. Retschitzegger. Workflow management based on objects, rules, and roles. *IEEE Data Engineering*, 18(1):11–18, Mar. 1995.

114. S. Kounev and A. Buchmann. Improving data access of J2EE applications by exploiting asynchronous messaging and caching services. In *Proceedings of the International Conference on Very Large Data Bases (VLDB)*, Hong Kong, China, Aug. 2002.

115. H. Kreger. *Web Services Conceptual Architecture (WSCA 1.0)*. International Business Machines Corporation (IBM). http://www-4.ibm.com/software/solutions/webservices/pdf/WSCA.pdf.

116. V. Krishnamoorthy and M. Shan. Virtual transaction model for workflow applications. In *Proceedings of the International Symposium on Applied Computing (SAC)*, Como, Italy, Mar. 2000.

117. B. Lampson and H. Sturgis. Crash Recovery in a Distributed Storage System. Technical report, Computer Science Laboratory, Xerox, Palo Alto Research Center, Palo Alto, CA, USA, 1976.

118. C. Lee and A. Helal. Context attributes: An approach to enable context-awareness for service discovery. In *Third IEEE/IPSJ Symposium on Applications and the Internet*, Jan. 2003.

119. F. Leymann. Web Services Flow Language. Version 1.0. Technical report, International Business Machines Corporation (IBM), May 2001.

120. F. Leymann and D. Roller. Business Process Management With FlowMark. In *Proceedings of the IEEE COMPCON conference*, pages 230–234, San Francisco, CA, USA, 1994.

121. F. Leymann and D. Roller. *Production Workflow: Concepts and Techniques*. Prentice Hall, 1999.

122. F. Leymann, D. Roller, and M.-T. Schmidt. Web services and business process management. *IBM Systems Journal*, 41(2), 2002.

123. M. Lorch and D. Kafura. Symphony - a java-based composition and manipulation framework for computational grids. In *Proceedings of the 2nd IEEE/ACM International Symposium on Cluster Computing and the Grid*, 2002.

124. D. Lowe. *Client/Server Computing for Dummies*. Hungry Minds, Inc. 2nd Edition, 1997.

125. N. Lynch. *Distributed Algorithms*. Morgan Kaufmann, 1997.

126. V. Machiraju, A. van Moorsel, and A. Sahai. Web services Management Network: An Overlay Network for Federated Service Management. In *Proceedings of 8th IFIP/IEEE International Symposium on Integrated Network Management*, Colorado Springs, U.S.A, Mar. 2003.

127. S. Madnick et al. Surviving and thriving in the new world of Web aggregators. Technical Report v20, Sloan School of Management, MIT, Oct. 2000.

128. T. Malone, K. Grant, K. Lai, R. Rao, and D. Rosenblitt. Semistructured Messages Are Surprisingly Useful for Computer-Supported Coordination. *ACM Transactions on Office Information Systems*, 5(2):115–131, 1987.

129. M. P. McCahill and F. X. Anklesaria. Evolution of Internet gopher. *J.UCS: Journal of Universal Computer Science*, 1(4), 1995.

130. D. McGuinness and F. van Harmelen. W3C Working Draft: Feature Synopsis for OWL Lite and OWL. Technical report, W3C, July 2002.

131. S. McIlraith, T. C. Son, and H. Zeng. Semantic Web services. *IEEE Intelligent Systems*, 16(2), Mar. 2002.

132. M. Mecella, F. Presicce, and B. Pernici. Modeling e-services orchestration through Petri nets. In A. Buchmann and M. Hsu, editors, *Proceedings of the International VLDB Workshop on Technologies for E-Services.* Springer-Verlag, Hong Kong, China, Aug. 2002.

133. D. Menasce and V. Almeida. *Capacity Planning for Web Services*. Prentice Hall, 2001.

134. Microsoft Corporation. *ASP.NET Web: The Official Microsoft ASP.NET Site.* http://www.asp.net/.

135. Microsoft Corporation. *Microsoft Open Database Connectivity (ODBC) interface.* Microsoft Corporation. http://www.microsoft.com/data/doc.htm#odbc.

136. Microsoft Corporation. *Microsoft UDDI Business Registry Node.* http://uddi.microsoft.com/default.aspx.

137. Microsoft Corporation. *Message Queuing in Windows XP*, 2001.

138. Microsoft Corporation. *Web Services Routing Protocol (WS-Routing)*, Oct. 2001. http://msdn.microsoft.com/webservices.

139. Microsoft Corporation. *Microsoft BizTalk Server 2002 Enterprise Edition*, 2002. http://www.microsoft.com.

140. Microsoft Corporation. *Microsoft Transaction Server*, 2002. http://msdn.microsoft.com/library/.

141. T. Mikalsen, S. Tai, and I. Rouvellou. Transactional attitudes: Reliable composition of autonomous Web services. In *Workshop on Dependable Middleware-based Systems (WDMS 2002)*, Washington D.C., USA, June 2002.

142. R. Milner. *Communication and Concurrency*. Prentice Hall, 1989.

143. R. Milner, J. Parrow, and D. Walker. A calculus of mobile processes. *Information and Computation*, 100(1):1–40, Sept. 1992.

144. R. Mordani and S. Boag. *Java API for XML Processing*. Sun Microsystems, Inc., 2002. http://java.sun.com/xml/downloads/jaxp.html.

145. N. Mukhi. *Web Services Invocation Framework*. IBM developerWorks. http://www-106.ibm.com/developerworks/library/ws-wsif.html.

146. S. E. Mullender. *Distributed Systems*. Addison-Wesley, 2nd Edition, 1993.

147. National Center for Supercomputing Applications. *The Common Gateway Interface*. University of Illinois at Urbana - Champaign, IL, USA. http://hoohoo.ncsa.uiuc.edu/cgi/.

148. Netscape Communications Corporation. *Introduction to SSL*. http://developer.netscape.com/docs/manuals/security/sslin/index.html.

149. Netscape Communications Corporation. *Persistent Client State: HTTP Cookies*, 1999. http://wp.netscape.com/newsref/std/cookie_spec.html.

150. H. F. Nielsen et al. *Direct Internet Message Encapsulation (DIME)*. Internet draft, draft-nielsen-dime-02, June, 2002, http://www.ietf.org/internet-drafts/draft-nielsen-dime-02.txt.

151. Object Management Group. *Catalog of OMG CORBAfacilities Specifications*. http://www.omg.org.

152. Object Management Group. *Catalog of OMG CORBAservices Specifications*. http://www.omg.org.

153. Object Management Group. *CORBAservices: Common Object Services Specification*, 1997.

154. Object Management Group. *Unified Modeling Language Specification (Version 1.3)*, June 1999.
http://www.omg.org/technology/documents/formal/uml.htm.

155. Object Management Group. *Event Service Specification*, March 2001.
http://www.omg.org/technology/documents/formal/event_service.htm.

156. Object Management Group. *Java to IDL Language Mapping Specification. Version 1.2*, Aug. 2002. http://www.omg.org.

157. U. Ogbuji. Supercharging WSDL with RDF: Managing structured web service metadata. *IBM DeveloperWorks*, November 2000.

158. OMG CCM Implementers Group. *CORBA Component Model Tutorial*, Apr. 2002. http://www.omg.org/cgi-bin/doc?ccm/2002-04-01.

159. The Open Group. *Application Response Measurement. Version 1.2*.
http://www.opengroup.org/management/arm.htm.

160. Oracle Corporation. *Oracle 9i Application Server: An Oracle White Paper*, Sept. 2002. http://www.oracle.com/ip/deploy/ias/.

161. Oracle Corporation. *Oracle 9i Application Server: Business Intelligence Overview*, Mar. 2002. http://www.oracle.com/ip/deploy/ias/bi/bi_twp.pdf.

162. R. Orfali, D. Harkey, and J. Edwards. *Client/Server Survival Guide*. John Wiley & Sons, 3rd Edition, 1999.

163. S. G. Parker and C. R. Johnson. SCIRun: A Scientific Programming Environment for Computational Steering. In *Proceedings of the 1995 ACM/IEEE Supercomputing Conference*, 1995.

164. D. Platt. *Understanding COM+*. Microsoft Press, 1999.

165. M. Platt. *Microsoft Architecture Overview*. Microsoft Corporation, July 2002. http://msdn.microsoft.com/architecture/default.aspx.

166. J. Postel. RFC 318: Telnet protocol, Apr. 1972.

167. J. Postel and J. K. Reynolds. RFC 959: File transfer protocol, Oct. 1985.

168. PROMATIS GmbH. *PROMATIS*. http://www.promatis.com.

169. W. Reisig and G. R. (editors). *Lectures on Petri Nets I: Basic Models*. Lecture Notes in Computer Science. Springer-Verlag, 1998.

170. A. Reuter, K. Schneider, and F. Schwenkreis. Contracts revisited. In S. Jajodia and L. Kerschberg, editors, *Advanced Transaction Models and Architectures*. Kluwer Academic Publishers, New York, 1997.

171. RosettaNet. *RosettaNet: Lingua Franca for E-Business*.
http://www.rosettanet.org.

172. RosettaNet. *RosettaNet Overview*. RosettaNet, 1999.
http://www.rosettanet.org/background.

173. RosettaNet. *Understanding a PIP Blueprint*, 2000.
http://ibm.com/developerworks/library/ws-bpel.

174. M. Rusinkiewicz, A. Elmagarmid, Y. Leu, and W. Litwin. Extending the transaction model to capture more meaning. *ACM SIGMOD Record*, 19, Oct. 1990.

175. W. Sadiq and S. Kumar, editors. *Web Service Description Usage Scenarios*. World Wide Web Consortium (W3C), June 2002. This version of the W3C Working Draft is available at
http://www.w3.org/TR/2002/WD-ws-desc-usecases-20020604 The latest version is available at http://www.w3.org/TR/ws-desc-usecases.

176. A. Sahai, V. Machiraju, M. Sayal, A. van Moorsel, F. Casati, and L. J. Jin. Automated SLA monitoring for Web services. In *Proceedings of Management Technologies for E-Commerce and E-Business Applications, 13th IFIP/IEEE International Workshop on Distributed Systems: Operations and Management, DSOM 2002*, Montreal, Canada, Oct. 2002.

177. R. Salz. Transporting Binary Data in SOAP. http://www.xml.com/pub/a/2002/08/28/endpoints.html.

178. Z. Sheng, B. Benatallah, M. Dumas, and E. O.-Y. Mak. SELF-SERV: A Platform for Rapid Composition of Web Services in a Peer-to-Peer Environment. In *Proceedings of the International Conference on Very Large Data Bases (VLDB)*, Hong Kong, China, Aug. 2002.

179. A. Sheth, M. Rusinkicwicz, and G. Karabatis. Using polytransactions to manage independent data. In A. Elmagarmid, editor, *Transaction Models for Advanced Database Applications*. Morgan Kaufmann Publishers, 1992.

180. B. Sleeper. The Evolution of UDDI. Technical report, The Stencil Group, Inc., July 2002. http://uddi.org/pubs/the_evolution_of_uddi_20020719.pdf.

181. M. Sloman. Policy driven management for distributed systems. *Journal of Network and Systems Management*, 2:333, 1994.

182. Society for Worldwide Interbank Financial Telecommunication SCRL. *SWIFT*. http://www.swift.com/.

183. R. Srinivasan. Rpc: Remote procedure call protocol specification version 2. Technical Report RFC 1831, Sun Microsystems, Inc., Aug. 1995.

184. M. Stonebraker. Legacy systems - the Achilles heel of downsizing. In *Proceedings of the Third IEEE International Conference on Parallel and Distributed Information Systems (PDIS 94)*, Austin, Texas, September 28-30, 1994, page 108, 1994.

185. M. Stonebraker. Too much middleware. *ACM Sigmod Record*, 31(1):97–106, 2002.

186. R. Sturm and W. Bumpus. *Foundations of Application Management*. John Wiley & Sons, 1998.

187. R. Sturm, W. Morris, and M. Jander. *Foundations of Service Level Management*. Sams, 2000.

188. Sun Microsystems, Inc. *Java Servlet Technology*. http://java.sun.com/products/servlet/.

189. Sun Microsystems, Inc. *JavaServer Pages Technology*. http://java.sun.com/products/jsp/.

190. Sun Microsystems, Inc. *JDBC Data Access API*. Sun Microsystems, Inc. http://java.sun.com/products/jdbc/.

191. Sun Microsystems, Inc. *The Source for Java Technology*. http://java.sun.com/.

192. Sun Microsystems, Inc. *Simplified Guide to the Java 2 Platform, Enterprise Edition*, 1999. http://java.sun.com/j2ee/j2ee_guide.pdf.

193. Sun Microsystems, Inc. *Java Management Extensions. Version 1.2.*, Dec. 2002.

194. Sun Microsystems, Inc. *Java Message Service. Version 1.1*, Apr. 2002.

195. Sun Microsystems, Inc. *Sun ONE Architecture Guide*, 2002. http://wwws.sun.com/software/sunone/.

196. A. Tanenbaum. *Distributed Operating Systems*. Prentice Hall, Inc., 1995.

197. The Open Group. *Transaction Processing Titles*. The Open Group. http://www.opengroup.org/products/publications/catalog/tp.htm.

198. TIBCO Software Inc. *TIBCO Business Process Management solutions*, 2002.
http://www.tibco.com.

199. TIBCO Software Inc. *TIBCO Enterprise Application Integration solutions*,
2002. http://www1.tibco.com/solutions/tibco_eai.pdf.

200. D. Trastour, C. Bartolini, and J. Gonzalez-Castillo. A Semantic Web
approach to service description for matchmaking of services. In *Proceedings
of the International Semantic Web Working Symposium (SWWS)*, 2001.

201. D. Trastour, C. Preist, and D. Coleman. Using Semantic Web technology to
enhance current business-to-business integration approaches. In *Proceedings
of the International World Wide Web Conference (WWW03)*, Budapest,
Hungary, May 2003.

202. D. Tsichritzis. Form Management. *Communications of the ACM*,
25(7):453–478, July 1982.

203. UDDI Consortium. *UDDI Executive White Paper*, Nov. 2001.
http://uddi.org/pubs/UDDI_Executive_White_Paper.pdf.

204. W. van der Aalst. The application of Petri nets to workflow management.
The Journal of Circuits, Systems, and Computers, 8(1):21–66, 1998.

205. W. van der Aalst and K. van Hee. *Workflow Management: Models, Methods,
and Systems*. MIT Press, 2001.

206. W. van der Aalst and M. Weske. The P2P approach to interorganizational
workflows. In *Proceedings of the International Conference on Advanced
information Systems Engineering (CAiSE)*, pages 140–156, Interlaken,
Switzerland, 2001.

207. H. Verbeek, T. Basten, and W. van der Aalst. Diagnosing workflow processes
using woflan. *The Computer Journal*, 44(4):246–279, 2001.

208. Vitria. *BusinessWare: The Leading Integration Platform*, 2002.
http://www.vitria.com.

209. G. Vossen and G. Weikum. *Transactional Information Systems: Theory,
Algorithms, and the Practice of Concurrency Control*. Morgan Kaufmann
Publishers, 2001.

210. W3C. *Extensible Markup Language (XML) 1.0 (Second Edition)*, Oct. 2000.
http://www.w3.org/TR/REC-xml.

211. W3C. *XML Schema part 0: Primer*, May 2001.
http://www.w3.org/TR/xmlschema-0/.

212. W3C. *Web Services Architecture Requirements*, Oct. 2002.
http://www.w3.org/TR/wsa-reqs.

213. WebMethods. *WebMethods Enterprise Integrator: User's Guide*, 2002.

214. WebRatio. *WebRatio–Model driven code generation of Web applications*.
http://www.webratio.com/.

215. J. E. White. RFC 524: Proposed mail protocol, June 1973.

216. G. Wiederhold, P. Wegner, and S. Ceri. Towards megaprogramming: A
paradigm for component-based programming. *Communications of the ACM*,
35(11):89–99, 1992.

217. A. Wise. Little-JIL 1.0: Language reports. Technical Report
UM-CS-1998-024, University of Massachussets, Amherst, MA, USA, 1998.

218. D. Wodtke and G. Weikum. A formal foundation for distributed workflow
execution based on state charts. In *Proceedings of the 6th International
Conference on Database Theory*, Delphi, Greece, 1997.

219. D. Wodtke, J. Weissenfels, G. Weikum, and A. Kotz-Dittrich. The Mentor project: Steps towards enterprise-wide workflow management. In *Proceedings of the International Conference on Data Engineering (ICDE)*, New Orleans, LA, USA, 1996.

220. D. Worah and A. Sheth. Transactions in transactional workflows. In S. Jajodia and L. Kerschberg, editors, *Advanced Transaction Models and Architectures*. Kluwer Academic Publishers, New York, 1997.

221. Workflow Management Coalition. *Workflow Management Coalition*. http://www.wfmc.org.

222. World Wide Web Consortium (W3C). *SemanticWeb*. http://www.w3.org/2001/sw/.

223. World Wide Web Consortium (W3C). *Web-Ontology (WebOnt) Working Group*. http://www.w3.org/2001/sw/WebOnt/.

224. P. Yendluri. RosettaNet Implementation Framework (RNIF) 2.0. Technical report, RosettaNet, 2000. http://xml.coverpages.org/RNIF-Spec020000.pdf.

Index